Authoritarianism and the Crisis of the Argentine Political Economy

Authoritarianism and the Crisis of the Argentine Political Economy

WILLIAM C. SMITH

STANFORD UNIVERSITY PRESS   1989
STANFORD, CALIFORNIA

Stanford University Press
Stanford, California
© 1989 by the Board of Trustees of the
Leland Stanford Junior University
Printed in the United States of America

CIP data are at the end of the book

To María de Lourdes and
Gabriela Lucía

Acknowledgments

THIS STUDY of the Argentine political economy is the product of a prolonged gestation period of research and reflection. I began the research for this book during two years spent in Buenos Aires in the mid-1970s. The first, dissertation version of this study was completed in July 1980. Two weeks later I arrived at the Federal University of Minas Gerais in Belo Horizonte, Brazil, planning to spend one year as a Fulbright professor. But Brazil was irresistible and I remained nearly five years. Although Argentina was still my first passion, fascination with things Argentine had to compete with learning Portuguese, teaching Latin American politics to Brazilian graduate students, and studying the history, culture, and politics of my new country. Not until late 1987, when I was resident in Miami, did I undertake the radical transformation of an unwieldy dissertation of nearly 800 pages into a book.

As usually happens with large projects stretching over many years, numerous friendships were formed and debts incurred. I gratefully acknowledge the support given by my professors at Stanford University. Particular gratitude goes to Richard Fagen, whose friendship, patience, and understanding as an adviser I value highly. I also thank Barry Ames (then a visiting scholar at Stanford's Bolívar House), who saved me from several egregious errors, and Charles Drekmeier, who never lost his good humor while plunging into the alien territory of Latin American politics. Frank Bonilla, my first adviser at Stanford, I thank for his example as an intellectual who combines exemplary scholarship with concern for the implications of research for the lives of people.

While in Argentina I received friendship and invaluable intellectual stimulation from many sources. To Marcelo Cavarozzi and Oscar Oszlak, colleagues at the Centro de Investigación en Administración Pública (CIAP) of the Torcuato Di Tella Institute and then at the Centro de Estudios de Estado y Sociedad (CEDES), I owe many intellectual debts which are only imperfectly recognized in this book's citations. Thanks are also due for welcoming me back to CEDES for briefer visits in 1983 and 1987. I am especially grateful to my *amigos queridos* Lila Felicitas Milutín, Ricardo Milutín, Luis Ros, Susana Canela, and Juan Noel Grau for sharing their insights into Argentine society, and I thank them for accepting my wife and me into their families. I reserve special esteem for the late Don Miguel Milutín, a patriot in the best tradition of Argentine democratic politics and a wonderful *compañero de vino tinto*.

Among these Argentine friends and colleagues Guillermo O'Donnell merits particular mention. I fondly remember our many stimulating discussions attempting to make sense out of the Argentine riddle. Because O'Donnell and I were both writing on the same general questions, we agreed to refrain from reading the other's text until both had been completed. I thank him for his very generous reference in his own book to the dissertation version of my study. After sending my own manuscript to Stanford Press, I finally had the pleasure of reading O'Donnell's book, and I concur with his judgment that despite the inevitable coincidences, the different emphases of our texts make them more complementary than overlapping.* His study of the 1966–73 period is clearly a major extension of his earlier pioneering and influential work on bureaucratic-authoritarianism.

While at Stanford, I was fortunate to establish enduring friendships with an extraordinary group of Brazilians, including Malori José Pompermayer, Edgar Pontes de Magalhães, Benício V. Schmidt, Evelina Dagnino, Glaura Vásquez de Miranda, and Isaura Belloni. During my Brazilian sojourn these friendships deepened and new ones were established with Eli Diniz, Bernardo Sorj, Aurea Dreifuss, Fabio Wanderley Reis, Celson José da Silva, Otávio Dulce, Vera Alice Cardoso, and many others.

---

* See O'Donnell's comments in *Bureaucratic-Authoritarianism: Argentina, 1966–1973, in Comparative Perspective* (Berkeley: University of California Press, 1988), p. xiii.

The intellectual fervor and the impressive scholarship produced by the Brazilian academic community in the early 1980s made a major impact on me. Although my dissertation remained unopened during these years, the time spent reading and debating questions of theory and history with my students and colleagues substantially changed my thinking about politics and the state in Argentina and Latin America. I feel these changes are reflected positively in this book.

My research and writing was generously supported early on by a Foreign Area Fellowship from the Social Science Research Council and the American Council of Learned Societies. The final writing was funded in part by a grant from the Corporate Affiliates Program at the University of Miami. I am grateful for their support. An early version of Chapter 9 appeared in *Generals in Retreat: The Crisis of Military Rule in Latin America*, edited by Philip O'Brien and Paul Cammack (Manchester, Eng.: Manchester University Press, 1985). Portions of Chapter 10 were published in *Lost Promises: Debt, Austerity, and Development in Latin America*, edited by William L. Canak (Boulder, Colo.: Westview Press, 1989).

I have received particularly valuable written comments on the entire manuscript from Steven E. Sanderson, Roberto Patricio Korzeniewicz, and Jeff Stark. Peter Ranis, Scott Mainwaring, and Lisa Fuentes also made useful criticisms of individual chapters. David Dye was an extremely demanding critic of the earlier incarnation. Peter J. Kahn, Associate Editor at Stanford Press, did a marvelous editorial job and I thank him for shepherding the manuscript to publication. I am grateful to all of them and relieve them of responsibility for remaining errors of fact or interpretation.

I dedicate this book to María de Lourdes Baeza, for her encouragement of my initial interest in Latin America and for opening new cultures that have enriched me tremendously, and to my daughter Gabriela Lucía Baeza-Smith, who is the wonderful product of our complex life together.

W.C.S.

Contents

Tables and Figures

FIGURES

Authoritarianism and
the Crisis of the
Argentine Political Economy

ONE

Thinking About Authoritarianism in Argentina

FOR MUCH of the last two decades, Argentine citizens have been living a nightmare. In 1966, a weak civilian government was overthrown and Argentina's first military-sponsored experiment in authoritarian rule began. The pompously named Revolución Argentina remained in power until 1973. After nearly three years of disastrous leadership by Juan Perón and María Estela Martínez de Perón, another, even more radical and cruelly repressive military project—the so-called Proceso de Reorganización Nacional—assumed state power. During the ensuing "dirty war" at least 9,000 people died, victims of official terrorism, while tens of thousands more were consigned to a twilight zone inhabited by the "disappeared." Many hundreds of thousands more fled their country into political or economic exile.

Belying its promises to create a dynamic free-market economy, the Proceso managed to destroy much of Argentina's industrial base and to saddle future generations with a huge external debt. The election of Raúl Alfonsín in 1983, coming as the dénouement of the Malvinas conflict with Great Britain in the South Atlantic, finally returned Argentina to shaky civilian rule.

Argentina's violent and frequently terrifying history poses a number of paradoxical and disturbing questions. Why has one of Latin America's wealthiest and most developed nations failed so tragically in reconciling economic modernization with democratic politics? Why have authoritarian regimes failed even more disastrously than those led by civilian politicians? And as the

Alfonsín government nears the end of its constitutional mandate, what are the prospects for the consolidation of Argentina's still fragile democracy?

In addressing these and related questions, my primary objective is to reconstruct and make sense of the crisis of the Argentine political economy. This is not an exercise in economic determinism. I do not deny the importance of political culture or of political parties, the rules of electoral competition, and related institutional questions. I simply believe that a focus on the political economy promises what in Spanish might be called a "privileged" perspective on the factors that have undermined democratic politics and aborted authoritarian projects for the radical reorganization of society from above.

The term "political economy" refers to the mutual interaction of "state" and "market." Neither politics nor markets can ever exist in pure form. The contradictory logics of politics and the market always co-exist, with the state, property arrangements, and the price mechanism jointly determining the structures of political power and economic production, the articulation of society into social classes, and the associated distribution of income, wealth, and life chances. As used in this study, "political economy" does not refer to the interpretation of historical processes in light of a particular *theory* (such as game theory, collective action theory, or Marxist theories). Nor does it refer to the application of a particular *methodology* from formal economics (such as the rational actor model) to make sense of historical events.[1] Instead, I use the term in a broader, more eclectic fashion to refer to a set of *questions* posed by the interaction of state, class, and accumulation, questions that I believe can best be studied through historical case studies employing a variety of theories, methodologies, and empirical materials.

While I hope that this study sheds some light on more general theoretical issues of political economy as well as on classical questions of political sociology such as the conditions for legitimate authority, I have chosen not to "test" any general theory of Latin American politics or economic development. Instead, my fundamental concern is to highlight the specificities of, and to tease out the internal logic embedded in, particular historical configurations in recent Argentine history.

Politics and Economics in Explanations of the "New Authoritarianism"

The approach taken here departs from the influential bureaucratic-authoritarian (BA) paradigm first proposed by Guillermo O'Donnell in the early 1970s. The BA model sought to link a specific economic problem (the exhaustion of the "easy" phase of import-substitution industrialization) and the crisis of a specific political model (populism) with the emergence of a *sui generis* state form—the BA regime. By challenging classical Marxist explanations of military dictatorship as well as the modernization paradigm's claim of a positive causal relationship between economic development and democracy, the BA model fundamentally transformed the way political scientists and sociologists viewed the military regimes that took power in Brazil (1964), Argentina (1966 and 1976), Peru (1968), Uruguay (1973), and Chile (1973).[2] In doing so, the BA model made significant contributions to our knowledge about authoritarian forms of domination and their social and economic correlates. Subsequent theoretical reflection and empirical research, however, have identified a number of deficiencies in fact and logic and have called into question many of the BA model's basic postulates.

Several general objections to the bureaucratic-authoritarian paradigm should be mentioned. First, the causal linkages and the connections between the logic of accumulation and economic strategies are much less determinate than the model suggests; the range of possible alternative economic strategies is considerably broader than envisioned in the model. Second, not all Latin American economies have gone through the sequence of stages suggested by the model, nor has the timing always been that specified by the model. Third, the bulk of the empirical evidence fails to support the hypothesized correlation between different phases of economic development and the emergence of particular regime types. And, fourth, the "new wave" dictatorial regimes that took power in the 1970s in Argentina, Uruguay, and Chile have pursued economic policies that differ in fundamental ways from those implemented by the "original" authoritarian regimes in Brazil and Argentina in the 1960s; to characterize both sets of regimes as "bureaucratic-authoritarian" is to obscure rather than to elucidate the political and economic attributes of these different variants of military rule.[3]

In view of these criticisms, the notion of a close correlation between economic phases and specific political arrangements cannot be sustained. The relations between the political and economic spheres are simply too loose and unpredictable. In fact, broadly similar structures of production and similar modes of insertion in the world-economy have been associated with quite different political regimes and forms of political domination, and vice versa.[4]

Successive, ad hoc attempts to respecify the BA model to accommodate deviant cases have only led to growing frustration about the entire enterprise. One critic has observed that "as a result there was an air of crisis about the state of the debate even before the regimes of the type concerned themselves began to crumble."[5] The transitions from military regimes to civilian rule in Peru (1980), Argentina (1983), Uruguay (1985), and Brazil (1985) further undermined the central postulates of the BA model.[6]

State-Led Restructuring

Several European and Latin American scholars have recently put forth the tentative outlines of an alternative interpretation of Latin American military rule focusing on the "restructuring" of the political economy.[7] In contrasting this approach with the BA model, Cammack notes that rather than concentrating

upon the relationship between contemporary military regimes and the dominated classes, or upon the nature of the alliance in which such regimes enter with domestic or foreign groups, [this perspective] inquires into the extent to which they consciously set out to restructure the economy (in order to provide a new basis for accumulation) and the polity (in order to create the conditions for the emergence of a truly hegemonic domestic ruling class). It focuses, then, upon explicit projects aimed at restructuring capital and, at a sociopolitical level, at restructuring the dominant class itself.[8]

This restructuring perspective, in contrast to the BA model, does not seek to identify a "modal pattern" applicable to the region as a whole, nor does it draw selectively upon various cases to produce an analytical model with a logic of its own. Instead, it provides a common framework within which theoretically informed analyses of contemporary authoritarian regimes can explicitly take into account the specificity and internal logic of each case under study.[9]

The BA model identifies the tasks of the new military regimes as the elimination of the "threat from below" and the "normalization" of the economy through the adoption of orthodox stabilization measures. The restructuring perspective agrees that these are important tasks but goes further to identify a much more ambitious agenda for these regimes, namely the wholesale reorganization of the state apparatus, the class structure, prevailing patterns of capital accumulation, and the country's mode of insertion in the world-economy. As Chilean sociologist Manuel Antonio Garretón has pointed out, although these regimes are initially impelled by a short-term logic of reaction and counterrevolution in response to popular challenges, they are in fact bearers of a longer-term "foundational logic" whose object is nothing less than the construction of a "new order."[10]

From this perspective, it is understandable that the implantation of authoritarian regimes provokes the resistance of the subaltern classes, who are the object of systematic political exclusion while being asked to bear the brunt of economic policies designed to control inflation and increase savings and investment. What is less obvious, and what the restructuring perspective specifically calls to our attention, is that the foundational logic of these regimes, crystallized in state-led projects for the "reorganization from above" of capital, are also bound to provoke major conflicts between the state and the dominant classes. The identification of the state as the subject, object, and determinant of political struggles and class conflicts, therefore, emerges at the center of any analysis of state-led restructuring.[11]

As my study of the Argentine case will make clear, the struggles within the state apparatus and among the various fractions of capital are equally as important as, if not more important than, the state's handling of the "threat from below." In this regard, to see the state as a cohesive, unitary actor or as the "instrument" of a united ruling class is to fail to understand that successful restructuring requires that state elites distance themselves from the dominant classes and resist attempts by specific sectors of capital to bend state policies to their own particular economic interests. To "discipline" the dominant classes may even require the political exclusion of their political representatives from the bureaucratic agencies charged with formulating and implementing economic policies.[12]

Moreover, it is not only the need to attract foreign capital, or the conflicts pitting large domestic and transnational industrial firms against embattled competitive-sector manufacturers, that limit the state's "relative autonomy" from dominant-class interests and influence its capacity to implement a coherent economic strategy. In Argentina, as we shall see, the conflicts between urban capital and the still-powerful agricultural sector, and between agrarian interests and the regime, were fundamental both in determining the longevity of authoritarian rule and in shaping the specific dynamics of the regime's transformation.

The restructuring approach also sheds light on another problem. Military regimes in the Southern Cone and Brazil have been brutally effective, at least in the short run, in repressing and excluding the subordinate sectors of society. However, they have been much less successful in consolidating their power and legitimating their rule on a permanent basis.[13] Focusing on the attempted reorganization from above of the mechanisms of capital accumulation may help explain this apparent anomaly. Military and civilian technocratic elites develop their own bureaucratic interests and frequently resist pressures for the representation of private-sector interests with a fervor that almost rivals their opposition to the reemergence of autonomous political spaces for the political parties or the organized labor movement.

The role of the armed forces in crystallizing a distinct "state interest"[14] helps explain why the military may decide to withdraw from direct control of the state apparatus as well as why authoritarian rule frequently acquires a momentum of its own that persists long after the "threat from below" has been vanquished. The paradox is that in order to pursue projects for restructuring the economy to benefit capital, these regimes are frequently led to exclude the dominant classes' political representatives from participation in decision-making. Although opposition from the political parties and subordinate sectors of civil society frequently plays a crucial role in challenging authoritarianism, as long as these regimes retain the loyalty of the dominant classes—and the military, of course—their hold on power is not endangered. When this loyalty fades, or when discontent resulting from the exclusion of these sectors reaches unsustainable levels,[15] as ultimately happened in the two authoritarian experiments studied in this book, the stability of the regime is in serious jeopardy.

Finally, I should note, to identify military-authoritarian regimes with projects for restructuring the political economy does not imply that these regimes are capable of carrying those projects to a successful conclusion. Notwithstanding the successes achieved by the post-1964 Brazilian regime or the major transformations effected by the Pinochet regime in Chile since 1973, state-led restructuring projects face huge, virtually insurmountable obstacles. Failure may be the most probable outcome. The collapse of the Revolución Argentina and the Proceso de Reorganización Nacional demonstrates that a seemingly invincible logic of state power allied with powerful social forces is certainly no guarantee of success.

Authoritarianism, Democracy, and Class Compromise

What is the connection between authoritarianism and democracy? Does the failure of authoritarian rule make democracy more likely? How has democracy emerged elsewhere and can Argentina replicate its achievement?

The emergence of political democracy in capitalist societies in North America and Western Europe in the twentieth century was a paradoxical historical outcome not expected by either Marxists or classical liberals; both camps thought that these two radically different logics of social organization were inherently contradictory and thus subversive of one another.[16]

In fact, political democracy emerged in the context of specific historical conjunctures, for example, amid national mobilizations to wage war and/or divisions among the dominant classes that opened the way for progressive political alliances among the middle classes, workers, and, in some cases, rural producers. In the successful cases, the outcome was the expansion of the franchise and citizenship to the subaltern classes. This resulted in a significant ideological deradicalization and attentuation of class-based political conflict. These new political constellations were consolidated in North America and Western Europe in the post-1930 period by means of a major expansion of state intervention in the economy guided by Keynesian-inspired welfare state policies.[17]

The institutionalization of this "democratic class compromise" was the product of decades of strategic conflict among state elites, capital, and organized labor over the conditions of capital accumulation and the distribution of the economic surplus.[18] The search for institutional arrangements to reduce the "predictable uncertainties" democracy poses for politicians, labor leaders, and entrepreneurs under capitalist relations of production played an essential role.

This compromise was only possible when the leaders of organized labor agreed to control the unruliness of their rank and file by accepting capital's control over productive assets. In making this major concession, labor leaders had gradually realized that barring a socialist transformation, improvements in the material well-being of their constituency were contingent upon reasonable guarantees for capital regarding the profitability of its investments. Labor elites constrained working-class militancy in the hope that a substantial portion of capital's profits would be saved, reinvested, and converted into technological modernization, greater labor productivity, and expanded production, thus making it possible for part of future profits to be distributed to workers in the form of higher real wages.

In addition to organized labor's adoption of an essentially reformist strategy, this emergent class compromise also required capital's acceptance of the legitimacy of the institutions of political democracy, such as parties, parliaments, unions, and collective bargaining, and the post-liberal state's role in regulating aggregate demand. Together, these institutions and policies created a political marketplace: workers exercised their citizenship rights, while political parties and state elites responded to their demands for material improvements, to ensure the reproduction of political legitimacy on a democratic basis.

A fundamental corollary to an effective class compromise was that investment not be left to the exclusive control of capitalists. In exchange for their participation in this compromise, organized labor, liberal and leftist parties, and reformist state elites demanded greater public control over investment decisions. Only if capitalists saved and invested at appropriately high levels would it be rational for labor elites to restrain working-class militancy in exchange for an assurance of future wage increases.

Class compromises in advanced capitalism were not the result of shared political culture or a liberal-pluralist consensus. On the contrary, they generally resulted from protracted (and frequently violent) conflict between labor and capital.

Neither the acceptance of capitalism by workers, nor the acceptance of democracy by capitalists constitutes a "consensus." . . . Acceptance is not a mental state, nor a previously accepted obligation, but an aspect of behavior imputable to [class] organizations. . . . The classes consent to a specific modality of social organization when they select strategies that lead to a compromise, and they choose those strategies when, given the situation of conflict, they permit the best realization of their interests.[19]

But political democracy has never been an affair solely involving the resolution of structural conflicts among state elites, organized labor, and entrepreneurs. The full consolidation of class compromises has only occurred when key sectors of the middle class have allied themselves with subaltern groups, thus effectively tilting the balance in favor of institutional arrangements based upon representation and electoral competition.[20]

Thus, the possibility of a class compromise depends on the calculations that state elites, entrepreneurs, and workers, along with party politicians and middle-class representatives, make regarding the risk or degree of certainty that the other actors will uphold their part of the bargain. The magnitude of this risk will be a function of the extent of class organization, the level of institutionalization of capital-labor relations, and the risk of investment. Risk is reduced when capital, labor, and the key middle-class sectors are well-organized as collective actors with a legal or de facto monopoly of representation empowering the leadership of their respective organizations to oblige their members to respect the terms of the compromise.

Similarly, a well-institutionalized system of labor relations, in which the state has the legal authority and the bureaucratic capacity to enforce the class compromise, substantially reduces the risks to both capital and labor. Investment is inherently risky. When uncertainties rooted in the economy—such as the fluctuation of relative prices (including the price of labor), domestic and international competition, dislocations due to technological modernization, and so on—are moderate and predictable, and hence acceptable to capital, the risk of investment declines and the likelihood of a class compromise correspondingly increases. A similar calculus operates in the decision by labor elites and representatives of the middle class to accept the compromise.

Class compromise under capitalism is not the only alternative, of course. Labor and leftist parties may attempt a socialist transformation. Capital may use its superior resources and access to the state's coercive power to impose a nondemocratic solution to labor militancy; such authoritarian solutions have been all too common in Argentina and elsewhere in Latin America. Finally, when neither labor nor capital has the political power to impose unilateral solutions, and when a compromise is rejected, a sociopolitical stalemate may emerge. This stalemate, referred to by Gramsci as a "catastrophic equilibrium" and by Huntington as "praetorianism," is characterized by an erosion of regime legitimacy and high levels of class conflict poorly mediated by parties and representative institutions.[21] Mediocre economic performance and wild cyclical fluctuations are both cause and effect of this unstable equilibrium, which is of course suboptimum for capital, labor, and the middle class, as well as contrary to the self-interest of political elites and destructive of political stability under both democratic and authoritarian regimes.

Although schematized, this discussion of class compromise and the alternatives to it resonates well with the decades of political turmoil and economic turbulence that will be analyzed in subsequent chapters. But, for various reasons, this is not surprising. In terms of its productive structure, system of class stratification, and social relations, Argentina is more akin to the advanced areas of the world-economy than it is to most other Latin American societies. Along with other semiperipheral nations such as Brazil, Spain, Portugal, and Greece, Argentina shares many structural traits with North America and Western Europe. Like these nations, Argentina has been sharply constrained by fewer economic resources with which to support a democratic class compromise.

Given its extensive, although disarticulated, manufacturing sector, the primordial role still played by agro-export activities, and its large and politically mobilized middle and working classes, Argentina—perhaps even more so than other semiperipheral nations—has been particularly vulnerable to the logic of international competition that presses for constant technological innovation, as "core" economic activities typical of advanced nations in one phase of the world-economy undergo "peripheralization" in the next phase.[22] Partly as a function of the exigencies of international competition, in these nations state intervention in extracting and guiding the investment of the economic surplus performs an extraordinarily crucial role in promoting the upgrading of productive activities. The fate of any regime's economic policy naturally will partly depend on the success of this state function. Therefore, with limited economic resources, and reliant upon the productive success of business and industry, state elites in semiperipheral nations are particularly hard-pressed to effectively organize and discipline entrepreneurial interests, however necessary that may be for the implementation of the social-welfare and income-redistribution policies required by any democratic class compromise.

Argentina thus confronts the same social and economic exigencies that earlier had led advanced capitalist societies to grope toward a class compromise facilitating the coexistence of a market economy and democracy. In contrast to North America and Western Europe, however, the functioning of the Argentine political economy and its precarious insertion in world markets have not been conducive to democratic outcomes. Or, as we shall see, to stable authoritarian ones, either. The labyrinthine course of Argentine politics offers abundant testimony to the collective inability of state elites and social classes in Argentina to coexist peacefully, let alone fashion a viable class compromise.

The Argument and the Format

The attempt to comprehend the dynamics of Argentine politics and economics without oversimplifying an extraordinarily complex reality has produced a difficult book. The format combines a chronologically ordered narrative interwoven with theoretical analysis of the legitimation and accumulation problems facing authoritarian forms of domination, and the extrication scenarios encountered when authoritarian experiments fail.

Chapter 2 provides an historical overview of the formation of the Argentine state and its role in articulating the class structure and fostering capital accumulation. I argue that Argentina's failure to establish a stable and legitimate political order can be traced to the manner in which the political economy has been structured historically around two poles of accumulation—one agrarian and the other urban and industrial—with contradictory relations with the world market. The early consolidation of a hegemonic class, the Pampean agro-export bourgeoisie, provided the basis for extensive urbanization and precocious industrial development and gave rise to a large and prosperous middle class and a well-organized working class that long enjoyed relatively high wages. The Depression and World War II created the conditions that challenged Pampean hegemony and led to the emergence of a populist class compromise presided over by Juan Perón. But Peronism could not overcome the structural constraints stemming from Argentina's relation to the world market. Military and semidemocratic civilian regimes in the immediate post-Peronist period equally fell victim to cyclical crises of the economy. A new style of dictatorial rule emerged in 1966 as a consequence of these intractable economic problems and the exhaustion of the political initiatives of the dominant classes, who turned to the armed forces for salvation.

The initial phase of the Revolución Argentina and the revamping of the state apparatus attempted by General Juan Carlos Onganía are described in Chapter 3. Here I examine the development of a new "language of the state" designed to legitimate military rule, and proposals for major innovations in the organization of the state bureaucracy aimed at enhancing the technical capacity and relative autonomy of state elites. This period was also marked by clashes pitting a band of "nationalist" ideologues espousing corporatist formulas against military and civilian "liberals" with a very different political and economic agenda.

The new strategy of state-led restructuring implemented by Economy Minister Krieger Vasena in hopes of overcoming the Argentine economy's deeply rooted structural impasses is discussed in Chapter 4. Essentially, the new strategy broke with conventional import-substitution industrialization by promoting domestic production of intermediate goods, capital goods, and ancillary infrastructure; by expanding production in the consumer durables sector; and by providing incentives for the export of manufactured goods. In analyzing Krieger's policies I lay the groundwork for the chapters that follow. I treat the *politics* of economic transformation through the lens of the leading organizational actors, rather than focusing only on economic *policy*, as more conventional analysis does. This interpretation stresses the interaction between state policies, the business cycle, and the response of key entrepreneurial groups in order to highlight the constraints on Krieger's project of capitalist restructuring.

In Chapter 5, I explain the working class's deepening alienation from post-Peronist politics and probe the political, economic, and organizational factors explaining the organized labor movement's fragmentation and weakness in responding to the imposition of authoritarian rule. After tracing the labor movement's changing relations with the Onganía regime, I describe the political strategies followed by rival "participationist" and *clasista* factions within the labor movement. In this analysis, I underscore the dilemma faced by labor elites in seeking redress of class issues while also serving as the political representatives of a heterogeneous Peronist movement.

Chapter 6 focuses on the *cordobazo*, an unprecedented and largely spontaneous mass urban uprising that took place in May 1969 in Argentina's second-largest city. While a confluence of factors led to the collapse of the Onganía regime, I argue that the *cordobazo* was clearly the catalyst that triggered deepening military factionalism and accelerated the evaporation of bourgeois support for authoritarian rule. The *cordobazo* also initiated a period of mounting mass mobilization and increasingly radical opposition, the long-term consequences of which were to profoundly shape Argentine politics for the next decade and more.

I open Chapter 7 with a theoretical discussion of "reformism" and "transformism" as alternative solutions to the political crisis afflicting Argentina in the early 1970s. Following Onganía's ouster, a second phase of the military's "revolution" unfolded under the leadership of General Roberto Levingston. This experiment in military reformism under nationalist banners reversed Krieger's strategy by calling for the "Argentinization" of the economy. Additionally, Levingston's brief, nine-month tenure was marked by his determined opposition to pressures for a democratic opening and by a renewed commitment to authoritarian rule. This attempted "deepening of the revolution" spurred the rebirth of civilian reformism led by the Peronists and the Radicals. Consumed by its own contradictions, and confronted by an increasingly vocal opposition, Levingston's government was replaced by that of General Alejandro Lanusse in March 1971.

During the stormy period of the early 1970s, the political sphere—where struggles for power among rival leaders, social forces, and institutional actors were played out—acquired an extraordinary autonomy and logic of its own. In Chapter 8, I probe the causes of this autonomy by focusing on how a specific "state interest" based on the military's own professional interests led to political liberalization and the abandonment of the original project of state-led restructuring. General Lanusse proposed a "Great National Accord" (GAN) in a bold attempt to limit, and if possible reverse, the political defeat the *cordobazo* and the subsequent expansion of democratic and revolutionary opposition had inflicted on the military and the dominant groups. The GAN's strategic objectives were to extricate the military from the direct exercise of state power while simultaneously stifling *clasista* labor militancy and crushing the burgeoning revolutionary guerrilla movement. The ensuing "war game" pitted two military strategists, Alejandro Lanusse and Juan Perón, against once another, and opened the way for Peronism's electoral victory in 1973.

The 1976–83 period witnessed the apotheosis of Argentine authoritarianism. This is the subject of Chapter 9. Following a brief discussion of the short interregnum under the Peróns, I concentrate on the Proceso, Argentina's second experiment in authoritarian rule. In common with other "new wave" authoritarianisms of the 1970s in the Southern Cone, the Proceso exemplified the foundational logic of radical restructuring of state, society, and economy in a particularly pure form. Tracing the evolution of Economy Minister Martínez de Hoz's "capitalist revolution," I explain the rampant financial speculation, deindustrialization, shrinkage of the labor force in the manufacturing sector, and massive foreign debt fostered by the Proceso. This chapter concludes by explaining how the Malvinas debacle, which was fought by the same military that had waged a "dirty war" against its fellow citizens, led to the collapse of the Proceso.

The government of Raúl Alfonsín and the return to civilian rule are the topics of Chapter 10. Alfonsín and his Radical party came to power in December 1983 following the defeat of Peronism in openly competitive democratic elections. My purpose in this concluding chapter is not to provide a detailed account of the Alfonsín years, but rather to assess the prospects for the emergence of a democratic class compromise in Argentina. I conclude that the Alfonsín regime's policies of "heterodox shock" embodied in the Austral Plan and its attempt to forge a "social pact" with capital and labor have been only partially successful in overcoming the authoritarian legacy and in reconciling democratic politics with social justice and economic modernization.

Still, the record of the Alfonsín years would appear to demonstrate that both political elites and the mass public share a deeper commitment to democratic values and institutions than ever before, and a somewhat greater awareness of the immense difficulties in promoting economic growth. Unfortunately, however, my argument suggests that many years of costly sacrifices lie ahead before Argentines can hope to overcome decades of political turbulence and economic decline and consolidate a viable class compromise.

TWO

Cycles of Crisis and Transformation in the Argentine Political Economy

IN 1916, on the centennial of its independence from Spain, Argentina had great prospects for joining the ranks of the most privileged core nations of the world-economy. Compared to other "new nations" with temperate agricultural economies, Argentina stacked up well. An abundance of natural resources, scant population, and great riches ranked it among the wealthiest of nations, with a per capita income of $700 compared to $1,800 for the United States, $1,300 for Australia, and $1,000 for Canada.[1]

By the 1950s, however, Argentina had entered a period of relative stagnation and never regained its status as an emerging nation poised to join the ranks of the developed countries of the world. Table 2.1, which compares Argentina's per capita product with that of a group of selected countries, graphically illustrates this prolonged period of relative decline. As the data indicate, Argentina's relative decline did not begin until fairly recently. Argentina's per capita product was 71 percent of the group average in 1929, 74 percent in 1939, and still 68 percent in 1950. By 1983, Argentina had slipped to only 27 percent of the average for all 28 countries. Argentina's relative decline is not surprising if one considers that from 1929 to 1983, its economy grew at an annual rate of less than 1 percent per capita, while the other countries achieved 2.5 percent annual growth.

Table 2.2 shows us when Argentina's relative decline occurred. After a small relative improvement during the Great Depression, 13.6 percent of the decline took place in the 1940s,

TABLE 2.1

Ratio of Argentine Per Capita Product to That of Other Countries and Regions, Selected Years, 1929–83

Country or region	1929	1939	1950	1960	1970	1975	1983
United States	.38	.33	.23	.24	.24	.23	.15
Temperate agrarian societies[a]	.45	.44	.34	.34	.34	.27	.20
European industrial societies[b]	.47	.54	.49	.35	.32	.24	.18
Backward European societies[c]	1.08	1.04	1.30	.80	.65	.49	.34
Japan	1.16	1.33	2.50	.90	.49	.37	.20
Latin American "dual" societies[d]	2.95	2.72	2.72	2.18	2.16	1.84	1.37
Chile and Uruguay	1.15	1.40	1.16	1.29	1.20	1.66	.97
South Africa	1.54	1.33	1.47	1.64	1.28	1.15	.83
Average	.77	.74	.68	.53	.48	.38	.27
Argentina's ranking	18	18	16	20	21	21	25

SOURCE: Llach, *Reconstrucción o estancamiento*, p. 27.
[a] Australia, Canada, and New Zealand.
[b] Germany, Belgium, France, Great Britain, Holland, Norway, Sweden, and Switzerland.
[c] Austria, Spain, Finland, Greece, Ireland, Italy, and Portugal.
[d] Brazil, Colombia, Mexico, and Peru.

TABLE 2.2

Argentina's Loss of Relative Position in Product Per Capita

(*Percent*)

Country or region	1939 vs. 1929	1950 vs. 1939	1960 vs. 1950	1970 vs. 1960	1975 vs. 1970	1983 vs. 1975
United States	−22.8%	−41.5%	+2.1%	+2.5%	−3.4%	−36.9%
Temperate agrarian societies[a]	−6.5	−38.5	−0.4	+0.8	−27.5	−27.9
European industrial societies[b]	+25.6	−16.6	−48.7	−12.5	−25.3	−22.5
Backward European societies[c]	−4.5	+35.1	−68.1	−20.5	−21.8	−20.2
Japan	+17.4	+122.0	−166.7	−43.4	−12.1	−17.2
Latin American "dual" societies[d]	−14.6	0.0	−34.2	−1.3	−20.3	−29.6
Chile and Uruguay	+138.9	−133.3	+72.2	−50.0	+255.6	−177.8
South Africa	−29.0	+19.5	+23.7	−50.5	−18.8	−45.1
Average	+6.8%	−13.6%	−34.1%	−11.4%	−22.7%	−25.0%

SOURCE: Llach, *Reconstrucción o estancamiento*, p. 29.
[a] Australia, Canada, and New Zealand.
[b] Germany, Belgium, France, Great Britain, Holland, Norway, Sweden, and Switzerland.
[c] Austria, Spain, Finland, Greece, Ireland, Italy, and Portugal.
[d] Brazil, Colombia, Mexico, and Peru.

followed by a very large 34.1 percent fall in the 1950s. Moderate per capita annual growth of 2.7 percent in the 1960s corresponded with a modest 11.4 percent relative decline. The 1970s and early 1980s were disastrous: 22.7 percent of the total decline occurred from 1970 to 1975, and a further 24 percent from 1975 to 1983.[2] It is worth noting that the precipitous economic decline of the 1950s coincided with the crisis and overthrow of Peronism, while the even more dramatic reversals of the 1970s took place during massive social convulsions, triple-digit inflation, and a brutal "dirty war" waged by a military dictatorship against its own citizenry.

To provide the proper historical context for analyzing Argentina's contemporary politico-economic crisis, this chapter will examine the watershed of the 1930s and then turn to the key decades of the 1940s and 1960s and the events that led, in the mid-1960s, to Argentina's first experiment with state-led economic restructuring under authoritarian aegis.

Pampean Hegemony in an Oligarchical Order

The Argentine state that emerged after the defeat of Juan Manuel de Rosas's autocratic reign in 1852 was the most modern to be found in Latin America. Indeed, according to Jorge Sábato's provocative thesis, this state was "the product of the deliberate and conscious will of a social group which, to a certain extent, was *ahead* of the necessities of the epoch." In spite of the prevailing laissez-faire ideology, the state played a strategic role in attracting foreign capital, promoting necessary infrastructure development, guaranteeing massive inflows of immigrant labor, managing the foreign debt, and in general developing policies designed to further the agro-export economy's expansion.[3]

As the country rode the crest of a wave of very rapid economic and demographic expansion during the last quarter of the nineteenth century, the basic contours of modern Argentina began to emerge. This unprecedented expansion was founded upon Argentina's rapid integration into the world-economy, the consolidation of capitalist relations, and the formation of a modern bourgeois state. Prosperity during this phase of *desarrollo hacia afuera* ("outward-oriented development") was based on the large differential rents on a world scale generated by the comparative advantages enjoyed by Argentina's famous *pampa húmeda* in the production of primary products for export. The backward and forward linkages of the agro-export sector gave impetus to a precocious, although limited, industrialization based on high wages and a sizable domestic market.[4]

Capitalist expansion generated considerable differentiation of the class structure. The most notable consequence of the growing complexity of society was the consolidation of the Pampean bourgeoisie and the emergence of comparatively large urban and rural middle-class groups, tied to import-export activities, production for the internal market, or the expansion of the state bureaucracy. With few exceptions, the existence and prosperity of these urban and rural middle-class groups, and the incipient formation of an urban working class, were closely linked to the export sector dominated by the Pampean bourgeoisie. As a result, both the middle sectors and the working class generally defended free trade liberalism and acted as "consumers" by opposing high tariffs on imports and other measures favoring industrialization.[5]

The political and ideological consequences of this prosperity and early broadening of the class structure were crucial. Although the Pampean beef and grain producers were in permanent conflict with other classes, they almost never had to confront the rest of society as a bloc. Argentina's economy did not generate a "principal antagonist" to question the privileged position of the Pampean bourgeoisie. This allowed a flexible network of oligarchical state institutions to establish their legitimacy over contending social forces, while the Pampean producers consolidated their hegemonic leadership over the various regional bourgeoisies and over society as a whole.[6]

Pampean hegemony and state legitimacy did not, however, imply an absence of class conflict. Rather, they transferred conflicts from the economic and social arenas into political disputes over participation and representation within the oligarchical state. Particularly after the economic crises of the early 1890s, the narrowness of representation and participation led to mounting pressures for political reform from dissident sectors of the oligarchy, the middle sectors, and labor unions. The most significant manifestation of this opposition was the Unión Cívica Radical, which staged unsuccessful uprisings against the system of oligarchic politics in 1893 and 1905.[7]

Reacting to these pressures, the more progressive and farsighted elements of the oligarchical political elite advanced a strategy of transformism. Their premise was that political co-optation and incorporation of the opposition would strengthen commitment to the rules of oligarchical politics upholding the values of decision-making by consensus. In practice, adherence to the rules meant that the traditional political elite would continue to enjoy a virtual monopoly of substantive power, preventing the state apparatus from being used to pursue economic policies contrary to the logic of the agro-export economy.[8]

This strategy materialized in the 1912 Sáenz Peña Law, which established universal, secret, and obligatory suffrage for males at 18 years of age.[9] In the ensuing elections of 1916, the Unión Cívica Radical succeeded in winning the presidency for its standard-bearer, Hipólito Yrigoyen: the Conservatives, convinced there was no real threat to their interests, had bickered among themselves, failing to present a united front. The generally stand-pat policies adopted during Yrigoyen's first term in office (1916–22), as well as the maintenance of consensus-style decision-making, meant that although real wages improved substantially, Pampean dominance went unchallenged. Politics largely remained a "struggle *within* the political class, without changes in the government being translated into significant changes in the distribution of income, in property, or in the access to power by the other classes."[10]

Gradual liberalization of the oligarchical state continued without trauma until Yrigoyen's reelection to the presidency in 1928. By then, new circumstances led conservative elites to perceive Yrigoyen's return to the Casa Rosada and, indeed, political democracy itself as grave threats to fundamental oligarchical interests. Three broad changes led to the legitimation crisis of the liberalized oligarchical order. First, the Radical party attempted to broaden its mass constituency in a more populist direction by appealing to urban workers. Second, the Radicals increased their majority in the Chamber of Deputies and seemed poised to achieve a future majority in the Senate, thus posing a threat to the remaining bastions of Conservative representation in the state. And third, a related increase in the acrimony of public-policy debates hinted at deepening polarization along class and regional cleavages.[11]

The international economic disruptions heralded by the October 1929 stock market crash in New York accelerated and exacerbated the political crisis. The chain of causation from external economic crisis to the breakdown of democracy and the oligarchical order was not direct and mechanical, but was mediated by the contradictory policies pursued by the Yrigoyen regime, policies that in turn contributed to the hardening of bourgeois and middle-class opposition.[12]

The collapse of the export sector triggered growing unemployment, on the one hand, while the attempt to bolster internal demand through deficit financing further accelerated inflationary pressures, on the other. The collapse of markets and prices threatened to force a default on Argentina's overseas debt. This would have meant disaster for the agro-export economy, for it would have disrupted the Pampean bourgeoisie's external market and investment relationships. The expected day of reckoning was not long in coming, as landed interests, spearheaded by the Sociedad Rural Argentina, and commercial and industrial groups, represented by the Unión Industrial Argentina and the Cámara de Comercio, stepped up their hostility to Yrigoyen and the Radicals.

The Yrigoyen government's response to the Crash not only alienated powerful bourgeois interests but also caused the loss of middle-class and popular support. Reacting to criticisms voiced by the dominant groups, the government belatedly cut public spending, an action which eroded its ability to maintain popular support through political patronage. When disaffected elements of the army and the civilian opposition denounced Yrigoyen's so-called "arbitrary and despotic" policies, middle-class and working-class constituencies had little reason to rally to the Radicals' defense. Finally, on September 6, 1930, a symbolic show of force was sufficient to topple the Yrigoyen regime,[13] thereby ending nearly seventy years of civilian politics and gradual liberalization of the oligarchical order.

The Restructuring of State Power in the 1930s

The fall of the Radical regime, together with the Great Depression, initiated a long period of economic and political instability. Argentina's exceptional degree of integration into the world-economy guaranteed that the impact of the Great Depression on international trade would force a major departure from the model of outward growth that had given Argentina one of the highest per capita incomes in the world. The central axis of this reorientation was the transition to greater state regulation of the economy, and the establishment of a new pattern of "inward-oriented growth" based upon industrialization tied to the domestic market, which replaced agro-export production as the dynamic hub of Argentine capitalism. Events from 1930 to 1943 played a crucial role in this transition.

The objective behind the 1930 coup was to reestablish elite power by returning to the pre-1912 political arrangement, whereby the masses had been allowed only limited representation and participation in national politics. Elites were divided, however, over how best to restore the oligarchical order. The Crash and the ensuing violent contraction of international commerce touched off a crisis in those semiperipheral nations which, like Argentina, were most dependent on the inflow of foreign capital and the demand in the core countries for their exports. For Argentina, a debtor nation whose exports accounted for nearly 30 percent of gross domestic production, the sharp drop in its volume of exports and the worsening of its terms of trade with the industrial economies were a potential disaster.

The right-wing Catholic nationalist faction that assumed power immediately after the coup attempted to reorganize the state along quasi-Fascist corporatist lines but soon foundered because of its adherence to economic orthodoxy. It was replaced by General Augustín P. Justo through fraudulent elections in 1932. The Justo administration inaugurated an eleven-year period known as the Década Infame ("infamous decade") during which the Concordancia—a coalition of strange bedfellows consisting of conservatives, anti-Yrigoyen Radicals, and technocrats—ruled through the systematic practice of "patriotic fraud." The Concordancia was content with preserving a veneer of parliamentary democracy without any attempt to seek broader legitimation.[14]

Policymakers in the Justo government perceived that even the prompt recovery of the industrialized economies of the United States and Europe probably would not restore Argentina's traditional pattern of international trade. Guided by a new generation of competent *técnicos* whose policies were "more enlightened than those followed in more advanced countries," the government, seeking greater legitimacy, made a partial break with liberal orthodoxy, which counseled that the best course of action was to balance the budget, honor Argentina's overseas commitments, and simply wait for better times. The new strategy, set forth in a Plan for Economic Restructuring, called for "writing off the external stimulus" and promoting domestic industry. Argentina had discovered its own home-brewed, *avant la lettre* version of Keynesian countercyclical stimulation of domestic demand through public works.[15]

This strategy impelled the expansion of state intervention in the economy through the creation of a Central Bank in 1935, the establishment of New Deal–style regulatory boards for marketing rural products such as meat, grain, wine, cotton, and wool, plus the creation of new policy instruments such as income taxes, foreign-exchange controls, new industrial credit schemes, and so on. State intervention to promote capital accumulation was decisive in reorienting the economic surplus from the agrarian to the industrial sector. Not only did state policies increase profit rates in manufacturing activities to the detriment of rural producers, but they also raised the absolute level of profits in the import-substituting sectors.

These changes facilitated a shift in the structure of production and resulted in rapid import-substitution industrialization. Of course it is difficult to distinguish between the impact of state policies and that of changes in international trade, but it is nevertheless true that while domestic production only accounted for 40–50 percent of total consumption of manufactured products during the previous three decades, this figure increased to over 63 percent by the late 1930s and to over 80 percent by the early 1940s.[16]

On the whole, therefore, industrial expansion during the 1930s signified a remarkably successful recovery from the impact of the Depression. The economic turnaround was related to an authoritarian restructuring of state power. State elites, and more particularly economic policymakers, began to act more autonomously on the basis of a differentiated "state interest,"[17] an interest shaped by the challenge of the Great Depression. The emergence of a distinct state interest gave these elites the maneuvering room they needed to guide the transition toward a

modified model of capital accumulation. The structural transformations of the economy associated with import-substitution led
to a broader alliance of social forces, extending beyond the traditional dominant class of agrarian origin to include industrial
entrepreneurs. Although the interests of Pampean landowners
remained hegemonic within this more complex alliance, state
tutelage and economic policies not only went beyond their immediate interests, but obliged them to make major concessions
to other groups, particularly foreign financial and industrial
interests.[18]

In this process, state policies furthered a process of internal
cleavage within the dominant agrarian class. From the early
1930s on, the *invernadores* or "fatteners," by capitalizing on official favoritism and the Roca-Runciman Pact with Great Britain,
which guaranteed a quota for Argentine "chilled" beef in British
markets, became the senior partner in the new alliance. In
contrast, the *criadores* or "breeders," who suffered a severe
economic setback because of the collapse of their export markets, were relegated to a marginal role in the new phase of
accumulation.[19]

Industrial entrepreneurs, acting through the Unión Industrial, gave few indications of challenging the political ascendancy of the *invernadores*. The political logic underlying this
broadened alliance, as well as the state's central role in its
emergence, came out of the crisis of the world market and the
rapid economic diversification then taking place. In this complex
equation, the ultimate success of capitalist restructuring depended on the ability of state elites to constantly juggle the interests and demands of the members of the agro-industrial bloc.

This challenge became particularly difficult in the late 1930s
and early 1940s, during a recession brought on by balance-of-
payments problems and heightened insecurity about future international trade occasioned by the onset of World War II. A
Plan of Economic Reactivation was proposed to meet the new
situation. While the Plan's most immediate goal was to protect
agriculture by buying up crops, it also was intended to avoid unemployment (of resources as well as of labor) and, through
public works spending, to avoid a precipitous fall in aggregate
demand. However, the Plan also proposed to go beyond countercyclical considerations by vigorously promoting industries

capable of exporting to the world market. Promotion of manufactured exports was a remarkably advanced idea for the period
and in fact threatened to transgress the bounds of the project of
limited industrialization in force since 1933. Still, while implicitly going beyond the "spontaneous" import-substitution of the
previous decade to a more systematic—and statist—accumulation strategy, the economic authorities were still primarily concerned with protecting the power of Pampean landholders.[20]

This attempt to revamp the economy by promoting industrialization, even though it protected agrarian interests, failed to
evoke the necessary political support. Only the Unión Industrial, of the groups within the still-inchoate dominant coalition,
expressed strong support for the Plan of Economic Reactivation; the members of the Sociedad Rural, by contrast, accepted
the short-run countercyclical measures (i.e., buying up surplus
crops) but were unenthusiastic about the Plan's pro-industry
thrust, which they viewed as too radical and contrary to Argentina's "agrarian vocation." This failure to articulate a more coherent accumulation strategy revealed the vacillation of state
elites. It also demonstrated the growing fragility of Pampean political and ideological predominance and a shortsighted inability
to transcend economic-corporate interests.[21]

A second factor undermining Pampean hegemony was the ex-
ponential growth of the working class, which, by doubling to
almost a million persons by the early 1940s, became the largest
class in Argentine society. Accordingly, after 1935, organized labor's capacity for mobilizing its rank and file, as measured by
the incidence of strikes and the number of strikers, increased
substantially. In fact, labor's weakness in this period has been
much exaggerated, when it was labor's comparative strength under adverse conditions that was most striking. Despite this,
however, most strikes still ended in defeat. By the early 1940s
only 20 percent of industrial workers were organized into unions.
Moreover, the fact that real wages stagnated during the 1930–
43 period, while employment in manufacturing experienced a
quantum jump, was indicative of a large shift in the distribution
of national income in favor of capital.[22]

These transformations in the class structure and in the political economy soon carried the Concordancia to the brink of crisis.
Roberto Ortiz, Justo's successor in the presidency, realized that

the changes wrought by the economic recovery threatened to dismember the regime's narrow social base. At the same time, attempts to co-opt opposition forces by curtailing the more objectionable aspects of "patriotic fraud" were set aside, and fraud and corruption were reinstituted on an even grander scale than witnessed in the past.[23] The return to rule by fraud—aggravated by the failure of the Plan, and combined with labor's exclusion from a share in the benefits of economic growth and its lack of its own autonomous channels of political participation—fed a deepening crisis of the Concordancia.

When it became clear that conservative elites planned to rig the upcoming presidential elections, the armed forces carried out a coup on 4 June 1943. The goals of the new military regime were quickly defined as antiparty and "eminently Argentine" in orientation: "No politician—whatever his affiliation—will be summoned to collaborate with the government. . . . The political parties are not important now." In the military's view, a strong regime, free of the "venality, fraud, peculation, and corruption" of the past, was required to guide Argentina through the World War.[24]

Peronism and the Limits of Populist Class Compromise

Peronism emerged from the 1943 coup through a convergence of interests created by the process of import-substitution. The army, the rapidly expanding working class, and industrial entrepreneurs found common ground under its banner. Within the framework of such a convergence, each group nevertheless pursued primarily economistic objectives. The goal of the working class was the improvement of its immediate material conditions (wages, working conditions, etc.). Industrialists also operated primarily on an economic-corporate level and "saw society from their factories, as a collection of consumers." The military, for its part, had been propelled toward assuming political power by "professional contradictions" with the civilian-run Concordancia and its pro-Allied foreign policy; military officers consequently "saw society from their cannon sights, as a collection of potential recruits."[25]

It fell to Colonel Juan Domingo Perón to weld these disparate groups into a coherent political movement. Perón rapidly became the central figure of the military regime, first serving as Labor Secretary and then becoming Vice President as well. On October 17, 1945, an unprecedented mass mobilization organized by labor unions (with the participation of Eva Duarte, soon to become Evita Perón) confirmed Perón's status as Argentina's new strongman. Perón was to be elected president in 1946 in one of the freer contests in Argentine history, defeating the Unión Democrática, a coalition of Radicals, Conservatives, and Communists, with a clear 54.8 percent majority.

The Peronist regime confronted a difficult economic situation. The Argentine economy was nearing the limits of a model of industrial expansion based on domestic production of previously imported finished goods; to avoid stagnation, further growth would depend on widening the internal market and redistributing income, or, alternatively, on shifting emphasis toward promotion of traditional and manufactured exports. The option chosen was the first. Once in the presidency, Perón advanced a project of industrial reconversion based on increased internal consumption, virtually ignoring the export sector.[26]

Perón's economic policies were successful in increasing gross domestic product 25–29 percent between 1943 and 1948. Aided by favorable terms of trade, the total availability of goods and services (domestic production plus imports) increased an even more impressive 45 percent in the same period.[27] This growth spurt was made possible by an unusual combination of domestic and international conditions. First, large increases in consumer demand were immediately and apparently effortlessly achieved via income redistribution to labor. Second, the end of the war found Argentina with sizable foreign-exchange reserves, which allowed the state to subsidize the importation of needed machinery and raw materials.

This combination papered over, for a short while at least, important contradictions which later hindered accumulation and which became painfully apparent by the end of the decade. Increased domestic consumption of foodstuffs, semistagnant rural output, large increases in imports, and Perón's costly program of nationalizing foreign-owned infrastructure (e.g., British-owned railroads) soon combined to produce a growing foreign-exchange crisis by the end of the 1940s.[28]

Imports declined by one-third in 1949 and continued to be

TABLE 2.3

Growth Rate of GDP, Inflation Rates, and Foreign-Exchange Reserves,
1946–55

	GDP growth rate (%)	Cost of living index (%)	Wholesale price index (%)	Change in foreign-exchange reserves[a]
1946	8.3%	17.7%	15.8%	–
1947	13.8	13.5	3.5	–
1948	1.2	13.1	15.5	–
1949	−4.6	31.1	23.0	−269
1950	1.6	25.5	20.2	+166
1951	4.0	36.7	49.1	−333
1952	−6.3	38.7	31.2	−173
1953	7.0	4.0	11.6	+279
1954	3.8	3.8	3.2	−33
1955	6.9	12.3	8.8	−175

SOURCE: Díaz Alejandro, *Essays on the Economic History of the Argentine Republic*, Table 7.1, p. 352; Table 7.2, p. 353; and Table 124, p. 528.
[a]Change in net Central Bank reserves in millions of U.S. dollars.

depressed for several years; the economy went into a period of stagnation. Inflation, which had been comparatively low in international terms, jumped to an average annual rate of over 30 percent from 1949 to 1952, before stabilization measures and economic recovery brought it under control during 1953–55. This period of initial rapid accumulation and the subsequent crisis can be observed clearly in Table 2.3.

Industrial entrepreneurs are frequently ignored as key participants in Perón's populist class compromise.[29] Perón first attempted to cultivate industrial support in the 1946 electoral campaign for the presidency, but met with rejection. Also in 1946, when he offered the Unión Industrial, industry's representative body, the same status as the national labor confederation, the Confederación General del Trabajo (CGT), he was again turned down. After some years without an official interlocutor, Perón, in classic corporatist fashion, moved to create the Confederación General Económica (CGE) as industry's officially recognized class organization. By and large, however, the largest and most dynamic firms refused to affiliate with the new organization, and the CGE was dominated by small and medium-sized firms, especially from the interior provinces.[30]

In spite of a slightly more pro-business tilt in the regime's policies in the early 1950s, few industrialists, aside from those in leadership positions in the Confederación General Económica, could be considered ardent supporters of Peronism. In fact, "from the viewpoint of the industrialists there were too many wage increases, too much social legislation, too much labor indiscipline, too much statism, too much personalism, too many attacks on middle class values."[31]

But even if there is little evidence supporting a claim for the industrial bourgeoisie's dominance within Peronism, it does not contradict the clear fact that Perón's economic project accorded entrepreneurs substantial benefits. The impact of Peronist economic policies on industrial entrepreneurs can be seen as part of a complex, contradictory process of industrial deconcentration and centralization of production. The industrial bourgeoisie began to divide into two groups. On one side were found a large number of small and medium-sized entrepreneurs, many operating family-owned firms characterized by considerable competition; on the other were found a relatively small group of firms, mostly organized as modern corporations, which had considerable capacity to achieve monopoly or oligopoly rents due to their technological superiority and ability to set prices.[32]

The political significance of this vertical cleavage within the industrial bourgeoisie was that it hastened the crystallization of anti-Peronist opposition among both fractions, neither of which felt that the regime was responding adequately to its needs. Intensified anti-Peronist sentiment among the industrialists then set the stage for a political and ideological convergence between industrialists and the Pampean bourgeoisie, as well as between both these groups and antiregime sectors within the Catholic church, the political parties, and the military itself.

The basis of the rapprochement between the industrialists, especially the modern firms in the dynamic sectors, and the agrarian interests was their common support for liberalization of the tight state control exercised over the economy. Industrialists were motivated by a need to seek new forms of association with foreign capital, especially that of transnational firms and international financial institutions, in order to acquire needed investment and technology for modernization. Significant labor constraints (wages, loss of control over the shop floor, etc.) also pushed them in the same direction.[33]

In short, for the industrial bourgeoisie, Peronism represented a system of state tutelage and concessions which was accepted—albeit grudgingly, along with political marginalization—as long as prosperity continued and expansion of the internal market allowed further accumulation. Peronism, therefore, should be seen not as the political representative of a non-hegemonic "national bourgeoisie" but as a patchwork of state-engineered compromises, a system which became increasingly onerous to all sectors of the bourgeoisie by the early 1950s. Though it was a remarkably resilient patchwork, its ideological limits were narrower than they appeared.

Peronism was the most radical of Latin American populisms to have captured state power before the late 1960s. The Peronist ideological discourse was founded on a melange of contradictory elements that passed through various incarnations: an initial emphasis on military concerns and aspirations of a corporative nature; a phase of *laborismo* tinged with anticapitalist overtones; a period of greater stress on organic corporatism and a view of the state as the arbiter of relations between labor and capital; and finally, in its period of disintegration, a vacillation between rigid control over all spheres of institutional life and opportunistic concessions first to one group, then to another.[34]

A central feature in the ever-changing ideology of Perón and his regime was the aspiration to create an "organized community" in which the working class would be firmly subjected to state tutelage. At the same time, Perón made it clear that reforms had to be consonant with Argentina's capitalist economy. To transgress the limits imposed by the economy in extending social justice was "to march toward economic cataclysm," he explained; "not to go far enough, [was] to march toward social cataclysm."[35]

A second constant in the ideology of populist compromise was the regime's attempt to base the state's legitimacy vis-à-vis the working class on Perón's claim that the state was on their side and that, with their loyalty, capitalism could be made to work for all Argentines. The regime's goal, Perón stated, was the "humanization of capital," to be achieved by "suppressing the capitalist economy of exploitation and replacing it with a social economy, in which there are neither exploiters nor exploited and where each person receives just recompense according to his capacity and his efforts."[36] Of course these ideas did not arise by chance: they responded to growing fears about a future threat of Communism, which this discourse attempted to forestall.

Espousing these sentiments, and abetted by his wife Evita's powerful presence, Perón actively promoted labor's incorporation into an inclusive system of state corporatism, dispensing social justice by intervening in labor conflicts on the side of the workers, raising real wages, and sponsoring the extension of social services. Efforts to contain socialist and communist unions led the administration to encourage parallel unions, resulting in a growth of total union membership. As a result, organized labor more than doubled in size between 1946 and 1950, increasing from 877,333 to 1,992,404; by 1954 unions represented some 2,256,580 workers, or 42.5 percent of all workers, a very high figure by international standards.[37] But relations between the regime and its principal social base were far from tranquil.

From 1946 to 1949 a syndicalist wing of Peronism, independent of the regime but not against it, attempted to channel organized labor's growing political power and militancy into the Partido Laborista. As state control over labor expanded, however, *laborismo* lost its institutional base and ceased to represent an alternative to the weakening of labor autonomy achieved by co-opting and incorporating the union leadership into the state. Thus, by 1949–50, the leadership of the Confederación General del Trabajo and of many of the most powerful unions had come under the sway of loyal Peronists who owed their positions of authority more to the state's labor bureaucracy than to their own membership.[38] Particularly in view of the lack of effective incorporation of entrepreneurs, labor's political incorporation also provided a strong position for union organizations at the level of the state apparatus.

However, one important caveat is required to round out this picture. In spite of labor's loss of organizational autonomy, workers did not meekly accept the modest decline in real wages and living standards occasioned by the downturn in the economy in the early 1950s. Working-class politics found other outlets in wildcat strikes, absenteeism, and production slowdowns. While rank-and-file protests and acts of labor indiscipline were primarily directed against recalcitrant employers, dissatisfaction was also directed against the union leaderships for their quiescent attitude in protecting labor's earlier gains, as well as against the regime's shift in economic policy, which required wage restraint in order to fight inflation and revive flagging bourgeois confidence in the regime.[39] These forms of rank-and-file protest pointed out that trade-union leaderships, in the last instance, derived their political legitimacy and bargaining power from the ability to control grass-roots militancy. Control and militancy are features of any form of political incorporation, and that practiced by Peronism was a veritable art form.

These arrangements were undermined as Perón's administration responded to the economic crisis through recessionary policies. Perón had "abandoned the workers' nation" to a certain extent, but the regime did as much as possible—within the increasingly narrow limits of the populist compromise—to protect labor's earlier conquests. The bind was that while capital pressed for greater labor productivity and viewed labor's gains as a threat, economic stagnation was for labor a threat to the very foundation of the "conquests" achieved since 1943. Post-1950 economic policy shifts were a consequence of the state's mounting inability to resolve the contradictions between its need to maintain legitimacy vis-à-vis its principal social support, the working class, and its equally imperative need to respond to bourgeois demands to cease its populist demagoguery and move to put the process of capital accumulation on a firmer footing.

This dilemma was ultimately resolved (or postponed) when the military overthrew the regime on September 20, 1955. Rather than risk resistance, Perón chose to leave for exile aboard a Paraguayan gunboat.[40] He was not to return to Argentina until seventeen years later. As a political force, however, Peronism was far from exhausted, and in fact proved to be an unconquerable nemesis for all post-1955 regimes, military or civilian.

Economic Cycles, Democratic Breakdown, and Military Intervention

The decade following Perón's fall from power was marked by a new phase in the world-economy. Along with Brazil and Mexico, Argentina saw its domestic market rapidly internationalized as the country was reinserted into an emerging transnational economy in which patterns of production, finance, and trade were articulated by transnational corporations acting on a world scale. For the largest Latin American economies, these transformations signified a new pattern of "associated-dependent" development in which rapid expansion was combined with growing subordination to the advanced core regions of the world-economy.[41] The corollary to these economic transformations was the realignment and accelerated diversification of the Argentine class structure. The sum of these parallel processes led to the emergence of a new grouping of industrial capital and financial institutions made up of transnational corporations and the largest and most dynamic fractions of Argentine capital.

Salient to this phase of capitalist expansion was a rather confusing mixture of stop-go growth cycles, high inflation, and trends toward greater inequality of income distribution. During these years, the economy as a whole grew at an average annual rate of 3.5 percent. The annual rate of inflation averaged around 33 percent per year, compared with 16 percent in the 1943–55 period. The erratic evolution of the economy is clearly visible in Table 2.4.

TABLE 2.4

Annual Percent Change in Macroeconomic Indicators, 1951–66

(*Constant 1960 pesos*)

	Total GDP	Industrial GDP	Cost of living index	Gross domestic investment	Supply and demand	Change in international reserves[a]
1951–55	3.1%	1.6%	19.1%	9.3%	3.0%	–
1956	2.8	6.9	13.1	−5.8	1.4	18
1957	5.1	7.9	25.0	12.5	5.8	140
1958	6.1	8.4	31.4	9.6	5.9	−214
1959	−6.4	−10.3	113.9	−11.3	−6.9	119
1960	7.8	10.1	27.1	47.3	9.3	174
1961	7.1	10.0	13.7	9.6	8.3	−162
1962	−1.6	−5.5	26.2	−8.0	−1.9	−296
1963	−2.4	−0.4	25.9	−18.0	−4.7	118
1964	10.3	18.9	22.1	26.0	10.8	−23
1965	9.1	13.8	28.6	7.3	8.2	91
1966	0.6	0.7	31.9	−7.2	0.3	32

SOURCES: Data in the first five columns are from Banco Central, *Sistema de cuentas del producto e ingreso de la Argentina*, vol. II, Table 34, pp. 118–19, and Tables 55–58, pp. 182–89; data in the last column are from Mallon and Sourrouille, *Economic Policymaking in a Conflict Society: The Argentine Case*, Table 1–3, p. 18.

[a]Millions of U.S. dollars.

A second characteristic of the transnationalization of the economy was the unprecedented inflow of foreign investment. From 1958 to 1966, $630 million in new foreign investments were authorized, with U.S. investment in Argentina nearly tripling in less than a decade, rising from $427 million in 1960 to nearly $1.2 billion in 1968.[42] More than 90 percent of all U.S. investments (and a similar proportion from other sources) in Argentina during these years went into the most rapidly expanding sectors of the manufacturing industry—chemicals and petrochemicals, transportation, metallurgy, machinery, electrical equipment, and petroleum.

Argentina's full incorporation into this latest phase of the world-economy produced the rapid structural shifts within the industrial sector depicted in Table 2.5. These shifts were intimately related to processes of concentration, centralization of capital, and denationalization of the key industrial sectors. Transnational firms, together with large locally owned firms (many of which were associated with foreign capital through portfolio investment, technology, management interlocks, etc.), rapidly gained control over the most profitable and dynamic sectors of the Argentine economy.[43]

The growing transnational presence was facilitated by policies that removed state control over foreign exchange, prices, and wages in favor of greater reliance on market forces, thus spurring the reallocation of all types of economic resources. The combined effect of the resulting horizontal and vertical income shifts primarily benefited the large national firms, multinational companies, and the Pampean agro-export producers, while pe-

TABLE 2.5

Sectoral Composition of Industrial Gross Domestic Product, Selected Years

(*Percent*)

Sector	1950	1958	1964	1966
Traditional	52.5%	43.4%	35.3%	34.9%
Dynamic	29.8	41.3	52.1	51.9
Intermediate	10.9	10.1	8.0	8.8
Others	6.8	5.2	4.6	4.4
Total	100.0%	100.0%	100.0%	100.0%

SOURCE: Calculated from Banco Central, *Sistema de cuentas del producto e ingreso de la Argentina*, Vol. II, Table 39, pp. 128–31.

TABLE 2.6

Indicators of Labor's Participation in the Economy, 1951–66

	Labor's share of GDP (%)	Index of exploitation[a]	Real wages (1960 = 100)	Change in real wages (%)
1951–55	48.2%	108	111	–
1956	45.3	121	121	+4.6%
1957	43.8	128	121	+0.2
1958	44.4	125	127	+4.9
1959	37.7	165	94	−25.8
1960	38.0	163	100	+6.4
1961	40.8	145	112	+11.6
1962	39.8	156	107	−3.8
1963	38.8	158	108	+0.8
1964	38.7	158	121	+12.0
1965	40.6	146	132	+8.4
1966	43.8	128	133	+1.4

SOURCES: The first two columns are calculated from Banco Central, *Sistema de cuentas del producto e ingreso de la Argentina*, vol. II, Table I, pp. 50–51; the last two are calculated from Sigaut, *Acerca de la distribución y niveles de ingreso en la Argentina, 1950–1972*, Table 16, p. 57.
[a] Capital's share of GDP ÷ wage and salary share of GDP × 100.

nalizing most of urban labor, the professional sectors of the middle class, and the state itself, which suffered recurrent fiscal crises. The "big trade-off" between economic efficiency and fair income distribution acquired sharper contours. The bottom 60 percent of all income recipients experienced a notable decline in their share of national income, while the middle 30 percent suffered a small loss. The top 10 percent achieved a substantial increase.[44]

The data presented in Table 2.6 indicate that there was a similar deterioration in the functional distribution of income between labor and capital. Wages and salaries as a percent of GDP declined from around 48 percent in the second half of the Peronist decade to about 38–39 percent in the early 1960s, before improving slightly under the Radicals' expansionary policies.

With a general idea of the economic transformations occurring in the 1955–66 period, we can now turn to corollary changes in the class structure and realignments at the level of social forces. Notwithstanding their growing economic predominance, the new transnationalized sectors of Argentine industry and finance found it exceedingly difficult to win consent for their leadership from the Pampean bourgeoisie. Nor were they able to successfully subdue the weaker fractions of urban industrial capital and organized labor. The stop-go growth cycles of the Argentine political economy explain part of the transnationalized sector's political weakness. It should be noted that the content and the outcomes of these stop-go cycles were fundamentally shaped by the constitution of social forces and their patterns of conflict and alliance, rather than the other way around. Politics was always in command.

As the Argentine economy advanced beyond the "easy" phase of industrialization toward the production of durable goods and capital goods, it became increasingly import-intensive. This meant that even modest growth rates of 3–4 percent soon exhausted the available foreign exchange, thus inexorably leading to IMF-style stabilization policies that produced both recession and inflation. Hence, stable economic growth came to hinge on the provision of sufficient foreign exchange. Since Pampean exporters remained the principal source of foreign exchange, they logically argued that they needed greater incentives (higher domestic prices and reduced export taxes) in order to produce more for the export market.[45]

Urban industrialists, along with the middle class and the workers, naturally disagreed with this orthodox solution to the crisis. Instead, a number of economists and industrialists of diverse ideological views called for the rapid modernization of meat and grain production for export and the conversion of rural producers into highly productive agro-industrial entrepreneurs. The income transfers required for the capitalization of rural producers had to come from the urban sector—namely from the public sector, urban capital, or consumers. Given the correlation of political forces, this meant that workers, the middle class, and the weaker fractions of urban capital probably would foot the bill.

For multinational firms and large domestic capital, and the upper strata of middle-class consumers, however, a reliable source of foreign exchange could provide a secure flow of needed imports, allow the free repatriation of profits overseas, and cement ties with international financial markets. Greater production of primary products could also assure cheap foodstuffs for domestic consumption, thereby keeping wages under control. Thus, industrialization could continue and the stop-go cycles be overcome.

Despite its appealing economic logic, such an alliance between the dominant industrial groups and rural producers never emerged, at least not on a stable basis. Whenever tentative steps were taken toward its formation, they invariably failed. One reason was that the newer segments of industrial capital, who had struggled to consolidate their entrepreneurial leadership in the postwar phase of economic expansion, embarked on a recurrent series of pendular shifts, attempting first to ally themselves with Pampean producers, and then abandoning that alliance in favor of a go-it-alone strategy of pursuing maximum economic benefit for themselves.[46]

This pattern of pendular swings on the part of the most transnationalized fractions of industrial capital repeated itself during each of the four economic cycles from 1951 to 1972. When expansion threatened to produce a balance-of-payments crisis in 1952, 1959, and 1962–63, stabilization plans were enacted that touched off recessionary contractions and massive income transfers. In each case, state policies reflected tentative efforts to form an alliance between the two "upper" fractions of the bourgeoisie. Invariably, however, the fragility of this alliance was revealed in the subsequent expansion phases—1953–58, 1960–61, 1964–65, and 1968–72.

Economic cycles, while shaping the parameters framing the political practice of economic agents, did not alone explain the failure to consolidate a stable alliance between the dominant industrial and agrarian groups. The organizational and ideological characteristics of both fractions also reinforced the predominance of economic-corporate orientations and the inability of the transnationalized groups, acting through the Unión Industrial and the Asociación Coordinadora de Instituciones Empresarias Libres (ACIEL, the Association of Free-Enterprise Institutions) to act as a "conquering bourgeoisie" vis-à-vis agrarian interests, the subordinate classes, and the state.

The behavior of the Unión Industrial Argentina and the ACIEL free-enterprise coalition during the 1955–66 period illustrates this point: the UIA vacillated in bringing industrialists' influence to bear on state economic policies and engaged in constant quarrels with other fractions of capital, including not only the Confederación General Económica, the representative of smaller firms in the competitive sector, but also its partners in the ACIEL free-enterprise coalition. The UIA's inability to project a leadership role for the transnationalized bourgeoisie was complemented by a pervasive lack of political realism. For its part, the Sociedad Rural, along with the traditionalist sectors of the ACIEL, remained wedded to a stubborn defense of large devaluations and income transfers without a corollary interest in agro-industrial modernization.[47]

A final element in the social stalemate was the tenacity of the competitive fractions of urban capital and organized labor. Under the impetus of both the transnationalization process and recurrent stabilization plans, these two sectors came together during the downward side of economic cycles in a "defensive alliance" to protect their common interest in state tutelage and policies of high wages, easy credit, and low food prices.[48] However, this alliance, bringing the CGT and the CGE together in transitory pacts of convenience, was strongest during the recessionary phase of the cycle; once expansion was under way again, conflicts between labor and capital eroded the alliance's cohesion.

Economic cycles and the vacillating political behavior of the social classes undermined the stability of the fragile institutions of competitive politics put into place after Peronism's fall. The military liberals who gained control over the "Liberating Revolution" had two overarching goals: freeing the private sector from the straitjacket of state controls, and purging all Peronist influence from national politics.

They made significant progress toward the first goal, beginning with a neo-liberal economic plan reestablishing market mechanisms in foreign commerce and then by joining the Club of Paris, the World Bank, and the International Monetary Fund.[49] Progress in "cleansing" the body politic of Peronism proved infinitely more difficult—and ultimately impossible. As part of a general political offensive directed against organized labor, the military and its civilian allies pursued a "divide and conquer" strategy in an attempt to foster non-Peronist unions. This effort not only failed but had the opposite effect, namely to foster a new militant leadership, unite workers in a spirit of solidarity,

TABLE 2.7

Indicators of Socio-Political Protest, 1956–66

	Strikes	Political demonstrations	Revolutionary "direct action"[a]
1956	37	4	107
1957	118	10	158
1958	124	49	73
1959	206	35	347
1960	134	14	223
1961	215	21	169
1962	181	42	309
1963	143	38	87
1964	265	115	215
1965	291	109	173
1966	263	159	158

SOURCE: "Archive on Socio-Political Protest in Argentina, 1956–1974."
[a] Includes bombings, all assassination attempts (whether successful or not), kidnappings, "armed propaganda," and other acts.

and rehabilitate Peronism as the focus of working-class allegiance. This was evident in a significant increase in labor militancy, and in the birth of the so-called "Peronist Resistance," which gave a new emphasis to more direct forms of political protest.[50] An idea of the magnitude of labor militancy and other forms of protest can be gleaned from Table 2.7.[51]

The most graphic indication of the military's inability to create a stable anti-Peronist majority came from the electoral arena. In the vote for representatives to the 1957 Constitutional Convention, the largest single bloc consisted of blank votes ordered by Perón from exile. Peronist strength was also underscored by the division of Radicalism into two rival parties—the Unión Cívica Radical del Pueblo (UCRP), representing the more traditional wing, and the Unión Cívica Radical Intransigente (UCRI). This division of the electorate was continued in the presidential elections of 1958, with the variation of Perón's decision to enter into a secret pact with Arturo Frondizi, the *intransigentes'* candidate, in exchange for promises to legalize Peronism and to follow populist economic policies. With Peronist support, Frondizi received 53 percent of the popular vote and Ricardo Balbín, the UCRP candidate, only 34 percent. In the legislative elections the UCRI received 42.4 percent and the UCRP 24.7 percent.[52]

Frondizi's government was a study in contradictions. His economic policies were based on *desarrollismo*, an eclectic combination of liberalism and populism. Its premise was that in order to free Argentina from the confines of the international division of labor, state policies should pursue vertical economic integration by creating an infrastructure and promoting basic industries (steel, chemicals, paper, machinery, etc.). This "nationalist" program was to be financed, however, with massive injections of foreign capital. The *desarrollistas* insisted that this was no contradiction, because foreign capital posed no threat as long as it was properly supervised by the state and served to further autonomous national development.

Frondizi's developmentalist strategy appeared to possess all the necessary elements required to promote a new stage of industrialization under the hegemony of the transnationalized groups. According to Mallon and Sourrouille,

Entrepreneurs need not fear foreign competition, although in other respects the economy would remain open; agricultural proprietary rights would not be tampered with; the military could have their domestic production of strategic materials and strong regional economies resistant to infiltration from envious neighboring countries; nationalists could find succor in the strongly anti-imperialist rationale of the strategy once they overcame their prejudice toward foreign capital; and wage earners would soon find that the most effective way to improve their real incomes was through rapid growth in overall output and employment.[53]

However, the strategy had one crucial weakness, namely that it was an all-or-nothing gamble that could lead to greater labor discontent and electoral disaster if an economic boom were not quickly forthcoming.

The implementation of a rigorous stabilization plan under IMF auspices created a positive business climate that attracted a massive infusion of foreign investment. The ensuing economic boom was short-lived, however. Soon Frondizi's policies confronted renewed foreign-exchange constraints, forward momentum was lost, and the economy entered into a deep recession in 1962 and 1963.

The second aspect to Frondizi's strategy involved the conciliation and co-optation of organized labor, but this was even less successful. In spite of initial overtures to labor, the decline in real wages (− 25.8 percent in 1959; see Table 2.6) and repression of strikes (for strike frequency, see Table 2.7) convinced the Peronist-dominated labor movement that they could not trust the regime.

Nor did Frondizi fare much better in gaining capitalist support. His decision in 1958 to reverse the military's abolition of the CGE's legal status led directly to the formation of the free-enterprise ACIEL group. ACIEL was alienated by Frondizi's appeals for labor support, his "softness" toward Peronism, and his failure to provide channels for permanent business input in economic decision-making.

In a bid to prevent any other party from attempting an electoral pact with Perón, Frondizi allowed the Peronists to run their own candidates in the 1962 midterm elections. The ensuing Peronist resurgence proved too much for the military, who ousted Frondizi from the presidency, annulled the elections, and replaced him with a civilian figurehead president.

Following Frondizi's ouster there was a flare-up of military factionalism that dated from the post-1955 politicization of the officer corps and deterioration of military professionalism. The first coherent faction to emerge, the so-called *colorados*, combined extreme economic orthodoxy with near-fanatical anti-Peronism. The second faction, the *azules*, while also harboring suspicions about civilian politicians, favored a quick return to constitutional rule. Led by General Juan Carlos Onganía, the *azules* stood for the military's "spirit of self-preservation," defined as defense of its corporate interests, internal cohesion, and autonomy from partisan political struggles. The *azules* and the *colorados* engaged in constant bitter disputes over national policy leading to unprecedented armed conflicts in September 1962 and April 1963.[54]

The victory of the *azules* in these conflicts initiated a process of professionalization within the armed forces as well as closer relations with the U.S. military, a reorganization of the military's organizational structure, and, most importantly, an ideological shift marked by doctrines emphasizing "national security and national development." The notion that the armed forces had to assume a "mission beyond the merely military" found its most coherent expression in a rising concern with "revolutionary warfare" and "internal subversion." The real "enemy" no longer was external aggression or even an internal military threat, but rather political or ideological dissent and economic underdevelopment, both of which threatened the "breakdown of national internal cohesion."[55]

The "Onganía Doctrine," as this new posture was christened, was soon put to the test, in the aftermath of the 1963 elections. Although the Unión Cívica Radical del Pueblo (UCRP) won these elections, the legitimacy of the new government headed by Arturo Illia was questioned from the very outset. Illia's 25.4 percent of the votes cast was hardly a show of popular support, particularly considering that Peronism alone (blank votes plus the votes won by various neo-Peronist parties) won 24.5 percent. Clearly the political fragmentation visible since 1957 had continued unaltered.[56]

Coming into power in such inauspicious circumstances, the Illia regime dedicated itself to following the tenets of "good government" and leading the economy out of the 1962–63 recession. The latter goal was pursued by means of expansionary fiscal and monetary policies and by promoting foreign trade in order to avoid balance-of-payments problems. In the short run this strategy was successful; by late 1965, however, the economy went into a slump combining stagnant output and rising prices.

But the real failure of the Illia regime was less economic than political. Governing in the best tradition of Radicalism, Illia gave liberal democracy one of its fairest tests in Argentine history. The press operated without restrictions, unions were free from state intervention, the rights of the political parties and the autonomy of interest groups were respected. Illia also exemplified the worst in the Radical tradition, namely a narrow partisanship that antagonized the other parties and alienated the social forces whose cooperation the Radicals needed to govern.

Actions of the CGT and the CGE, representing the sectors that stood to gain the most from Illia's moderate nationalism and policies favoring the internal market, reflected this alienation. The CGT opposed Illia from the very beginning of his term, arguing that he had been elected by fraudulent and illegitimate means through Peronism's proscription. Labor manifested its opposition to Illia through so-called *planes de lucha* ("struggle plans") consisting of general strikes, factory occupations, and demonstrations (see Table 2.7). Prominent labor leaders also engaged in anti-regime conspiracies with the military. The CGE was more supportive of Illia's economic policies, but preferred to keep its distance from an increasingly isolated regime.

Moreover, the representative organizations of the dominant class—the ACIEL, the UIA, the Sociedad Rural, etc.—were actively hostile to Illia and his government. Motivated by the reluctance of the Radical party's technocrats to consult with or give representation to private-sector interests, they centered their destabilization efforts on accusations of "electoral demagoguery" and Illia's refusal to repress "subversive" labor agitation.[57]

The solid Peronist victory in the 1965 midterm elections brought the Illia government under mounting pressure from all sides. The economy went into a mild slump, a situation made worse, in the private sector's opinion, by the government's refusal to modify its nationalist opposition to foreign capital and the IMF. Business spokespersons and the conservative press began to call for a coup against the regime in thinly veiled terms, even going so far as to specify the most likely target dates.[58] Finally tipping the scales against Illia was the impact of the regime's accelerating legitimation crisis on the state itself, particularly the threat it posed for the military.

Military strategists became convinced that if the situation were allowed to continue, the armed forces' cohesion, and the level of military professionalism achieved since 1963, would be at risk. Illia's forced retirement of General Onganía in 1965, combined with prognostications of a probable Peronist victory in the upcoming 1967 elections, was influential in determining the timing of the planned coup. The Army General Staff actively began to make operational plans to remove Illia from power. By mid-1966, the prevailing view among the military was that a coup of the familiar intervene-and-exit variety, turning power over to "reliable" civilian politicians, was no longer sufficient. What was needed, many believed, was a "revolution" to sweep aside the entire "corrupt" system of political parties and competitive politics.[59]

Following meticulous preparation, the military removed President Illia from the Casa Rosada at 5:00 A.M. on 28 June 1966. After dissolving the Congress and the political parties, the three commanders-in-chief appointed General Juan Carlos Onganía to the presidency.

Illia's overthrow certainly seemed to have an air of ineluctable tragedy. The June 1966 coup was not inevitable, however. Rather

it was the result of different social forces and political actors—
the military, the business community, organized labor, and the
parties—*opting* for a nondemocratic, corporatist response to the
crisis of the Argentine political economy.

The Politico-Economic Crisis in Perspective

This chapter has examined the structural crisis of the Argentine political economy in hopes of discerning some of the reasons for the failure to create a legitimate political order. Prior to
1930, a relatively broad-based, semicompetitive oligarchical system existed and had even undergone substantial liberalization
under Yrigoyen and the Radicals. This historical outcome had
been possible thanks to the large differential rents generated by
the production of beef and grain for export to world markets.
The 1930s changed all of that. Although perhaps milder than
elsewhere in Latin America, the Depression nevertheless made
it impossible for Argentina to regain its earlier privileged status
within the world-economy, even though the subsequent economic recovery was fairly rapid.

After the Depression, neither liberal democracy nor a strong
and enduring authoritarian system emerged. The material root
of the failure to construct a new hegemonic system lay in the
manner in which the post-1930 political economy was structured
around two different poles of accumulation—one agrarian and
the other urban and industrial—with contradictory relations
with the world market.

By the early twentieth century Argentina was firmly anchored
in what had become a relatively stable semiperipheral zone of
the world-economy. Like other semiperipheral nations at that
time, such as Spain, Portugal, Greece, and Mexico, Argentina
had within its borders a mixture of "core" and "peripheral"
productive activities. These activities were not fixed, however.
Constant change occurred as a function of technological innovations and international competitive pressures. In fact, because of international competition, activities typical of advanced
nations in one phase of the world-economy frequently underwent "peripheralization" in the next phase. For this reason,
state intervention in semiperipheral economies was fundamental to projects of development striving to upgrade the mix of

activities by promoting the introduction of "core-like" productive activities.[60]

This brief excursus is not meant to imply that an abstract
global logic, acting as an external demiurge, was somehow responsible for the restructuring of state power and the reorientation of state structures and economic strategies in Argentina.
To the contrary, changes in the world-economy in the 1930s and
the postwar period merely opened up opportunities for semiperipheral countries like Argentina. Whether or not these opportunities were seized upon, possibly leading to ascension to
core status, was an entirely different matter. In Argentina, as
elsewhere, there was no doubt that change, indeed major transformations, had to occur. But the precise nature of these transformations—and their political and social consequences—were
largely determined internally by the country's specific articulation of state and society and attendant patterns of class conflict
and sociopolitical struggle.

As we have seen, there were two major changes in the nature
of class rule in the 1930s. First, the state assumed a new and
more autonomous role in the organization of the economically
dominant classes; this was achieved through the creation of a
more heterogeneous but also more unstable coalition of propertied groups, with industrialists joining agro-export interests in
an uneasy partnership. And, second, there occurred a sharp
erosion of state legitimacy and bourgeois hegemony vis-à-vis
the subaltern sectors of society; this erosion was particularly significant with respect to the urban working class. That class, from
the 1930s forward, began to constitute itself as the principal antagonist to the existing order.

The role of the state in transforming the productive system
during the long Peronist decade, from 1943 to 1955, was perhaps
even more fundamental than during the Depression. Peronist
policies certainly promoted industrial expansion, albeit in ways
that had very contradictory outcomes for a satisfactory insertion
in the changing world-economy. By 1950, total state spending
adjusted for inflation had jumped 87 percent over the level of
1940–44; by the end of the Peronist reign, state expenditures
had increased an additional 16 percent. Much of this spending
went to support activities in public services (airlines, railroads,
shipping, energy, communications, etc.) and other areas (for-

eign trade, insurance, banking) that traditionally had been dominated by foreign capital along with a few local interests. The
state's role in infrastructure and heavy industry were particularly significant in widening the internal market and in facilitating accumulation and private profitability in the newest industrial sectors. The expansion of state intervention in the realm of
production thus complemented Peronism's populist emphasis
on allocation policies benefiting the urban population.[61]

Some of the limits of state-organized national capitalism on
the semiperiphery appear, however, when one examines Peronism's interventionist role in distributing the country's economic surplus. The state was instrumental in appropriating a
sizable portion of the surplus generated by the rural sector and
then transferring it to urban areas. The principal mechanisms
for effecting this transfer were control over relative prices and
control over foreign trade. During the economy's initial growth
spurt in the 1940s, state control over agricultural prices consistently discriminated against rural producers. This boosted
consumption of beef and grains by the urban population and
helped to maintain low labor costs for urban industrialists. Similarly, control over foreign trade allowed the state to manipulate
exchange rates to the benefit of industrial importers.[62]

The net short-run effect of these transfer mechanisms was to
widen the domestic market. However, by the early 1950s, the
cumulative effect began to constrain further accumulation by reducing incentives for further import-substitution in intermediate and capital goods sectors. And braking these dynamic sectors slowed employment generation and reduced the backward
linkage effects of the entire scheme for industrial promotion.

Despite these negative factors, the transfer of surplus from
the rural sector to the benefit of urban labor and industry had
one important advantage: it served to finance industrialization
while simultaneously promoting income redistribution, all without requiring radical alteration of property rights, a not incon-
siderable plus for the maintenance of the populist compromise.
Unfortunately, however, the goose that laid the golden egg disappeared when Argentina's international terms of trade began
to deteriorate precipitously after 1949, and when bad droughts
in 1951 and 1952 reduced both the volume and purchasing
power of exports. From the point of view of many entrepre-

neurs, this made it urgently necessary to reduce real wages and labor's share of national income in order to generate greater savings and boost investment.[63]

The Peronist regime was vulnerable to these pressures precisely because of the pro-labor tilt inherent in the populist class compromise: state elites had failed to create strong mechanisms of corporatist representation for capital to counterbalance organized labor's institutional presence. Lacking legitimate mechanisms, disaffected industrial and agrarian groups tended to adopt confrontational strategies in defending their interests; the state was *too* autonomous from capitalist interests. Conversely, labor's political incorporation significantly eroded the regime's autonomy vis-à-vis its principal base of support, thereby constantly embroiling state elites in the intense conflicts among different sectors of the Peronist movement.

After 1955, this legacy of institutional weakness and incoherence on the part of the state apparatus meant that labor and the competing sectors of capital both were able to successfully resist attempts to subordinate them to state policies. Consequently, the efforts of civilian and military governments alike to control inflation, boost profitability, and increase investment met with very uneven success. Gains achieved during the recessionary phases of the business cycle were largely negated during the expansionary phases.

The most modern industrial firms came to believe that the chief obstacle to the consolidation of their leadership over society and the state was not so much economic as political. The defensive capacity of organized labor, frequently in de facto alliance with still potent competitive industrial-sector entrepreneurs, and backed by middle-class consumers, was surprisingly strong. While not capable of fully reversing state policies, these groups did regularly succeed in blocking their full implementation.

The resulting social confrontations led to deepening public cynicism about democratic politics. Growing frustration fed the belief (promoted by many business groups and nurtured by the mass media) that fundamental, even "revolutionary," change was necessary. Many Argentines, perhaps even a majority, thus retreated from democratic politics in the mid-1960s and in effect deliberately opted for an authoritarian solution.

THREE

The State and the "Argentine Revolution"

TO UNDERSTAND the vicissitudes of the Argentine Revolution it is necessary to analyze the installation phase of the new political regime put into place following the 28 June 1966 coup. We begin by examining the initial emplacement of the new authoritarian system, concentrating on its ideology, innovations in political institutions, and competing economic programs. Together, these factors formed a project for the wholesale restructuring of the state itself.

If the order ushered in by military might was to be successful in overcoming the structurally rooted impasse of Argentine politics and economic development, new methods of political control had to be created. The polity's relations with civil society had to be reformulated for the state's bureaucratic institutions to regain greater autonomy vis-à-vis the contending entrepreneurial groups and the subaltern classes. Only a much strengthened state could carry forward a coherent project for transforming Argentine capitalism.

The new rulers immediately began to reinforce state power by strengthening the repressive apparatus—the military, police, judicial system, and penal institutions. Equally important were legal-institutional innovations in the operation of the state's planning agencies intended to insulate the process of economic decision-making from disruptive conflicts within the entrepreneurial class. The Argentine state could only make possible the political organization of the dominant groups by disciplining the centrifugal tendencies created by economic competition, ideological cleavages, and organizational fragmentation.[1]

The New Language of the State

The "philosophical" pretensions of the military and civilian *golpistas* were graphically revealed in their very first documents and proclamations. As was the case with similar military-inspired projects that emerged throughout Latin America in the 1960s and 1970s, this ideological discourse found its most characteristic expression in a new "language of the state"[2] that combined elements taken from the military's recently acquired technocratic managerialism with elements of organic-statism and corporatism, concepts that have time-honored pedigrees in Latin American political and legal thought.[3]

The ideological core of the authoritarian project was expressed in its purest and most complete form in the "Act of the Argentine Revolution" (*Acta de la Revolución Argentina*) and in several complementary addenda and declarations issued by the new president, General Juan Carlos Onganía. The founding documents wrestled with the frequently contradictory demands facing the new leadership in the realms of legitimation and capital accumulation. Consequently, notwithstanding their vagueness, repetitiveness, and high-flown rhetoric, these documents set forth the conceptions and aspirations behind the authoritarian project and presaged its intended course.[4]

The founding ideology first of all sought to provide a rationale explaining the coup and the demolition of Argentina's fragile democratic institutions. Interestingly, given the military and elitist nature of the new regime, the critique of the preceding Radical government centered on the inadequacy of group and interest representation under it. It was alleged that the "real" majority of the country had been denied representation in the state while the "general interest" had been trampled on and ignored by "special interests," who in turn had betrayed the confidence of the nation by their constant manipulation of "electoralism."[5]

Moreover, according to this partisan view, the absence of a stable and representative system stemmed not simply from the venality of bureaucrats and the political parties, but even more fundamentally from the rupture of the nation's "spiritual unity" caused by the very institutional structure of the state. Cited, therefore, were "rigid political structures and anachronistic economic structures that destroyed and obstructed the efforts of the community."[6]

The military *golpistas* sought to portray themselves as the disinterested and impartial guardians of the state and nation, above class or corporate interests, and denied any responsibility for the sins of the previous order, which had "created propitious conditions for a subtle and aggressive Marxist penetration of all areas of national life . . . that place the Nation in danger of falling before the advance of collectivist totalitarianism."[7]

However, concern with the legitimacy needs of the new regime precluded an exclusive emphasis on the vices of Argentina's flawed democracy. A new and brighter future was also promised. This future was to emanate from the enlightened rule of the armed forces, acting, "as in all decisive stages of our history," to assume responsibility for carrying out a "substantial transformation" of Argentine society. "Representative democracy" would be eventually reestablished at some future, but unspecified, date. As the regime's ideologues put it, "the Revolution doesn't have a timetable, but it does have objectives."[8]

The founding documents also attempted to come to grips with the other pressing need of the new regime—the imperative of modernizing Argentina's shaky capitalist economy. The notorious difficulty of confronting this question continued to plague the new rulers, contributing to incessant conflicts within and among the different apparatuses of the state and the business groups. These conflicts not only jeopardized the goal of a "substantial transformation" of the economy, but also held out the constant danger of violating the equally important legitimation requirements of the authoritarian project.

Turning first to the more obvious question of policies affecting capital accumulation, the ideologues of the regime set forth a confusing and contradictory blueprint that mandated a reduction in the role of the state in the productive process while simultaneously announcing a far-reaching plan of state economic intervention. The clarion call for a return to a "market system of free choice" was based on a conventional conception of the limited role of the state in a capitalist political economy. This was not a "night watchman" view of the state, however, but a rather more "mercantilist" perspective that specifically charged the state with the task of eliminating the "obstacles, interferences, and rigidities" that hindered private economic activity.[9]

Hence, there came to be an intermingling of liberal orthodoxy, mercantilism, and technocratic interventionism—all reflecting an intense debate raging in Argentine academic and business circles. These early disagreements foreshadowed later, more rancorous differences over economic policy that eventually came to test the cohesiveness of the various factions contending for dominance.

In another area of clear importance to an altered project of capital accumulation, that of labor policy and relations with the subordinate sectors of society in general, the regime's discourse simultaneously held out a threat and extended an olive branch to the Argentine working class. This ambivalence reflected the military's desire to incorporate the powerful unions and the large urban working class in support of the new regime. A decision to reform existing labor and welfare legislation in accord with "present needs" and the "national interest" was announced. This thinly veiled threat to curtail the autonomous political and organizational power of the Peronist movement was balanced by an explicit pledge to "limit the state's control over labor organizations to a minimum" in return for a cooperative, non-hostile attitude toward the regime. Here could be found familiar corporatist notions of a "just equilibrium between the interests of the Nation, of labor, and of the enterprise."[10]

Concern with the other aspect of the accumulation problem, that of reorganizing the internal structures of the state, was accorded a secondary priority in these early formulations of public policy. Several imperatives were, however, apparent at this early stage: the necessity for rigid political and military control over the administrative agencies of the state; for greater state penetration of civil society in order to repress and/or co-opt any opposition; and for the expansion of direct military participation in the affairs of the state.

The military ideologues of the "new professionalism" saw an interrelationship between their economic and security goals and their obligations. According to the military doctrine developed by the *azules* prior to the coup, national development and national security (viewed primarily as a response to internal subversion) were mutually contingent, in that each was a necessary condition for the attainment of the other. Consequently, great emphasis was placed on the modernization and restructuring of the armed forces that had begun in 1964 (in collaboration with

the U.S. military) under then army commander General Onganía. In short, by virtue of their privileged position in the new
authoritarian system, the armed forces firmly proclaimed their
determination to expand their activities to include virtually all
aspects of the "socioeconomic battlefront."

New State Structures

The structures of domination created during the installation
phase transformed the ideology just described into legal norms,
institutions, and political practices. The comparison with military rule in Brazil is instructive. Civil society in Argentina was
much more complex and well-articulated than in Brazil. The
greater sophistication and solidity of political organization and
ideology typical of all social classes in Argentina resulted in a
political system that was considerably more radical, authoritarian, and "revolutionary" than the one created by the Brazilian
military following their 1964 coup.

The political disorganization and demobilization of civil society was the primary goal of the initial reforms. Authoritarian
elites proceeded systematically to eliminate the institutions and
political practices of what was seen as a corrupt system of political parties, elections, and state agencies controlled by self-
serving bureaucratic interests. President Onganía and his political staff rapidly implemented a series of authoritarian measures
including the following points: first, the removal from office of
political appointees of the previous regime, including many
middle- and upper-level bureaucrats and technocrats; second,
the dissolution, outlawing, and seizure of the monetary and
physical assets of all political parties regardless of ideology or
even of their support for the coup, plus a prohibition on the
formation of new parties and penalties for political activities by
party leaders; third, the elimination of national and provincial
legislative institutions, as well as other elective bodies, and the
ouster of all provincial public officials and functionaries with political sympathies; fourth, the removal of all judges from the Supreme Court and the imposition of severe limitations on judicial
autonomy; fifth, a campaign against the press, the universities,
and those manifestations of popular culture considered to be
"decadent" by the regime's moral censors.[11]

The measures used to dismantle the preexisting political institutions were reinforced by two additional coercive decree-laws issued in 1967. Both were specifically military in origin and represented long-standing aspirations of the armed forces. The first, the "Law for a Civilian Defense Service" (*Ley de Servicio Civil de Defensa*), exemplified the hypertrophy of the Argentine concept of "national security." This decree-law defined threats to national security so broadly as to include virtually anything that affected the "vital interests or the integrity of the state" or that even "interfered with or perturbed . . . internal order, the welfare of the community, and the normal and full functioning of the activities and services that have to do with the development of the Nation." [12]

The second military-inspired measure, the "Law for Defense Against Communism" (*Ley de Defensa contra el Comunismo*), was an extremely vague piece of legislation seen by many sectors, including some supporters of the regime, as likely to foment indiscriminate witch-hunts designed to silence public opinion by harassing the outlawed political parties and by severely controlling the more combative sectors of organized labor. [13]

Equal in importance to these repressive legal structures were institutional innovations designed to enhance the relative autonomy of the new regime and to build support among fractious entrepreneurs for a project to restructure the economy. The most important institutional departures centered on a coordinated effort to strengthen the executive branch of the state.

The centralization and expansion of executive power was embodied in a reorganization of the complex and unwieldy ministerial structure. These reforms, engineered by the Interior Minister and his political staff, redistributed areas of responsibility and reduced the number of cabinet-level ministries from eight to five: Interior, Economy, Foreign Relations, Defense, and a newly created Ministry of Social Welfare. In addition, fifteen secretariats were established and placed under the authority of the cabinet ministers. The scope of the jurisdictional power of the new ministries and secretariats was greatly enhanced, giving them total control (at least in theory) over the judicial system, culture and education, internal politics, foreign policy, communications and propaganda, provincial and local government, and public order and security. [14]

The strengthening of President Onganía's political staff began with the creation of an autonomous bureaucracy, the Presidencia de la Nación, charged with the management of the entire public administration. This presidential bureaucracy, located in the Casa Rosada, was given a special high-priority mission: rationalization of the state's administrative agencies. Such rationalization was designed to effect a major qualitative change in the level of technical and scientific knowledge at the top of the state apparatus, and to further extend central oversight over all the financial, economic, and administrative functions of the state.[15]

The modernization and rationalization of the state apparatus was to be completed with the establishment of a new planning system of obvious military design—the so-called "System for National Planning and Action for Development and Security" (*Sistema de Planeamiento y Acción para el Desarrollo y la Seguridad*). Congruent with the managerial thrust of the new professionalism, the *Sistema* was touted as an example of modern scientific management by means of an integrated, logically coherent system, founded upon a hierarchical set of principles ranging from the most abstract conceptual level down to the smallest operational element in the most distant region of the country. The ultimate goal of the *Sistema* was to design a new "national project" to guide Argentina into the twenty-first century. According to General Osiris Villegas, a leading military intellectual and the first head of the newly formed National Security Council (CONASE), the *Sistema* was not to be merely another layer of bureaucracy grafted onto existing structures, but rather the core of a novel type of state uniquely capable of coordinating economic development and national security.[16]

The *Sistema* consisted of two institutional complexes: the National Security Council (CONASE) and the National Development Council (CONADE). After the disasters of earlier military interventions and the internecine conflict between *azules* and *colorados*, the CONASE's objective was to put an end to constant military factionalism. It was supposed to accomplish this by providing an institutionalized channel, subject to a clear-cut chain-of-command, through which the officer corps could make its positions known and thus have input directly into the core of the decision-making structures of the state.

To complement the CONASE, the CONADE, which had been created in 1964 as part of the Alliance for Progress, was originally seen as the cornerstone of the new regime's attempt to eliminate "politics" and to technocratize the processes of state decision-making. It was an effort by the authoritarian elites to constrain the influence of conflicting entrepreneurial interests and bring them under state control. Therefore, whereas CONASE was the most complete expression of the negative, disorganizing mechanisms of political control and demobilization, CONADE was a coherent attempt to manifest positive selective mechanisms essential to the distillation of the "collective interest of capital."

Contending Projects of Accumulation

Lifting the technocratic veil to peer behind these new institutions, we find that the installation period was characterized by sharp internal divisions and struggles within the state among representatives of the rival entrepreneurial groups and bureaucratic interests. At stake in these bitter disputes was control of the policymaking apparatus. Three main groups, reflecting the interests of different social forces and projects of accumulation, initially competed for control: the proponents of liberal, pre-Keynesian economic orthodoxy, who will be referred to as *ortodoxos*; a diverse collection of more pragmatic, business-oriented moderates; and a fairly close-knit group of *técnicos* who sought to promote a more "progressive" orientation to state economic policies. CONADE, then in a period of reorganization, was not an important actor at this early stage.

Two prominent brothers, General Julio Alsogaray, one of the most influential *golpistas* in the army, and Alvaro Alsogaray, twice Minister of Economy in previous governments, were the primary representatives of the more extreme liberal *ortodoxos*. The Alsogarays were a truly formidable political, military, and ideological force; the regime's founding ideological discourse carried their heavy imprint in its emphasis on the dangers of "statism," the glories of unfettered free enterprise, and the necessity for a restrictive monetary policy.[17]

In the aftermath of the coup, General Alsogaray was appointed to the key post of General Secretary of the recently created Presidencia de la Nación, placing him in a strategic position to influence Onganía's still unformed economic ideas. Onganía, however, was eager to assert his independence from military control and soon returned General Alsogaray to his normal military duties. Alvaro Alsogaray was likewise passed over for the key post at the Economy Ministry, and was conveniently sent into "golden exile" as Argentina's ambassador in Washington, D.C.

Onganía's later efforts to maintain his autonomy vis-à-vis the more extreme *ortodoxos* were foreshadowed in his immediate appointment of Jorge Nestor Salimei, a moderate, as Minister of Economy.[18] This decision was reinforced by the naming of Adolfo Raggio, a respected agronomist, as Secretary of Agriculture, and of Franciso Rodolfo Aguilar, the owner of a metallurgical firm, as Secretary of Industry and Commerce. Salimei and Aguilar were affiliated with the Confederación General Económica, the organization representing small and medium-sized firms of national origin. Raggio was a member of the more nationalist wing of the Sociedad Rural Argentina, representing the powerful livestock and agricultural interests in the *pampa húmeda*.

The Salimei team's business affiliations were widely interpreted as signifying the political arrival of "nationalist" fractions of the Argentine bourgeoisie, i.e., fractions not compromised by association with the powerful transnational groups.[19] Although this was an exaggeration, these appointments, and the intense *ortodoxo* opposition they provoked, did signal future difficulties for the authoritarian system in balancing the conflicting interests of different economic groups.

Salimei's nominal control of the economic policymaking machinery of the state did not signify a threat to established interests. In fact, Salimei embarked upon a very cautious and practical course. His pragmatism was readily apparent in the regime's principal policy initiatives designed to bring about a rapprochement with international capital. For example, Illia's nationalist stance in defense of the YPF state petroleum monopoly was reversed through contracts signed with Pan American Oil and Cities Service.[20]

The technocrats were the final group in this three-way struggle for control over economic policy. By virtue of their academic orientation and lack of direct links to any particular business group, the technocrats were obliged to conduct their struggle for influence on state policy primarily by means of well-argued economic analysis. Although they were clearly the weakest of the three protagonists, the fate of the technocrats was particularly revealing of the different ideologies in play and of the manner in which rival economic interests were reproduced, in mediated form, within the economic policy machinery of the state.

The leading member of the group of academic technocrats was Felipe Tami, a "social Christian" businessman who was appointed to head the Central Bank. Tami brought with him into the Bank many professional economists, several of whom had foreign postgraduate training. The Tami Group (sometimes called the Di Tella Group because of its ties to the prestigious Instituto Torcuato Di Tella) was known for its apolitical orientation, lack of strong links with the traditional political parties, and general commitment to the more progressive positions of the Catholic church. Furthermore, its sympathies with the structuralism advocated by the Economic Commission for Latin America (CEPAL), and its opposition to utopian plans to "administer" the Argentine economy, were cause for suspicion on the part of Onganía, Salimei, and the Alsogarays, who viewed the Tami Group as vaguely "leftist" in orientation.[21]

The Tami *técnicos* explicitly rejected the extreme monetarism and the "shock treatment" for the economy called for by the *ortodoxos*. They argued that an exclusive focus on anti-inflationary policies was both erroneous and dangerous. The technocrats also advocated tax reform, promotion of agricultural production, and reform of the system of land tenure, all of which aroused immediate opposition from the dominant industrial and agricultural interests. Their primary objective was to achieve greater equity and to foster income redistribution with balanced growth and full employment. They also sought to use state power to modernize the agricultural sector in order to increase productivity and earn more foreign exchange. An equally crucial difference between the *técnicos* and their opponents concerned their attitude toward foreign capital. The Tami technocrats were strongly opposed to any policy of economic development based upon a narrow alliance linking state enterprises and large domestic firms to transnational capital.[22]

As the battle within the economic apparatus heated up in the second half of 1966, the lines became sharply drawn between the moderate reformism of the *técnicos* of the Central Bank and the pro-international-capital stance of the doctrinaire *ortodoxos*. In this context, the *técnicos* outlined two opposed theories about the Argentine economy which, in their view, "reflected different interpretations of economic reality . . . linked to divergent orientations about economic policy as a whole." The first position, that of the *ortodoxos*, they dubbed the "drastic" solution; it held that it was necessary to put a quick halt to inflation through strict monetary restraint. The alternative "progressive" solution, as the technocrats labeled their preferred approach, argued that braking inflationary pressures too rapidly would be counterproductive, and would result in a recessionary crisis with prohibitively high social and political costs. In an indirect attack on Alvaro Alsogaray, who as a previous Minister of Economy had implemented anti-inflationary policies of the monetarist variety, the *técnicos* charged that the "drastic" stabilization advocated by the *ortodoxos* had been responsible for the economic crises of 1959, 1962, and 1963; each of these episodes had resulted in markedly higher inflation than before, combined with recession, unemployment, and increased foreign indebtedness.[23]

The Tami technocrats resigned en masse in November 1966, after Onganía decided to adopt the "drastic" approach of the *ortodoxos*, including devaluation of the peso, elimination of export taxes on agricultural products, and new Central Bank credit and lending policies. The resigning *técnicos* charged that the economic authorities and, by implication, President Onganía himself were responsible for the "confusion" and "incoherence" of official policy. This was evidenced, in their view, by the clear contradictions between the slogans of "modernization" and "structural transformation" and the reality of what were really recessionary policies favoring entrenched industrial, commercial, and agricultural interests.[24]

The victory of the *ortodoxos* signified the defeat not only of the Tami technocrats but of intermediate figures such as Minister of Economy Salimei, who had attempted to avoid identification with either "drastic" or "progressive" policies. Salimei's departure was the most visible consequence of a reaccommodation of political forces within the regime that culminated in a cabinet reshuffle in late December 1966. The economic project of his successor, Adalberto Krieger Vasena, is the subject of the next chapter.

Although conflicts over economic policy were crucial, the cabinet crisis was triggered by "unrest" in the army. Many officers felt deceived and were coming to believe that Onganía's failure to take decisive action on the economic front was responsible for the malaise engulfing the regime and destroying its revolutionary elán.[25]

Nationalism and the Corporatist Utopia

While the struggles taking place over control of economic policymaking were crucial to the evolution of the authoritarian system, an apparently less significant process led to the emergence from within the regime of another major project of domination. As the post-coup euphoria faded away into conflicts and recriminations, the nationalist-controlled political apparatus gradually became an important locus of intermediation among disparate social forces which, as soon became apparent, were to be allocated a decidedly subordinate place in the project of accumulation then taking form. The bearers of this alternative project were to be found among a fascinating collection of nationalist politicians, ideologues, and businessmen who had been swept into power on Onganía's coattails.[26]

In contrast to the battles raging over economic policy, the political-ideological apparatus presented a deceptive image of stability and coherence. In reality, however, the apparent control by the right-wing nationalists was endangered from the outset by the existence of two rival camps: a more extreme, ultra-Catholic group headed by Interior Minister Enrique Martínez Paz, and less sectarian nationalists more interested in the exercise of political power than in doctrinal purity. Mario Díaz Colodrero, the head of the Secretariat of Government, the apex of the newly expanded presidential bureaucracy, became the principal spokesman for these moderate nationalists and acted as the director of the entire political apparatus.[27] The more extreme nationalists suffered a major erosion of their power when retired General Guillermo Borda replaced Martínez Paz as Interior Minister in the December 1966 cabinet shake-up.

The ascendancy of Díaz Colodrero was in large measure a consequence of the wholesale colonization and staffing of the state's political agencies by a semisecret sect called the Ateneo de la República. The ideology of the Ateneo was less anti-Semitic and less in the thrall of Argentina's "destiny" as a regional great power than the more extreme variants of Catholic nationalism. The Ateneo nationalists were also distinguished by their conciliatory, paternalistic attitude toward the working class and the Peronist masses.[28]

This flexible stance was reflected in Díaz Colodrero's pledges to carry out a policy of "social accord" to bring together all those sectors with a truly "revolutionary vocation." In addition to the various nationalist groups, Díaz identified urban workers, nationalist businessmen, and middle-class professionals as the groups that could coalesce behind nationalist banners.[29]

Onganía himself was the most visible standard-bearer of nationalist aspirations. This role came naturally, given the president's utopian vision of Argentina's future grandeur as a regional power. The appeal to Díaz Colodrero and his nationalist ideologues was obvious: the authoritarian project explicitly gave the political apparatus the predominant role as the regime's ideological guardian and architect of its social policies.

Onganía's utopian vision was made explicit in his famous "Theory of the *Tres Tiempos*": an "economic" period, a "social" period, and a "political" period. The principal goal of the economic stage was the rapid modernization and restructuring of the country's productive system and the achievement of a more competitive insertion in the world-economy. After this "economic miracle" there would follow a period of vaguely defined social reforms, leading to the regime's institutionalization and the "return to representative and republican democracy." This last stage would consist of a carefully controlled process of decompression, with selective grants of representation and participation to business and organized labor.[30]

The overarching mission of the political apparatus, according to this logic, was to control the tempo of "institutional reorganization" with an iron hand in order to contain civil society's "impatience." Elections and the reemergence of parties could be permitted only after elite-controlled political structures had been firmly established at the new national, provincial, and local levels.[31]

The nationalists, emboldened by these vague but passionate plans, attempted to seize the initiative from their liberal authoritarian adversaries by proposing an alternative to representative government. Behind the banners of Congresalismo and Participacionismo, Díaz Colodrero launched a coordinated effort involving the presidency, the Interior Ministry, the Ministry of Social Welfare, and the Labor Secretariat in a nationwide campaign to promote a so-called Representative Congress of Production, Commerce, and Consumption (Congreso Representativo de la Producción, el Comercio y el Consumo). In classic corporatist fashion, the Congress was portrayed as the natural arena for the "genuine participation" of society's so-called "intermediate organisms."[32]

The use of these hoary corporatist shibboleths represented an attempt to advance beyond the nationalists' traditional rejection of liberal democracy and representative institutions. According to Italian, French, and Spanish academics brought to Argentina by the government, the industrialized nations had progressed beyond classical liberalism; electoral politics and parliamentary institutions were but facades behind which the executive branch of the state supervised bargaining among powerful interest groups. By selectively utilizing concepts then in vogue in the social sciences (the "end of ideology," the importance of "functional groups," and so on), the nationalists argued that Argentina should follow the trend toward corporatism and adopt the "scientific" mode of politics practiced in the "advanced democracies."[33]

Buenos Aires and the most modern sectors, however, were not receptive to this message. The most fertile ground for corporatism was to be found in the interior of the country. Accordingly, Díaz Colodrero and the nationalists devised a "provincial strategy" to co-opt local notables, especially neo-Peronists and conservatives. This "social opening" was seen as a politically profitable way to take advantage of the acute economic difficulties in the interior provinces resulting from orthodox economic policies.[34]

The ultimate objective of the provincial strategy was a major state-directed realignment of political forces to destroy the traditional political parties. The strategy was to produce three new political alliances, each linked to and beholden to the state: first, a neo-liberal party composed of the remnants of traditional conservatism, still strong in some areas of the interior; second, a "non-extremist" party of the center-left, which included elements of moderate Peronism and traditional Marxist parties; and third, a Social-Christian party. The last-named party was the intended beneficiary of the nationalist strategy and would be based upon those sectors of Catholic nationalism sensitive to social and economic reforms and those sectors of organized labor and the various provincial populist movements that had in the past favored a strategy of "Peronism without Perón."[35]

Despite their organizational charts and the expenditure of large sums of money, the nationalists never achieved anything commensurate with their expectations. The problem was that the repetition of a medieval mystique, backed by repression and limitations on cultural and political freedoms, was simply incapable of legitimating authoritarian rule in a complex country like Argentina. Placed on the defensive, Díaz Colodrero and General Borda, the Interior Minister, grudgingly admitted that ". . . communitarian participation does not replace or exclude the exercise of traditional political rights" to vote and participate in party activities. By mid-1968, declining support for the regime registered in public-opinion polls showed that the populace was unconvinced by denials that the nationalists harbored fascist and totalitarian designs.[36]

Having failed to find acceptable interlocutors in their proposed "dialogue with the Argentine community," Díaz Colodrero, General Borda, and the other nationalists had two alternatives: either to capitulate before their antagonists, or to "deepen the Revolution." With scarcely any hesitation, they embarked upon the latter course.[37]

In September 1968, General Borda, speaking at the Escuela Superior de Guerra, declared that the regime had decided to initiate the second of the *tres tiempos*. The "social period" was to last approximately three years, culminating in something similar to the French model of national planning, with a Social and Economic Council that would "enrich" republican institutions with "new forms" of representation. Reversing their previous refusal to even consider a "political plan" (the Revolution had "objectives" but no timetable), the regime's strategists now began to toy with proposals to "constitutionalize" Onganía's presidency, perhaps by limiting his mandate to one six-year term, with his successor to be chosen by the military Junta. These attempts to give the regime greater legitimacy provoked broad condemnation from party, union, business, and civic organizations. When authoritarian liberals in the military also voiced reservations, the plans were quickly shelved.[38]

In late 1968 and early 1969, as groups in civil society became more outspoken, Onganía was forced to assume a much more active political role in defending the regime's corporatist project. But the president's new high public profile backfired. The impression created was that, after nearly three years in power, Onganía was not even able to control his own collaborators, much less deliver on his own promises of political reform and economic modernization.[39]

Guerrilla activity now showed signs of increasing, police repression was necessary to put down several small protests in the interior provinces, criticism from the leadership of Argentina's conservative Catholic church became more pointed, and even pliant union leaders began to reconsider their truce with the regime.

Sensing the danger, the nationalists in the political apparatus made a bold bid to "surround Onganía with a wall of popular support capable of dissuading all subversive movements, civil or military." To the dismay of supporters of the regime, however, this bid failed to recognize the errors of the past. On the contrary, Onganía and the nationalists proposed the most grandiose version of the *comunitarista* ideology yet to emerge. On the occasion of the annual meeting with provincial governors on 6 May 1969, Onganía announced a far-reaching plan to completely bypass the party system and short-circuit electoral politics. *Consejalismo*, as this plan was dubbed, was little more than a rehash of past corporatist blueprints: provincial governors and local notables would erect new political structures to link the state and society by means of so-called "intermediate groups."[40]

Most of the governors, along with the rest of the nation's political elite, were reported to be "disillusioned," "shocked," and "betrayed" by Onganía's dogged restatement of what were seen as "fascist" slogans and by his refusal to come to grips with the crisis of legitimacy engulfing his regime.[41]

If the nationalists had failed to create a corporatist legitimacy for the regime, the question remained whether the political parties could take advantage of the opportunity to press for a return to civilian rule. Or had the nationalists succeeded in destroying the country's party system and traditional political movements?

For a while, at least, the parties—their legal status lost, their electoral and parliamentary arenas abolished, their activities prohibited, and their leaders harassed and occasionally imprisoned—virtually disintegrated and all but ceased to exist. In practice, they were reduced to criticizing the regime through books, journals, and speeches, plotting with their friends among the military, and making and breaking pacts among themselves. Victims of the general demobilization of civil society, the parties suffered the same fragmentation, disorientation, and retreat that afflicted many other civic institutions.

Of course the 1966 coup had not been without its supporters among the parties. Juan Perón and Arturo Frondizi, for example, both victims of earlier military conspiracies, initially had kind words for the new regime. Frondizi praised the military coup and called for an "alliance of classes and sectors" to promote rapid industrialization. To show his dedication to carrying out the "national revolution," the ex-president even disbanded his own party, the Movimiento de Integración y Desarrollo.[42]

Similarly, Perón at first pronounced the military coup "unobjectionable" because, as he said, political chaos justified harsh measures. However, he strongly criticized the intention to carry out "an exclusively military action that would give birth to a government of force." He reminded the armed forces that "in Argentina no one can govern without the support of the *pueblo*." By late 1966, when it became clear that Onganía had no interest in an alliance with the aging exile, Perón's wait-and-see attitude hardened into total opposition.[43]

With Perón's passage to the opposition, the resistance by the parties and the traditional political elite began in earnest. Though the main protagonists would be adherents of Peronism and Radicalism, their strategies fell into three broad categories that were related only indirectly to the conventional left-right ideological spectrum: they will be referred to as *golpistas, frentistas*, and *revolucionarios*.[44]

The *golpistas* proclaimed their allegiance to a "democratic solution" of Argentina's problems. This camp included the center-right wing of the Radicals led by Ricardo Balbín; ex-president General Pedro E. Aramburu (who thought of himself as a South American Charles De Gaulle) and his Unión del Pueblo Argentino (UDELPA); and Alvaro Alsogaray, the defender of unfettered free enterprise and orthodox economic policies. While Balbín and the Radical *golpistas* were firmly rooted in civil society, Alsogaray and Aramburu represented those sectors of Argentine society whose electoral presence had always been practically non-existent.

The strategy of the *golpistas* was founded upon what they viewed as fundamental internal cleavages within the regime, particularly the divisions between liberals and nationalists. Their ultimate objective was to restore Argentina's traditional political institutions, appropriately "strengthened" and "modernized" in light of the new requirements of capital accumulation. They believed that these objectives could be best accomplished through a liberal military coup directed against Onganía and the nationalists.[45]

The *frentistas* did not believe an effective military coup against Onganía to be feasible. Hence, the main thrust of the *frentista* strategy centered on the creation of a broad civilian political front, perhaps in tactical alliance with dissident military officers, in order to invert the balance of forces favoring the dictatorship. Although the Communists, the Christian Democrats, and the "national left" played active roles, the most conspicuous standard-bearers of this strategy were Juan Perón and ex-president Arturo Illia. Despite repeated attempts, however, mutual suspicions and recriminations prevented the hoped-for "Perón-Illia Pact" from getting off the drawing board.[46]

As the label indicates, the *revolucionarios* proclaimed their "revolutionary vocation," but the revolution they had in mind was similar to that of the authoritarian regime. This diverse collection of political forces ranged from extreme right-wing groups to the left-leaning remnants of the Intransigent Radicals, led by Oscar Alende, and Frondizi's *desarrollistas*. They were prepared to offer Onganía their support in exchange for the regime's adoption of their preferred policies. In contrast to the *golpistas*, however, they strongly opposed *ortodoxo* economic policies. In Frondizi's case, the solution for the regime's political crisis was obvious: the naming of a *desarrollista* economic team with Frondizi himself playing the role of Onganía's chief political strategist.

The ambitions of the *revolucionarios* were constantly frustrated. They could neither overcome *ortodoxo* ascendancy over economic policy nor counter right-wing nationalist suspicions of their alleged "leftist" sympathies.[47] By early 1969, the parties and the traditional political elite were too divided to force a change in the political situation. The immediate challenge to Onganía came not from the parties, but from growing divisions within the armed forces.

Fragmentation in the Military

The armed forces, as sponsor of and ultimate source of power in the new order, were caught in the crossfire of the struggles and contradictions described above. The military's problems stemmed from the fact that they had not been accorded a clear-cut role in the authoritarian system. To begin with, the *Acta de la Revolución Argentina*, the basic legal claim to legitimate authority, did not provide a mechanism for selecting Onganía's successor, stating only that "in the case of incapacity or death of the President, his successor will be designated by common agreement of the Commanders-in-Chief of the Armed Forces." Herein lay the crux of the institutional conflict that would permanently plague the regime: while Onganía rejected any special status for the armed forces in affairs of state, the military insisted that their role in the 1966 coup had given them the right and duty to oversee the political process and to exercise vigilance over their appointees to the presidency.

These two views found their expression in conflicting versions of the *azul* doctrine elaborated in the early 1960s. Onganía's version explicitly stressed the military's limited "reserve function," while the version of top-ranking officers, never clearly expressed and only articulated in moments of crisis, emphasized that the president was the armed forces' appointed "delegate." Onganía vehemently rejected the "delegate" view, which made him subordinate to the Junta that had placed him in power. This, the president said, would amount to "co-government," which was unthinkable and unworkable.[48]

There was more to Onganía's stance than a narrow defense of his personal and institutional power. It will be recalled that the National Security Council (CONASE) had been created to institutionalize military participation in decision-making. The problem was, however, that the president never really trusted CONASE and was little disposed to allow the officer corps to use it to voice their concerns. Onganía's fear was that if the armed forces took the responsibility for "overseeing" difficult governmental decisions, they would inevitably be transformed into a replica of Argentine society, with its political rivalries and contradictory social forces. Further, the politicization of, and the emergence of factions within, the military would endanger the authoritarian project itself, a project whose very survival and chances of success ultimately depended on the relative autonomy of the state from civil society.

Onganía's "reserve function" version of *azulismo*, therefore, was an attempt to prevent military factionalism. The price to be paid, however, was a long and tortuous struggle between Onganía and the military, which led to the alienation and frustration of important segments of the officer corps, who felt they were being denied a voice in the direction of a revolution carried out in their name and on which their honor depended. Herein, some feared, lay the seeds of the military's conversion into a kind of praetorian guard of the new authoritarian order.[49]

In his memoirs General Alejandro Lanusse aptly summed up the military's relations with Onganía:

According to the more-or-less tacit rules of the game, the President had to appear as a civilian and it was good that he did not wear a uniform, except for military ceremonies. The true character of the regime was not accepted—only two years later did it begin to be said that the Armed Forces were the repositories of power—and it was only admitted, decorously, that that general who held at the same time the functions of titular head of the Executive Power and responsibility for Legislative Power, the general who designated governors and ministers without consulting anyone, was the head of an administration of military origins. This notwithstanding, that administration appeared to be the result of an elaborate interpretation of republican legality and of the doctrine of the subordination of the Military to civilian power.[50]

At least four major military factions played important roles in the politics of the authoritarian project: first, the *onganistas*, who supported their leader's patriarchal and traditionalist variant of nationalism and his autocratic vision of the reorganization of the state and society; second, the authoritarian liberals, who distrusted Onganía's nationalist and corporatist tendencies, while generally supporting plans for economic modernization; third, the authoritarian nationalists, who shared Onganía's objective of restructuring the state and society, but who were fearful of the "sellout" (*entreguismo*) of national sovereignty to international capital; and fourth, the *profesionalistas*, who upheld the ideal of a strictly apolitical military, but who in practice tended to go along with the prevailing correlation of forces within the armed forces.

The real political consequences of these internal alignments flowed from the interaction between the military's own internal organization as a complex bureaucratic institution and its structural role as the state's "repressive apparatus" and ultimate source of power and authority. Military factionalism acquired political significance from the armed forces' interactions with the class conflicts and political cleavages present in the state and society. These interactions articulated the military's affinities with different classes, social sectors, and ideologies, making it an active participant, not a mechanical reflection of external forces.

Thus the armed forces' political posture and policy alignments could not be reduced to calculations of profit margins, to the need for a healthy business climate to attract foreign investment, or to the predilections of the International Monetary Fund and the World Bank. Like the state's political organs, the armed forces defined their "mission" in terms of the "nation" and the "national interest." As long as orthodox economic policies were perceived as consonant with the maintenance of internal order, with respect for national sovereignty, and, most importantly, with the cohesion and integrity of the state and the armed forces, nationalist officers might grumble but would pose no significant danger to plans to effect the modernization of Argentine capitalism. If, however, these conditions were violated, or were perceived as being violated, large sectors of the officer corps were potentially susceptible to politicization and the temptation to form alliances with disaffected entrepreneurs, the political parties, and organized labor. In short, the military, like the political apparatus, was compelled to legitimate its role in the authoritarian project before the entire society, not just the narrow segments limited to the dominant business groups. How did this imperative play itself out?

The replacement, in late 1966, of army commander General Pascual A. Pistarini, a *profesionalista* manager without great political skills or ambitions, with General Julio Alsogaray, an officer with many political connections, placed the army under control of the military liberals, the faction with the closest ties to the economic authorities and to local big business and transnational capital. Despite Onganía's nationalist excesses, the shift toward economic orthodoxy begun also in late 1966 meant that the military liberals found little in the regime's policies to merit strong opposition.[51]

The nationalists were not so complacent. In fact, growing anti-liberal sentiment in the officer corps spawned several nationalist factions. One faction, usually labeled *desarrollista*, had a marked affinity with civilian currents of the same persuasion. These military "developmentalists" feared that denationalization of the economy, anti-labor policies, and subservience to international financial institutions might touch off dangerous social and political unrest. The most prominent exponent of the argument that economic liberalism represented a potential threat to national security was General Osiris Villegas, the head of CONASE. General Villegas's concern with "social harmony," the "just distribution of wealth," and the "vital interests of the Nation" converted the charges against economic orthodoxy into legitimate topics of military discussion.[52]

A second anti-liberal faction went beyond rejection of economic orthodoxy to include a far-reaching questioning of the social and political future of the Onganía regime. The emergence of this faction demonstrated the interaction between ideological differences and conflicts of a strictly institutional nature concerning promotions. President Onganía was determined to force the early retirement of General Adolfo Cándido López, head of the Institutos Militares and an influential nationalist officer at the strategic Campo de Mayo army base near Buenos Aires. General Alsogaray had no sympathy with General López's politics, but was determined to resist Onganía's interference with his prerogative as the army commander. Onganía prevailed, but he paid a high price. After his ouster, General López initiated highly publicized negotiations with civilian nationalists, Peronists, *desarrollistas*, the clergy, and others in an effort to create a broad civil-military opposition front of classic populist characteristics.[53]

Although General López's burst of national-populist nostalgia failed to win broad public support, his actions succeeded in irreversibly transforming the ideological climate within the military. Henceforth all factions had to consider the question of popular appeal in competing for control over the future of the authoritarian experiment. General López's populist-oriented campaign thus opened the door to a "state of deliberation" among the officer corps, thereby contributing to a growing fragmentation that undermined the military's cohesion and sense of professionalism.[54]

Nationalist officers like General López were an irritant, but the real threat to the unstable equilibrium between Onganía and the armed forces came from the growing alienation of the authoritarian liberals. The immediate cause of the rift was the threat to liberal hegemony over economic matters represented by the corporatist offensive unleashed by Onganía and the nationalists in the political apparatus. Onganía's response was to attempt to mollify liberal officers by offering the three service chiefs expanded "participation" in the naming of high-ranking functionaries.[55]

The rapprochement was only partial and proved short-lived. Rumors of liberal and nationalist conspiracies rose to a fever pitch. In a long meeting with the army leadership on May 21–22, 1968, Generals Julio Alsogaray and Alejandro Lanusse pressured the president for quick affirmative steps to return to "representative democracy," and defended the military's role as the interpreter of the Argentine Revolution. Onganía countered by refusing to countenance military demands for major policy changes, and defended the nationalists' corporatist political project.[56]

This atmosphere of polarization and recrimination was intensified further following General Alsogaray's Army Day address, in which he denounced what he referred to as the nationalists' "unconfessable objectives." The army commander pointedly defined the military's political doctrine as ". . . markedly anti-

totalitarian" and "fundamentally based on liberty and eminently democratic concepts." The allusion to Onganía himself
was clear to all.[57]

Onganía answered General Alsogaray's challenge on television the same day. He firmly defended his right to act as the sole
interpreter of the military pact of 1966 and issued a call for renewed faith in his leadership: "If the Argentine Revolution were
to be ended after having achieved only the modest goal of paci-
fying the country, correcting errors, and overcoming difficulties
[by permitting] a complete return to the past, it would com-
mit an irreparable fraud, a cynical deception of the younger
generations."[58]

Unconvinced, the military liberals continued to press for an
explicit commitment to the regime's institutionalization and for
a clear-cut definition of the military's role in top-level economic
decision-making. Giving voice to the concerns of the dominant
entrepreneurial sectors, they interpreted Onganía's defense of
corporatist schemes as a direct threat to continued orthodoxy in
economic affairs. Their worst fears were borne out in August
1968. First, President Onganía forced Alvaro Alsogaray's resignation as Argentine ambassador in Washington. Next, Onganía
demanded General Julio Alsogaray's resignation along with those
of the like-minded chiefs of the navy and the air force.[59]

The success of Onganía's gambit depended on his choice of
General Alejandro Lanusse as the new army chief. General Lanusse's alternatives were two: to become Onganía's "military
bodyguard," attempting to prevent further military fragmentation, or to be drawn into the same dilemma confronted by his
predecessor. That dilemma implied the politically impossible
task of supervising the regime according to liberal criteria, or
acquiescing in Onganía's autocratic vision of presidential authority and grandiose plans for a corporatist utopia.

General Lanusse gradually assumed an increasingly critical
stance vis-à-vis Onganía and the corporatist thrust of the regime.[60] The waning months of 1968 and the first quarter of 1969
witnessed intensified unrest on the part of both military liberals
and nationalists. The most dramatic events centered around
a series of coup conspiracies involving both active-duty and
retired officers. Although these conspiracies were easily contained, the fact that Onganía had to resort to using the Secretaría

de Informaciones del Estado (SIDE), the presidency's own intelligence service, to harass and expose military conspirators
offered eloquent testimony to the regime's declining support
within the military. Onganía's efforts to halt the military's politicization and fragmentation had failed.[61]

The Ubiquity of Politics

The complex narrative of this chapter highlights several important points. First, politicians and political parties may have
been prohibited, but politics, defined as the clash of competing
interests and ideologies and the struggle to control the state and
influence public policies, proved ubiquitous. Second, significant
parts of the state machinery could not be subordinated to orthodox economic policy imperatives. In fact, the state's political and
ideological agencies managed to articulate an alternative project
of domination. Ultimately, however, the corporatist project undermined the regime's precarious unity and alienated powerful
political and economic groups.

The nationalists' failure highlights two interesting paradoxes.
For one thing, fear of losing control over the political process
paralyzed the will of the political apparatus; instead of mobilizing popular support against the liberals' economic policies, the
nationalists remained wedded to notions such as "communitarianism" that were as anachronistic as they were elitist. Second,
despite their failure to create an alternative legitimacy, the nationalists' success in repressing anti-regime opposition made the
regime's institutionalization along corporatist lines less urgent.
After all, with social peace seemingly assured, what incentive
was there for Onganía, the military, and the dominant business
groups to make the populist concessions necessary to create a
"party of the revolution"?

Turning to the armed forces, we find that the officer corps'
vulnerability to politicization was a consequence of its structural
characteristics and insertion in a state criss-crossed by class
cleavages and conflicting ideologies. Military sensitivity to the
regime's legitimation requirements—heightened by the closure
of most legal channels of political expression and participation—brought rival factions closer to the ensemble of competing

class interests exerting pressure on the regime. Naturally, this process of politicization violated the tenets of a vigilant professional officer corps jealously guarding its own autonomy and always ready to defend the integrity of the state.

These events also shed light on the oft-touted virtues of military-sponsored authoritarian forms of domination, namely their greater freedom from the worrisome constraints of electoral competition, and their greater autonomy from narrow sectorial interests. These factors allegedly give authoritarian regimes greater capacity to pursue unpopular policies without regard to political considerations.

Such arguments are only partially borne out by the Argentine case. Powerful domestic economic and financial interests, allied with powerful international groups, successfully pressured President Onganía to reject Salimei's pragmatic policies as well as the Tami group's "progressive" alternative program. The victory of the *ortodoxos* demonstrated the political weakness of competitive sectors of the domestic entrepreneurial class, who found themselves severely weakened and displaced from the center of the accumulation process by the economic crises of the early 1960s and the advancing internationalization of the economy. It remained to be seen, however, whether authoritarian elites could also bring the more powerful industrial, financial, and agricultural groups into line.

In any case, the new regime's installation phase gave ample proof that politics could not be abolished by authoritarian edict, and the military could not rule the country from some empyreal realm. Nevertheless, as we shall see next, the authoritarians' initial efforts to restructure state power during the installation phase did pave the way for the implementation of a new project of capital accumulation.

FOUR

The State-Led Project of Capitalist Restructuring

THE POLITICAL CRISIS and cabinet shakeup that brought the Argentine Revolution's installation phase to a close in December 1966 provided a new cohesion to the Onganía regime and helped to launch a bold new economic project. President Onganía appointed Adalberto Krieger Vasena, a leading industrialist and agri-businessman with extensive ties to transnational interests, to head the Economy Ministry, giving him such vastly expanded power that he became the regime's second most influential figure. One leading journal praised Onganía's choice as "the right man for the job" and noted the "tranquillity which invaded the business world" upon his appointment.[1]

Krieger Vasena sought to overcome the structural impasses that had plagued the Argentine economy since the late 1940s by realizing three basic goals: first, the deepening of the industrial structure through local production of intermediate inputs, capital goods, and ancillary infrastructure; second, the expansion of the consumer durables sector; and third, the promotion of nontraditional exports.[2] This strategy constituted a major break with past import-substitution programs in two important respects. First, despite important elements of continuity with programs pursued piecemeal by other post-1955 economic teams, never before had similar policies been part of such a coherent global strategy for long-term economic restructuring. Second, and perhaps most significant, the authoritarian context in which the new strategy was conceived and implemented gave the Krieger team an extraordinary degree of relative autonomy vis-à-vis civil

society, including greater freedom from pressures from entrepreneurial interests.

These ambitious goals necessarily implied a very active role
for the public sector in guiding the process of economic growth.
Under Krieger, interventionist state policies entailed boosting
the rate of domestic savings and attracting foreign capital for
investment in the most modern, dynamic, and technologically
sophisticated industrial sectors; encouraging business mergers
and joint ventures between local firms and transnational companies; and promoting the transfer of economic surplus from
the popular classes and the subordinate fractions of industrial,
commercial, and agrarian capital to the dynamic industrial and
financial sectors.

The economic authorities deliberately set out to reward the
most "efficient" economic units and sectors, frequently those
owned by or associated with foreign capital. Consequently,
Krieger's tenure (December 1966 to June 1969) witnessed increased concentration and centralization of capital, coupled with
denationalization of many important sectors of the economy.
From the point of view of the economic authorities, these were
certainly desirable outcomes. The problem was, however, that
Krieger had pledged to "avoid income transfers from one sector
to another."[3] The contradiction between Krieger's promise of
equity for all sectors and the logical effects of his own economic
strategy was at first obscured by a brief phase of economic expansion. When the full implications of Krieger's project to re-
shape the Argentine political economy became more visible,
however, the stability, and indeed the survival, of the country's
first experience with the new authoritarianism was called into
question.

Our analysis of Krieger's new strategy lays the groundwork
for the chapters that follow. Emphasis will be placed on the
politics of the strategy's conceptualization and implementation,
through consideration of the perspectives of the leading organizational actors, rather than on an analysis of the strategy as
economic *policy*, with the accent on technical questions, as is
usually the case with more conventional approaches. This approach will allow us to better capture the interaction between
policies, the economic cycle, and the response of key entrepre-

TABLE 4.1
Evolution of the Principal Economic Variables, 1965–70

| | Percent rates of change from December to December, average of one year compared to average of preceding year | | | | | Participation of salaried workers in gross product | |
| | Inflation rate | | | | | | |
	Cost of living	Wholesale prices	Gross domestic product	Employment[a]	Real wages[b]	Without employer contribution to retirement	With employer contribution to retirement
1965	–	–	9.1%	–	5.7%	38.1%	40.7%
1966	31.9%	20.0%	0.6	0.9%	1.1	41.0	43.7
1967	29.2	25.8	2.6	0.6	0.3	42.2	45.5
1968	16.2	9.5	4.4	3.0	–10.0	40.9	44.4
1969	7.6	6.1	8.5	2.1	2.2	40.5	43.9
1970	13.6	14.1	5.4	1.0	3.7	42.0	45.3

SOURCES: The first two columns were calculated from the Ministerio de Economía y Trabajo, *Informe Económico* (I and II Semester 1974), Tables 26 and 27, p. 46. The next three were calculated from Banco Central, *Sistema de cuentas del producto e ingreso de la Argentina*, vol. I, Table 56, p. 184; Table 47, p. 104; and Table 51, p. 174, respectively. The last two are from Diéguez and Petrecolla, "La distribución funcional del ingreso y el sistema previsional en la Argentina, 1950–1972," Table 5, p. 438.

[a]Based on the unemployment rate.

[b]Nominal salary of a *peon*, according to contracts, deflated with the cost of living index.

neurial interests, and it will also permit us to highlight the constraints impinging on the project of state-led restructuring.

The Unveiling of the Krieger Strategy

The accomplishments of the new project in its efforts to revitalize Argentina's chronically troubled economy are summarized in Table 4.1. The new strategy brought about 21.5 percent expansion of the gross domestic product in real terms between 1966 and 1970, an average annual cumulative growth rate of 5.2 percent. This was significantly above the 3.2 percent annual average growth rate that had been attained in Argentina since 1950. The growth was made possible in part by the increase in gross domestic investment from −7.2 percent in 1966 and 4.5 percent in 1967 to 10.7 and 21.4 percent in 1968 and 1969, respectively. These years also saw a sharp braking of the inflationary forces endemic to the Argentine economy. From approximately 30 percent annual inflation in the 1965–67 period (the peak of the earlier economic cycle), the increase in the cost of living was brought down to 7.6 percent in 1969, while wholesale price increases declined from the 20–25 percent range to less than 10 percent in 1968 and 1969.[4]

The Argentine experience stands in sharp contrast to that of Brazil, where the 1967–73 "economic miracle" was preceded by recession and a sharp decline in both real wages and the standard of living of the popular sectors. In Argentina, the Onganía regime could claim, with some justification, that economic expansion and control over inflation had not significantly affected the standard of living of the majority of the population. Unemployment remained low and the total number of salaried workers actually increased somewhat between 1966 and 1970. Real wages did fall somewhat (3.8 percent for single workers), but the functional distribution of income between capital and labor did not change appreciably and may have even improved slightly if compared to the 1960–65 period. Given what had come to be considered "normal" for Argentina, the regime could indeed claim that these achievements were substantial.

The keys to the regime's economic performance lay in significant, indeed occasionally radical, departures from past policies and the tactical skill with which the new strategy was carried out. Upon assuming power, Krieger's two immediate priorities were gaining the confidence and support of the International Monetary Fund, the World Bank, private international banks, and the transnationals, and consolidating his control over the economic apparatus (purging holdovers likely to dissent from his views and appointing business-oriented pragmatists to key posts). Strengthening ties to the U.S. government, especially the Department of Commerce and the Treasury Department, was also a top priority.

Krieger moved first to assert his control over the budgetary process. This was accomplished by adopting a modified version of World Bank proposals that emphasized severe controls on public spending (entailing cuts in salaries and social welfare), while redirecting overall spending to accord with plans for infrastructure and directly reproductive investments.[5] The ideological shift reflected in budgetary policies was crucial to Krieger's bid to win the support of the international community and to restore Argentina's favorable "investment climate." As a reward for Argentina's acceptance of the strictures of the IMF and the World Bank (and perhaps to boost Krieger's stock in the local business world), the IMF approved an initial credit agreement of $83 million.

The second challenge Krieger had to confront was an attempt by General Osiris Villegas, the head of the Sistema Nacional de Planeamiento, to assert his primacy in economic policy matters. The National Development Council (CONADE), which had played a negligible role during the installation phase of the Onganía regime, tried to put its vaunted "mechanics of national leadership" into operation through an attempted putsch directed at Krieger Vasena and the Ministry of Economy. The CONADE technocrats were overmatched, however, and found themselves bereft of support either from within the state or from private interests. The defeat of CONADE's bid for dominance over macroeconomic policymaking eliminated a potential rival source of power within the state apparatus and consolidated Krieger Vasena's status as czar of the economy.[6]

Having overcome these political obstacles, Krieger set out in March 1967 to implement economic policies that were neither orthodox monetarist (strict control over the money supply) nor structuralist (forcing a realignment of relative prices). The key to

Krieger's strategy was its analysis of inflation. According to the new diagnosis, uncontrollable price rises in the previous decade had been the result of cost-push inflation, meaning that the traditional view of demand-generated inflation was mistaken. Excessive demand was fundamentally a problem of expectations on the part of different sectors that attempted to maintain or improve their share of national income relative to each other. Political weakness, instability, and inept public policies were thus seen as the causes of cyclical economic crises, which were marked by a vicious circle in which difficulties in the external sector, inflation, and economic stagnation fed on one another.

This diagnosis of inflation, and a hard-boiled political realism based on the unhappy experiences of previous governments, led to a quite heterodox strategy that was a precursor of the strategies of *concertación* that would emerge in the 1970s and 1980s.[7] Krieger's strategy called for state control over the money supply, wages and prices, and bank credit to the private sector. The annual increase in nominal wages permitted by the economic authorities was to be held below the previous year's inflation rate. Expansion of credit to the private sector was to be equal to or greater than the increase in nominal wages. Finally, the rate of expansion of the money supply was to be held below the increase in credit to the private sector in the previous year. The parameters of economic policy are presented in Table 4.2.

Until 1970, the Krieger team was fairly successful in adhering to its original plan. Credit policies were kept in line with the overall strategy throughout the period and were particularly favorable to private-sector profitability in 1968 and 1969. Monetary policy was also kept within the prescribed parameters. Wage restraint was successful as long as organized labor was maintained under control. By 1970, however, the authorities were no longer capable of maintaining wage restraints and confronted an escalation of the wage-price spiral as a result of the growing political crisis engulfing the Onganía regime.

Looking more closely at Krieger's policies, we are able to distinguish between short-term tactics designed to normalize the economy and a long-term strategy for economic restructuring. In the first half of 1967, Krieger sought to stimulate capital accumulation, and the external sector was to play the role of the principal dynamic agent in this phase of growth. Krieger

TABLE 4.2

Parameters of Economic Policy, 1965–70

(*Percent*)

	1965	1966	1967	1968	1969	1970
Wage increase	36.0%	33.3%	29.7%	4.6%	9.9%	17.8%
Inflation in previous year	27.3	27.8	22.8	24.5	10.7	7.6
Parameter of wage policy	1.32	1.20	1.30	**0.19**	**0.93**	2.34
Increase in bank credit	27.3	36.0	32.8	44.4	27.0	19.4
Wage increase	36.0	33.3	29.7	4.6	9.9	17.8
Parameter of credit policy	0.76	**1.08**	**1.10**	**9.65**	**2.73**	**1.09**
Increase in money supply	29.0	33.6	36.2	25.0	11.2	19.4
Increase in bank credit	27.3	36.0	32.8	44.4	27.0	19.4
Parameter of monetary policy	1.06	**0.93**	1.10	**0.56**	**0.41**	1.00

SOURCES: Wages and inflation data from INDEC, *Boletín Estadístico Trimestral*; credit and money supply from Ministerio de Economía y Trabajo, *Informe Económico* (I and II semester of 1974), Table 46, pp. 78–79.

NOTE: Figures in boldface indicate outcomes within prescribed parameters.

pursued a rapprochement with foreign investment capital by providing incentives for increased agricultural exports and by encouraging greater utilization of installed capacity in the manufacturing sector. The same policies were pursued in the second half of 1967, but once increased internal savings began to diminish the urgency of foreign investment, domestic investment and production assumed the dynamic role.

An early example of Krieger's tactical versatility during this initial phase was the enactment of a so-called "imperfectly compensated devaluation." The peso was devalued by about 37 percent, from 255 to the dollar to 350 to the dollar, and the devaluation was accompanied by an increase in export taxes on primary goods. The major objectives of this unorthodox policy were the attraction of a large influx of international capital and the generation of investor confidence in the stability of the currency.[8]

This measure—which deliberately deprived agricultural exporters of the large income transfers typical of past devaluations—was in large part responsible for the unremitting hostility of Pampean producers to Krieger's policies. Conversely, by holding down the price of food (and hence of wages), while transferring a portion of the surplus generated by rural producers to the city for investment at subsidized interest rates, Krieger benefited urban industrialists. These policies were also appealing to international capital, attracted by monetary stability and promises of policy predictability. The solicitousness of Krieger's team toward foreign investors in 1967 was due not only to Argentina's need for a quick injection of investment capital, but also to the acknowledgment of the instrumental role that foreign capital would have to play by way of a political demonstration effect. Foreign capital investment was required to convince local capitalists that foreign governments, industrialists, and bankers had confidence in the authoritarian project, and particularly in its economic leadership. However, when the expected influx of foreign investment did not arrive in the quantities necessary to boost economic activity, Krieger was forced to reconsider his tactics.[9]

A second major initiative came in the area of tax reforms, which were integral to Krieger's drive to reduce the budget deficit. The plan was to simultaneously stimulate private-sector economic activity (in order to help absorb the bloated labor force employed by the state) and generate higher revenues by increasing tax rates and modifying the structure of taxation. This reform was complemented by offering a major tax break to the private sector, which included the opportunity to deduct 100 percent of the cost of industrial and agricultural machinery from a firm's tax bill. Such an incentive represented a very substantial state subsidy designed to stimulate private investment as rapidly as possible, even though this conflicted with other elements of the grand strategy then unfolding.[10]

While the devaluation and the tax reforms were of undeniable importance, the real centerpiece of the Krieger strategy was the expansion of state intervention into relations between labor and capital through wage and price controls. The new economic team understood the politics of a successful stabilization program. Experience had demonstrated that previous regimes, both civilian and military, had foundered upon their inability to force modifications in the expectations and behavior of capitalists and workers with regard to future wage and price increases. The Krieger team resolved to try a new approach.

In contrast to classic IMF-style stabilization programs, Krieger's anti-inflation program focused on controlling nominal wages and salaries through a firm "incomes policy." The state moved to replace traditional collective bargaining with a far-reaching decree law. The new law, which followed previous anti-labor measures such as mandatory arbitration and state intervention of unions, limited increases in nominal wages according to a complex formula.[11] The goal was for this technocratic approach to defuse the wage issue and reinforce the image of the state's neutrality by imposing "equal sacrifices" on all sectors of the labor force.

The Krieger team also benefited from the past failures of price controls. The cornerstone of the new price policy was the decision to impose controls exclusively over the industrial sector, concentrating on the negotiation of price agreements with the largest domestic and transnational manufacturing firms. These large firms were expected to exercise price leadership and impose discipline throughout the rest of the economy. The vehicle for this discipline was a plan for "voluntary" price agreements between the state and the largest firms in key economic sectors. Participating firms would be required to maintain their prices at the level in effect at the time of their incorporation into the agreement. This was the "sacrifice" the industrial sector would make to promote economic stabilization.[12]

The combined effect of peso devaluation, tax reforms, and the incomes policy emboldened Krieger and his team to risk a definite break with the more extreme *ortodoxos* over the management of monetary policy. Allowing moderate expansion of the money supply held out a significant political advantage over alternative policies, namely the promise that inflation could be brought under control in the brief span of one year.[13] In Krieger's view, inflation had to be whipped before ambitious pledges to transform the Argentine economy structurally could be fulfilled.

The final economic policy initiative adopted in 1967—a new credit policy to stimulate consumption—revealed much about the political and economic constraints shaping the new strategy of development. By authorizing commercial banks to open new lines of credit of up to 350,000 pesos to consumers, the new Central Bank policies sought to stimulate personal consumption so as to absorb excessive inventory in the consumer durables sector. (Additionally, the credits could only be used for purchases from firms participating in the price-control agreement.)[14] However, the expansion of consumer credit implied the paradox of stimulation during a stabilization program. In this instance, the risks of feeding inflationary pressures had to be subordinated to the more pressing political necessity of avoiding a recession in the strategic consumer durables sector and widening entrepreneurial support for the authoritarian regime.

Despite sluggish growth and the disappointing response of foreign and domestic investors, the success of the reforms in bringing inflation under control convinced the authorities of the appropriateness of their chosen strategy. Krieger and his collaborators viewed their problem as basically political: in spite of all the concessions that had been offered as atonement for the past sins of economic policies, the magic element of "investor confidence" had still not been forthcoming, at least not with the rapidity originally anticipated. What else was to be done?

The Krieger team's answer to this question was to move even further in the direction of abandoning the more outmoded tenets of economic orthodoxy. In the process, they ignored the criticisms of influential entrepreneurial groups alarmed by "statism" and the evils of deficit spending. In a display of the state's autonomy from its capitalist supporters, the economic strategy for 1968 was to dramatically increase the public sector's role in maintaining aggregate demand. This was to be done by boosting utilization of existing installed capacity and by placing less emphasis on attracting foreign investment or inducing domestic investment.[15] The goal, however, remained the same as before— economic stabilization.

The politics of this pragmatic shift in favor of greater state intervention said much about the internal and external alliances underlying the authoritarian project. Krieger's increasingly heterodox policies provoked strong domestic opposition, but he counterbalanced this criticism with the crucial support he received from the international financial community through the World Bank and the International Monetary Fund. This "international connection" was vital to the economic authorities (and

Krieger himself) because it provided a much-needed political counterweight to the criticism of orthodox economists and their business supporters, as well as to the attacks of both liberal and nationalist factions within the armed forces.[16]

The turnaround in the economy seemed to justify Krieger's heterodoxy. In fact, in 1968 and 1969 the state's forceful role in stimulating aggregate demand was further expanded through an active fiscal policy. A reduction in current expenditures, combined with steady increases in capital expenditures, began to bring deficits under control and to further the structural shift in state spending initiated in 1967. By 1969 capital expenditures had increased more than 30 percent in real terms over 1967 levels; current expenditures had declined from about 79 percent of total spending in 1966 to less than 65 percent; and capital outlays jumped dramatically from only 21 percent to over 35 percent. The state was clearly doing its part to cut waste and to further productive investment.[17]

These successes were viewed by Krieger and his collaborators as having prepared the terrain for productive use of savings by the private sector. It was difficult for the economic planners to resist being carried away by their own optimism, for they were convinced that 1969 would be the year of economic takeoff, the beginning of an "Argentine Miracle" that would vindicate Krieger's break with orthodoxy and redeem the Onganía regime's pledge to carry out a structural transformation of the economy.[18]

The Entrepreneurial Response to Restructuring

The Krieger team's sense of victory was reinforced by the enthusiasm for its general objectives, policies, and policy instruments expressed by the principal entrepreneurial organizations. Both modern and traditional interests strongly supported efforts to curtail organized labor's legal and institutional bases of power and to depoliticize capital-labor relations.[19] Most sectors of capital and their respective class organizations also applauded the announced intention to reduce the fiscal deficit by rationalizing state enterprises and administrative agencies, restructuring state spending so as to directly boost productive expenditures, and cutting back on current expenditures for wages and administrative overhead. Their support was tempered, however, by the fear that Krieger was actually "soft" on the fiscal deficit.

This attachment to strict fiscal orthodoxy contained the seeds of future conflict between the entrepreneurs and the state. Most entrepreneurs did not accept the heterodox thrust of the Krieger program's commitment to use the state budget as an instrument to transform the economy. Their preference for privatization and dismantling of the state sector made it difficult for them to accept that the collective interest of the private sector would perhaps be well served by a selective expansion of the state's power to manage and plan economic activities.[20]

The declarations of the Unión Industrial, the Cámara de Comercio, and the Sociedad Rural were particularly enthusiastic about the peso devaluation, the liberalization of the foreign-exchange market, and other policies designed to make the Argentine economy more "open" to foreign investment and technology. These organizations strongly favored all measures for attracting foreign investment, assuring easy repatriation of profits, and getting back into the good graces of the IMF and the World Bank. The traditionally liberal organizations also supported the instruments geared toward achieving monetary stabilization and control of inflation. These goals were seen as complementary to that of liberalizing the economy in general, rewarding the most efficient and innovative units of capital, and putting an end to "artificial" state protection of firms that were unable to compete in the most recent phase of transnational development.

But Argentina's businessmen did not respond to Krieger's strategy as a homogeneous bloc. To facilitate our exposition, we will first consider the reaction of agrarian producers and then turn to the industrial sectors' response and the larger question of hegemony within the entrepreneurial class as a whole.

Agrarian interests shared the general concern over the expansion of the state's role in the economy, but the increasing subordination of agricultural producers to the urban industrial and financial sectors caused considerable friction. However, this conflict did not automatically lead to a clear-cut confrontation between urban and rural interests, or between agricultural producers and the economic authorities. Rather, there was only a gradual awareness on the part of the agricultural sector that the new project of accumulation did not contemplate their restoration as the leading economic and political force in Argentine society. The resulting frustration gave rise to a contradictory response: on the one hand, the agrarian fractions led by the Sociedad Rural and the conservative media such as *La Prensa* continued to applaud the liberal discourse of the regime, while on the other they began to inject an increasingly strident tone into their criticisms of the new economic project.[21]

The agrarian interests' initial criticism centered most directly on the state's appropriation of the windfall profits generated by the increase in export taxes which had accompanied the 37-percent devaluation of the peso. Very soon, however, there began to emerge a more general critique of Krieger's brand of technocratic Keynesianism. This critique, expressed in the language of defending "free enterprise," laid the foundations for the subsequent disaffection of the agricultural sectors with the authoritarian project. The tone for this ideological challenge was set early in 1967 by the president of the Sociedad Rural. Denouncing "twenty-five years of sterile and ruinous struggle" between left- and right-wing ideologues, which had resulted in a "regime of exaggerated state interventionism in the economy," the leader of the SRA launched an indirect attack on the economic authorities: "*Dirigismo* is the principal cause of national stagnation and backwardness. The growth of the state has been inverse to the growth of wealth. . . . In spite of this, demagogues and socialistic ideologues call for state interventionism, the nationalization of public services, the statization of industry, and the control of economic activity in general."[22] Notwithstanding this criticism, however, the Sociedad Rural, the Bolsa de Comercio, and other organizations such as the Confederación de Asociaciones Rurales de Buenos Aires y La Pampa (CARBAP), representing the middle agrarian bourgeoisie, were initially at pains to recognize the authorities' reinforcement of the basic property rights of rural landowners.[23]

Soon, however, agrarian interests moved even more rapidly and aggressively to reject the implied bid for hegemony on the part of the transnationalized groups and their allies within the economic apparatus. Conflicts over two major issues defined the terms of the struggle within the dominant groups and between the rural producers and those sponsoring the Krieger accumulation strategy. Both issues involved the state's ability to force the agricultural sector to subsidize the "urban alliance" consisting of industrialists, labor, and the state itself.

The first issue centered on policy toward the external sector in the face of declining prices for Argentina's agricultural exports. During 1968 the economic authorities gradually reduced export taxes on certain agricultural products: from 18 percent on corn, meat, and wool to 8 percent on corn, 10–15 percent on meat, and 12 percent on wool. But agrarian producers were not placated, and they protested the relative, and in many cases absolute, decline in their real income. The Sociedad Rural demanded a complete end to export taxes as part of a "just incomes policy." Going even further, the SRA rejected the system by which the state set prices for agricultural products. Krieger quickly responded by adopting a tough public stance as the champion of the "national interest" versus the "selfish" interests of the rural producers, declaring that the economic authorities would remain "inflexible" before unjustified pressures.[24]

In this increasingly acrimonious conflict between the agrarian producers and the Minister of Economy, the SRA and its allies (the "men of the *campo*," as they styled themselves) articulated a double-pronged strategy of opposition. On the one hand, the rural organizations moved to smooth over their own rivalries in order to present a united front of opposition to state policies, and on the other, they began a public and private campaign condemning their lack of representation within the state apparatus.

A second issue provoked even more serious opposition from the agrarian bourgeoisie. Ever since the early 1960s, agricultural economists and other policymakers had put forward proposals to stimulate greater productivity in the agricultural sector by penalizing large landowners who failed to introduce technological improvements. The reasons for these proposals were obvious: with virtually stagnant agricultural production and a growing urban population demanding cheap foodstuffs, Argentina found it almost impossible to increase the surplus available for export. The resulting foreign-exchange bottleneck gave the agrarian bourgeoisie, particularly the Pampean producers of cattle and wheat, significant political and economic power. The problem was that many rural producers preferred to reap easy profits derived from large differential rents on a world scale rather than modernize techniques of production that had remained essentially unchanged since the turn of the century.[25]

The instrument chosen by the Krieger team to assure sufficient foreign exchange was a modification of the existing system of taxation on land. The new system (the so-called *impuesto a las tierras aptas para la explotación agropecuaria*) was designed to penalize unproductive land use and to reward landowners willing to assume the risks of technological modernization. Moreover, the new system lowered considerably the minimum income subject to taxation, so that many rural producers who had not previously paid income taxes now became taxpayers.

This tough stance vis-à-vis the rural sector allowed Krieger again to pose as the defender of the "national interest," to the approbation of the urban sectors. Krieger thereby reaffirmed the authorities' growing disregard for the agrarian bourgeoisie, enhancing the state's relative autonomy vis-à-vis that sector and attempting to subordinate agriculture to the collective interest of capital as interpreted and reflected by the strategy in place since 1967.

The initial reaction of rural producers to this attack was defensive, but an ideological offensive was soon launched that focused on the political motivations behind the tax and its alleged "ultimate consequences." The large Pampean agricultural producers seized upon the emotion-laden issue of "agrarian reform," charging that "the announced innovations could result in an alteration of a system that has solid foundations in the way of life adopted in Argentina and the Free World." [26] At an Extraordinary Assembly of the Sociedad Rural called to debate the new tax system, the government's policies were denounced as "unconstitutional" and "confiscatory." The Assembly's formal declaration warned against "foreign philosophies" and the "collectivist foundations" of the state's agrarian policy, a policy that it said violated the precepts of "Western and Christian civilization." [27]

CARBAP, the Sociedad Rural's main rival, with more than 60 rural societies and 22,000 affiliates in the provinces of Buenos Aires and La Pampa, went even further in denouncing the state's tilt away from the interests of rural producers. Wrapping themselves in patriotic garb, the leaders of CARBAP warned Onganía in these terms:

Confronted with this imminent hard blow to agriculture, we denounce before your Excellency, now in our character as Argentines, [the fact] that national financial interests and the international interests to which they are linked are preparing themselves to take over at despicable prices the ownership of the land which [government] functionaries have cheapened. Should we be too surprised? Have they not already installed themselves in control of the most important banks? Must we resign ourselves to the triumph of financial interests over the authentic entrepreneur, over national savings? Will we have to witness the destruction of the basic pillar on which the agrarian family rests? Your Excellency, do not ignore these facets of the problem, because we believe that they are a key aspect of the present Argentine reality.[28]

The conflict between the large agricultural producers and the Krieger team became further complicated by mounting class tensions in the countryside flowing from an increasingly aggressive stance on the part of many smaller rural entrepreneurs. The most politically active of the smaller producers were represented by the Federación Agraria Argentina (FAA), which consistently opposed policies favoring the big latifundistas. With their production primarily oriented toward domestic consumption, these producers had long been subjugated by the large cattle and grain interests tied to the export market. The FAA, unlike the representative organizations of the dominant agricultural sectors, strongly supported the state's effort to restructure and modernize agricultural production, even favoring Krieger's tax schemes for rural property.[29]

In fact, the FAA advocated a project of rural development that would promote more modern, capital-intensive techniques of cultivation by changing the structure of land ownership, introducing modern technology, modernizing the marketing and processing of agricultural products, expanding rural infrastructure and education, increasing credits to efficient producers, and so on. The FAA also called for increased state intervention on behalf of the capitalization of agriculture, following the example of the advanced capitalist countries, who had "liberated themselves from orthodox ideological attachments."[30]

It is in response to this two-front struggle—against both Krieger's economic policies and the Federación Agraria—that the "nationalist" offensive of the large Pampean producers of the Sociedad Rural and CARBAP may be most fruitfully interpreted. The SRA and CARBAP attempted to link their rivals in the countryside to the "collectivist designs" of the Minister of Economy and to the United States, Argentina's traditional rival in international markets for agricultural commodities. The policies of the Ministry of Economy were now denounced as "socialistic expedients" designed to further U.S. agricultural interests.

The Question of Hegemony

Turning now to consider the urban sector's response to the restructuring project and the question of hegemony, we must begin with a brief overview of the political and institutional organization of Argentina's entrepreneurial class. The transnationalization of production and markets since the mid-1950s had made the Argentine class structure exceedingly complex, giving rise to a multitude of cleavages affecting both the propertied classes and the rest of society. A new fault line that deepened internal divisions within the business community resulted from the emergence of new firms and sectors that differed in the extent of their ability to participate fully in the latest phase of industrial expansion.[31]

Those segments of industrial and financial capital involved in the transnationalization of the productive system came to be differentiated from the domestic entrepreneurs in the more competitive sectors. In political and ideological terms, this cleavage roughly corresponded to the long-standing divisions among organizations representing the different business groups that had crystallized in the immediate post-Peronist period. At the level of their organizations, entrepreneurs were divided into two opposing camps: the Confederación General Económica (CGE), grouping the more traditional, competitive sector of domestic industrialists who had emerged during the early phases of import-substitution; and the umbrella group called the Asociación Coordinadora de Instituciones Empresarias Libres (ACIEL), which brought together the largest and most powerful commercial, agricultural, financial, and industrial interests.

Figure 4.1 provides a schematic depiction of the different segments of capital and their organizations. The fractions of capital actively asserting their claim for hegemony over the class as a whole were primarily represented in the Unión Industrial Argentina (UIA), which counted among its members all the major transnational corporations as well as the largest national firms,

FIGURE 4.1

Leading Entrepreneurial Organizations

Dominant fractions/Hegemonic contenders	Subordinate fractions/"Traditional" national sectors
"Modern" transnationalized sectors *Industry* UIA* *Finance* ABRA* ABA*	*Industry* CGE *Agriculture* CARBAP CRA FAA
"Traditional" national sectors *Agriculture* SRA*	*Commerce* CAC* BC*

NOTE: Asterisks indicate organizations belonging to ACIEL. Full titles are as follows: ABA, Asociación de Bancos Argentinos (split from ABRA in 1972); ABRA, Asociación de Bancos de la República Argentina; BC, Bolsa de Comercio; CAC, Cámara Argentina de Comercio; CARBAP, Confederación de Asociaciones Rurales de Buenos Aires y La Pampa; FAA, Federación Agraria Argentina; SRA, Sociedad Rural Argentina; UIA, Unión Industrial Argentina.

and the Asociación de Bancos de la República Argentina (ABRA), whose membership included the major foreign banks operating in the country. The still influential agrarian interests of the *pampa húmeda*, represented by the Sociedad Rural, were the other main contenders for hegemony.

The key to the power potential of the social forces represented by the ACIEL and the CGE was their composition as umbrella organizations. Tables 4.3, 4.4, and 4.5 facilitate analysis of these two camps by comparing the numbers of their affiliates, the sectors of economic activity they represented, and their regional concentration. All these factors influenced the political practice of the different fractions of capital and the ultimate fate of Krieger's project. The sectorial breakdown is revealing of the strengths and weaknesses of the two principal organizations: industry—53.5 percent affiliated with the CGE, 32.1 percent with ACIEL; commerce—65.1 percent with the CGE, 11.3 percent with ACIEL; agriculture—76.0 percent with the CGE, and 22.2 percent with ACIEL.

The regional concentration of affiliates throughout the country is as important as the number of affiliates and their sectorial distribution. Table 4.4 illustrates the preponderant concentration of ACIEL affiliates in the Federal Capital, the province of Buenos Aires, and in Córdoba and Santa Fe, the two other most industrialized provinces. Although the majority of the CGE's af-

TABLE 4.3

First-Grade Business Organizations by Affiliation and Economic Sector, 1969

	Industry		Commerce		Agriculture		Construction		Other		Total	
	No.	Pct.	No.	Pct.	No.	Pct.	No.	Pct.	No.	Pct.	No.	Pct.
CGE	413	53.5%	432	65.1%	557	76.0%	11	12.8%	107	49.8%	1,520	61.5%
ACIEL	248	32.1	75	11.3	163	22.2	–	–	25	11.6	511	20.7
Non-member	111	14.4	157	23.6	13	1.8	75	87.2	83	38.6	439	17.8
Totals	772	100.0%	664	100.0%	733	100.0%	86	100.0%	215	100.0%	2,470	100.0%

SOURCE: Calculated from Confederación General Económica, *Memoria Anual, 1970,* Appendix.

TABLE 4.4

Distribution of First-Grade Business Organizations Affiliated with the Asociación Coordinadora de Instituciones Empresarias Libres (ACIEL), by Region and Economic Sector, 1969

	Industry		Commerce		Agriculture		Construction		Other		Total	
	No.	Pct.	No.	Pct.	No.	Pct.	No.	Pct.	No.	Pct.	No.	Pct.
Federal Capital and Province of Buenos Aires	199	80.2%	50	66.7%	56	34.3%	–	–	19	76.0%	250	48.9%
Core provinces[a]	22	8.9	16	21.3	42	25.8	–	–	4	16.0	84	16.5
Peripheral provinces[b]	27	10.9	9	12.0	65	39.9	–	–	2	8.0	177	34.6
Totals	248	100.0%	75	100.0%	163	100.0%	–	–	25	100.0%	511	100.0%

SOURCE: Calculated from Confederación General Económica, *Memoria Anual, 1970,* Appendix.
[a] Cordoba and Santa Fe.
[b] All other provinces.

TABLE 4.5

Distribution of First-Grade Business Organizations Affiliated with the Confederación General Económica (GGE), by Region and Economic Sector, 1969

	Industry		Commerce		Agriculture		Construction		Other		Total	
	No.	Pct.	No.	Pct.	No.	Pct.	No.	Pct.	No.	Pct.	No.	Pct.
Federal Capital and Province of Buenos Aires	200	48.4%	222	51.4%	123	22.1%	7	63.6%	49	45.8%	601	39.5%
Core provinces[a]	51	12.4	58	13.4	281	50.4	–	–	18	16.8	408	26.9
Peripheral provinces[b]	162	39.2	152	35.2	153	27.5	4	36.4	40	37.4	511	33.6
Totals	413	100.0%	432	100.0%	557	100.0%	11	100.0%	107	100.0%	1,520	100.0%

SOURCE: Calculated from Confederación General Económica, *Memoria Anual, 1970*, Appendix.
[a] Córdoba and Santa Fe.
[b] All other provinces.

filiates were also located in the heart of the country, the CGE had significant representation from less industrial and more backward areas in the interior, as shown in Table 4.5.

Claiming to represent 90 percent of the nation's entrepreneurs throughout the interior provinces, the CGE raised the banner of federalism to attack the dominance of the economic groups centered in Buenos Aires and the developed core region. The UIA, representing modern industry, responded that its member firms accounted for 90 percent of total manufacturing sales, 95 percent of total employment, 96 percent of wages and salaries, 85 percent of capital goods production, and 91 percent of the physical volume of production.[32] In terms of economic power alone, it thus appeared that the social forces represented in the ACIEL should have easily established their political leadership. But the CGE was stronger than might be suspected, while sharp disagreements among its members made the ACIEL something of a paper tiger.

The weaknesses of the groups represented in the ACIEL were certainly not apparent at first glance. In the 1955–69 period, around 75 percent of all businessmen in high posts were affiliated with the ACIEL; the only exception was during the Illia administration, when ACIEL members held 50 percent of the top posts. During the Onganía regime, members of the ACIEL occupied 34 out of 42 top-level offices, or 81 percent. The CGE, by contrast, only had two representatives, whose tenure was limited to the first six months of the new regime. Moreover, ACIEL businessmen were not only dominant in the economic ministries, but also accounted for half of the top posts in key political agencies and two out of five top posts in the Defense Ministry.[33]

Considering this picture, business's enthusiastic support for the ouster of the Illia government was hardly surprising. Businessmen saw their aspirations echoed in the initial ideological discourse of the new authoritarian regime.[34] The dominant industrial, agricultural, and commercial groups applauded the appointment of Krieger Vasena and saw him as further evidence of the Onganía regime's strong response to political instability and economic stagnation. Many representatives of these social forces even adopted the rhetorical style of the regime's official ideologues, identifying their interests as those of the new state and the nation as a whole. Early in 1968, the director of the Argentine Chamber of Commerce (CAC) captured well the general enthusiasm of these forces about the direction of the new regime:

The Argentine Revolution . . . has not been a simple change in government. Much more than that, it has had as its objective the modification of the political, economic, and social systems and structures that have blocked Argentina's progress . . . and that have kept it from reaching the place to which it aspires in the concert of the most advanced nations of the world. This great transformation of Argentina, in which we are all involved in a common effort, government and the private sectors, labor as well as business, is based on the principles of liberty, order, hierarchy, and discipline that will contribute to assuring the stability of all the institutions that harmoniously come together to achieve the reestablishment of the moral and spiritual values of the Nation.[35]

The sectors of local capital represented by the Confederación General Económica took a very different stance, one of strong opposition to virtually all the policies enacted by the new authorities. Dusting off the remaining vestiges of its anti-imperialist ideology from the 1940s and early 1950s, the CGE forcefully condemned Krieger's overtures to foreign capital. In particular it protested the denationalization of the banking and financial sectors, but noted that "this process of absorption extends to other sectors of the national economy."[36] This denationalization, the CGE charged, was detrimental to domestic control over economic decision-making and national sovereignty. The CGE also charged that the state's monetary and credit policies would drain capital away from the country through profit repatriation, paving the way for a future foreign-exchange shortage and a slowing of industrial development.

The authorities' handling of the peso devaluation and liberalization of the exchange market had also contributed to takeovers by transnational firms and foreign banks. Indeed, according to the CGE, these actions "signified in practice the equivalent of a subsidy for foreign capitalists who dedicate themselves to buying up Argentine firms at bargain-basement prices." The CGE thus called for tougher laws controlling foreign investment to protect national capital, saying "we insist on the necessity of creating an effective defense against all types of absorption, of banks as well as of national firms."[37]

By early 1969, polarization in the business community began

to accelerate rapidly, with the most modern industrial and financial fractions pressuring the economic apparatus to pursue the Krieger strategy without regard to the interests of other groups in society. These sectors were concerned that the "extraordinary achievements" obtained by Krieger's policies had, in their view, almost exclusively benefited the state itself, rather than the private sector. To boost capital formation and to make Argentine industry more competitive in world markets, the Unión Industrial called upon the state to implement policies that would transfer resources from less to more efficient sectors and from consumption to capital investment. Failure to adopt these measures, it warned, would result in "strangulation of the possibility of expansion and modernization of industrial firms." Moreover, the UIA and its affiliates affirmed that "definitive triumph can only be reached by deepening and extending the [Krieger] reforms as a whole." In effect, the UIA demanded that the state pursue a policy favoring the interests of the modern industrial sector in an even more open and direct manner.[38]

The economic authorities' response to these demands was to deflect concrete, technical criticisms of specific policy measures, and to use the "international connections" so carefully cultivated by the Minister of Economy to shunt aside opposition from both nationalist and *ortodoxo* critics within the regime. At the same time, they tried to convince the most dynamic fractions of the bourgeoisie to rally around the economic project, which all agreed would ultimately promote their interests and consolidate their position as the dominant group in Argentine society. In this endeavor, Krieger Vasena continued to receive invaluable support from his external allies in the international financial community. Such support was dramatically evidenced in October 1968, when Krieger was elected president of the annual joint meeting of the International Monetary Fund and the World Bank.

To complete the panorama of positions taken by the different fractions of capital during the period, it is necessary to probe further the stance assumed by small and medium-sized industrial and commercial entrepreneurs (now strengthened by the addition of the Federación Agraria), represented by the Confederación General Económica. The CGE's fundamental disagreement with Krieger's policies was based on the fact that smaller entrepreneurs were not participating equally in the process of capitalist expansion. It was necessary, said the leadership of the CGE, for the state to promote even more economic expansion benefiting capital as a whole, and not just the large transnationals and their domestic counterparts: "We call for much more ambitious goals . . . we propose a growth of much greater volume."[39]

This call for more "ambitious" goals translated into an appeal for measures protecting small and medium-sized capital from the "unfair" competition of foreign capital and big local capital. Demand for state protection of the domestic competitive-sector firms was articulated in a discourse in which foreign capital was portrayed as "anti-national." Accordingly, the state should act to protect the legitimate interests of the "patriotic" local entrepreneurs—interests that were seen as congruent with the "national interest."[40]

In summary, by early 1969 the balance of social forces within the dominant groups presented a complex picture. On the one hand, the transnationals and the largest and most dynamic local industrial firms and financial groups continued to further their position of economic dominance. On the other, however, mounting opposition to state policies on the part of subordinate fractions of industrial and commercial capital and the dissonant objectives of dominant agricultural interests revealed that after three years the authoritarian model still had not consolidated a stable system of bourgeois hegemony over the state or civil society.[41]

Unresolved Dilemmas

Krieger's project to restructure the economy, though at first applauded, thus soon met with mounting resistance from many sectors of Argentina's fractious bourgeoisie. Three main tendencies had emerged: the position of the modern industrial and financial fractions represented by the UIA and the Bankers' Association; the position of the agricultural sectors led by the SRA and generally supported by other organizations such as CARBAP and the CRA; and the "nationalist" position adopted by the CGE, representing the more traditional, competitive industrial and commercial groups linked to the domestic market.

The first two positions—spearheaded by the UIA and the SRA, respectively—articulated a common concern with a tendency toward increased state intervention and an exclusive focus on the external sector. Here, however, a divergence appeared, with the leading industrial interests in the modern sectors calling for a continuation and deepening of the current policy, while rural interests began to criticize their own growing subordination to the needs of urban industry and finance.

Confrontation was by no means inevitable. There remained a possibility that a workable compromise—expressed perhaps in a more orthodox economic strategy—could be forged between the modern industrial and financial groups and the traditional agricultural interests. In contrast, possibilities for an amicable agreement with the third major fraction of capital, that represented by the Confederación General Económica, were very remote. The CGE had assumed a strong opposition stance that foreshadowed future attempts to create a defensive alliance of national capital in concert with the middle sectors and organized labor.

The incipient disarray of the major social forces constituting the social base of the authoritarian project was intimately related to the difficulties encountered by Krieger Vasena in implementing a new model of accumulation. Despite their continued use of the rhetoric of modernization and transformation, the attention of policymakers became increasingly focused on short-run policy considerations geared toward maintaining the level of aggregate economic activity and avoiding the alienation of important international and local groups.

This subordination of economic policy to political concerns was indicative of the very limited degree of relative autonomy the state (and particularly the economic apparatus) had been able to achieve. It also spoke to the dominance of economic orthodoxy within the most important local and transnational groups of the private sector. Failure by the economic authorities to respond to these pressures would have been interpreted as a "failure of nerve" or "lack of seriousness" and would have convinced all economic agents—capital, workers, middle sectors—that inflation would continue unabated, thus rendering even more difficult the tasks of modernizing the economy and maintaining political stability.

Another facet of this dilemma was illustrated by the state's problematic relationship with foreign capital—a relationship of "mutual indispensability."[42] The question of timing was crucial here. The original strategy of promoting private-sector expansion to close the gap in the state's finances (more growth meaning larger revenues) ran into trouble when foreign capital failed to arrive and when domestic investment stagnated as a result of local capital's reluctance to move alone. Herein lay the crux of the problem confronting the restructuring project: even with a prestigious economic czar like Krieger Vasena serving as guarantor, international capital had to believe firmly in the future stability of their local allies before investing, and yet investment was needed before future economic expansion could confirm the wisdom of their trust. This explains the extreme vulnerability of the economic authorities who espoused the new development policies in the initial years of the authoritarian project.

Given the external sector's mediocre performance, domestic investment had to be the main catalyst of the expansion required to avoid stagnation and recession. Therefore, the state was forced to partially reverse its original strategy and stimulate the economy. It was now the confidence of the local capitalists that had to be won, through a demonstration of economic orthodoxy, before foreign investment capital would flow into the country. The reality was that foreign capital was reluctant to make long-term investments and preferred taking quick profits from currency speculation in "hot money" until internal economic expansion was well under way and political stability was achieved.[43]

Even Krieger's relatively brief delay in learning this lesson meant that the achievement of the key requirement in his long-term strategy for restructuring the Argentine economy—the elimination of inflation as a brake on accumulation—remained in jeopardy. Failure to solve this problem had important repercussions for the relationship between the state and entrepreneurs, threatening the hegemonic aspirations of the modern groups by alienating the agricultural sectors and industrialists in the competitive sectors. This difficult dilemma vividly illustrated the importance of sequence, timing, and the intimate interconnections among class alliances, economic policy instruments, and economic outcomes.

As the implications of Krieger's restructuring strategy became clearer, the injured sectors of the entrepreneurial class began to mobilize and to contest the direction of the authoritarian project more actively. Capitalists were not alone in their discontent, as shall be seen next.

FIVE

Working-Class Politics and the State

THE ONGANÍA REGIME faced many challenges in dealing with the working class that were broadly similar to those confronted twenty years earlier by Juan Perón. But there were also some fundamental differences. Like Perón, Onganía needed to subordinate the working class to his own project, and, as Perón had done, he attempted this by employing a variety of neocorporatist mechanisms. Perón largely succeeded in the political incorporation of labor. But post-Peronist governments, civilian and military alike, could not sustain this feat. A key feature of Perón's legacy was an "organized working class" that now wielded tremendous political and economic bargaining power and was fully prepared to defend aggressively its corporate interests, even if this meant clashing with the state and the military. Onganía and his nationalist political apparatchiks understood that to succeed in restructuring state and society on the basis of an ambitious corporatist architecture, the working class's impressive capacity for autonomous organization and political action had to be destroyed or at least transformed radically. And, in fact, the positive reactions of many prominent labor leaders to the 1966 coup encouraged their efforts to transform Argentina's unruly workers into a "support class" for the authoritarian regime.[1]

That this project had any realistic prospects at all was eloquent testimony to the working class's deep alienation from post-1955 Argentine politics. A parallel could be drawn with the late 1930s and early 1940s. The workers' political and economic exclusion under the Concordancia had paved the way for Perón's project to make the unions the foundation of a new system of legitimate domination. But the obstacles confronting Onganía were much more formidable. Although politics cannot be understood simply as an epiphenomenal manifestation of the economy, the logic of the Argentine political economy in the 1960s certainly made it extremely difficult for state elites to conciliate the interests of both labor and capital.

During the so-called "easy" stage of import-substitution, state policies subsidizing the industrial sector at the expense of Pampean agriculture had made a large and sustained rise in the real income of urban workers and the salaried middle class compatible with the profitability expectations of entrepreneurs. This was no longer possible. The new pattern of accumulation inaugurated with the transnationalization of the economy in the mid-1950s, particularly the implantation of the automobile sector and a sophisticated manufacturing sector, signified the virtual completion of the expansion of the domestic market for consumer non-durables. Henceforth, efforts to achieve the vertical integration of the productive system in the consumer durable and capital goods sectors would generate chronic inflation, large and erratic shifts in income redistribution, and stop-go growth cycles punctuated by periodic balance-of-payments crises.

In recognition of these new circumstances, Krieger Vasena and many leading entrepreneurs cogently argued that further industrialization hinged on limiting the economic rewards accorded labor while also requiring its political demobilization and limiting its participation in the shaping of state policies. To accomplish this, of course, the trick was to overcome labor's exceptional level of organizational development, high degree of political consciousness and sophistication, and long history of political and economic militancy, which were without equal in Latin America.[2]

Peronism's undisputed hegemony over the labor movement as an anti-Marxist force for class collaboration in defense of a now utopian development model gave the nationalists some reason for optimism. The more astute among Onganía's political staff realized that it was a mistake to see in Peronism a catalyst for revolutionary upheaval. In fact, despite its militant rhetoric and occasionally violent tactics, they understood that Peronism

was an important factor accounting for the low degree of ideological polarization in Argentina, especially when compared to
Chile or Uruguay, where the labor movement's anti-capitalist
thrust was threatening to dominant class interests.[3]

How the ambiguous relations between the Peronist-domi-
nanted working class and the Onganía regime were played out
is the focus of this chapter. Onganía's strategy of attracting
"friendly" leaders while dividing, repressing, or ignoring the
rest bore its first fruits by polarizing organized labor into competing tendencies, apparently just as interested in combating
each other as in standing up to the regime. Soon, however, this
strategy not only undermined the position of the more pliant
union leaders, it also led directly to the emergence of more radical challengers bent on leading the working class into a major
confrontation with the authoritarian project.

The Structural Bases of Working-Class Heterogeneity

The situation in 1966 in some ways resembled the 1943–45
period, which saw the emergence of Peronism and the first
sustained attempt at labor's political incorporation. As in that
earlier period, the working class of the mid-1960s had experienced a decade of stagnant standards of living. The working
class's position in the economy and the polity had been undermined by crucial transformations in the labor market and the
structure of employment since the early 1950s.[4] These transformations were marked by an absolute and relative decline in the
rural labor force, together with a large expansion of employment in the secondary sector from 1947 to 1960, followed by a
much slower increase during the following decade. More specifically, a moderate increase in the blue-collar labor force employed in manufacturing occurred between 1947 and 1960, followed by stagnation and relative decline as a proportion of the
economically active population between 1960 and 1970. Finally,
the tertiary sector grew rapidly throughout the entire period,
especially after 1960. These trends are presented in Tables 5.1
and 5.2.

The new pattern of accumulation based upon rapidly rising
labor productivity negatively affected the distribution of income, with all wage and salary earners experiencing a substan-

TABLE 5.1

Structure of Employment by Sector, 1947, 1960, and 1970

(*Millions of employed workers*)

	1947		1960		1970	
Sector	No.	Pct.	No.	Pct.	No.	Pct.
1. Agriculture	1.7	26.7%	1.5	19.7%	1.4	16.1%
2. Secondary[a]	1.9	30.2	2.7	36.0	3.0	34.4
2.1 *Industry*	1.6	25.0	2.1	27.8	2.1	23.9
3. Tertiary[b]	2.7	43.1	3.3	44.3	4.4	49.4
Total	6.3	100.0%	7.5	100.0%	8.8	100.0%

SOURCE: Calculated from Llach, "Estructura ocupacional y dinámica del empleo en la Argentina," Table 1, p. 582.

[a]Includes manufacturing, industry, mining, construction, electricity, gas, and water.

[b]Includes commerce and finance, transportation, and other services.

TABLE 5.2

Percent Changes in Sectoral Composition of Employment,
1947–70

Sector	1947–70	1947–60	1960–70
1. Agriculture	−10.6%	−7.0%	−3.6%
2. Secondary[a]	4.2	5.9	−1.7
2.1 *Industry*	−1.1%	2.8%	−3.9%
3. Tertiary[b]	6.2	1.1	5.1

SOURCE: Calculated from Llach, "Estructura ocupacional y dinámica del empleo en la Argentina," Table 2, p. 583.

[a]Includes manufacturing, industry, mining, construction, electricity, gas, and water.

[b]Includes commerce and finance, transportation, and other services.

tial decline of about 10 percent in their share of the gross domestic product from the early 1950s to the mid-1960s. The situation of the working class in the strategically important manufacturing sector eroded even more sharply. Table 5.3 reveals that labor's share of industrial GDP declined from over 50 percent in the early 1950s to around 35 percent in the early 1960s.

During this period, considerable differentiation within the working class occurred due to the increased dispersion of the wage distribution, as the mean wage declined while the gap between the best and worst paid industrial workers grew. In fact,

TABLE 5.3

*Functional Distribution of Gross Domestic Product
Between Labor and Capital and Real Wages in the
Industrial Sector, 1950–73*

Year	Percent of income to labor[a]	Percent of income to capital[b]	Index of real wages[c] (1966 = 100)
1950	55.4%	44.6%	87.6
1951–55	51.5	48.5	81.4
1956–60	40.5	59.5	83.8
1961–65	34.9	65.1	87.0
1966	38.4	61.6	100.0
1967	42.7	57.3	99.6
1968	41.4	58.6	92.2
1969	40.8	59.2	95.3
1970	41.7	58.4	98.8
1966–70	41.0	59.0	97.2
1971	42.1	57.9	102.4
1972	36.9	63.1	95.2
1973	40.0	60.0	101.5

SOURCE: Calculated from Banco Central, *Sistema de cuentas del producto e ingreso de la Argentina*, vol. II, Table 4, pp. 56–57, and Table 52, pp. 176–79.
[a] Wages and salaries plus employers' contributions to Social Security divided by GDP.
[b] GDP minus income to labor, the total divided by GDP.
[c] Nominal wages deflated by the cost-of-living index.

a dramatic process of internal stratification in the industrial labor force was intensified in the late 1950s, following large infusions of transnational capital into the more dynamic, capital-intensive consumer durables and capital goods sectors. The large productivity gains attained in these new, more technologically advanced sectors were partially translated into wage increases substantially higher than the industry average. The data in Table 5.4 reveal that in 1955 real wages in the so-called "static" sectors, such as foodstuffs and textiles (typically dominated by small and medium-sized competitive firms), were still above the industry average, and above wages in such recently installed "dynamic" sectors as automobiles, transportation equipment, and petrochemicals (typically dominated by large monopoly or oligopoly firms).[5]

Following Perón's ouster, however, the impact of state policies geared to promoting foreign investment and curtailing labor

TABLE 5.4

Wage Differentials in Real Annual Wages Across
Industrial Sectors, Selected Years, 1950–73

	Dynamic sectors vs. industry total	Static sectors vs. industry total	Static sectors vs. dynamic sectors
1950	−7.8%	+8.6%	+1.4%
1955	−11.1	+14.6	+3.0
1960	+20.1	−4.3	−25.2
1965	+34.6	−17.8	−58.5
1970	+43.1	−18.3	−69.2
1973	+34.6	−19.0	−59.1

SOURCE: Calculated from Banco Central, *Sistema de cuentas del producto e ingreso de la Argentina*, vol. II, Table 52, pp. 176–79.
NOTE: Nominal annual wages were deflated using the cost-of-
living index; 1960 = 100.

militancy contributed to rapidly widening wage differentials; by
1965, wages in the dynamic sectors were 35 percent above the
industry average and nearly 59 percent above those paid by
workers in static industries. The short-lived economic recovery
during the Onganía years produced an improvement in labor's
overall share of national income (see Table 5.3), but wage differentials were widened even further. By 1970, following the application of policies canceling collective bargaining, the imposition
of obligatory arbitration, and other "reforms" of the labor market, workers in the rapidly growing dynamic sectors received
wages 43 percent above the industry average and fully 69 percent over the wages received by their counterparts in the slow-
growing, competitive sectors.

Political Fragmentation and Labor Strategies

Concomitant with its deepening structural heterogeneity and
declining share of national income, labor in the post-1955 period also confronted the closing of its legitimate channels of
political participation and representation. New political strategies emerged as a consequence, as the labor movement sought
to protect its political power and safeguard its hard-won social
and economic conquests. But, contrary to its image as an intransigent, backward-looking force, the "new Peronism" that

emerged after its leader's overthrow was not bent solely on destabilizing governments and blocking economic progress. To the contrary, Peronism's militant oppositionist posture in the period leading to the 1966 military coup was "generated and nurtured by its adversaries" and can "only be understood as the antithesis of both the heterogeneous social and political front that coalesced in 1955 and of the several regimes which failed to consolidate" after 1955.[6]

During the brief Revolución Libertadora (Liberating Revolution) that followed Perón's overthrow, the military followed two distinct strategies vis-à-vis the working class. First, General Eduardo Lonardi declared a conciliatory policy of *ni vencedores ni vencidos* ("neither victors nor vanquished") in a futile attempt to don Perón's mantle as a popular leader with mass support. Following Lonardi's ouster in November 1955, General Pedro F. Aramburu initiated a full-scale assault on Peronism and the workers. The Peronist party was dissolved, the Confederación General del Trabajo was intervened, some 60,000 union leaders were barred from holding office in the labor movement, and all Peronist symbols and slogans were outlawed, as was mention of Perón's name. In what was hoped to be a *coup de grace*, Perón's Law of Professional Associations was annulled in an attempt to destroy the source of union power.[7]

But Armaburu's efforts to destroy the CGT and liquidate Peronism as a political force backfired. Instead, there emerged a younger, more militant generation of union leaders and a renewed symbolic identification of Peronism with popular struggles, a combination that provided the embattled working class with a powerful unifying force. Peronist dominance was expressed through the clandestine labor central known as the 62 Organizaciones,[8] which was crucial in carrying out a wave of strikes and mobilizations in 1956, 1957, and 1958. Together with party militants, union activists thus assumed a leading role in the Resistencia Peronista launched in response to government repression. Although the Peronist-controlled unions were unable to prevent an erosion of real wages, or to block capital's efforts to introduce technological improvements and undercut the unions' control of the factory floor, the long-term effect of these strikes was significant because they "reinforced a threatened mass movement and achieved [Peronism's] recognition as the trade union and political interlocutor of the organized working class."[9]

Arturo Frondizi, who won the 1958 presidential elections with Perón's support, attempted to carry out an ingenious but extremely risky strategy. Frondizi's economic project of *desarrollismo* dictated a rapprochement with foreign capital and the most dynamic and modern domestic financial and industrial groups in order to increase investment and incorporate advanced technology. But Frondizi also sought popular consensus by attempting to co-opt the union leadership in the hope of "integrating" the workers in a non-Peronist polity. An ultimately irreconcilable contradiction emerged from the fact that the policies required to respond to labor's corporative demands (a return to one union per industry and recognition of the CGT as the single national confederation, an end to the electoral proscription against Peronism, and so on) clashed frontally with entrepreneurial demands for the liquidation of Peronist "totalitarianism," liberalization of the economy, and drastic reduction in wages to control inflationary pressures.[10]

The precarious equilibrium between the Peronist union movement and the anti-Peronist bourgeoisie exploded in Frondizi's face. In 1959, the cost of living jumped nearly 120 percent, industrial output dropped 8 percent, and real wages fell 26 percent. One and a half million workers went out on strike and 10 million working days were lost. Frondizi responded with a state of siege and strong police and army repression.[11] Although 1959 was a high point of labor militancy and the culmination of the Peronist Resistance, "the objective result of labor conflicts was defeat rather than victory. These defeats marked the turning of the tide as far as working-class mobilization and confidence was concerned."[12]

The partial demobilization of the working class after 1959 resulted in the emergence of a new, more pragmatic trade union current known as *vandorismo*—after Augusto Vandor of the powerful Metalworker's Union. Under Vandor's aegis, Peronism consolidated its organizational and ideological identity and defined a new politico-economic strategy for the labor movement.

The Peronist party apparatus, deprived of its role as legitimate political interlocutor by proscriptions that made it difficult to compete effectively in the electoral arena, was easily eclipsed by the union leadership. Consequently, the Peronist labor movement came to function both as the political representative of a heterogeneous mass movement and as the corporative representative of the working class. Organized labor's ultimate weapon was the use, or the threat, of its capacity to destabilize the government in power. This gave birth to a strategy of permanent political pressure—the so-called *juego doble*—in which the union leadership combined aggressive political bargaining with North-American-style business unionism.[13]

Under Vandor's leadership, this strategy was utilized repeatedly in the early 1960s, but with mixed results. Strike activity declined precipitously and never returned to 1959 levels.[14] The waning of the Resistencia was paralleled by a growing reliance on negotiations with the state and a concomitant negligence of the grass-roots organization of the workers. Heading huge organizations with impressive financial resources,[15] the *vandoristas* acted as "union bureaucrats" and began to relinquish union influence in the factories while distancing themselves from rank-and-file concerns.

More radical political goals and strategies, such as those outlined in the La Falda (1957) and Huerta Grande (1962) programs,[16] failed to hide the predominance of a ruthlessly pragmatic strategy exemplified by the slogan *golpear y negociar* ("hit and negotiate"). *Vandorismo* turned militant union tactics into a finely calibrated tool in a sophisticated bargaining strategy with business and the state. The Plan de Lucha orchestrated by the CGT (which had regained its legal status under Frondizi) in 1963 and 1964 exemplified this sophisticated strategy. This "struggle plan" was drafted with little input from the rank and file, whose job was simply to follow instructions. Mobilizations, strikes, and factory occupations were carefully modulated as part of the leadership's pressure tactics.[17]

The principal demands of the Plan de Lucha were economic, but the clear objective was to destabilize the recently elected Radical government headed by Arturo Illia. Once again allowed to participate in electoral politics, Peronists in the Congress reacted to the Radicals' maladroit attempt to weaken the CGT and depoliticize organized labor by consistently sabotaging government initiatives. This further exacerbated an already poisoned atmosphere and facilitated the work of *golpista* propagandists, who had a field day arguing that "subversion" had led the nation to the brink of political chaos.

Following a Peronist victory in the 1965 congressional elections (Peronists polled 38 percent of the vote to the Radicals' 30 percent) and the failure of Perón's attempt to return from exile, organized labor's internal contradictions led to a major political crisis. The immediate spark was Vandor's decision to challenge the exiled caudillo's leadership by extending union power into the electoral arena in a clear bid to establish a "Peronism without Perón." In response, a rival clique led by José Alonso led a schism referred to as the 62 Organizaciones de Pie Junto a Perón ("standing alongside Perón") to defend Peronist orthodoxy.[18]

The labor movement thus confronted the crisis of the Illia government as warring factions, almost all of which actively pursued contacts with the military in preparation for a coup, which came in July 1966. The Peronist labor leadership, like General Onganía, apparently believed in the resurrection of the 1940s "alliance of the Army and the People."

While the new economic and political constraints stemming from ongoing transformations in the Argentine political economy certainly limited the feasibility of Onganía's corporatist project, the forces fragmenting the working class opened up interesting new possibilities. The same factors also impinged upon the range of options open to the union leadership. As in the past, two basic strategies were available: political autonomy vis-à-vis the state apparatus, or heteronomy characterized by reformism and collaboration with state elites.[19]

Wage deterioration and the blockage of labor's political participation favored the autonomous strategy, with possible variants ranging from a cautious refusal to accept subordination to state elites to a more radical or even revolutionary confrontation with the state and capital. Reformism, on the other hand, was more congruent with the political restrictions on working-class participation, but it also confronted a basic obstacle, namely the limited material rewards the economic authorities were willing or able to offer in exchange for labor's support for the new regime. Reformists, therefore, were faced with pressures to abandon labor militancy—and even their identification with Peronism—

by progressively becoming more apolitical and subordinate to "friendly" sectors of the state apparatus. All of these variants were attempted at one time or another over the course of the next years.

State and Labor During the "Honeymoon"

Immediately after the coup, while civilian and military liberals and the different fractions of capital sought to destroy the existing union structure and to crush labor's capacity to resist their plans for the restructuring of Argentine capitalism, Onganía and his nationalist political staff faced a different imperative. Their goal was not to destroy the labor movement but to subordinate and integrate the working class into their own rival project.[20] There were various ideological underpinnings for these paternalistic aspirations. One showed the endurance of a nostalgic wish for an "alliance of the Army and the People." Another drew upon Catholic social doctrines emphasizing a "just equilibrium between labor and capital." These ideas also had affinities with Peronism's reformist and class-collaborationist thrust. The nationalist project envisioned not so much an "interventionist" or "entrepreneurial" state, which would actively foster capital accumulation, as a strong, paternalistic state jealously defending its sovereignty "above the class struggle" and "selfish" sectoral interests.[21]

Seeking to domesticate labor and convert it into a support class for the regime, the nationalists in the political apparatus attempted first to unify organized labor under the control of pliant union bureaucrats, and then, when that failed, to atomize and weaken the CGT by acting upon the principle that "the greater the number of unions, the greater the possibilities of dividing union power." In its essentials, this strategy differed little from the policies of other post-1958 regimes, which had employed the tactic of granting legal recognition (*personería gremial*) to new unions in order to erode the unity of organized labor.[22]

The unifying strategy was tried first. Employing a rhetoric of "participation" to describe a non-democratic form of intermediation through corporative channels, state elites immediately began to search for cooperative interlocutors within the CGT leadership. They were aided by existing political differences separating the two rival wings of Peronist unionism and their leaders, José Alonso and Augusto Vandor. While Alonso had been much more intimately involved than Vandor in the pre-coup negotiations with the military, both rivals hastened to welcome the end of constitutional rule.[23] With a few minor exceptions, the rest of organized labor fell into line, echoing the language of the press release issued by the CGT one day after the coup: "At the beginning of a new national historical stage, the CGT, conscious of its responsibility, proposes solutions and demands the participation due it in the true process of Argentine progress."[24]

It soon became apparent that state intervention in the CGT's internal affairs was designed to tilt the balance in favor of Alonso in the upcoming election of the CGT's new national authorities. Vandor, expressing a more cautious attitude toward the new regime, and branding his rivals as opportunists and *oficialistas*, moved to shore up his support with the more progressive sectors of organized labor. However, the *vandoristas* were defeated in the CGT's National Congress, which elected an ally of Alonso, Francisco Prado, of the important *Luz y Fuerza* electrical workers union, as General Secretary. Prado immediately sought close relations with entrepreneurs and the Onganía regime.[25] So far, the unifying strategy seemed to be working.

But business interests had been watching the nationalists' rapprochement with labor with alarm, and quickly stepped up their attacks on the "totalitarian" CGT. Business pressure ultimately undercut the nationalists' efforts to unify the CGT, contributing to the vindication of Vandor's more arms-length approach. This allowed Vandor to assume a leading position in the first post-coup strikes—by the powerful SMATA auto workers union of Córdoba and by his own Metalworkers Union—as well as in the labor protests against obligatory arbitration and the intervention of several key unions.[26]

The honeymoon between organized labor and the Onganía regime came to an abrupt end with a general strike in mid-December 1966. This first major confrontation with the regime shut down 70 percent of establishments in the key sectors of industry, commerce, and transportation. As a consequence, Onganía was forced to retreat and temporarily delay his rationalization plans for state enterprises.[27] The *vandoristas'* euphoria over their success in short-circuiting the alliance between the regime and the Alonso-controlled CGT was reinforced by the cabinet crisis and shake-up of late December 1966, which displaced Economy Minister Salimei and Interior Minister Martínez Paz, both viewed as hostile to labor. This success created a false sense of strength among the trade union leadership and contributed to their decision to go on the offensive for greater economic and political concessions from the state and from capital.

The Plan de Acción *and the State's Counterattack*

The period of direct confrontation from mid-December 1966 to March 1967 was decisive in shaping the future evolution of the authoritarian experiment. The most salient factors behind labor's offensive were the deterioration of real wages, which led the rank and file to demand more aggressive action from their leadership; state intervention in key unions; Vandor's fear of being outflanked on the left by more militant sectors; Perón's own shift to more strident opposition; and Vandor's desire to definitively displace his rival, Alonso. Vandor was playing for high stakes, but if successful he expected to return to his accustomed place as labor's *caudillo* at the center of negotiations with the state and the bourgeoisie.

Vandor's gamble culminated in the decision by the CGT's Central Committee to launch a so-called Plan de Acción, similar to the earlier Plan de Lucha, beginning with "agitation" and partial strikes, continuing with a general strike, and culminating in a series of 48- and 72-hour strikes. Vandor reasoned that the nationalists, then locked in battle with the *ortodoxos* within the state and lacking support in public opinion, would be forced to either adopt a more conciliatory stance or resort to violent repression, further eroding their already narrow political base. In either case, the *vandoristas* believed, the labor movement could come out ahead and perhaps cement a more favorable *modus vivendi* with Onganía, thus countering the influence of the new economic team headed by Krieger Vasena and forcing a pro-labor shift in the regime's economic policies.[28]

The nationalists desperately sought to avoid a showdown, but hard-liners within the military—led by General Osiris Villegas, the head of the National Security Council, and supported by Krieger and the major business organizations—responded in extremely tough fashion to Vandor's offensive. General Villegas warned union leaders that the regime would brook no strikes, occupations, or demonstrations that threatened law and order and the maintenance of labor discipline. Under CONASE's direction, an escalating series of reprisals was implemented beginning with a threat to "interrupt the dialogue" with the CGT, and continuing with the prohibition of all street demonstrations, the freezing of the bank accounts of several unions by the Central Bank, and the threat of severe sanctions to civil servants who supported the CGT's actions. The regime's hard-line response culminated in the suspension of the *personería gremial* of the five influential unions that had most strongly supported the Plan de Acción. Finally, in early March, the counterattack was completed with the approval of a harsh decree-law (the *Ley de Servicio Civil de Defensa*) providing for the militarization of the labor force in times of national emergency.[29] The message was unmistakable. If the unions and the working class wanted a role in the new authoritarian project, they had to "collaborate" and abandon militant Peronism and combative trade-union tactics. Hence, "the attempt at an alliance between the 'People and the Army' had reversed in an unexpected way for the labor movement: the bourgeoisie and the Army *against* the People."[30]

The defeat of labor's offensive was total. Faced with an implacable state, ready and willing to take repressive action including the destruction of the CGT, Vandor and the other union leaders capitulated quickly and called off a planned general strike.[31] This devastating defeat opened the way for the early successes of Krieger's economic policy and the parallel offensive of the dominant entrepreneurial groups. The defeat also set the stage for efforts by the parties to capture the workers' allegiance in broader alliances, while it exacerbated the labor movement's existing internal cleavages and thus further weakened the working class's capacity for autonomous political action. In the short run, the economic authorities as well as Onganía and the nationalist political managers had emerged strengthened from labor's defeat.

Labor's Retreat and Truce with the State

The nationalist apparatchiks quickly moved to domesticate the unions, seeking to take advantage of labor's demobilization. Their immediate objectives were to prevent labor from forming part of an Illia-Perón pact and to block an anti-government union delegation from participating in the June 1967 meeting of the International Labor Organization in Geneva, Switzerland. Their long-term objectives included the imposition of corporatist labor controls and the use of the unions to undercut *ortodoxo* influence over economic policy, both as preludes to a global shift in the balance of forces within the state to a more favorable direction for nationalist hegemony.

Rubéns San Sebastián, the Labor Secretary and principal architect of the regime's labor policies, clearly set forth the regime's three conditions for organized labor's "participation." First, the union leadership would have to proclaim publicly its faith in Onganía's "national revolution" and the regime's economic and political programs. Second, unions should abstain from ties or alliances with all political parties and factions, including Peronism. Third, the unions had to accede to union elections to give voice to the rank and file, thus ensuring the "authenticity" and "representativity" of union leadership. The CGT, however, would have to agree to a prolonged recess in its institutional life by postponing selection of new national officers.[32]

In exchange for meeting these conditions, San Sebastián promised greater concessions to pliant labor leaders. But if the union leadership should refuse the regime's offer of "participation" and *apertura social* ("social opening"), he let it be understood that the state would not hesitate to dismantle the CGT and severely limit the economic power enjoyed by the union bureaucracies.

The leadership thus faced a difficult dilemma. If they acceded to the state's blandishments, they ran the risk of alienating their rank and file, who would be angered by their political capitulation and the loss of bread-and-butter rewards. If they resisted, they ran the even greater risk of certain repression at the hands of a state now sure of itself in the wake labor's recent defeat. Labor's ensuing political fragmentation occurred along the lines of the previously mentioned option between autonomy or reformism.

The reformist option assumed two different forms, both characterized by a desire to reach an accommodation with the general economic restructuring advocated by the state and the dominant fractions of capital.[33] They diverged, however, over their willingness to accept union subordination to state control and to sacrifice the rank and file's immediate economic interests. One tendency—immediately dubbed *colaboracionista* or *participacionista*—advocated a strategy of alliances with the nationalists in order to lobby against Krieger Vasena's economic policies. The *colaboracionista* analysis stressed the division in the Onganía regime between nationalists and liberals, each pushing rival projects, and argued that this gave the working class a chance to redefine the regime's composition and direction along the lines of a military-union entente. Accordingly, the *colaboracionistas* wanted to refrain from dangerous (and in their view, unnecessary) confrontations, especially strikes, or other militant trade-union tactics.[34]

The *colaboracionistas*—who coalesced into a faction known as the Nueva Corriente de Opinión—were led by several very able union bureaucrats, including Juan José Taccone of the powerful Luz y Fuerza electrical workers union and Rogelio Coria of the Construction Workers Union. Taccone had long been a defender of European-style worker participation in management. He also was an opponent of "political wheeling-and-dealing" and labor's addiction to *planes de lucha* which, he said, carried labor to the "portal of power" only to leave it in the "third subbasement."

Vandor and his followers made up the second variant of labor reformism. Vandor's strategy was determined by the failure of the Plan de Acción, which convinced him that the state was too strong and cohesive for his old strategy based on *golpear y negociar*. Accordingly, the *vandoristas* now argued that organized labor should be ready to bargain with the state while waiting for a future conjuncture more favorable to the unions. The key difference between Vandor and the *colaboracionistas* was the former's insistence on safeguarding at least a modicum of political independence vis-à-vis the state. This was a safeguard, Vandor argued, against an uncontrolled mass mobilization from below against *both* the state and capital *and* an undemocratic union leadership unable or unwilling to defend the workers' long-term economic interests.[35]

When Taccone assured the Onganía regime that the *colaboracionistas* did not have "any urgency about a political plan because it would only be a trap of conditioned democracy,"[36] this was just what the nationalists wanted to hear from labor. Consequently, San Sebastián abandoned negotiations with Vandor and henceforth threw the regime's support to the almost slavishly pro-regime *colaboracionistas*, who were favored with state patronage and minor economic concessions to offset the rigors of Krieger's policies.[37]

The Birth of a Revolutionary Alternative

Of course, *vandoristas* and *colaboracionistas* were not alone in defining organized labor's response to authoritarian rule: there were forces in favor of a strategy of militant autonomy. This current, known as *clasismo*, was spearheaded by a new, post-1955 generation of union leaders less socialized into the corporatist labor practices favored by "labor bureaucrats" such as Alonso and Vandor. The new leaders were formed in the context of deepening structural heterogeneity and political fragmentation of the working class, growing business hostility, and labor's exclusion from meaningful participation in the state. *Clasismo*, with its potentially revolutionary connotations, had long antecedents in the history of Argentine labor, but previous *clasista* tendencies had been smothered by state repression or by populist co-optation.

One of the first inklings of a more radical tendency within the organized labor movement under the Onganía regime surfaced in a critique of reforms and union "paper shufflers" by Amado Olmos of the Sanitation Workers Union. According to Olmos, labor's defeat in March 1967 derived from factors dating back at least to the Frondizi government (1958–62) and probably as far as labor's subordination to the state under Peronism. The problem was "legalism" and a political practice based on "negotiation and not on struggle." To Olmos, leaders like Vandor

turned out to be the best *tramitadores de expendientes* (paper shufflers) rather than the best combatants. . . . To every blow we responded not with struggle but with a plea for legal protection (*recurso de amparo*). . . . Rather than expressions of a will to struggle, our strikes were a way to give vent to the discontent of the rank and file and to pressure the public authorities to open new negotiations. In doing this we once again defended legality, ignoring that this legality was not that of the people, nor of the workers or of the fatherland, but the legality of colonialist privilege. . . . That path could only lead to disaster and, in an unsuspected but inevitable way, disaster arrived [in March 1967].[38]

With the bulk of the working class still demobilized, and with Perón placing his bets on alliances with other political forces or with factions within the military, Olmos's call for "new ways of thinking and new methods of struggle" was slow to find supporters. The *clasista* strategy of political autonomy only emerged as an important political alternative for the working class and the popular sectors in March 1968, when the CGT held a so-called "Normalizing Congress" at the end of its imposed year-long "recess." The Congress ended in a split when it was unable to reach a consensus between autonomists and reformists over the seating of delegates. The reformists called for the exclusion of delegates from unions that had been "intervened" by Labor Secretary San Sebastián; the autonomists demanded that all delegates be admitted and that the CGT adopt a more militant stance. The former, a minority led by Vandor and Alonso, walked out after denouncing the majority as "usurpers and agents of provocation." Claiming to be labor's legitimate representatives, this grouping—*vandoristas*, followers of Alonso, members of "non-aligned" unions, and *colaboracionistas*—formed the CGT de Azopardo. Those who remained established the autonomist CGT de los Argentinos.[39]

The CGT de los Argentinos quickly articulated an ideology and strategy of working-class autonomy more radical, militant, and uncompromising than anything seen in the union movement since the 1930s. Raimundo Ongaro, the head of the new movement and the long-time leader of a leftist printers union, the Federación Gráfica Bonaerense, instilled a high moral tone of radical defense of union democracy and rank-and-file interests, declaring that he would always "prefer honor without unions to unions without honor."[40] The radical populist discourse of the CGT de los Argentinos became even clearer in its May 1 document entitled "The CGT with the Fatherland and the Argentine People": "They asked us to bear another winter. We have borne ten. They demanded that we rationalize ourselves: by doing so we are losing conquests won by our grandfathers. . . . And when there is no further humiliation or injustice that we have not suffered, we are ironically asked to 'participate.' "[41]

The CGT de los Argentinos firmly rejected Onganía's demand for apolitical unionism, characterizing the offer of "participation" as tantamount to working-class capitulation, an ideology that reveals "the true face of free enterprise, of the free sellout." It continued: "The official philosophy of the regime, behind the illusory division between 'nationalists' and 'liberals,' is incapable of hiding the deeper reality, that of the monopolies in power."[42] The peculiar alchemy of populist evangelism and anti-imperialism combined to give the CGT de los Argentinos its revolutionary potential, which the *clasistas* defined in fairly orthodox Marxist terms:

[It is the working class's] historic mission to destroy the capitalist system. The government of General Onganía is the expression of this system. Dictatorial in form, "*gorila*" in tradition, "sellout" in content, it is beyond all redemption. . . . There will be no pact between the working class and General Onganía. . . . The CGT de los Argentinos does not propose holding elections, nor does it support any candidates—civilian or military. . . . We reject the entire system and all the alternatives it offers. . . . We are not ready to negotiate our truth, our rights, or our dignity. Besides, we are convinced that the process of history leads inevitably toward the triumph of the people.[43]

Notwithstanding this revolutionary rhetoric, the CGT de los Argentinos did not adopt a vanguard strategy, but proposed instead a broad-based opposition including "all sectors, with the single exception of the sellout minorities and the corrupt leaders." Reflecting the familiar tendency of Argentine populism to search for allies within the military, the new movement reminded the armed forces that they did not have to be "guardians of one class, the hangman of another." Instead, a direct appeal was made to the military to honor their "duty and vocation to defend the Fatherland."[44]

The rival CGT de Azopardo, with Vandor in the lead, reacted to this radical challenge by accentuating its conciliatory stance and proclaiming its "goodwill" toward the Onganía regime, which it called upon to assume its proper role at the "apex of [national] understanding and as the executor of the mandate" given it in June 1966. The leaders of the CGT de Azopardo used Peronism's familiar tactic of postulating a rigid antinomy between themselves, the "true" leaders of the workers and the embodiment of "national values" (*lo nacional*), and the *clasistas*, who were pictured as "alien" to "the Argentine way of life" and a "false option" based on an unholy alliance with Marxism and other "foreign ideologies" propagating the struggle of one class against another. Accordingly, Vandor and his allies did not venture beyond quite moderate demands on the regime for wage increases, freedom for detained union leaders, restitution of legal recognition for intervened unions, and so on.[45]

Although there remained divergences between Vandor and the *colaboracionistas*, both could agree on a show of "responsibility" designed to appeal to the political apparatus, nationalist military officers, and middle-class groups opposed to Krieger's economic policies. The contrast with the "revolutionary" option defended by the CGT de los Argentinos could hardly have been more clearly delineated.

Toward Confrontation

While each current claimed to be the legitimate heir to the Peronist tradition, each also proposed a different ideology and strategy for the working class. These differences stemmed from their differing perceptions concerning which fractions of the bourgeoisie shared sufficient common interests with the working class to form a viable political alliance.

The CGT de los Argentinos, composed of members and sympathizers of the Peronist left, the Communist Party, and the left in general, held that its objective of overthrowing the regime would find its natural allies among the democratic sectors of the "small and medium bourgeoisie" that faced ruin from economic concentration and denationalization. In contrast, the strategic objective pursued by *vandorismo* was the institutionalization of labor's independent power to influence state policies within the parameters of a project of rapid capitalist modernization. Therefore, Vandor's preferred allies as interlocutors within the state were the most dynamic fractions of the industrial bourgeoisie, the principal agents of the new project of accumulation.[46]

These differences in strategic conception were grounded in important structural differences. One key contrast between the CGT de Azopardo and the CGT de los Argentinos was the marked predominance of industrial, blue-collar unions in the former and of service-sector unions in the latter. In terms of total number of affiliated workers there was no significant difference: 496,000 versus 561,000, respectively. However, the principal leadership roles in the CGT de los Argentinos were held by unions representing state-sector workers: white- and blue-collar workers and civil servants (ATE, UOEM, UPCN), telephone workers (FOETRA), and railroad workers and engineers (Unión Ferroviaria, La Fraternidad). These unions alone accounted for 443,000 members.[47] Workers in the state bureaucracy and state enterprises were those most negatively affected by Krieger Vasena's policies directed toward administrative rationalization and increased productivity, and many of these worker's unions had been intervened or had their legal status suspended.

In contrast, the core of the CGT de Azopardo included large blue-collar unions in the industrial sector, such as the metalworkers, textile workers, and garment workers, plus workers in the important construction industry and the Luz y Fuerza electrical workers. These were among the most powerful unions in terms of economic resources and location in the productive structure. In addition, virtually all were in the private sector (the meat workers were the only important exception).

The unions affiliated with the *clasista* tendency, in contrast to the *vandorista* and *colaboracionista* unions, generally had considerably smaller memberships, were typically established either before the advent of Peronism (e.g., the railroad engineers) or after Perón's fall, and tended to be stronger in the interior than in the industrial core around Buenos Aires. The cumulative impact of these differences produced a younger leadership (in organizational and bureaucratic terms) less influenced by forma-tive experiences under the corporatist umbrella of the state and, hence, more open to Marxist ideology and/or a more "revolutionary" variety of Peronism.

The unions of the reformist tendency, whether *vandorista* and *colaboracionista*, faced serious structural constraints that tended to preclude both pure bread-and-butter unionism and radical militancy. Instead, because of their strength, they were called upon by the state and the bourgeoisie to participate in the institutionalized mechanisms of negotiation and conciliation joining all three. Also, as mentioned previously, the closing of the normal political channels meant that reformist leaders had to assume a dual role as both representatives of a particular social class and political agents of the Peronist movement; this dual responsibility accentuated the inclination of both reformist tendencies to seek constant compromises with the state and capital.

In contrast, leaders adhering to *clasismo* were more responsible to the rank and file than their reformist counterparts on positions about everyday labor struggles and contract negotiations. This had contradictory effects. On the one hand, the small size of most of these unions and their meager financial resources might have counseled caution in dealing with the state and management. On the other hand, however, their more democratic leadership style and closeness to their "bases" may have predisposed them to more militant, or even revolutionary, strategies. The reformist leaders, and especially such powerful "labor aristocrats" as Vandor, Taccone, and Coria, given their greater autonomy from rank-and-file demands and corresponding dependence on state elites and employers, had much more at stake in confronting the regime and acted accordingly.

The dilemmas facing reformist leaders were evident in the failure of the CGT de Azopardo to convert its conciliatory stance into tangible benefits for the workers. Onganía's paternalistic ambivalence toward labor and his continued support of Krieger's economic policies repeatedly undermined the best efforts of San Sebastián and the *colaboracionistas* to win rank-and-file support for the regime. In spite of this, however, the *colaboracionistas* were gradually obliged, under increasing pressure from their membership, to seek refuge in the shadow of the state apparatus in order to preserve their privileges. The reformists naturally sought to portray their dependence on the state in a positive light. For example, after a private meeting in early September 1968 between President Onganía and the key leaders of the reformist sector, Rogelio Coria, the leader of the Nueva Corriente de Opinión, optimistically proclaimed that, "When this process began I was the only '*participacionista*.' Later there were three, then five, now more than thirty. I do not doubt that the rest will 'jump the fence' more rapidly."[48]

Even systematic intervention in union elections by Labor Secretary San Sebastián and the lavish use of patronage to reward pliant leaders, however, failed to legitimate a subservient *colaboracionista* leadership. Not surprisingly, in fact, the state's manifestly anti-labor policies did much to undercut the appeal of *colaboracionismo* to rank-and-file workers. This was evident in the failure of the political apparatus to secure a return to collective bargaining and substantial wage increases.[49]

The regime's inability to domesticate labor also fueled renewed pressures from big business to dismantle the CGT. This furthered the nationalists' desperation to marshal their dwindling labor support in order to resist the mounting attacks of civilian and military liberals. All came to naught, however, because Onganía could not bring himself to grant his would-be *colaboracionista* allies real political power. According to the president, labor's participation in the state must remain only "technical," limited to the "study of problems," without becoming either "political or verbose."[50]

Vandor fared even worse than rival *colaboracionistas* in wringing concessions from the state. The government's decision to negotiate only with declared allies was intended to erode Vandor's base of support and win over his followers to the pro-regime line championed by Coria and Taccone. Vandor responded to official hostility not with militant tactics but by attempting to woo Perón away from his earlier rather ambiguous support for the *clasistas* in order to further his goal of unifying the CGT under *vandorista* control. This "putting on the Peronist *camiseta*" (and the abandonment of earlier flirtations with the notion of "Peronism without Perón") paid some dividends in consolidating Vandor's position, while also contributing to Perón's anti-regime strategy of opportunistic zigzagging between *golpismo* and calls for the formation of a broad opposition front.[51]

Vandor's move toward more open opposition was motivated

in part by his fear of being outflanked on the left. In 1968 the militantly *clasista* CGT de los Argentinos faced a determined effort by the regime to crush it. After Raimundo Ongaro organized protests against the visit of President Jorge Pacheco Areco of Uruguay, the regime accused the labor leader of inciting rebellion, stepped up harassment of the fledgling organization , and decreed numerous interventions in its affiliated unions.[52]

The CGT de los Argentinos responded with a strategy of mass mobilization linking worker's struggles with the protests of small businessmen, student resistance to the restructuring of the university system, the emerging Third World Priests Movement, and other popular causes. This strategy culminated in the launching of a broad-based Frente Cívico de la Resistencia in June 1968. The Frente assumed a leading role in promoting a series of demonstrations marked by mass arrests in Buenos Aires and cities throughout the interior provinces of Córdoba, Rosario, Tucumán, Jujuy, La Plata, Corrientes, Santa Fe, and the Chaco. This was followed up in August by "lightning acts" in large industrial *barrios* to mobilize the public against the regime and against the conciliatory position of *vandorismo* and *colaboracionismo*.[53]

The biggest labor challenge to the Onganía regime during this period broke out in late September 1968 with a general strike by workers employed by Yacimientos Petrolíferos Fiscales (YPF), the state oil monopoly. This militant movement, involving some of the best-paid workers in the country, followed an independent line with ties with both Vandor and *clasista* currents. The regime finally resolved to crush the strike movement by force in early November with 200 workers dismissed and 4,000 investigated by the intelligence services for their union and political activities.[54]

In response to growing mobilization against the regime, Vandor, now with Perón's more explicit backing, began in early 1969 to lead the CGT de Azopardo toward more open confrontation with Onganía. As signs of widespread opposition from other sectors of society multiplied, Vandor reluctantly entered into contact with *clasista* unions in an attempt to isolate the now largely impotent *colaboracionistas*. In mid-May 1969, amid mounting tensions, Vandor's own powerful Metalworkers

Union held its National Congress in Mar del Plata. Vandor seized the occasion to declare war on the regime. Decrying denationalization by "international monopolies" and recalling labor's "happy and prosperous hours" under Peronism, Vandor skillfully jockeyed to take advantage of Onganía's mounting troubles and strengthen his own position within the labor movement.[55]

Toward New Forms of Popular Resistance

The failure of *vandorismo* and the *colaboracionistas* to win an effective foothold in the authoritarian state was apparent by early 1969. What was less clear, however, was the impact of this failure on the immediate economic interests of the working class. The share of wages and salaries in industrial gross domestic production recovered significantly during the Onganía years (see Table 4.3). This was due less to an effective labor movement than to Krieger's brief economic boom, however. There can be little doubt that the biggest price paid by the working class was not economic (although widening wage differentials clearly penalized the lowest paid workers) but political. Union democracy was dealt a serious blow, the labor movement's political unity was shattered, workers' demands were met with repression, and workers' interests were systematically excluded from representation in shaping state policies.

The failures of the reformist currents opened the way for a more radical alternative. However, despite its far-reaching impact on the ideological polarization of popular opposition to the Onganía regime, Ongaro's radical *clasismo* and his revolutionary strategy of mass mobilization were only partially successful. State repression, the unrelenting hostility of adversaries in the labor movement, and internal organizational weaknesses and rhetorical excesses all took their toll. Perón's withdrawal of his earlier, tentative support and tilt toward Vandor only accelerated the deterioration of the CGT de los Argentinos. By the end of 1968 Ongaro's movement had been severely weakened and remained an important political force only in the interior, especially in Córdoba. Still, by early 1969, it was evident that the Argentine Revolution had not succeeded in taming the working class and incorporating the labor movement into the authoritarian project. Soon, much sooner than anyone could have foreseen, new, more radical Peronist and Marxist revolutionary options, together with new forms of mass resistance to authoritarianism, would emerge to contest the reformist-controlled labor movement's role as the principal opposition force in Argentine society.

SIX

The *Cordobazo*, Popular Resistance, and Entrepreneurial Reaction

WITH PRESIDENT ONGANÍA and his nationalist political managers and *colaboracionista* labor leaders locked in a mutual embrace of mounting impotence, and with an uneasy truce between *vandorismo* and *clasismo*, the stage was set for one of the most dramatic events in recent Argentine, or for that matter Latin American, history—the *cordobazo*, an anti-regime uprising of formidable proportions.[1] The events of 1969 constituted a fundamental watershed, a point of inflection in the course of the authoritarian project, marking the collapse of attempts to modernize the economy under state direction and restructure state and society along different principles of domination. In this sense the *cordobazo* signified the beginning of the end for the Onganía regime.

One way in which the changed atmosphere was immediately made manifest was an increase in labor militancy through strikes and demonstrations. While this was reason enough for concern on the part of the regime, tension was heightened further by the blossoming of revolutionary groups who engaged in armed struggle through bombings, kidnappings, and assassinations. The new social ferment soon affected the economic realm by both undermining the confidence of dominant entrepreneurial groups in the prevailing economic policy and obliging the regime to be more attentive to labor's demands.

Soon thereafter a boom in meat prices on the world market posed the issue of the distribution of new and unexpected profits. When Onganía's economic policymakers took measures that were contrary to the hopes and interests of domestic producers, the rural sector coalesced to protest the gains going to foreign firms at the expense of the "national interest." Once again, the military could not stand aside from such broad-based civil discontent. While debates and conspiracies waxed and waned within the ranks of the military, the commander-in-chief, General Alejandro Lanusse, sought to maintain institutional cohesion, even as his patience with President Onganía ebbed away. When, in the face of all-too-palpable failures, Onganía could merely parrot his hackneyed corporatist dreams, the die was cast for one more changing of the guard.

The Cordobazo *as a Mass Uprising*

Beginning on 29 May 1969, and continuing for roughly a week, the interior city of Córdoba, with a population of approximately 750,000, was the scene of a largely spontaneous explosion of protest against the Onganía regime. This uprising capped a month of rising protests by students in Corrientes, Rosario, and Córdoba, as well as parallel protests by workers both in Córdoba and throughout the interior against a series of measures approved by Krieger Vasena at the urging of powerful economic groups.[2] These measures included the end of discounts to workers in the interior provinces (so-called *quitas zonales*) and of the so-called *sábado inglés*, thereby increasing the workweek by four hours.[3]

The *cordobazo* was a true mass uprising in which thousands of people invaded the streets and established barricades to confront the forces of order. Smaller groups engaged in sniper activity and the throwing of Molotov cocktails. At its height, the rebellion encompassed 150 square blocks as the protesters surged toward the center of the city to attack state institutions and offices of the transnationals in an uncoordinated assault on the "heart, brain, and pocketbook of the bourgeoisie."[4] When confronted by superior force, the rebellion retreated from "zones of struggle" to "zones of popular resistance" in the neighborhoods. Finally, after local police proved insufficient, special army troops were called in to quell the uprising and restore order.

The damage done by protesters and troops was very heavy and centered on public buildings and the headquarters of foreign firms and banks. Official estimates put the total economic cost at 5 billion pesos, or 85 percent of the municipal budget and 15 percent of the provincial budget. The repression eventually required upwards of 5,000 special army troops to supplement local police already totaling some 4,000 men.[5]

How can these dramatic events be explained? To what extent did the *cordobazo* reflect a larger crisis of the authoritarian system? To begin with, Córdoba's rebellion was primarily the result of its own specific characteristics, shaped of course by national political and economic developments. As the best study of the *cordobazo* argues, "Córdoba appears . . . as the weak link in the chain of Argentine capitalism. Sufficiently weak to feel with greater severity and profundity the crisis that affects the [entire] country, and sufficiently strong to be able to react."[6] In effect, this popular upheaval took place in Córdoba rather than in Buenos Aires or elsewhere because of the peculiarities of Córdoba's pattern of industrialization, the exceptional unity and strength of Córdoba's working class and the corresponding divisions and weaknesses of its bourgeoisie, and the province's especially weak and illegitimate political institutions.

By the mid-1960s Córdoba was an industrialized region. In 1966 the province accounted for 5.5 percent of national manufacturing output, and the industrial and service sectors had far outstripped agriculture's contribution to the region's economy.[7] However, this industrialization was extremely recent, uneven, and fragile. Moreover, it was based on the "monoproduction" of the automobile industry, which only dated from the mid-1950s. The greatest spur in economic expansion came as a consequence of Frondizi's rapprochement with foreign automobile companies, who invested heavily after 1959.

The domination of auto production was a mixed blessing. Rather than serving as a dynamic growth pole for the local economy, it accentuated the province's dependence on Buenos Aires, where the foreign firms established their headquarters and most of their final assembly lines. As a consequence, whereas in 1960 Córdoba accounted for 60 percent of Argentina's automobile production, by 1969 only 20 percent of the national total was still produced in the province. At the same time,

TABLE 6.1

Class Structure in Córdoba and Greater
Buenos Aires

(*Percent of economically active population*)

Class	Córdoba	Buenos Aires
Bourgeoisie	16.0%	11.5%
Petty bourgeoisie	17.9	8.1
"Auxiliaries" to		
the bourgeoisie	7.6	8.4
Working class	58.5	71.9
Total	100.0%	100.0%

SOURCE: Balve et al., *Lucha de calles, lucha de clases*, Table 6,
p. 167, on the basis of the 1960 Census.

the rest of the regional economy became increasingly vulnerable
to the boom and bust cycles afflicting the automobile industry
and allied activities such as electronics, farm machinery, and
cement.

Córdoba's class structure reflected the province's distorted
pattern of industrialization. This can be seen in the composition and political practice of both the bourgeoisie and the working class. Table 6.1 reveals that the bourgeoisie in Córdoba
formed a larger portion of society than was the case in greater
Buenos Aires. The same was true of the petite bourgeoisie (arti-
sans, merchants, etc.). This reflected both the more rural nature of Córdoba's economy and the comparatively lower degree
of economic concentration. In contrast, the working class in
Córdoba, proportionally speaking, was considerably smaller
than its *porteño* counterpart, indicative of the region's incipient
industrialization.

A number of factors made for an exceptionally strong and
combative working class. In addition to constituting the numeri-
cal majority of the population, the workers formed a "young"
and comparatively homogeneous proletariat whose most dynamic element consisted of industrial workers, many of whom
(45–50 percent) were employed in a handful of huge, foreign-
owned auto plants.[8] The recent development of the auto industry also meant that organized labor in Córdoba was led by union
elites socialized in the post-1955 period of constant struggle with
the state and capital, rather than in the more state-corporatist

pattern of labor relations of the Peronist period. A final factor was the unions' strong shop-floor organization, which, paradoxically, had been promoted by management itself. Not unexpectedly, therefore, Córdoba was a bulwark of *clasismo* and the radical CGT de los Argentinos.

In contrast to the strength, unity, and combativeness of its working class, Córdoba's bourgeoisie in the late 1960s found itself weakened and sharply divided. The region's relatively recent dependent industrialization had resulted in a general restructuring of the regional bourgeoisie. The largest rural producers had already lost their traditional economic and political predominance, while urban merchants and small-scale industrialists were being threatened by the inexorable processes of concentration and centralization of ownership and production. Most importantly, the locus of economic and political power had shifted out of the province to Buenos Aires and even abroad as the transnational auto firms made decisions shaping the future of the local economy in the context of worldwide strategies of production, marketing, and profit-maximization.[9]

The expansion of big industrial and financial capital strengthened external control over the most profitable sectors of the local economy and drained away capital toward Buenos Aires and abroad. Although this dominance of "absentee" capital gave the appearance of a conflict pitting the "good guys" against the "bad guys" and the "locals" against the "outsiders," it was really a contest for hegemony, a struggle among entrepreneurial groups over which would assume the leading role in directing the region's development.

By themselves, the peculiarities of Córdoba's industrialization and the non-hegemonic balance of social forces were necessary though not sufficient causes of the mass uprising of May 1969. The particularly anachronistic political institutions imposed on Córdoba following the 1966 coup added a further salient ingredient. Through their control over the state's political apparatus, the nationalistic political managers had turned Córdoba into a laboratory for testing their "provincial strategy" and implementing their blueprint for corporatist restructuring of state and society. The ensuing struggle for political power replicated the national contest then raging between the nationalists on one hand and the *ortodoxos* and economic technocrats on the other, as well as the conflicting constellations of class and social forces that each represented.

At the provincial level this contest resulted in an "oligarchical restoration" whose most conspicuous representative was Carlos Caballero, the nationalists' right-wing appointee as provincial governor. Caballero, his clerical followers, and the social forces they represented were the "inheritors of the old aristocracy without money, but influential in justice, in education, in the university, and in the government bureaucracy." Their own economic base undermined by rapid industrialization, and unable to cement a political alliance with the ascendant industrial and financial groups (which in any case enjoyed direct linkages to the state at the national level), the forces behind Caballero's corporatist project could only aspire to be "circumstantial owners of formal political power." [10]

The illegitimacy of Caballero's corporatist experiment and the high potential for violent political crisis offered an instructive example of the consequences flowing from the destruction of the preexisting mechanisms of political intermediation and democratic management of sociopolitical conflict following the 1966 coup. Bereft of political parties and an electoral arena, the authoritarian institutions operative in Córdoba converted mere dissent into open anti-system opposition. Disaffected groups were obliged to seek direct redress, thus heightening the likelihood that social conflicts would erupt onto the political scene in violent forms. Here we come full circle to our original query. The proposition that Córdoba was the "weak link in the chain of Argentine capitalism" points to the fact that Córdoba was simultaneously "different" from the rest of the country while also "typical" in that it stood at the point of condensation of the contradictions and weaknesses of the entire authoritarian project.

In this atmosphere of a latent crisis of authority, percolating just below the surface of Córdoba's everyday life, what began as just the latest in a month-long series of labor and student protests in Córdoba and elsewhere in the interior ended by exploding the tranquillity of Onganía's much touted "consensus of the silent majority." In fact, the *cordobazo* took the regime almost completely by surprise. Although the president and his nationalist advisers were reluctant to recognize the new reality, the repercussions of the mass rebellion for Krieger's carefully nurtured economic model were felt almost immediately. The transnationals and their local allies in Buenos Aires and Córdoba were less hampered by the ideological blinders that so distorted the regime's perception of the *cordobazo*. The bourgeoisie was not alone in appreciating the new political realities, however.

Labor Militancy and Mass Protest

In the aftermath of the *cordobazo* many disparate groups suddenly realized that the image of the Onganía regime as an all-powerful repressive machine was no longer valid. In fact, the new reality was more akin to the pre-1966 situation of hegemonic crisis or "mass praetorianism" in which the state was unable to mediate social contradictions effectively. As Huntington reminds us, in such situations "social forces confront each other nakedly . . . and each group employs means which reflect its peculiar nature and capabilities. The wealthy bribe; students riot; workers strike; mobs demonstrate; and the military coup. . . . [All] these forms of direct action are found on the political scene."[11] After the *cordobazo* each new strike or demonstration created the sensation of a new confrontation, of a recurrence of the events of May. Some longed for, and others feared, a national conflagration, a true *argentinazo*.

Widespread realization of the regime's vulnerability fed the audacity of many groups who now perceived the possibility of effective opposition. The web of intricate relationships between the dominant fractions of capital and the state became increasingly diaphanous in the confrontation between the "people's violence" and the repressive violence employed to quell the outburst of resentment and rebellion to which the *cordobazo* gave vent. This sudden crystallization of the class nature of the authoritarian project ended a brief lull in the mass protest and political violence that had been endemic in post-1955 Argentine political life. The transitory, "successful" phase of the authoritarian project was now to be followed by a resurgence of mass protest and the emergence of a new revolutionary opposition.

The catalytic role of the *cordobazo* in touching off a new wave of militant forms of opposition can be empirically shown through the use of data on strikes, demonstrations, and revolutionary activities.[12] Figure 6.1 gives a panoramic picture of the

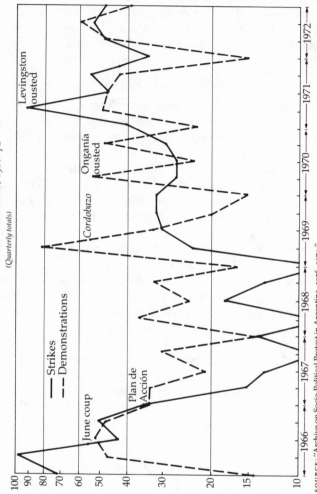

FIGURE 6.1

Strikes and Political Demonstrations, 1966–72

(Quarterly totals)

Strikes
-- Demonstrations

June coup

Plan de
Acción

Cordobazo

Onganía
ousted

Levingston
ousted

100
90
80
70
60
50
40
30
20
15
10

1966 — 1967 — 1968 — 1969 — 1970 — 1971 — 1972

SOURCE: "Archive on Socio-Political Protest in Argentina, 1956–1974."

NOTE: Strikes include those by blue- and white-collar unions, mixed unions, national confederations, and simultaneous national-level strikes; demonstrations include those of Peronists, Radicals, the center, left, and right parties, students, and all unions.

Three values could not be shown in the figure: 4th quarter 1967, 5; 2nd quarter 1968, 5; and 1st quarter 1969, 8.

evolution of strikes and political demonstrations. Both of these militant but generally nonviolent forms of protest declined in frequency after the 1966 coup, with the trough especially noticeable following the state's defeat of the Plan de Acción. The political parties, less directly affected by state control than the unions, also reduced their level of public activity. The period from early 1967 to the end of 1968 was, therefore, one of successful political demobilization. The reversal of the state's advance over the subordinate sectors of society is verified by the increase in strikes and demonstrations evident from March 1969 forward. Following the *cordobazo,* a growing willingness to confront state repression was evidenced by a trend toward even greater militancy on the part of the working class and the political parties.

A more disaggregated analysis of strike activity emerges from Tables 6.2 and 6.3. The decade before the 1966 coup witnessed a sustained increase in working-class militancy, with peaks in the 1964–66 period. The drastic decline in strikes in 1967 and 1968 was reversed in 1969, with a pronounced inflection in the trend that was accentuated in subsequent years. The decline in strike activity in 1967–68 was more pronounced for white-collar unions. However, beginning in 1969 white-collar unions regained their pre-1966 role. Moreover, state-sector white-collar workers were in the vanguard of labor militancy, reflecting the resistance to Krieger's rationalization policies.

The greater militancy of white-collar workers and the negligible level of strike activity in the service sectors is confirmed in Table 6.4. These data also show that workers in the dynamic industrial branches led the labor struggles in the strategic manufacturing sector of the economy.

Looking at the total universe of strikes from the point of view of the union structure tells much about the differences between the *clasista* militants and the forces of labor reformism. There was a complex inverse relationship between rank-and-file militancy and the strength of the labor bureaucracy at the level of the national CGT and union confederations. From the fall of Perón to June 1966, strikes declared at the factory level ("wildcat strikes") and the local level accounted for slightly more than half of all strikes, with the rest declared by the CGT or national-level union organizations. Under the Onganía regime, this figure

TABLE 6.2

Strikes in Argentina, by Type of Union, 1956–72

Type of union	Average 1956–60	Average 1961–65	1966	1967	1968	1969	1970	1971	1972
Blue-collar	58	72	67	36	25	30	41	54	33
White-collar	61	129	120	13	15	38	67	151	123
State	43	93	82	7	10	28	32	110	95
Private	10	26	17	3	4	5	20	26	20
Mixed	8	10	21	3	1	5	15	15	8
National confederation	4	5	6	7	1	14	8	15	13
Simultaneous, nationwide	52	66	62	13	8	16	31	51	37
Total[a]	139	228	263	68	50	93	116	237	187

SOURCE: "Archive on Socio-Political Protest in Argentina, 1956–1974."

[a] The figure for total strikes counts each strike only once, because a given strike might simultaneously be called by a national confederation, be adhered to by a local union, and occur on the same day nationwide.

TABLE 6.3

Strikes Called by Blue-Collar, White-Collar, and State-Sector White-Collar Unions, 1956–72

(*Percent*)

	Blue-collar strikes as pct. of all strikes	White-collar strikes as pct. of all strikes	State-sector white-collar strikes as pct. of all strikes	State-sector white-collar strikes as pct. of white-collar strikes
1956–60	41.7%	43.9%	30.9%	70.5%
1961–65	31.6	56.6	40.8	70.1
1966	25.5	45.6	31.2	68.3
1967	52.9	19.1	10.3	53.8
1968	50.0	30.0	20.0	66.6
1969	32.3	40.9	30.1	73.7
1970	35.3	57.8	27.6	47.8
1971	22.8	63.7	46.4	72.8
1972	17.6	65.8	50.8	77.2

SOURCE: Calculated from Table 6.2.

NOTE: In order to obtain a more accurate measure of the differential propensity toward strike activity of blue-collar and white-collar unions, strikes called by national-level organizations and mixed-member unions were not included.

jumped to two-thirds, reflecting the increasing use of state repression, the retreat of the *colaboracionistas* and *vandoristas*, and the new militancy of rank-and-file workers.[13]

Regional factors play a significant role in explaining why the *cordobazo* occurred in the interior rather than in Buenos Aires. Table 6.5 permits a closer look at these factors by focusing on differential levels of strike activity by region. What is most notable is the decline of activity in Greater Buenos Aires in the 1967–71 period and the corresponding rise in both the industrialized provinces (Buenos Aires, Córdoba, Santa Fe) and the rest of the interior, where a mainly agricultural economy and social structure predominated.

The contrast between the regime's early success in controlling labor militancy and the post-*cordobazo* period is also apparent in strike data from the Federal Capital. In the coup year of 1966, over 904,000 workers engaged in labor conflicts, with 1.9 million workdays lost. By 1968, however, both the number of workers affected and the number of days lost to strikes had declined dramatically to 27,000 and 24,000, respectively, reflecting labor's defeat at the hands of the state. Beginning in 1969, however, a

TABLE 6.4
Strikes in Selected Economic Sectors, 1966–72

Sector	1966	1967	1968	1969	1970	1971	1972
Manufacturing	41	21	17	24	28	31	21
Traditional sectors	12	2	3	3	4	6	2
Intermediate sectors	7	5	2	3	2	4	2
Dynamic sectors	22	14	12	18	22	21	17
Mining	6	2	1	0	1	11	0
Power and light	3	0	4	0	2	7	2
Construction	2	2	0	1	3	1	2
Commerce	1	0	0	0	0	0	0
Telephone	10	0	0	1	1	6	1
Banking	0	0	0	1	2	7	5
Other blue-collar	14	6	2	3	6	5	3
State-sector (white-collar)	51	0	3	14	22	91	62
State enterprises (blue- and white-collar)	11	7	3	12	0	2	8
University employees	7	0	0	1	7	4	22
Total	146	38	30	57	72	165	126

SOURCE: "Archive on Socio-Political Protest in Argentina, 1956–1974."

TABLE 6.5

Strike Activity Disaggregated by Region, 1956–72

| | Greater Buenos Aires[b] | | Industrialized provinces[c] | | Peripheral provinces[d] | | Simultaneous nationwide | | |
	No.	Pct.	No.	Pct.	No.	Pct.	No.	Pct.	Total
1956–60[a]	49	35.2%	31	22.3%	8	5.8%	51	36.7%	139
1961–65[a]	99	43.4	46	20.2	10	4.4	73	32.0	228
1966	94	35.7	60	22.8	47	17.9	62	23.6	263
1967	21	30.9	27	39.7	7	10.3	13	19.1	68
1968	16	32.0	17	34.0	9	18.0	8	16.0	50
1969	22	23.7	32	34.4	23	24.7	16	17.2	93
1970	30	25.9	39	33.6	16	13.8	31	26.7	116
1971	59	24.9	82	34.6	45	19.0	51	21.5	237
1972	80	42.8	36	19.3	34	18.2	37	19.8	187

SOURCE: "Archive on Socio-Political Protest in Argentina, 1956–1974."

NOTE: To arrive at the actual number of strikes in each region, it is necessary to add to the total given the number of simultaneous nationwide strikes; e.g., the actual number of strikes in Greater Buenos Aires in 1969 is 38.

[a]The average for these years.

[b]Greater Buenos Aires includes the Federal Capital and vicinity.

[c]The industrialized provinces include Buenos Aires, Córdoba, and Santa Fe.

[d]The peripheral provinces include the rest of the country, which is primarily agrarian.

reversal took place, with 123,000 workers affected and 251,000 workdays lost. Even though the number of conflicts increased only marginally, their "size" increased fivefold in terms of workers affected and tenfold in terms of days lost. Labor militancy continued to mount, peaking at 396,000 workers affected and 445,000 workdays lost in 1972.[14]

Revolutionary Opposition

The *cordobazo* also fueled the emergence of important revolutionary movements dedicated to guerrilla warfare that were without parallel in Latin America in terms of their characteristic combination of theoretical sophistication, mass appeal, and impact on the course of national politics. However, in their drive to become the "armed vanguard of the proletariat," the revolutionary organizations born in the late 1960s made a deeply ambiguous contribution to Argentine politics. While they helped to block the consolidation of the authoritarian regime, revolutionary violence provided a justification for state terrorism and left a legacy of militarization of politics, ideological polarization, pervasive cynicism, and a retreat into civic privatism.

In the mid-1960s the Argentine revolutionary left was weak and splintered into diverse Peronist and Marxist-oriented tendencies. Argentina had a long tradition of guerrilla struggles dating from the famous Resistencia Peronista begun in 1956, which had been closely linked to militant trade unionism. The urban and rural *focos* inspired by the Cuban Revolution and the example of "Che" Guevara, himself an Argentine, were also significant antecedents. The June 1966 coup breathed new life into the revolutionary left, particularly the diverse currents of the so-called "revolutionary tendency" of Peronism which increasingly "converged" on Guevarist ideology and the Cuban example.[15]

These antecedents were a powerful impetus propelling many students, intellectuals, and other sectors of the middle class toward involvement in radical politics, whether Peronist, Marxist, and/or Guevarist in orientation. The most active organizations included the Fuerzas Armadas de Liberación (FAL), founded in 1962 by disaffected youth from the pro-Soviet Communist Party but quiescent until the early 1970s; the Fuerzas Armadas Peronistas (FAP), which after a setback in Taco Ralo in 1968 reemerged in late 1969 with a Peronist-Guevarist orientation; the Fuerzas Armadas Revolucionarias (FAR), an offshoot of "Che" Guevara's failed Bolivian *foco*, which stepped up its activities in 1970 guided by a combination of Marxism-Leninism and Peronism; the Montoneros, a Peronist group inspired by Catholic radicalism that first emerged as a coherent organization in 1970; and the Ejército Revolucionario del Pueblo (ERP), founded in June 1970 as the military wing of the Revolutionary Workers Party (PRT). Of these guerrilla organizations, the Montoneros and the ERP were the largest, best armed, and most politically significant. They unleashed attacks against the state, the military, and institutions and individuals representing the interests of domestic and transnational capitalism.[16]

The upsurge, following the *cordobazo*, of guerrilla "direct action" tactics such as bombings, assassinations, kidnappings, and "armed propaganda" (e.g., the hijacking of milk trucks and the distribution of the contents in poor neighborhoods) is illustrated in Table 6.6. Here again, the same basic pattern was evi-

TABLE 6.6

Revolutionary "Direct Action," 1966–72

	1966	1967	1968	1969	1970	1971	1972
Bombings	141	141	77	302	287	330	539
Assassination attempts[a]	12	2	2	9	42	60	50
Kidnappings	0	0	1	1	2	7	9
"Armed propaganda"	1	2	2	15	36	42	39
Other acts	4	1	2	14	80	169	100
Total acts[b]	158	146	84	341	447	608	737
Total deaths[c]	33	20	12	39	41	64	68

SOURCE: "Archive on Socio-Political Protest in Argentina, 1956–1974."

NOTE: Includes all acts by revolutionary organizations and individuals. After 1969 it includes all acts by the ERP, the Montoneros, other Peronist guerrilla organizations, and those which could not be attributed to any group.

[a]Includes all assassination attempts against both civilians and military personnel, whether successful or unsuccessful.

[b]For comparative purposes, the average total acts for the 1956–60 period was 141 per year, for 1961–65, 191 per year.

[c]Includes both the deaths of military and police personnel and the deaths of individuals or members of guerrilla organizations due to armed confrontations.

dent: an increase in revolutionary acts from 1956 to 1966, followed by a brief decline in activity in 1967–68 and a dramatic increase following the events of May 1969. The only variation was that in contrast to strikes and demonstrations, revolutionary acts after 1969 far outstripped all previous levels. This increasingly violent turn in Argentine politics clearly reflected the radicalization of the post-1966 period and the new strength and sophistication of the revolutionary organizations themselves.

The incidence of revolutionary actions carried out by guerrilla organizations is shown in Figure 6.2, thus allowing a closer look at the relationship between the single most important form of revolutionary violence and different political conjunctures. Perhaps even more than the data on strikes and demonstrations, these data portray the state's mounting difficulties, and ultimate failure, in making good on its promise to impose political stability and to establish a new hegemony congruent with a "healthy business climate." The brunt of the bombings, assassinations, and kidnappings carried out by the guerrilla organizations was borne by transnational capital, but military installations were also regular targets. The message was not lost, and the negative impact on the economic project, while difficult to measure, cannot be overestimated.

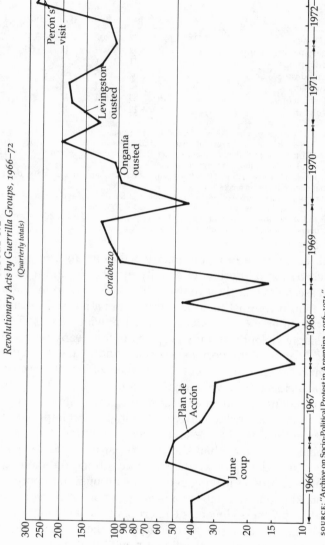

FIGURE 6.2

Revolutionary Acts by Guerrilla Groups, 1966–72

(Quarterly totals)

SOURCE: "Archive on Socio-Political Protest in Argentina, 1956–1974."

NOTE: Includes all bombings, kidnappings, and other acts of "armed propaganda."

The Cordobazo *and the End of the Boom*

The *cordobazo* and the gathering momentum of popular mobilization crystallized the mounting frustration and opposition to Krieger's strategy of state-led restructuring and the political and social exclusion practiced by the Onganía regime. In immediate economic terms, this placed in jeopardy the key goal of "social peace" through state control over wages and salaries, an achievement that was necessary to generate the savings and investment required for more rapid capital accumulation. The inability to enforce labor discipline removed an important motivation for capital, particularly the large industrial firms, to collaborate in upholding the price agreements that had been instrumental in controlling inflation. The possibility of a renewed spiral of cost-push inflation, in turn, threatened the entire system of economic policy so carefully erected by Krieger Vasena. Perhaps most important from the point of view of constructing a new system of domination, the state was directly confronted with the prospect of abandonment by its own social base and the rupture of the pact of domination binding the military, technocratic elites, and entrepreneurs. Most immediately, the social explosion in Córdoba forced Krieger Vasena's resignation as economic czar and de facto "super-minister" of the Onganía regime.

José María Dagnino Pastore, appointed Krieger's successor in June 1969, inherited a situation affording him precious little policy space in which to effect changes in the basic strategy followed since March 1967. By mid-1969 many sectors of the economy were rapidly approaching full utilization of installed capacity. This made it all the more imperative to avoid dramatic policy changes, and to follow instead Krieger's 1969 fiscal and budgetary policies in pursuit of the same goal: the use of state expenditures to support the existing high level of aggregate demand, while simultaneously avoiding an excessive stimulation of the economy, which might spark off a round of demand-pull inflation, and thus wreck the incomes policies so diligently set in place since 1967.

The political situation was equally delicate. The *cordobazo* and the consequent change in the makeup of the regime touched off a deep crisis of confidence on the part of the most powerful industrial and financial groups, who were concerned about the explosive wave of labor militancy among urban blue- and white-collar workers and the renewed activity of the political parties. The wage question was central to business concerns. Krieger's rigid incomes policy had held wages to a nominal increase of 4.6 percent in 1968. Dagnino Pastore was forced to approve increases more than 20 percent above rates prevailing prior to the *cordobazo*, and wages for 1969 as a whole increased nearly 10 percent. In 1970 wages jumped an additional 17.8 percent.[17] Despite the erosion of its ability to impose labor discipline, the regime steadfastly refused to countenance a return to collective bargaining.

Only in 1970, with the worst of the financial unrest calmed for the moment, could Dagnino Pastore attempt a partial reorientation of the economic strategy inherited from Krieger. From an emphasis on state expenditures for the financing of infrastructure construction, Dagnino Pastore moved to increase investment in basic industries in import-substituting sectors. These sectors were identified as those capable of producing at internationally competitive prices, thus taking a major step in the rationalization and restructuring of Argentine capitalism. This shift was designed to save much-needed foreign exchange, thereby permitting sustained growth without periodic interruptions caused by bottlenecks in the capacity to import capital goods, raw materials, and sophisticated foreign technology. In addition, it was hoped that the new measures might generate additional foreign exchange by launching an export drive in industrial goods such as steel, aluminum, copper, petrochemicals, and newsprint produced by these high-value-added sectors.

There was a sharp contrast, however, between this agenda of capitalist "deepening" and Dagnino Pastore's actual policy initiatives. In fact, in the period from the *cordobazo* to the fall of the Onganía regime in June 1970 there were no significant departures or innovations of the magnitude required to implement the proposed reorientation of economic strategy alluded to in public pronouncements. In fact, examination of Dagnino Pastore's tenure gives the strong impression of a technocrat out of his depth, attempting to hold together an increasingly rickety edifice constructed by a far more nimble predecessor. Moreover, rather than "sustained expansion," the record of Dagnino Pastore's stewardship of the economy reads more like a classical case of crisis management relying on a series of stopgap expedients and opportunistic variations on the Krieger model.

One novel aspect of policy pursued by Dagnino Pastore revealed the economic authorities' need both to confront the fiscal deficit and to face up to the dwindling support of the propertied classes. In early 1970 the economic authorities resorted to the seldom-used expedient of declaring a *blanqueo de capitales*. This "whitewashing" allowed holders of illegal or questionable "black" funds to make them legal by declaring them to the government. The incentive to holders of undeclared funds was the possibility of achieving greater flexibility in their use by paying taxes at a very low rate.[18]

Finally, Dagnino Pastore's handling of the external sector was indicative of the growing desperation and lack of policy space open to the authorities following the *cordobazo*. In order to stave off an even more threatening crisis of confidence on the part of the domestic propertied classes and international capital, the economic authorities adhered rigidly to Krieger's earlier pledge not to modify the exchange rates established in March 1967. This guarantee became the single most visible proof of economic "sanity" to nervous investors. The result was an increasingly overvalued peso. But by early 1970 business confidence had been shattered.[19]

The Evaporation of Entrepreneurial Support

Krieger Vasena's exit from power, his replacement by a less skillful manager of the difficult Argentine economy, and the wave of popular mobilizations begun with the *cordobazo* constituted a severe challenge to the attempts of the transnationalized industrial and financial sectors to establish close ties with the state apparatus, and implicitly questioned their leadership over the whole of the propertied classes and, ultimately, over the rest of society.

The accelerating unraveling of the pact of domination supporting the Onganía regime was reflected in the relative inactivity of the business umbrella group the Acción Coordinadora de Instituciones Empresarias Libres. ACIEL, whose mission was to express the consensus of the diverse sectors of the business community, was unable to adjust its strategy to contain pressures from the newly militant working class and middle sectors, the subordinate fractions of industrial and commercial capital represented by the CGE, and the newly emboldened agrarian producers.

In contrast, the sectors of national capital represented by the CGE continued their criticism of economic strategy and policies. The tone of the CGE's ideological offensive became more aggressive, and included more direct attacks on policies favoring international capital. The CGE charged that continued restrictions on credits to smaller firms, depressed wages contributing to soft demand for traditional industries, and tariff policies favoring imports over nationally produced goods, contributed to the rise in speculation and commercial bankruptcies that disproportionately affected national firms.[20]

However, the real threat to the authoritarian project and the hegemony of the transnationalized groups did not come from a failure of leadership on the part of dominant groups or from the opposition of national industrial capital. The disintegration of capitalist unity stemmed fundamentally from the continuing centrality of agriculture to capitalist accumulation and from the fact that the dominant sectors of rural capital were able to construct a unified front to directly confront the state and big industrial and financial capital.

Immediately following the *cordobazo*, the dominant fraction of rural capital, represented by the SRA, temporarily retreated from its earlier tactic of seeking to attract the small and medium producers to its side. Instead, the SRA sought a rapprochement with part of the regime by seeking an alliance with the Secretariat of Agriculture and Livestock, led by Lorenzo Raggio (a medium-sized landowner and member of both the SRA and the FAA). Such an alliance would allow the dominant Pampean producers to enter decision-making circles, which Krieger had closed to their representatives and interests.[21]

Simultaneously, the SRA moved to oppose more decidedly the entire strategy elaborated by Krieger Vasena and continued under Dagnino Pastore. Key to this more aggressive strategy was the SRA's increasingly insistent call for large intersectoral income transfers through which industry (and in turn the work-

ing class) would be forced to pay for an increase in profits flowing to large producers in the *pampa húmeda.*[22]

The SRA's brief strategy of opposition, and its tactic of putting
greater distance between the dominant agrarian producers and
the medium and smaller producers (represented by CARBAP
and the FAA, respectively), underwent a major shift toward
the end of 1969 and was completely reversed in early 1970.
The cause of this shift was a so-called "meat crisis."[23] The international market for Argentine meat products, which had been
depressed for several years, began to experience spectacular
growth during 1969, resulting in a 20-percent rise in producer
prices over the course of the year. There was intense conflict
among the different sectors of Argentine cattlemen and between
producers and the export firms to determine who would appropriate the extraordinary profits from the simultaneous boom of
external and internal consumption.

The principal actors in this conflict were aligned in two rival
camps. In the first camp were four large meatpacking plants, or
frigoríficos, which had long dominated the export of Argentine
meat. The second camp embraced a more disparate array of economic interests including the cattle producers themselves, small
and medium-sized nationally owned meatpackers (grouped in
the Cámara de Industrias Frigoríficas), and the powerful Cor-
poración Argentina de Productores de Carne (CAP), the country's twelfth-largest enterprise.

At issue was a contest to determine which camp would increase its share of the lucrative export trade. Naturally, this
struggle soon centered on control over state economic policy,
since the state would play the crucial role in the distribution
of future profits from the cattle industry. The stakes went beyond a struggle for market share, however, to encompass the
broader issue of the denationalization of Argentine agriculture
and foreign trade, as well as the subordination of the agrarian
bourgeoisie and nationally owned processing firms to the dictates of the new model of accumulation. The struggle between
these two constellations of economic interests was conducted
through the mediation of competing agencies of the Ministry of
Economy. Dagnino Pastore was anxious to cash in on the favorable international market and the chance to earn new foreign

revenues to fuel industrialization. The Ministry's official position, expressed through the Secretariat of Industry and Internal
Trade, advocated measures favoring the large meatpacking monopolies, which needed state assistance in regulating the price
of cattle sold to the slaughterhouses. This meant holding down
prices paid to the producers, while climbing international prices
increased producers' profit margins, and reducing the share of
the market controlled by CAP and the smaller nationally owned
frigoríficos.

This transparent alliance between foreign firms and the economic authorities galvanized the entire rural sector into defending itself, thus helping to overcome the tensions between large
and small agrarian producers. The mobilization of the *campo* and
its allies in the meat-processing sector assumed the form of a
much publicized and very intense propaganda campaign in the
first months of 1970. Reflecting growing disarray within the
state itself, a key leadership role in the ensuing conflict was
played by the second-in-command of the Secretariat of Agriculture and Livestock, Tomás Joaquín de Anchorena. Anchorena
was an important cattle producer, dairyman, and member of the
Sociedad Rural known for his outspoken nationalist sympathies.

Anchorena denounced the foreign monopolies and their "an-
tinational" designs against Argentine agriculture and loudly
criticized the economic authorities for "selling out" the national
interest. He said that he had accepted his post following the
cordobazo because he believed that Krieger Vasena's ouster meant
that important "changes could be introduced in the line of economic policy with respect to the *campo*." However, according to
Anchorena, transnational influence continued unabated and
Onganía and Dagnino Pastore had "sold an illusion to the men
of the *campo*." [24]

The avalanche of denunciations that engulfed the economic
authorities soon became virtually a daily phenomenon that significantly contributed to the Onganía regime's internal disarray.
By April-May 1970 the unification of the *campo* was achieved and
intrasectoral contradictions were momentarily set aside. Medium-sized rural capital and small producers alike joined the Sociedad Rural in the chorus of denunciation. [25]

The final assault on the regime's economic project occurred
on the eve of Onganía's fall. Virtually all the representative

organizations of the rural sector—the SRA, the FFA, CARBAP, the Confederaciones Rurales Argentinas (CRA), and CONINA-GRO, among others—united in a "coordinating commission" (Coordinadora) of agricultural interests to pose a frontal challenge to the regime. This declaration of opposition by the agrarian bourgeoisie reflected the depths of the rural sector's frustration and anger over the subordinate role allocated agriculture in the authoritarian project. Claiming to speak for the "totality of Argentine agriculture," the Coordinadora forgot the rural sector's early praise for the Argentine Revolution and bitterly complained that the denial of adequate voice and representation in the top policymaking organs had revealed the regime's "authoritarian" nature. Moreover, the Coordinadora rejected the primacy of industry, insisting that agriculture still remained "the dynamic factor of the economy and fundamental to the stagnation or progress of the country."[26]

By 1970, the political offensive of the agrarian bloc, together with the opposition of the industrial sectors represented by the CGE, had shattered the cohesion of the entrepreneurial class. This left the dominant industrial and financial groups and their allies within the state exposed and vulnerable to attacks from civil society and from dissident sectors within the state itself.

Particularly after the *cordobazo*, Krieger's strategy contributed to polarization and class conflict while at the same time failing to eliminate constraints on further accumulation and expanded reproduction of the model. The ultimate causes of the failure of the Krieger Vasena strategy, as well as its technical merits and demerits, remain the subject of heated controversy among economists and politicians. However, analysis of the twists and turns of economic policy and the reactions by the different entrepreneurial fractions underline several points that can now be spelled out in more detail. The main point to be emphasized concerns the extreme political constraints affecting the effort to assert the hegemony of the most transnationalized financial and industrial sectors.

Two problematic areas of economic strategy and policy can be singled out in this regard: inflation and the balance of payments. Failure to resolve these issues was to prove fatal. Paradoxically, from the point of view of the supporters of the Krieger strategy, the very success of the original plan in 1968–69 made it difficult

to maintain the original alliance behind the 1966 coup and virtually impossible to gain new allies. This was particularly evident in the case of the agrarian sectors, who protested their political and economic subordination. Rural producers resented
both the fluctuations in commodity prices and a price system
that subsidized industry through unequal exchange. Emboldened by the new political situation in the second half of 1969,
the agrarian bourgeoisie, especially the Pampean cattle producers, made a concerted effort to take advantage of world demand
to raise their domestic prices. This contributed to substantial
jumps in wholesale and retail price indexes in 1970, fueling demands for larger and more frequent wage increases, and forcing industry to abandon its lingering commitment to the price
agreements with the state. Sectoral clashes between urban industry and rural producers ensued, with prices gradually shifting in favor of the latter.

The second problematic factor undermining the Krieger strategy was rooted in the inherent import-intensity of the process
of industrialization followed in Argentina. The growing dependence on imported capital and intermediate goods to sustain import-substitution was a particularly acute problem due to the
recurrent balance-of-payments crises that interrupted economic
growth.

State policies actually compounded this basic obstacle. The
trade policy initiated in 1967 tried to slowly liberalize exchange
controls and to eliminate many import restrictions, while increasing state revenues through the imposition of taxes on agricultural exports. Ostensibly this policy was designed to promote
industrial exports and reduce Argentina's dependence on agriculture to generate the foreign revenues needed for more rapid
internal accumulation. But the goal of promoting industrial exports was never taken very seriously. The cutback on existing
promotional programs and the subsequent neutralization of the
1967 incentives (for the purpose of honoring Krieger Vasena's
promise to maintain a fixed exchange rate) meant that "once
again history repeated itself: a small increase in international reserves was enough to remove any priority from efforts tending
toward the expansion of [industrial] exports."[27]

Moreover, the elimination of many import controls under
pressure from the World Bank, the decline in tariff protection,

the government's limited capacity for (and interest in) regulating "dumping," and the intrafirm pricing practices of the transnationals, combined with the brief euphoria of the economic expansion of 1968 and 1969, produced huge increases in imports during the period. From $1.2 billion dollars in 1965, imports rose to $1.7 billion in 1970, a 41 percent increase in only five years. In particular, imports of capital goods consumed by industry increased 136 percent, thus contradicting the goal of deepening the industrial structure.[28]

Because such large increases in imports could not immediately be paid for, debts accumulated over debts and interest was paid with new debts. The foreign debt began to grow rapidly, from $3 billion in 1967 to nearly $5 billion in 1970 to over $6 billion in 1972. Naturally, the servicing of foreign debt and profit repatriation began to consume ever larger portions of total exports. In addition to placing limits on domestic economic expansion and spurring inflation, this process accelerated the decapitalization of the economy by transferring larger portions of the national product overseas. In short, Krieger Vasena's and Dagnino Pastore's policy of "repressed inflation" and their failure to deal with the foreign-exchange bottleneck not only contributed to the coalescence of factors which led to the eventual fall of the Onganía regime, but failed to deliver on the original promise of a "politics of production" capable of restructuring the economy and producing an "Argentine Miracle."

The regime's collapse was by no means inevitable; skillful leadership might have succeeded in regaining entrepreneurial support. But just when it faced its greatest trial, requiring a maximum of internal cohesion and resolve, the Onganía regime proved to be at its weakest and most disorganized. Onganía and his nationalist political staff demonstrated a deep incomprehension of the significance of the *cordobazo* and the magnitude of rising popular opposition. In response, Onganía announced new repressive legislation to strengthen the 1967 anti-Communist law and made it clear that he was prepared to deal harshly with any future popular rebellions. The official version of events placed exclusive blame on "professional agitators" and "extremists" controlled by Fidel Castro, Perón, "international Communism," or some improbable combination of all three bent on the destruction of the "Christian and Western world." An iron hand with subversion and firmness with the "incomformity" of naturally restless youth, the regime seemed to say, would be sufficient to weather the storm.[29]

When these palliatives proved inadequate, the business community arrived at very different conclusions. Viewing Dagnino Pastore's efforts to expand infrastructure and promote the capital goods sector as ineffectual, and facing a restrictive monetary policy that raised interest rates and reduced liquidity, industrialists and financiers halted or scaled down new investment projects, preferring to take capital out of the country to safer havens. Foreign investment virtually ceased and only "hot money" flowed into Argentina after May 1969.

Nor was the bourgeoisie's criticism limited to economic policy. Dominant groups also charged that the *cordobazo* reflected the state's vacillation and weakness before working-class demands. The nationalists' overtures and concessions to organized labor were roundly denounced as anti-democratic, corporatist, and a "threat to the Argentine Way of Life." The solution, they argued, was an immediate cessation of all attempts at alliance with the unions. Instead, the regime should make a concerted effort to crush the CGT and impose rigid controls over labor.

In contrast to the dominant fractions' call for an even more stringent application of Krieger's previous policies, the CGE was impressed with the breadth of popular opposition, even briefly considering using this discontent to displace *ortodoxo* management of economic policies. When this possibility evaporated, the CGE stepped up criticism of denationalization and the government's "sellout" to international capital.[30] Such criticism formed part of a new willingness on the CGE's part to espouse classic populist proposals for an alliance between "democratic entrepreneurs" and the working class and foreshadowed its future dialogue with the unions, the parties, and Juan Perón.

Although organized labor stood to gain much from the regime's weakness following the *cordobazo*, the reformist leadership was unable to play an autonomous role in the new conjuncture. Uncontrolled popular rebellions and labor militancy badly frightened the labor bureaucracy, threatening its privileged position and severely constraining its freedom of maneuver. Even though the radical challenge of the CGT de los Argentinos had receded,[31] the reformists were not strengthened.

Fearing both intensified labor militancy and state repression, *vandorismo* was torn between Perón's order from Madrid to intensify the struggle and its de facto alignment with the proregime *colaboracionistas*. The *vandoristas* were further weakened by the assassination of their leader, Augusto T. Vandor, by a Montonero guerrilla group on 30 June 1969.[32]

Riven by internal dissension, organized labor responded with a strategy of militant economism which the leadership hoped would placate rank-and-file grievances over declining real wages and lack of internal democracy. However, this policy implied continued acceptance of state tutelage, which assigned labor a subordinate role in the defense of the regime against mounting popular discontent and bourgeois challenges.

Popular uprisings by workers and students in the important industrial city of Rosario and in the smaller city of Cipoletti in the province of Río Negro further complicated matters and torpedoed Onganía's "social period" in which the state would show its "human face."[33] Harsh measures (some 14,000 railroad workers were placed under military jurisdiction) were taken by the army in September 1969 to put down the *rosariazo*. In response the *vandoristas* reluctantly called for a nationwide 36-hour strike. When, at the insistence of army commander-in-chief Alejandro Lanusse, Onganía approved threats to repress strikers and "wipe out" labor, the strike was called off.[34]

This episode further eroded the entrepreneurial class's confidence in the regime. The private sector was disturbed by the lengths to which Onganía and his political staff were willing to go to placate labor. Fears of the nationalists' "corporatist designs" were further exacerbated by the regime's continued insistence that wage increases be absorbed by employers in accordance with the 1967 price agreement. By late 1969 and early 1970, the regime's standing with the private sector had declined to such an extent that many firms ignored the price agreement altogether and shifted wage increases to prices, thus feeding inflationary expectations.

State intervention in the relationship between capital and labor had been welcomed when it meant a reduction in wages and an increase in profits, but in the new atmosphere of crisis such intervention was roundly denounced as a demagogic concession that would endanger stabilization efforts. Thereafter, tensions continued to grow as the regime and its erstwhile capitalist allies confronted one another in mounting antagonism on issue after issue.[35]

Politico-Military Crisis and Regime Collapse

The armed forces, like the rest of the state, were profoundly affected by the changes wrought by the *cordobazo*. The military's own organizational characteristics, its position in a state splintered by growing contradictions, and its complex affinity with the dominant social classes all made the officer corps particularly sensitive to repercussions of the regime's mounting legitimation problems.[36] Gradually this sensitivity coalesced in a broad consensus among the top leaders of the army and its sister services on the necessity of increasing their vigilance over the regime. If necessary, they would remove their "delegate" in order to protect their own corporate interests and defend the "Revolution." Thus began a drift toward a new round of direct military intervention, marked by the growing confrontation between Onganía and the army and its commander-in-chief, General Alejandro Lanusse.

In his memoirs, General Lanusse explained the mounting internal and external pressures on the army to abandon its "golden jail of mechanical obedience" and "blind and deaf professionalism" in which the military theoretically neither "governed nor co-governed."[37] In his Army Day address in the midst of the uprising in Córdoba, General Lanusse explicitly recalled Onganía's famous "West Point Speech" to warn that the army could not give its "unconditional support" to any regime, and he observed that military intervention could again be justified in "exceptional circumstances."[38]

The top military leadership's realization of the regime's vulnerability before a fractious and rebellious society was filtered through the prism of the need to dispel the armed forces' image as a repressive praetorian guard while also defending the national security.[39] Onganía responded to these concerns by steadfastly adhering to his own "reserve function" interpretation of military-state relations. In a stern lecture to the "military parliament" at the annual "comradeship dinner" on 7 July 1969, Onganía once again made vague and unconvincing promises to accelerate the "social period." He was more specific, and more persuasive, when he promised to unleash instant and massive repression "to protect life and property and to restore peace whenever the national being is threatened."[40] The president's sense of his messianic mission and his defense of his regime's "historic mandate" only aroused further fears that he intended to remain in power indefinitely regardless of civilian and military pleas for a "political solution."

The dramatic increase in tensions between Onganía and the military in the second half of 1969 hastened the politicization of the officer corps and fostered numerous conspiracies and intrigues involving both nationalists and liberals. The most notorious of the nationalist conspiracies centered on the activities of General Eduardo Rafael Labanca, commander of the 10th Infantry Brigade. Labanca and his followers engaged in a series of anti-regime plots with disaffected ultra-right officers. What made these particular plots such a red flag to Lanusse and the army liberals was Labanca's friendship and frequent contacts with Onganía.[41]

Although the army's intelligence service dealt effectively with these nationalist conspiracies, allegations of Onganía's support for the conspirators, coupled with the president's overtures and concessions to organized labor, further fanned the flames of liberal suspicions of an impending swing toward populism and corporatism. Needless to say, the liberals were not reassured by the symbolism of Onganía's decision in late 1969 to "consecrate the nation" to the "Immaculate Heart of the Virgin Mary."

Reaction to the regime's crisis among liberal sectors of the military took various forms, including conspiracies directed by retired officers to recruit active-duty officers willing to consider a coup against Onganía. Impatient with General Lanusse's carefully modulated criticism of Onganía's autocratic style and corporatist inclinations, ex-president General Pedro E. Aramburu and former army commander-in-chief General Julio Alsogaray openly engaged in anti-regime plots following the *cordobazo*. Aramburu, in particular, attempted to project the image of an Argentine de Gaulle, offering a "democratic" alternative to Onganía. His efforts were geared to forging an alliance with the political parties to push for elections as the best means to forestall radicalization and safeguard the interests of the military and the dominant classes. General Alsogaray's plotting was clearly more *golpista* in conception, reflecting the close ties between many of the more dogmatic military liberals and the business community, as well as their fears that popular mobilization might play into the hands of Perón or the revolutionary left. These liberal conspiracies, especially the so-called "Aramburu option," highlighted the regime's estrangement from the military and speeded up the emergence of opposition within the officer corps. Quickly this opposition came to be located in the institutionalized command structure of the army itself, i.e., in the hands of General Lanusse and his immediate staff.

General Lanusse confronted two imperatives that were at least partially contradictory. First, he was pressured to support a regime and a president placed in power by the military itself. Second, he had to defend the military's corporate interests— its hard-won professionalism and cohesion—against all external and internal pressures. Internal politicization and rampant factionalism, whether liberal or nationalist in orientation, violated the chain-of-command and seriously endangered Lanusse's ability to achieve either imperative. Consequently, Lanusse maneuvered carefully and skillfully to build up a coalition based upon strict observance of the command structure and loyalty to the commander-in-chief's prerogative to "speak for the institution."

General Lanusse's pragmatic strategy was akin to the army's political "retreat" of the 1963–66 period, when factionalism had been successfully suspended and institutional cohesion was reinforced as a prelude to confrontation with the Illia government. General Lanusse gradually became the defender of professionalism, while Onganía, the original architect of *azulismo*, found himself more and more isolated and dependent on his nationalist political staff, the dwindling number of military *onganistas*, and pro-regime labor bureaucrats. For these groups, defense of the "deepening of the Revolution" became the means to remaining in power.[42]

The Army General Staff began to draw up contingency plans as early as August 1969. These plans stressed the military's limited political options: either to push for a quick electoral opening and a decorous "return to the barracks" to head off mounting chaos, or to embark on some sort of national-populist adventure of "strong emotional content."[43] Rejecting both extreme solutions, General Lanusse insisted on a "slow transition" to civilian rule based on a plan for carefully controlled indirect elections to take place sometime between 1972 and 1976. Clearly, Lanusse and the top army command were in no hurry for a return to democracy.[44]

By the end of February 1970, General Lanusse had succeeded in marginalizing nationalist officers and generating a broad military consensus both for an immediate statement of the regime's political intentions and for an unambiguous rejection of all corporatist designs. In March and April 1970 the situation deteriorated visibly amid multiple difficulties, including a new crisis in Córdoba, the forced resignation of the director of the SIDE (the executive branch's principal intelligence service), the resignation of the Secretary of Agriculture and Livestock in connection with the "meat crisis," conflicts between the Interior Minister and the Federal Police, and the regime's failure to head off a nationwide strike by the CGT.[45]

Finally, at the end of April, the regime lost much of its remaining base of civilian support when ex-president Arturo Frondizi broke with Onganía by issuing a blistering attack that condemned virtually every aspect of the president's leadership. Frondizi charged that the "hope that the country placed in the government of Lt. Gen. Juan Carlos Onganía, leader of the Revolution, is exhausted. In these nearly four years, the Revolution has not been carried out; instead, the government has been turned over to the Counter-Revolution." Significantly, however, Frondizi's condemnation of Onganía's "reactionary and anachronistic" policies did not lead him to call for an electoral solution; instead, he appealed to the military to support an authoritarian solution, namely to "create the Revolution's political base in a vast accord of social sectors committed to structural change: the workers, the entrepreneurs, the politicians who are capable of adapting to the country's necessities, the intellectuals, the armed forces, and the church."[46]

Frondizi's attacks unleashed a psychological chain reaction within the military. Lanusse ordered the army's General Staff to analyze events in light of the break between Frondizi and his *desarrollista* followers and Onganía. A short document entitled simply "Situation" sharply criticized the "profound internal crisis of the government, caused by the lack of leadership over the revolutionary process, the coexistence of contradictory tendencies in its midst, and the absence of clearly defined orientations or policies."[47]

The point of no return was reached in a meeting between Onganía and the entire contingent of army generals on 27 May 1970. Called to heal the breach between the president and the army, the meeting had the exact opposite result. Onganía announced that he was "completely optimistic about the march of the process. . . . Each day the path is clearer." The president's so-called "political plan" was nothing more than the familiar refrain of "organizing the community by means of its structures." To the astonishment of the assembled generals, Onganía drew a series of triangles on a blackboard representing labor, capital, professionals, and the state, with the latter consisting of "structures of leadership" such as advisory councils and planning agencies. Each triangle was divided horizontally and vertically and linked to a grid with three basic political concepts—the "People," the "Country," and the "Republic." The president proclaimed that this intricate architectonic framework would culminate in the creation of an "organic community" free of the ills of liberal democracy. He warned, however, that his project would demand many sacrifices and that even "10 or 20 years" might not be long enough to bring this authoritarian utopia to full fruition.[48]

Only two days later, Lanusse's Army Day address sought to clearly distance the armed forces from the regime. Lanusse unambiguously defended military professionalism and highlighted the importance of the army's institutional cohesion, explaining to the officer corps that preserving unity was the *sine qua non* that permitted "the Army to exercise its influence as a united and powerful force in the face of any insinuation of distortion, interruption, or deviation of the normal development of the Revolution." The thrust of his message, however, was to assert the army's leadership role in healing social wounds by forging a Gran Acuerdo Nacional, or Great National Accord. In Lanusse's conception, the Gran Acuerdo was to be

a first step . . . necessary to defeat the old frameworks and prejudices that have divided our society into antagonistic sectors. It is the hour for all of us Argentines, without exception, to work with enthusiasm and

endangering not only the regime in power but also the entire panoply of political and economic institutions that had emerged during the most recent phase of capitalist modernization.

Although this crisis of hegemony was still incipient, its ominous dimensions underscored the fact that authoritarian forms of domination are at a great disadvantage compared to democratic-parliamentary political forms. Democratic regimes are protected by multiple layers of institutionalized defense mechanisms and a reserve of ideological loyalty that cushion and constrain crises and permit their administration. By the time authoritarian regimes confront an acute crisis of hegemony, on the other hand, they have usually done their best to destroy or render ineffective the means for achieving an orderly circulation of elites.

Although Onganía and his nationalist political staff took advantage of the crisis to partially displace the allies of the dominant entrepreneurial groups from direct control over economic policy, they were incapable of using their expanded control to redirect Argentine capitalism in a more nationalist and statist direction. Nor did they succeed in efforts to restructure state and society in order to create a new nationalist-populist social base. Finally, Onganía's maneuvers to ride out the storm were simultaneously "too much" and "too little," insufficient to prevent further radicalization and polarization and inadequate to placate those who feared the destruction of all that had been accomplished since 1967 in terms of economic stabilization.

Increasingly isolated and devoid of support from either the "classes" or the "masses," the Onganía regime remained in tenuous control only until the military perceived that Onganía's continuation in office threatened to lead to a major political disaster. The military then moved fairly rapidly to reinforce its threatened internal cohesion by finding an acceptable formula for replacing its "delegate" at the helm of the state. However, the magnitude of the crisis proved far greater than was apprehended in June 1970. The crisis would prove to be so intricately intertwined and interlaced with the deeper dimensions of class, accumulation, and state power that ever more costly lessons would have to be learned, and still more Byzantine projects, alliances, and political combinations attempted, before the Argentine Revolution had run its course.

SEVEN

Military Reformism and the "Deepening of the Revolution"

EVENTS REACHED true crisis proportions in the post-1970 period. The *cordobazo* transformed Argentine political life. The manner in which this crisis was resolved was to have far-reaching consequences not only for the Argentine Revolution itself, but also for the entire panoply of classes, institutions, and political forces present in Argentine society. However, these consequences were not immediately apparent. In fact, Onganía's ouster generated expectations for a quick return to the original project of capitalist restructuring and a renewed commitment to economic orthodoxy. Furthermore, with General Lanusse, a friend of the liberals with close connections to the most powerful economic groups, firmly in control of the army, it was hoped that the state's badly corroded social supports could be rebuilt.

Such expectations were soon dashed. Instead, the authoritarian experiment underwent its final disintegration: the military began a desperate search for a *salida política* or "political way out" of the deepening crisis, and the dominant entrepreneurial groups were forced into a precipitous retreat from the confident advance over state and society which they had begun so triumphantly in 1966. The search for a *salida* evolved through two clearly differentiated stages. First, there was a somewhat quixotic attempt, under the leadership of Onganía's immediate successor, General Roberto Marcelo Levingston, to stand Krieger's strategy on its head by articulating a model of "national capitalism." Second, following Levingston's fall from power, General Alejandro Lanusse deployed an aggressive political pragmatism and abandoned any overall model of accumulation, subordinating economic objectives to the more immediate political need to extricate the military from direct control over state power.

Reformism and Transformism

Antonio Gramsci's fragmentary notes on the concept of "organic crisis" offer a useful point of departure for analyzing this period. According to Gramsci, a profound political crisis generally occurs when the failure of a "major political undertaking" of the dominant groups in a society suddenly galvanizes "huge masses" into political mobilization on behalf of "demands which taken together, albeit not organically, add up to a revolution."[1] Many sectors of post-1970 Argentine society experienced just such a "general crisis of the state" and hoped or feared that a revolution was in the realm of historical possibility. These sectors searched urgently for ways to accelerate or to retard the crisis.

There are three possible "solutions" to a crisis of these proportions: revolution, reform, or "transformism."[2] Reformist *salidas*, if they are to provide long-term, "organic" responses to political crisis, must modify both the political form of domination (by incorporating representatives of the previously excluded groups through a "circulation of elites") as well as the content of the state's policies in the economic and social fields. If it has been successful at both endeavors, a reformist project can contribute to a reaffirmation of bourgeois rule and hegemony by broadening its social base and placing the state on a more stable foundation. The concept of "transformism," by contrast, is a little-known and very complex notion that evolved out of Gramsci's studies of the Italian Risorgimento and the "revolution-restoration" or "passive revolution" which gave birth to the modern Italian state.[3]

A transformist solution to an organic crisis also entails an "opening" toward excluded groups, but with very different implications and consequences. Transformism operates through the co-optation of both politicians and representatives of excluded groups ("molecular" transformism) as well as through the wholesale "absorption" of "entire groups" (i.e., parties, unions, other corporative organizations, etc.) into the ranks of the political class staffing the state. Though both reformist and transformist solutions may contemplate limited changes in the form of political domination, they differ in that the latter reject any "organic" responses, e.g., they resist significant change in patterns of accumulation and pertinent state policies.[4]

Political and economic events during the Levingston and Lanusse regimes were shaped by three alternative scenarios designed to extricate the military from state power, while offering guarantees for the continuity of the system as a whole: two variants of reformism, one military and one civilian, and one military-sponsored transformist project. Military reformism crystallized in Levingston's short-lived project of "deepening the revolution." To be successful, this version of reformism required detaching the military from transnationalized groups and realigning it with the "national" components of Argentine society, i.e., local entrepreneurs and organized labor. The civilian variant of reformism, already present in embryo even before the *cordobazo*, became an increasingly strong political force during Levingston's tenure. It was solidly rooted among the main political parties, the unions, and national entrepreneurs, who clamored for a more active state role in the economy to promote a latter-day version of the "populist" alliance. As its price for collaboration, civilian reformists demanded the liberalization and democratization of the political process, i.e., a total rupture with the autocratic practices of the Argentine Revolution.

Following the collapse of military reformism, and faced with the rising civilian challenge, the Lanusse regime and the armed forces confronted a narrowing range of political options. Convinced of the impossibility of a return to rigid authoritarian rule, Lanusse chose to launch the transformist Gran Acuerdo Nacional (GAN). The GAN's basic objective was to gain a margin of political maneuvering room that would permit the military to extricate itself from the center of the political maelstrom. This transformist project was essentially an intelligent defense premised on minimizing concessions to the subordinate groups in order to prepare for future capitalist modernization and restructuring under more propitious conditions.

From the point of view of the military and the dominant groups, each of these exit scenarios had to address three fundamental, non-negotiable questions: first, insurance of the "integrity" and continuity of the state and its key institutions, especially the armed forces as the branch most directly threatened by the collapse of the authoritarian project; second, protection of the basic national and international parameters of the political economy, especially the assurance of reasonable safeguards for the transnationalized business groups who, despite their political defeat and partial displacement in the wake of the *cordobazo*, still maintained a clearly predominant position in the economy; third, and central to the others, a realistic program to maintain strong political control over popular mobilization, especially in light of the threats posed by the *clasista* sectors of the working class and guerrilla groups bent on radicalizing Argentine society and eventually transforming it in a socialist direction.

Levingston and "National Capitalism"

When he was selected as Onganía's successor, General Levingston was an obscure officer representing Argentina on the Interamerican Defense Board in Washington, D.C. General Levingston seemed a perfect compromise candidate. He had no clear ideological leanings and was little-known even among his army peers, and he was considered a military intellectual, not a *tropero* with the experience of commanding troops. Therefore, he was not considered likely to repeat Onganía's attempts to perpetuate himself in power, nor to challenge General Lanusse's leadership within the army.[5] Argentines were introduced to their new president by the embarrassing device of press releases giving his *curriculum vitae*, since even the well-informed political elite had only the vaguest idea of his views or background.[6] The contrast with Onganía's status as a genuine military caudillo could not have been more clear-cut.

The transnationals and local businessmen reacted calmly to Levingston's appointment, trusting the military to control their little-known colleague. This favorable reaction reflected the liberal orientation imposed on the coup by Lanusse's leadership as well as the belief that the "only alternative to economic disorder" was to continue the plan initiated by Krieger Vasena.[7]

The problem was that maintaining the comparatively high rate of accumulation of 1969 would necessarily require large increases in the import bill for intermediate goods, increases which could not be paid for with the foreign exchange earned by agricultural exports. Moreover, the alternative of breaking into the industrial export market would require not only continued full employment of productive capacity in the basic goods sector (steel, cement, chemicals), but the more difficult task of expanding and reorganizing industrial production, the intermediate goods sector, and the ancillary communications and transportation infrastructure. This would mean an increase and redirection of state investments into areas where full returns could be delayed for at least 2–4 years. Herein lay the contradictions and tradeoffs confronted by any project of "continuity" with the original strategy.

Entrepreneurs in the dynamic industrial sectors most favored by the Krieger strategy naturally desired to continue the bonanza without any interruption. Rather than the costly development of local industries producing at non-competitive prices, the interests of the dynamic firms demanded a stable flow of cheap intermediate goods imports. Such a flow would allow Argentina to enter the world industrial export market without delay, while sustaining a high level of demand in existing sectors. On the other hand, this strategy would require heavy state subsidies for imported inputs and stringent efforts to freeze or even reduce real wages in order to assure competitiveness. It would also require the state to cast a benign eye on further concentration and centralization of industrial capital along with further denationalization of ownership and control.

However, the obstacles to the strategy of deepening and vertical integration were not primarily economic or technical but political in nature. Specifically, the new weakness and vulnerability of the state meant that it now had neither the internal unity nor the political autonomy to discipline labor and impose a common program on the quarrelsome and divided bourgeoisie. Thus it is clear that while continuity in the shape of further deepening and vertical integration of the economy may have been the "only alternative to economic disorder," such a project could hardly have been launched at a less propitious moment.

Given the pronounced erosion of the state's original authoritarian characteristics, virtually all classes and sectors found something to oppose in a project of continuity. The working class and the popular sectors would resist efforts to deprive them of the political gains won since the *cordobazo*. The Pampean producers would strenuously oppose any attempt to force them to foot the bill for industrial modernization through exports and cheap foodstuffs for internal consumption. The small and medium sized entrepreneurs would not passively accept their own demise and subordination, while no sector of business would voluntarily cooperate with a reimposition of price controls or efforts to raise tax revenues. Last but not least, the transnationals and their local associates would not agree voluntarily to a program of industrial exports that would contradict their worldwide production and marketing strategies.

On June 18, the same day that the new president was sworn in, the new Minister of Economy Moyano Llerena spelled out the regime's economic program, which strongly asserted the necessity of continuing the Krieger strategy. According to Moyano Llerena, the only other recourse was inflation, which was not only "irresponsible" but sure to lead to economic chaos and political instability.[8]

Bolstered by the support of the liberal sectors of the military, Moyano Llerena's reign as Minister of Economy began with a 14.3 percent devaluation of the peso to restore business confidence. As in 1967, this measure was accompanied by a compensating tax to deprive agricultural exporters of windfall profits. The new revenues would instead be transferred to a special fund for "eminently social goals," i.e., to assist industry in financing wage increases and to develop public works projects that would expand needed infrastructure and generate new jobs. The package was completed with reductions in import duties and plans to revitalize voluntary price agreements with leading firms.[9]

This program was a carbon copy of the 1967 strategy, but with two crucial exceptions. Conspicuously absent from official pronouncements was any promise to resuscitate Krieger Vasena's incomes policy. The failure to adopt a wage freeze reflected the realistic judgment that the union leadership was already finding it extremely difficult to restrain rank-and-file militancy. Consequently, the regime feared that a harsh incomes policy would torpedo the orthodox package before it even got off the ground. The second missing ingredient was the praise and enthusiasm with which the business community had greeted Krieger's original program.

Bourgeois skepticism and unease were evident from the very beginning. Both the Unión Industrial and the Sociedad Rural, as well as the other members of the ACIEL free-enterprise grouping, charged that Moyano Llerena's policies, rather than restoring confidence, would actually undermine the business climate by demonstrating the economic authorities' weakness and lack of resolve. According to the Unión Industrial, even the devaluation was "technically inexplicable, since no urgent reasons existed" to justify going back on Krieger's promise that the 1967 devaluation would be the "last in Argentine history."[10]

In reality, these criticisms were only symptoms of deeper concerns harbored by the transnationals and local large industrial and financial interests. The Unión Industrial feared that the new economic team would succumb to the pressures for more nationalist economic policies and a hasty electoral scenario, gravely endangering the interests of the dominant economic groups. Thus while fear of "a *salida política* without a process of development" obliged the Unión Industrial to reluctantly support Moyano Llerena's policies, concern mounted about his ability to successfully engineer a return to the previous strategy of accumulation and about the regime's lack of political support.[11]

The Sociedad Rural adopted a more militant posture, which stemmed from the different interests of its membership and its more rigid pre-Keynesian definition of economic orthodoxy. To the SRA, "continuity" with the Krieger program simply meant a prolongation of the subordination of Pampean producers to the needs of rapid industrialization. In consequence, the Sociedad Rural adopted a strategy of frontal opposition, charging not only that the new economic policies would cause inflation, but also that Moyano Llerena and his team would lack the confidence of the "men of the *campo*," who were no longer willing to sacrifice profitability in exchange for mere promises. In a thinly veiled threat, the Sociedad Rural warned that if the new authorities did not quickly rectify their errors, the "juridical-institutional continuity of the state" itself might be in danger.[12]

The Confederación General Económica and the leading proponents of an export strategy of development also criticized Moyano Llerena's orthodox policies, but from a different angle. They attacked the economic team for following short-sighted policies that would lead to stagnation and inflation while encouraging additional foreign penetration to threaten the survival of national industry. Nevertheless, from the CGE's perspective, the regime was emitting some positive signals. For instance, Levingston publicly promised to control the process of denationalization of the financial and industrial sectors and to promote "deep structural reforms" in support of national capital.[13] This presidential rhetoric fed the expectations of the more nationalist sectors of Argentine business and further eroded support among the dominant groups for Moyano Llerena's policies.

The most articulate and politically significant critique of continuity and orthodoxy, however, did not come from the private sector but from within the state apparatus itself. This opposition emerged from the National Development Council (CONADE) through its new director, retired army general Juan Enrique Guglialmelli, a well-known nationalist and "maximalist" on development questions. General Guglialmelli had strongly opposed Moyano Llerena's appointment and just as strongly objected to the continuation of the Krieger strategy. He challenged orthodox policies at every opportunity, particularly on such sensitive issues as wage increases and labor relations.[14]

In mid-September 1970, Levingston surprised many observers, including the Junta that had placed him in the presidency, when he announced that he intended to remain in power for 4–5 years. Moreover, in a move directed against both Guglialmelli and Moyano Llerena, Levingston simultaneously announced the formation of a commission to take charge of short- and medium-term economic policy formulation.[15] Tensions surrounding future economic policy soon reached a crisis point. Bereft of the president's support and lacking the full confidence of the military (who were increasingly concerned with relieving social tensions), Moyano Llerena resigned in mid-October. Levingston immediately named Aldo Ferrer, then in charge of public works, as the new Minister of Economy, thus snubbing Guglialmelli's bid for the top economic post.[16]

In response, Guglialmelli tendered his resignation in early November, blaming economic orthodoxy for a "true sacking" of Argentina's economy. The intended audience for this resignation was the military. Addressing his uniformed colleagues, Guglialmelli criticized Ferrer's policies as only a "new and more sophisticated" version of the same old orthodox recipes: "The economic policy proposed by the new Minister . . . will lead, if not radically changed, to a confrontation among social sectors just when the unity of the Argentine people is more urgent than ever."[17]

Aldo Ferrer and Argentinización

By October 1970 support for the June coup was wearing thin. Uncertainty was compounded by the fact that Ferrer was virtually unknown in international business and financial circles. Domestically, his past political affiliations and reputation as a structuralist economist and a "left-wing *desarrollista*" provoked mixed reactions. Ferrer's image as a technocrat and a "new man" untarnished by links with "anti-national interests" and the economic establishment was generally congenial to nationalist opinion, while provoking liberal criticism in the mass media. Both hopes and fears were reinforced by Levingston's shift to a more nationalist discourse announcing the so-called *argentinización* of the economy.

Ferrer's initial public statements clarified the general outlines of the proposed reorientation of state policies. The new minister championed the "explicit support for national capital and private national firms to enter sectors of vanguard technology and basic industry, which are those of greatest dynamism."[18] Ferrer also called for moderate income redistribution to boost domestic consumption. This program for state intervention on behalf of national capital and income redistribution favoring the poorer sectors constituted eloquent proof of the new correlation of forces following the *cordobazo*. The program also crystallized the realization on the part of many technocrats of the urgent need to protect the state's autonomy in a context of rising tensions among the dominant economic groups and between labor and capital.

Still, the Levingston-Ferrer call for *argentinización* by and large did not go beyond the positions advanced earlier by the National Development Council or the CGE, showing strict limits to this new nationalism.[19] The new program did not question the goal of an "open" economy or Argentina's subordinate insertion into the world-economy, nor did it question the inevitability of further concentration and centralization as part of economic modernization. Fundamentally, therefore, this nationalism constituted a demand for a renegotiated dependency and greater participation for the state and national capital in the process of industrialization.

Ferrer's strategic objectives centered on deepening vertical industrialization, especially in the intermediate goods sector, by promoting manufacturing exports and by stimulating internal demand through wage increases and public works projects. This implied forging a new partnership between the state and national firms while placing limitations on the activities of international capital. Ferrer consistently disdained monetarist stabilization plans which, he asserted, led to "strangulation" of national capital, income concentration favoring the privileged minority, and foreign indebtedness. Instead, he announced, inflation would "be attacked at its roots: underdevelopment and dependency."[20]

The centerpiece of the *argentinización* project was an attempt to reorient and redistribute bank credit in favor of locally owned firms. Reserve requirements restricting loan operations were reduced, thus increasing credit available to the private sector. This increase in liquidity was given a nationalist thrust by mandating that new loans go exclusively to firms with a majority of national capital. In addition to aiding the financing of national capital's expansion, Ferrer's plan to *argentinizar el crédito* was designed to force transnational firms to increase their reliance on external loans and new investment from parent firms in order to bolster the Central Bank's foreign-exchange position. However, this reversal of previous state policies had two drawbacks. First, it would increase Argentina's already rapidly growing foreign debt, thus placing a new burden on the delicate balance-of-payments situation. Second, many transnational firms were able to take advantage of the situation by stretching out payment schedules to local suppliers and by raising the prices on essential inputs consumed by local purchasers.[21]

A second major piece of nationalist legislation, the so-called "'Buy National' Law" (*Ley de Compre Nacional*), was approved in late December 1970. This measure required state agencies and enterprises to channel purchases away from imported goods toward local basic industries using national technologies. The law was thus designed to make it possible for local industry to compete on an equal footing with the transnationals.[22] Implementation, however, proved extremely difficult. The microeconomic needs of individual state enterprises and the macroeconomic limitations of the state budget combined to severely limit the effectiveness of the *Compre Nacional* law, and therefore the actual degree of support for state-sponsored vertical integration and reduced dependency.

An additional major obstacle to a nationalist reorientation of economic strategy was the Ferrer team's inability to make fundamental changes in the fiscal policies inherited from Krieger Vasena, Dagnino Pastore, and Moyano Llerena. This was due primarily to the difficulties of taking effective command over the agencies involved and to the rigidities in spending and taxing policies imposed by mounting economic problems and worsening social tensions. By mid-1971, in fact, there was a full-blown fiscal crisis caused by deficit financing of current and capital spending. Conflicting accumulation and legitimation needs, especially the regime's overtures to labor and the middle sectors, further aggravated this crisis and blocked meaningful steps toward the type of state capitalism implied by Levingston's nationalist rhetoric. Consequently, Ferrer's attempt to reorient state policies was soon overrun by mounting difficulties with the external sector.

The success of the Ferrer project depended on resolving conflicting accumulation and legitimation needs on the wage and price fronts. Levingston's political fortunes and his plan to broaden political support depended largely on a favorable response from labor and local industrialists, while Ferrer's program was predicated on reactivating demand in the less dynamic consumer non-durable sector and, to a lesser extent, in certain branches of the durable goods sector. Both requirements were conducive to a more flexible incomes policy. Consequently, Ferrer proposed wage guidelines that would both sustain demand in these sectors and protect wages from inflation.[23]

Initially, Ferrer's intention was to revive and strengthen earlier price agreements with leading firms. When such "voluntary" measures proved insufficient to contain inflation, they were supplemented with new legislation creating a National Price Commission and empowering the Secretary of Industry and Commerce to fix prices on a list of goods including both strategic industrial products and items of popular mass consumption. Additional interventionist legislation gave the state expanded powers to regulate price and supply by overseeing commercialization and distribution, along with the authority to set maximum prices and profit margins. Ferrer's final price-control measure, the imposition of a *veda* prohibiting the domestic sale of beef on certain days so as to increase supplies for export, was also the most controversial, symbolizing the mounting opposition among entrepreneurs to his entire project. The storm generated by the *veda*, including an unprecedented four hours of televised debate from the "Situation Room" in the Casa Rosada, along with protests from virtually all other sectors of business and commerce, laid bare Ferrer's lack of support among the private sector.[24]

Entrepreneurial Reaction to Argentinización

From Ferrer's appointment in October until Levingston's fall twenty-one weeks later, the different fractions of capital and their representative organizations underwent a process of polarization and confrontation with the regime. This polarization, however, was different from the internal divisions that characterized the Krieger Vasena project, which had reflected the bid for hegemony by the transnationalized fractions on the basis of a long-term program to restructure Argentine capitalism.

Paradoxically, the halt of the political and economic offensive by the dominant groups initially strengthened the position of the Unión Industrial by bringing a new cohesion to the ACIEL's alignment of industrial, financial, commercial, and agricultural interests. Their opposition to *argentinización* assumed the form of an ideological critique of the expansion of the state's economic role. This critique focused on the issues of statism, nationalism, inflation, and the threat of "socialism" and "totalitarianism," rather than on specific policies.

The Unión Industrial adopted not only the issues but even the highly political and polemical language that previously had been more typical of the Sociedad Rural and the ACIEL's pre-Keynesian wing.[25] The Unión Industrial pointedly reminded Levingston that the organization was forced to "assume its responsibility to warn" the public that Ferrer's policies would "lead directly to the socialization of the means of production, that is toward the structuring of a society in which all economic, political, and union power is concentrated in an omnipotent state, managed and directed by a small number of individuals."[26]

In contrast to big capital's posture, the Confederación General Económica moved aggressively to take the political offensive. The CGE sought to capitalize on the political vacuum created by Onganía's ouster and the indecision of the first months of the Levingston regime by stepping up the polemical tone of its rhetoric in defense of the "national patrimony" against U.S. domination and local "sellouts" in high places. A corollary was a carefully modulated rapprochement with the CGT. This strategy of populist alliances and "dialogue with democratic forces" was constructed around defense of the national firm, the internal market, and full employment.

The first phase of the CGE's political offensive, lasting from May to October 1970, consisted of a series of regional meetings to mobilize the support of small and medium-sized capital in order to buttress the CGE's claim to represent some 800,000 entrepreneurs. This offensive culminated in Buenos Aires in late October, just after Ferrer's appointment, with the consolidation of the leadership position of José Ber Gelbard, the CGE's president. Gelbard's position at this time was that "without political solutions there will be no economic solutions, and without economic solutions there will be no possibility of social solutions."[27]

The second phase of the CGE's offensive roughly coincided with the launching of the campaign for *argentinización* of the economy. Under Ferrer, for the first time since 1955 the CGE enjoyed considerable representation in the top policymaking levels of the state. Although Ferrer was not particularly close to the Gelbard group, CGE members were appointed to positions in the Central Bank, the Banco de la Nación, the Banco Hipotecario, the Ministry of Social Welfare, as well as to several governorships. Although Gelbard had said that the situation was "more favorable than in many years," the CGE did not give Ferrer its total support, preferring a more cautious wait-and-see approach.[28]

By the beginning of 1971, the CGE began to distance itself more clearly from the Levingston-Ferrer project. The CGE's waning enthusiasm stemmed from the regime's rapid loss of vital military support and from the emergence of center-left political coalitions, a rise in labor militancy, and redoubled guerrilla activities. Such opposition made it apparent that Levingston's hope to "deepen the revolution" through the creation of a strong state-controlled political movement was in serious jeopardy. As the crisis grew, the CGE leadership astutely moved to upgrade its contacts with the moderate wing of Peronism, the CGT, and the middle-class political parties. None of the CGE leadership's basic demands could be granted by the regime: Levingston and Ferrer could not offer any credible guarantees—either of their own continuance in power or of their ability to implement the *argentinización* project.

The CGE's decision not to expend its political capital in a futile gesture on Levingston's behalf contributed to a progressive unraveling of military reformism. By early 1971 the regime was all but totally cut off from the important centers of power in civil society. In addition to the open hostility of the dominant groups, Levingston had to confront the political parties, organized labor, and the middle sectors, who had already begun to coalesce in a defensive alliance of civilian reformism. The regime's failure to consolidate itself was highlighted by strikes led by the radicalized, *clasista* sectors of the working class and by the increasingly bold attacks of the guerrilla organizations. The confluence of these forces reinforced the threatening image of rampant social disintegration and widespread subversion.

The "Deepening of the Revolution"

The Levingston interregnum revealed the difficulties inherent in military reformism in a complex society. In the immediate aftermath of Onganía's "relief from command," the commanders-in-chief of the three services sought to bolster the military's ideological and political unity and capacity to supervise state policies. The most important of these steps, consisting of a reform of the *Estatuto de la Revolución Argentina*, specified that henceforth the Junta would have to approve all laws and decrees of "transcendent significance." The motives for this move were clear: the military was determined to avoid a repetition of the conflict that had pitted it against Onganía. In theory at least, this reform expressed the military's intention to claim for itself an enhanced role as "co-executive" and "co-legislator" in a power-sharing arrangement with the president. This redefinition of power relations between the executive and the military was re-inforced by repeated public statements by members of the Junta on Levingston's limited mandate. In an exposition before the Army's High Command on 6 July, Lanusse declared that the armed forces "had not exchanged one blank check to Onganía for another to Levingston."[29]

The new cabinet (whose members were named by the Junta, not by Levingston) was extremely heterogeneous in composi-tion, ranging from Catholic nationalists to liberal *gorilas* turned *azules*, from middle-of-the-roaders with no clear identification to *desarrollistas* or neo-Peronists. Their one common characteristic seemed to be their support from different military factions and lack of a popular base. Trying to put a positive face on things, Levingston argued that in his regime were represented "all the extractions, all the ideological currents, all the political, social, and cultural expressions that exist today in our country."[30]

Rather than giving birth to a coalition government, the Junta's enhanced power and the ideological incoherence of the Leving-ston regime actually contributed to the Balkanization of the state apparatus. Reversing the centralist thrust of the Onganía pe-riod, each bureaucratic faction pursued its own strategy and timetable, while remaining free to attempt to veto proposals emanating from other factions. It was left to the Junta and the "military parliament" to arbitrate the ensuing conflicts.[31]

Levingston did not willingly accept this state of affairs. He attempted to resurrect Onganía's doctrine of the *tres tiempos* to argue that "revolutionary" changes in the economy were still prerequisites for institutional normalization. But he went even further than Onganía when he insisted on fundamental political changes before liberalization could be contemplated. Leving-ston's first address to the nation sought to dampen any overly optimistic hopes for quick elections by making it "absolutely clear" that the Argentine Revolution still had a mission to ac-complish, namely the fulfillment of "the revolutionary objectives of June 1966." He warned that "the revolutionary process will not be short" and that new organizations had to be created with leaders "more sensitive to national needs." An ambiguous promise for future elections at an unspecified date, to be carried out "without traps or proscriptions," only further clouded his intentions, sowing seeds of doubt among the military liberals and stirring opposition from the parties.[32]

Levingston's strategy for the prolongation of authoritarian rule was founded on the premise, widely shared among the military, that the traditional parties and their leaders were incapable of imposing national discipline and carrying out the country's modernization. Levingston and his political advisers reasoned that it was possible to capitalize on the parties' weakness to forge a new coalition at the margin of existing organizations. The primary targets were second- and third-ranking party figures who were offered the blandishments of official patronage in exchange for joining the "national revolution." Levingston's efforts to form *oficialista* political groupings immediately reverberated throughout the state apparatus, polarizing the cabinet into two camps: those in favor of "deepening the revolution" and those who supported accelerating the regime's institutionalization through a dialogue with the traditional parties and an eventual electoral *salida*.

While Levingston publicly advocated the "deepening" option, he maintained considerable ambiguity about his precise intentions. In a nationally publicized television address in late September, the president proposed a "progressive reopening of political activity" while also repeating Onganía's provocations against the political parties. He categorically stated that "for this government the dissolution of the parties, realized by the Argentine Revolution, is an irreversible decision"; he then promised to engage "in an intensive and fluid dialogue with the most representative figures," i.e., those willing to abandon their parties and collaborate in the formation of a new pro-regime political alignment. While Levingston's call for an "authentic nationalism" was frightening enough for the military liberals and their business allies, what was more disturbing still, so soon after Onganía's autocratic excesses, was Levingston's bombshell declaration that he planned to remain in power four to five more years.[33]

Levingston's embrace of economic nationalism and his efforts to create an *oficialista* "party of the revolution" provoked a major cabinet crisis in October that culminated in the resignations of Economy Minister Moyano Llerena and Brigadier General Eduardo McLoughlin, the Interior Minister. Levingston's willingness to risk this showdown reflected both his recognition of the contradictions between economic orthodoxy and political decompression, and his evident desire to prolong authoritarian rule. Levingston named a retired air force general and rightwing nationalist, Arturo Cordón Aguirre, as the new Interior Minister.³⁴ The appointment of Aldo Ferrer as Minister of Economy provided the previously missing economic rationale for Levingston's military reformism from above. The expulsion of liberals and the consolidation of nationalist control over the state apparatus marked the high point of state autonomy vis-à-vis the dominant economic groups.

Seeking to take advantage of his momentary strength, Levingston escalated his anti-party crusade against the old "partidocracy" and restated his determination to "go beyond the old structures." More ominously, in an address to 2,000 officers at the Colegio Militar, he referred to his regime as the "Government of the Armed Forces" (something that Onganía had never done) in order to remind the military that "In this government the prestige of a general of the Nation is not at stake, but the destiny of the Armed Forces is."³⁵

In the face of mounting opposition, Levingston undertook a dangerous radicalization of his basic strategy. This consisted of a year-end political offensive complete with publication of the long-awaited "political plan" and intense discussions with representatives of all the minor parties. During these negotiations, the president admitted his lack of popular support, but predicted that economic takeoff would soon spark the long-awaited "national revolution." Oscar Alende, head of the *intransigente* wing of Radicalism and one of the invited participants, put things in more realistic perspective when he warned that "if the president does not surround himself with nationalists . . . the liberals will sweep him away; he will not be able to contain the electoral imperative."³⁶

Levingston proceeded to "surround himself with nationalists" precisely in order to ward off mounting opposition both from the political parties and the unions and from military liberals. Levingston turned to left-nationalist politicians like Oscar

Alende, who supported Ferrer's *argentinización* policies and feared their relegation to political oblivion should the major political parties succeed in convincing the military to accept an electoral *salida*.

The regime's growing desperation and its declining support were manifested in the bombastic attacks directed against its opponents. In late January 1971, the Casa Rosada warned against anti-national interests and conspiracies, adding that these interests "are not always foreign" in origin. The communiqué explained that when nationalist economic measures were implemented:

it is logical to expect inflamed resistance and a growing offensive on the part of those who see their privileges reduced. . . . This reaction materializes in various forms ranging from the alarming rumor, the distortion of news and information, the malevolent creation of false expectations, to the point of inciting rebellion in order, above all, to compromise the Armed Forces. Things happen this way because the affected interests will not give in without attempting—by whatever means—to reverse the process. Whether intentionally or not, those who call for a premature electoral *salida* also contribute to this action, which would make us fall—once again—into one of the grossest forms of fraud and deceit.[37]

This transparent attack on General Lanusse (Levingston simultaneously ousted Social Welfare Minister Francisco Manrique, a close friend of Lanusse) only served to deepen Levingston's political isolation. The president appeared to sense the inexorability of events when, in a 3 March address before provincial economy ministers, he sounded a fatalistic note, remarking that because of his nationalist economic policies, his government "has had to confront a concentration of adverse forces . . . who do not want the revolution to deepen itself. History will judge their responsibility."[38]

The Rebirth of Civilian Reformism

One of the "adverse forces" Levingston no doubt had in mind was the opposition of the traditional political parties, which had grown since the *cordobazo*, spurred by the impact of the Krieger Vasena program, and which had gathered additional impetus following Onganía's fall. Juan Perón, for example, seeking to influence events from Spain, immediately responded to Levingston's appointment by strengthening his control over his own followers, naming Jorge Paladino as his "personal delegate" in Argentina and transferring the headquarters of his Movimiento Nacional Justicialista from Madrid to Buenos Aires. Paladino proceeded to impose unity on the fragmented Peronist movement by threatening a purge of all "traitors" who dared to negotiate with the regime. He also promised the faithful that "Perón's return will be soon," while warning that "in these conditions any type of dialogue [with the regime] is impossible."[39]

The Radicals took an equally strong opposition stand by vehemently rejecting Levingston's "irreversible dissolution" of the parties and his attempt to forge a new coalition of party figures drawn from the so-called "intermediate generation." Ricardo Balbín, the Radical's veteran leader, called upon the military liberals to honor their commitment to democratization while they were still able to control the process. According to Balbín, the Onganía regime had crumbled even before the opposition had organized itself—"we had not even begun to fight and he fell." The message was clear: if the military did not call elections soon, the Radicals and the other parties would use the "weapons of *civismo*" to overthrow the regime.[40]

The influence of civilian reformism increased significantly in late 1970 with the convergence of Radicalism and the moderate wing of Peronism in an opposition front that included smaller groupings such as the Partido Socialista Argentino, the Partido Radical Bloquista, the Partido Demócrata Progresista, the Partido Conservador Popular, and the followers of ex-president Aramburu. The Hora del Pueblo ("Hour of the People"), as the front was baptized, made its public debut on 11 November with a declaration calling for immediate democratic elections as the prerequisite for "national emancipation":

Our Argentina is today a territory occupied by foreign interests, with its key parts in the power of imperialism. . . . It no longer makes sense to discuss whether the priority is economic or political. The concrete, visible, and undeniable fact is that there can be no economic or political *salida* [under military rule] because Argentines cannot exercise political influence.[41]

Despite this radical rhetoric, the Hora del Pueblo coalition was far from revolutionary. All the military had to do, according to coalition spokesmen, was to join with the democratic sectors and set aside political and economic differences in a search for "harmony and agreement." They were clear, however, in insisting that the solution had to lead rapidly to an electoral process to be open to all, without exclusions based on ideology or the proscription of Peronism.[42]

The Hora del Pueblo's efforts to influence military liberals accelerated in response to mounting social unrest and the regime's evident decomposition. In order to appear a viable alternative, and to allay the military's fears about its commitment to control "subversion," the coalition accused Levingston of "dragging the country toward one of the most difficult crossroads in its history" and leading the nation down "the path of chaos, misery, and the most degrading colonialism." Even more explicitly, some Hora del Pueblo spokesmen engaged in red-baiting tactics, arguing that the military was forced to choose between the civilian opposition or subversive violence.[43]

While the Radicals concentrated their efforts on middle-class public opinion and the military liberals, Perón's main emphasis (for he also pursued contacts within the military) was on unifying the more militant forces under his command. Calling upon Peronists not to place any hope in the military (*"no transar con militares continuistas"*), Perón instructed Paladino and the Peronist left to "strengthen our followers and prepare them for the struggle that will overturn the dictatorship."[44]

A second, but far less significant, brand of civilian reformism also emerged in late 1970. The Encuentro Nacional de los Argentinos grouped the Argentine Communist Party and the left wings of the traditional parties into a popular-front-style opposition modeled upon traditional Communist strategy and influenced by the recent success of the Popular Unity in electing Salvador Allende in neighboring Chile. The Encuentro sought to build a grass-roots coalition for radical change in opposition to the elite strategy of its moderate counterpart.[45] These two versions of reformism based on party coalitions achieved significant public visibility and, especially in the case of the Hora del Pueblo, played a role in undermining the legitimacy of the Levingston regime.

Social unrest also contributed to the disintegration of the Levingston regime, just as it had hastened Onganía's fall. From

June 1970 to March 1971, strikes and demonstrations increased steadily in frequency and intensity, reaching their highest peaks of the entire 1966–72 period during the last months of Levingston's tenure. Revolutionary activity by Peronist and Marxist guerrilla organizations also continued to mount as the various groups sought to delegitimate the state and to gain a mass following.

Organized labor had not been consulted in Onganía's ouster or in the formation of the new regime, and its initial response to the appointment of Levingston was thus very cautious. Soon this stance began to harden as the CGT reacted against what it portrayed as the favoritism of foreign interests and the "great monopolies" and aligned itself with Perón's "Spring Offensive," which gave increased support to *clasista* forces within organized labor. This new hard-line attitude was expressed publicly in mid-September when José Rucci, the new CGT leader, issued a challenge to the military: either join the majority and support democratic reforms and a nationalist economic policy or be prepared to defend a "system tied to international monopolies in open attack on [Argentina's] sovereignty." The attitude that "there is nothing to negotiate with the government" set the stage for a wave of labor militancy in defiance of the regime.[46]

This shift on labor's part to a more combative strategy began to take its toll in a series of very successful nationwide strikes beginning on October 9 (77 percent absenteeism), continuing on October 22 (75–80 percent absenteeism), and culminating in a 36-hour strike on November 12–13 (80–98 percent absenteeism). The regime's attacks on "pseudo-leaders" and the intervention of the petroleum and telephone workers' unions controlled by Peronist hardliners underlined the fact that Levingston and Ferrer had failed to win working-class support.[47] This failure became even more evident in early 1971 with the initiation of collective-bargaining discussions, at which time Ferrer reneged on earlier promises and set limits on wage increases.

Underlying these tense relations in the early months of 1971 was a more complex reality. The CGT's hard line reflected both Perón's enhanced control over his labor lieutenants, as part of his orchestration of opposition to the regime, and the increased militancy of the labor rank and file. Despite the necessity of the CGT and the larger unions—as labor bureaucracies—to maintain effective relations with the state, there was no escaping the growing radicalization of demands from below for both material rewards and internal union democracy. Moreover, these demands were channeled through a more revolutionary discourse, with explicit emphasis on the necessity of radical transformations in class relations. These demands for a "profound and revolutionary change of structures" were expressed in the slogan "Neither Coup Nor Elections: Revolution."

The focal point of *clasismo* was located in Córdoba, and more specifically in two unions, STIRAC and STIRAM, organized in the huge Fiat auto and truck complex located in the suburb of Ferreyra. Beginning in the mid-1960s, STIRAC and STIRAM workers had waged a long struggle against a recalcitrant management. This conflict escalated rapidly in December 1970, leading to the occupation of a Fiat factory and the taking of hostages in mid-January with the participation of 3,000 workers. Their slogans calling for "revolutionary union politics" and a "revolutionary government directed by the working class that will liberate the country from national and foreign monopolistic oppression" also appealed to colleagues in other large transnational auto firms with whom they shared family and neighborhood ties as well as class solidarity. The situation cooled off somewhat in early 1971, but not before the Third Army Corps was forced to declare the area an emergency zone in order to control rebellious workers.[48]

However, the situation rapidly deteriorated again in early March, when Levingston replaced Bernardo Bas, Córdoba's relatively moderate governor, with José Camilo Uriburru, an extreme Catholic nationalist known for his reactionary politics. In Levingston's presence, the new governor startled and alienated all sectors of public opinion in Córdoba by proclaiming that those in power "speak with the word of God." He also denounced a "materialist conspiracy of the red flag" orchestrated by "sinister anti-Argentine" forces which had chosen Córdoba as the "national epicenter of its cowardly maneuver." Uriburru concluded by requesting that God grant him the "historical honor of cutting off the head of the venomous serpent with a single slice."[49]

In reaction to what the local newspapers termed a "return to the Dark Ages," there was an immediate and unanimous rejection of this revival of the most objectionable aspects of Onganía's corporatist dream of reorganizing Argentine society. While the media, the business community, and the military liberals denounced Uriburru, it was the working-class response that was crucial in transforming what might have been a momentary *cause célébre* into a far more fundamental and dangerous crisis.

In mid-March Córdoba's entire local economy was shut down by strikes and 130 factories were occupied, with important participation by public-sector employees and support from small shop owners, in a huge urban social explosion that recalled the event of May 1969. This episode of collective resistance, which was soon dubbed the *vivorazo* (from the Spanish word for serpent), lasted for several days, with police and troops occupying union locals and imprisoning and torturing leaders and activists in a reign of terror directed against students and working-class *barrios*. Smaller but similar uprisings broke out in Santa Fe, Salta, Río Negro, and elsewhere in the interior.[50]

What made the *vivorazo* and the growing social unrest so threatening was that they occurred in the context of a parallel upsurge in guerrilla activity. This reinforced the already widespread image of a slide toward internal subversion. From the point of view of the military and dominant groups, the panorama was indeed truly alarming. With the Peronist Montoneros and the Marxist Ejército Revolucionario del Pueblo (ERP) in the forefront, there was a general escalation of bank robberies, assaults on police, military installations, and transnational firms, assassination attempts, and other forms of "direct action." Increasingly, moreover, guerrilla activities acquired a new and even more threatening emphasis on spectacular actions intended to raise the political consciousness of the masses, especially among industrial workers and urban shanty dwellers in the *villas miserias*. The purely military side of the guerrilla struggle was secondary. Armed operations were designed not to inflict a military defeat on the enemy; rather, the "propaganda of the deed" was designed to build mass support for revolutionary contestation of the regime and the existing order.[51]

Dictatorship or Internal Security?

By early 1971, therefore, the Levingston regime was increasingly isolated on all sides. The class organizations of the dominant groups had rebelled against Ferrer's policies, while the "national bourgeoisie" hesitated and then failed to support *argentinización*. Meanwhile, the political parties emerged from their enforced slumber of the Onganía years. Finally, working-class militancy and guerrilla activity contributed to an image of social disintegration and political subversion. In short, the state was truly "floating" above social and class forces, but this autonomy betrayed not strength but profound weakness. Only the military and inertia, it seemed, maintained Levingston in power. And the military was deliberating while inertia was beginning to give way.

At the outset of the Levingston interregnum, it had seemed that the Junta enjoyed sufficient power over the president to control the direction and tempo of events.[52] The consolidation of Levingston's control over the cabinet and the corresponding nationalist shift in regime policies were greatly disturbing to General Lanusse and the military liberals among the top leadership, who interpreted these events as proof of the president's deliberate violation of the agreement that had placed him in power. Lanusse's response was to call for a political timetable for a referendum by late 1971 or early 1972. According to Lanusse's reasoning, the Junta faced the dilemma that the thesis of "no more blank checks" could lead to a dangerous confrontation with the president. The army, navy, and air force, in spite of disagreements on other issues, thus began to step up their opposition to Levingston's bid to consolidate his power. This pressure was manifested in their recommendations for the regime's institutionalization, sent to the president in November and December 1970, as well as in the increased frequency of political discussions among the general staffs of the three services. Significantly, all three services emphasized the need for political legitimacy in order to carry out a successful anti-guerrilla campaign and to cut the ground from under the more radical opposition parties.[53]

The centrality of threats of internal subversion found doctrinal expression in apocalyptic predictions that, ironically, pointed toward a political opening as the way out of a dangerous situation. In his memoirs, Lanusse gives the following synthesis of the army's strategic thinking:

[Argentina] was chosen by an international subversive conspiracy to begin a revolutionary war that it planned to extend to reach continental or, at least, subcontinental dimensions. If Argentina is able to contain the enemy and normalize itself constitutionally at the same time, making a strong, efficient, and modern democracy function, with the majority of public opinion identified with the system, . . . the insurrection will give ground not only in Argentina but also in the area as a whole. But if the Republic were to depend on force alone, with weak laws and rulers, subversion would be propagated because it would have achieved the political desideratum it looked for, which would make any tactical victory of the forces of order only a circumstantial and relative matter.[54]

To many military officers this prediction—based on Ernesto "Che" Guevara's call for "One, Two, Many Vietnams"—was borne out by the escalation of guerrilla activity and by the presence of revolutionary cadres in the widespread industrial strife that marked these critical months. This confluence of labor militancy and guerrilla upsurge (coupled with the appearance of "soviets" in Bolivia under General Torres and Allende's victory in Chile) undercut most of the remaining military sympathy for the "deepening of the revolution." The charges made by such pro-regime figures as Oscar Alende—alleging a "conspiracy" of high-ranking officers backed by "imperialistic monopolies"—only served to strengthen the hand of the military liberals.

From mid-February forward the pace of events accelerated dramatically. Lanusse met with top-ranking army generals to consider the following options: (1) Lanusse accepts total subordination to Levingston; (2) Lanusse overthrows Levingston; (3) Levingston removes Lanusse; or (4) the status quo is maintained. There was a consensus that the last option was clearly the worst. Lanusse used the occasion of his rotation into the presidency of the Junta to issue a not very oblique warning to the president. After stressing the military's internal cohesion, he reiterated his earlier support of a Gran Acuerdo Nacional as the best solution to the worsening politico-institutional crisis.[55]

Although the launching of the Gran Acuerdo was clearly designed to appeal to the moderate opposition grouped in the Hora del Pueblo, its main audience was the armed forces themselves. General López Aufranc, an ally of Lanusse's, expressed the military's dilemma: "The government of the Argentine Revolution has done important things, but it has not known how to create political bases; the population is tired." Aufranc argued that reliance on greater repression alone was futile and even counter-productive because a strategy of repression would require the armed forces "to have a cohesion and clarity of purpose that do not presently exist."[56]

The final showdown was touched off by the *vivorazo* and social explosions in Córdoba in March. Numerous long meetings between Levingston and the military leaders only produced sharp disagreements over lines of authority between the president and the Junta in the context of the armed forces' proper role in controlling social unrest. The reluctant coup finally reached the point of no return on 22 March, when Levingston refused to reconsider his intransigent position and attempted to relieve Lanusse of his post and to place him under arrest. Levingston went on television the same day claiming that Lanusse's removal was due to his failure to carry out orders given in January to prevent a new outbreak of violence in Córdoba. He also falsely stated that the navy and air force chiefs agreed with him and that Lanusse had accepted his removal.[57]

When General Cáceres Monié, whom Levingston named to take command of the army, called upon Lanusse to resume his post, Levingston's fate was sealed. With the support of the navy and the air force, the army removed Levingston from the Casa Rosada at 2:10 A.M. on 23 March. In a communiqué, the armed forces stated that the Junta was "reassuming political power until the completion of the process of the Argentine Revolution."[58] There were no signs of any military support for the deposed president and no demonstrations on the part of those meager political forces that had supported Levingston and the "deepening of the revolution." The public passively witnessed the demise of military reformism with scarcely a voice or eyebrow raised in protest.

The ignominious failure of military reformism offered persuasive testimony to the elective affinity in contemporary Argentina between authoritarian rule and a very particular constellation of class and state actors. As Levingston and Ferrer learned too late, the regime they had inherited, a regime founded upon a logic of transnationalization of markets and production calling for greater integration with the world-economy, was bound to face immense obstacles in suddenly changing direction and raising the banners of economic nationalism and state capitalism. Authoritarian political structures could not be maintained intact, much less "deepened," while drastically transforming the economic and class contents of the original project. Military reformism had been a viable political formula under Perón in the 1940s, and perhaps was still feasible in the 1970s in Peru, Ecuador, Bolivia, or Panama, but it was simply no longer capable of governing the manifold complexities of modern Argentina.

With Levingston's "revolutionary" options exhausted, the armed forces reluctantly contemplated the necessity of extricating themselves from direct responsibility for state power. How such an "escape act" fell to a more nimble military strategist, General Alejandro Lanusse, is the topic of the next chapter.

EIGHT

The Military's Extrication Crisis and the "Gran Acuerdo Nacional"

FOLLOWING Levingston's overthrow, General Lanusse and the more lucid sectors of the military recognized that it was illusory to think that the authoritarian system could be maintained without far-reaching changes. The deep divisions among the dominant classes, the rebirth of civilian reformism, the resurgence of labor militancy, the outbreaks of popular rebellions, and the rise in revolutionary violence all gave rise to a political crisis far more threatening than the one that had led to military intervention in 1966.

The complex political events of these stormy years cannot be reduced to epiphenomenal reflections of an economic logic. The political sphere, where struggles for power among rival leaders, social forces, and powerful institutional actors were played out, acquired an extraordinary autonomy and logic of its own. Following the fiasco of military reformism through a "deepening of the revolution," the rival projects of party-led reformism, orchestrated by Juan Perón, and military-sponsored transformism, symbolized by Lanusse's Gran Acuerdo Nacional, dominated the political scene.

The Gran Acuerdo Nacional, as envisioned by General Lanusse and the military liberals, was a bold attempt to limit, and if possible reverse, the political defeat the *cordobazo* had inflicted upon the armed forces and the dominant groups. The GAN pursued two related strategic objectives. First, it sought the incorporation of its reformist interlocutors into a broad political accord spelling out the concessions and changes in state policies necessary to shore up the existing order. Second, it attempted to forge a civil–military consensus supporting implacable opposition to the revolutionary changes espoused by Peronist and Marxist guerrillas and *clasista* forces in the working class.

These objectives required a certain liberalization of the regime, but the full democratization of the state and civil society was rejected. In fact, Lanusse and his military and civilian allies hoped that controlled liberalization from above might block, and serve as an effective substitute to, real democratization.

The GAN and the Logic of Military Transformism

The logic of the Gran Acuerdo was visible from the day of the coup against Levingston. At that time, in addition to naming Lanusse as the new president, the Junta pledged to end fraud and repression and to establish a politics of *juego limpio*, or "fair play," leading to elections and a "full restoration of democratic institutions." Lanusse was quick to caution, however, that the military would not brook a "return to the past" or a "leap into the void," code phrases for Perón's return. Lanusse warned that elections could not be held unless the parties accepted a prior agreement with the military. He also defined the next government as one of "transition and consolidation," thus implying that full democracy was still as much as five to eight years down the road.[1]

As proof of the military's sincerity, Arturo Mor Roig, a prominent Radical politician who had been president of the Chamber of Deputies before the 1966 coup, was named to head the Interior Ministry and given responsibility for liaison with the political parties. Echoing Lanusse's pledge to "overcome the antinomies of the past," Mor Roig announced the renewal of party activity as the first step toward consolidation of a "modern, stable, and efficient representative democracy."[2]

These democratic pronouncements were complemented by a reversal of the Onganía-Levingston penchant for dialogue with the "parties without votes" while ignoring the major parties. Mor Roig initiated a series of high-level discussions with senior party leaders, including Jorge Paladino, Perón's "personal delegate" in Argentina. Mor Roig's interlocutors expressed cautious support for the regime's promise of liberalization, while warning that, in Paladino's words, there was "very little time margin . . . to try to get the people's support. . . . [The] new government has to say now to the people that in such and such year and day they will be able to freely elect their legitimate and constitutional authorities."[3]

This turn of events greatly alarmed the dominant domestic and transnational entrepreneurial interests. Disturbed by the prospect of losing their privileged access to the regime, the major business groups began to clamor for "representation" and "participation" in the new government. Their chief apprehension was that the resurrection of electoral politics would force the government to adopt "populist" economic policies. This, they emphasized, contradicted their own highest priority, namely adherence to economic orthodoxy and reversal of the "socialization" of the economy allegedly initiated under Levingston.[4]

The warm relations of the new government with the "national bourgeoisie" represented by Confederación General Económica stood in sharp contrast to the reaction of the dominant groups. In mid-April 1971 Lanusse received the top leaders of the CGE for amicable discussions in the Casa Rosada. Afterward, CGE president José Ber Gelbard waxed eloquent in support of the GAN, predicting that the new government would return the CGE and national capital to their rightful position in the center of economic policymaking. Declaring that Lanusse placed "tremendous importance" on the CGE's views, he noted that "our language is utilized almost verbatim by the political sectors and by the government."[5]

Capitalizing on proposals by the CGE and the CGT for a "social pact," Lanusse and Mor Roig engaged in an on-again, off-again courtship with the parties, labor, and entrepreneurs. First, they took advantage of the dismantling of the Ministry of Economy and the elevation of the secretariats of finance, industry, commerce, mining, agriculture, and labor to full ministerial status. Based on the new patronage possibilities, regime spokesmen floated the possibility of a coalition government. Second, regime strategists proposed the creation of a Social and Economic Council (Consejo Económico y Social, CONES) to advise on economic matters. As a neo-corporatist body, CONES promised to open up the state apparatus to subordinate groups and give them input into the decision-making process. Similarly, in early September 1971, Lanusse's announcement of a "social and economic truce" fed the hopes of the CGT, the CGE, and the parties for influence over a government policy leading to an acceleration of the electoral calendar.[6]

Simultaneously, the new regime initiated an *aggiornamento* of the political parties and other "community organizations" to pave the way for their absorption into the transformist project. The first step was the formation of two commissions, one to negotiate the terms of the GAN and the conditions for elections—the Comisión Coordinadora del Plan Político—and the other to study the necessary reforms of the Constitution—the Comisión Asesora para el Estudio de la Reforma Constitucional.[7]

Next, in early July 1972, Mor Roig announced a so-called "Organic Law of Political Parties." While legalizing the political parties, this law also augmented state control of their internal structures and methods of candidate selection, favored the larger parties, and promoted the formation of multiparty alliances. Mor Roig explained in a speech at the Escuela Superior de Guerra that the regime wanted to limit the number of political parties to five—Peronism, Radicalism, a neo-liberal conservative grouping, a front of provincial parties, and a party of the moderate "national left"—in order to reduce fragmentation and favor the emergence of moderate government.[8] Regime strategists saw these measures as prerequisites for a possible Lanusse candidacy.

The fact was that, despite their differences, Lanusse and the major parties in the Hora del Pueblo coalition needed one another. Their mutual dependence was reinforced by the mounting economic crisis. Lanusse urgently needed a veneer of legitimacy that could only come from the parties; similarly, the major parties, which were interested in elections and in regaining a foothold in the state apparatus, understood Lanusse's need to avoid a recession. In recognition of this symbiotic relationship, Lanusse reluctantly announced an electoral calendar: the campaign would commence officially in October 1972; elections would take place on 25 March 1973; and the next government would assume power on 25 May 1973. The parties, the CGT, and the CGE in exchange gave their tacit support to Lanusse's economic program, even though they continued to refuse cabinet posts.[9]

The regime's bid to transform Argentine politics was not limited to restructuring the party system. It also included a highly professional publicity campaign in the mass media, appealing for "confidence" and "faith" in the regime's democratic intentions. This public relations blitz defined the Gran Acuerdo as "a game that we all should play" and "the great game that all of us Argentines will win."[10]

The GAN's early successes with the Hora del Pueblo, the unions, and the CGE fed the fears of anti-Peronist sectors that Lanusse and Mor Roig were proceeding entirely too rapidly with liberalization. Anti-Peronists underwent a process of polarization to the right, or *gorilización*, in reaction to what they perceived as a manifest contradiction between Lanusse's impeccable anti-Peronist credentials and his promises not to negotiate with "criminals" or subversive elements, on the one hand, and rumors of secret talks with Perón, the "fugitive tyrant," on the other. The decision by Lanusse and the Junta to return Evita's cadaver to Juan Perón in Madrid in early September 1971 reinforced their suspicions. Far from undermining Lanusse, however, right-wing, anti-Peronist resistance to the GAN probably added to the president's standing with the forces clamoring for liberalization.

An abortive coup attempt by disgruntled nationalist army officers in two important army units in Azul and Olavarría in the province of Buenos Aires in early October 1971 further cemented the ties between Lanusse and the moderate civilian opposition. The regime orchestrated a successful campaign to publicly portray the coup (and by implication all anti-GAN opposition) in terms of "democracy versus fascism," equating the "nationalist" banner of the uprising with "obscurantist, reactionary" attempts to block democratic elections. Forces as disparate as the CGE, the CGT, and the Communist Party, on one hand, and the Sociedad Rural, the Unión Industrial, the Cámara Argentina de Comercio, on the other, unanimously condemned the rebellious officers. This chorus was led by the Hora del Pueblo, which charged that the coup had been "a crass attempt originated by groups of Nazi-Fascist mentality to prevent the people's return to power and the country's institution-

alization."[11] The regime paid a price for civilian support, however. Lanusse's occasional threat to carry out an *autogolpe* and
return to full dictatorial rule progressively lost credibility. The
president's own survival and that of the moderate elements of
the regime became increasingly contingent on a successful electoral solution.

Military Professionalism and the Dialectic of Mobilization and Repression

The parties and the business community were indispensable
in negotiating the *acuerdo*, but the military still played a central
and decisive role. The armed forces faced the difficult task of
reconstructing the original ideology of the authoritarian project
and reevaluating the hierarchy of values and commitments com-
prising its day-to-day operational code. With General Lanusse
in the forefront, the top military leadership proposed a virtual
inversion of their original formulation of "economic development" as the goal and "internal security" as the means of attain-
ing it. Few officers could any longer argue convincingly for the
indefinite postponement of the "political period" while waiting
for an economic miracle.[12]

Early in his regime, Lanusse enjoyed substantial but far from
unconditional support from army generals, navy admirals, and
air force brigadiers. The abortive nationalist coup of October,
however, resolved the internal situation in the three services
in Lanusse's favor. The coup had been premised on a "detona-
tor theory," which assumed that latent, anti-GAN opposition
within the officer corps could be mobilized by a relatively small
rebellion. However, when the *golpistas* failed to spark a larger
uprising, loyal army troops successfully forced a surrender after
only seventeen hours.[13]

Bringing internal factionalism under control was only a first,
albeit absolutely necessary, step. For the GAN to succeed, the
officer corps had to be persuaded not only to defend the regime
by force of arms, but also to promote the president's underlying
political strategy actively. Lanusse's task was to breathe new life
into the armed forces' sense of professionalism and *esprit de
corps*, which had been gravely undermined under Onganía and
Levingston.

This task was facilitated because, in contrast to his predecessors, Lanusse simultaneously held the post of army commander-in-chief, thus eliminating many sources of conflict between the president and the army. Moreover, Lanusse received indispensable backing from two strategically placed allies: army generals Tomás Sánchez de Bustamante and Alcides López Aufranc. Sánchez de Bustamante played a key role in promoting the cohesion and the reprofessionalization of the officer corps and in defending the army's political independence vis-à-vis both civilian liberals and military nationalists. General López Aufranc's martial rhetoric and his reputation as a hard-line admirer of Brazil's authoritarian regime contributed to the new wave of professionalization by giving the army greatly expanded repressive functions. López Aufranc constantly reminded the officer corps of their role as fighters in defense of the state:

We are a combat team. . . . We have the arms of the country and we use these green uniforms to kill our enemies . . . our external enemies . . . and the ideological enemy composed of Argentines, of people born in the country but whose hearts and minds have been won over by ideologies foreign to our democratic and Christian sentiments and who are trying to exchange [Argentina's] blue and white flag for a red rag.[14]

López Aufranc gave this repressive role a novel twist by emphasizing the army's duty to "reeducate the people" before allowing them to cast ballots. He made it clear that those who most needed "reeducation" were the working classes, who had to be weaned from their allegiance to Perón.

The military's renewed political managerialism went beyond mere rhetoric, as shown in a new "Law for the Repression of Terrorism" that reinforced the already draconian legislation enacted under Onganía. This "passage to the offensive in the struggle against subversion" was designed to confront both the rebelliousness of the civil servants, especially schoolteachers, whose protests threatened to paralyze the state, as well as the radicalization and mobilization of students and other middle-sector groups.[15]

This repressive "other face" of the GAN entered into an escalating dialectic with the democratic expansion occurring in civil society. Mounting popular resistance to military rule during

1971 and 1972 was manifested in an increase in the number and magnitude of strikes, many led by militant white-collar workers, with government employees and workers in state enterprises in the vanguard. What was particularly disturbing was the inability of national union and CGT officials to control the dramatic increase in the number of wildcat strikes called by rank-and-file workers and local union organizations. A significant broadening of the social base of popular opposition during this period was accompanied by experimentation with different forms of popular opposition, ranging from traditional strikes and occupations to newer forms of civil disobedience such as marches, sit-ins, and hunger strikes.[16]

The so-called *mendocinazo* in early April 1972 illustrated this dialectic between popular resistance and the military's "professional" repression. With schoolteachers and white-collar workers in the lead, the capital of the prosperous agricultural province of Mendoza suddenly erupted in spontaneous protest. The chief motivation for the uprising was the action of an unpopular governor appointed from Buenos Aires who decreed large hikes in public utility rates. The significance of the *mendocinazo* was precisely that such a rebellion could take place in a conservative bastion of bourgeois culture. When the local police forces were overrun, a "regional emergency" was declared, and the army intervened with an intimidating display of force and a massive propaganda campaign to "reeducate the people."[17]

The crescendo of revolutionary violence also contributed mightily to the general disorder engendered by this dialectic of repression and resistance. Assaults on military installations, bank "expropriations," and bombings of both public and private property became commonplace in many regions of the country. The most spectacular guerrilla operations occurred in the months following the *mendocinazo*. For example, the Ejército Revolucionario del Pueblo (ERP) and the Fuerzas Armadas Revolucionarias (FAR) carried out an extremely bold assassination of a highly visible, pro-GAN military figure, General Juan Carlos Sánchez, the commander of the important Second Army Corps headquartered in Rosario. Other key targets included the executives of transnational companies. For example, the ERP assassinated Oberdan Sallustro, the director of FIAT Argentina, which was then engaged in a bitter and protracted struggle with the *clasista* STIRAC-STIRAM unions.[18]

Popular rebellion and the escalation of guerrilla activity provoked a significant shift in the military's political practice. This
change explicitly committed the military leadership to Lanusse's
own belief that the Gran Acuerdo was not a "retreat" or a "defeat," as the nationalists argued, but the "natural culmination of
the Argentine Revolution." Therefore, the army, the navy, and
the air force had to ensure that the government to be elected in
1973 would result in a "strong and stable" regime in which the
armed forces would be guaranteed a strong voice. The "battle
for democracy" was one and the same as the "battle against
subversion."

The Politicization of Economic Policy
Under the GAN

Economic strategy during the Gran Acuerdo was strongly
shaped by two necessities: to confront the growing threat to the
state (and the military's privileged position in it), and to protect
the capitalist parameters of the Argentine social order. Accordingly, the regime's strategic objectives could no longer be determined by the logic of deepening or even stabilizing the
economy, or by the promotion of the immediate political and
economic interests of the dominant economic groups.

The extremely close relations between the state and the dominant fractions of industrial and financial capital cemented in
the Onganía–Krieger Vasena period was an early casualty. The
Lanusse regime steadily expanded its margin of maneuver with
respect to the dominant business groups. Even erstwhile military liberals put distance between themselves and the dictates
of economic orthodoxy defended by the powerful business
community.

Concomitant with the state's expanded relative autonomy
from the dominant economic groups was its simultaneous loss
of bargaining power vis-à-vis Pampean agro-export producers
and the weaker fractions of domestic industrial and commercial
capital, the urban middle classes, and the working class. This
opening to groups that had previously been unable to penetrate
the state apparatus directly resulted in the rapid dismember-
ment of the centralized bureaucratic institutions created since
1966. This disaggregation of state institutions occurred as each
class, fraction, and sector clamored for representation at each

stage of policy formulation and implementation. Group competition, as expressed in bureaucratic cliques and rivalries, turned
the state into a veritable battleground for the adjustment of contradictory interests.

Initially, Lanusse retained Aldo Ferrer as his Minister of
Economy. But Ferrer faced an impossible situation. His previous
strategy of *argentinización* was no longer viable, but he had no
coherent alternative program. As the major macroeconomic variables escaped his control, Ferrer responded by making concessions to virtually all groups: wage increases for labor, lax en-
forcement of price controls and new credits for business and
commerce, devaluations and increased price supports for exporters, government-guaranteed "swaps" to enable the transnationals to obtain risk-free external loans, pump-priming public works investments to appease the construction sector, and so
on. Ferrer's most notable achievements, such as the *Compre Nacional* legislation, were rapidly abandoned.[19]

This opening-up of the economic policymaking apparatus led
to a more direct reflection of class contradictions within the
state. This new form of "bureaucratic class struggle" grew up
around issue after issue. And since "final" decisions were always subject to revisions and reversals, the state was transformed into a highly politicized arena characterized by constant
zigzags, interminable bargaining, inflated rhetoric, and inevitable tradeoffs among diametrically opposed interests. Maintaining this highly unstable equilibrium of compromises required the constant intervention of the armed forces. As referee,
coach, and the most powerful player in the Gran Acuerdo,
Lanusse became a master tactician highly skilled in the use of a
national-populist rhetorical discourse carefully conceived to appeal to the regime's opponents. To sell the GAN as an authentic
solution, and not merely a hasty retreat to the barracks, Lanusse
urgently needed "revolutionary transformations" in the economic field.[20]

Ferrer was the first casualty of the politicization of economic
policymaking. Following the dismantling of the Ministry of
Economy, overall authority for policymaking was entrusted to a
series of lackluster *técnicos* of generally orthodox liberal inclinations. Juan Quilici served briefly as Finance Minister until September 1971, when he was replaced by Cayetano Licciardo, who

remained in his position until October 1972. His successor was Jorge Whebe, who resembled a capable but unimaginative accountant more than a planner concerned with implementing a coherent economic strategy.

This period witnessed a realignment of state forces resulting in two more-or-less identifiable camps. The "institutionalists" (*institucionalistas*) generally embraced the GAN's goal of a negotiated solution to the political crisis. The "stand-patters" (*quedantistas*), on the other hand, feared that such a solution would lead to a "return to the past" in which Peronist dominance had resulted in economic disorder.[21]

The two leading agencies representing *quedantismo* were the Finance Ministry and the Central Bank. Secondary, supportive roles were played by the ministries of Foreign Relations and Justice. The *quedantistas* portrayed themselves as guardians of scientific rationality defending the "business climate" and Argentina's international reputation. The Finance Ministry generally reflected Lanusse's own brand of pragmatism, oriented to the regime's immediate political needs. The central bankers, on the other hand, practiced what their critics called cynical "economic terrorism" to defend the interests of the "traditional economic Right." The president of the Central Bank would open the cycle by urging a "return to Krieger Vasena, but with social sensibility"; soon, however, this so-called "popular liberalism" (virtually identical to traditional pro-business orthodoxy) gave way to dire predictions of an impending economic apocalypse. The only solution, they alleged, was for the middle sectors and workers to tighten their belts and for Argentina to "live within its means." When this defense of "economic sanity" ran the risk of directly criticizing the GAN, the regime, and even Lanusse himself, the cycle began again, but with a new finance minister and a new president of the Central Bank.[22]

The second alignment, the *institucionalistas*, supported "national-populist" economic policies. The *institucionalistas* were more numerous but their political support within the state bureaucracy was located in less powerful agencies such as the Ministry of Industry and CONADE, with the "political" ministries of Interior, Social Welfare, and Labor playing an important secondary role. The Ministry of Agriculture and Livestock played an ambiguous role, first siding with one faction and then the other, depending on the issue and the position of agrarian producers. Along with Lanusse, they realized that the political crisis could not be resolved on the basis of "popular sacrifice." Therefore, they opposed orthodox stabilization policies. Political necessity, they believed, called for expansionary policies as a "democratic bridge" to the moderate political wing of Peronism, the CGT, the CGE, and the Radicals, whose support of the GAN was required to prepare an electoral solution. The *institucionalistas* tacitly resigned themselves to high inflation as a necessary price for avoiding a dangerous recession. Their goal was to moderate sociopolitical struggles by rewarding first one group or sector then another. For them, a "social accord," rather than orthodox stabilization, became the regime's overriding objective.[23]

The struggle between the *quedantistas* and the *institucionalistas* served Lanusse well as he attempted to finesse an extremely difficult political situation. Unwilling to pay the high costs of a return to a more directly repressive form of rule, Lanusse and his allies found internecine bureaucratic struggles and the deepening tug-of-war over income shares reasonable ways to manage the crisis while seeking to channel dissent away from the military and regime toward the electoral arena. Inflation during the Gran Acuerdo period reflected the intensification of the conflict among social classes—basically between labor and capital, but also among the different fractions of capital—over the appropriation of the social product. Inflation thus became a "peaceful civil war" in which each class or fraction used all the means at its disposal to leap-frog over its adversaries in order to force an income transfer in its own favor.[24] Therefore, despite the risks involved, Lanusse found inflation-generating policies highly rewarding because they transferred the costs to succeeding regimes while facilitating the achievement of immediate political objectives.[25]

The consequences of Lanusse's attempt to reconcile the GAN's strategic political objectives with the exigencies of managing the economy were readily apparent. As Table 8.1 demonstrates, none of Lanusse's four economic teams could tame mounting inflationary pressures. Monthly variations in the cost of living reveal that during the so-called "social and economic truce," announced at mid-year, the inflation index registered its largest monthly increase, a jump of 11.9 percent in December 1971. The

TABLE 8.1

Ministers of Economy and the Rate of Inflation, 1966–73

Minister	Period[a]	Annual inflation rates when leaving office[b]	
		Wholesale prices	Cost of living
Salimei	July-Dec. 1966	22.6%	29.6%
Krieger Vasena	Jan. 1967–May 1969	5.1	6.6
Dagnino Pastore	June 1969–May 1970	11.6	12.7
Moyano Llerena	June-Sept. 1970	14.5	14.7
Ferrer	Oct. 1970–Apr. 1971	34.1	29.8
Quilici	May-Sept. 1971	46.0	39.6
Licciardo	Oct. 1971–Sept. 1972	77.6	59.2
Whebe	Oct. 1972–May 1973	65.7	75.9

SOURCE: De Pablo, "Precios relativos, distribución del ingreso y planes de estabilización: la experiencia de la Argentina durante 1967–70," p. 61.

NOTE: The Ministry of Economy was abolished in May 1971 under Lanusse; the persons named after that date were the principal figures in designing economic policy.

[a]Calculated on the basis of the last complete month in office.

[b]Corresponds to price increases in the 12 months ending in the last complete month in office.

period of "popular liberalism" from January to August 1972 witnessed a modest containment of inflationary pressures through restrictive monetary policies. Finally, during the period of "electoral economics," from September 1972 to March 1973, when economic policy was subordinated almost completely to immediate political exigencies, monthly inflation ranged from 5 to 9 percent.

The Lanusse regime also presided over a sharp reversal of relative prices. Under Onganía and Krieger Vasena the structure of relative prices had consistently operated to transfer income from rural producers to urban industry, especially to the most dynamic domestic and transnational firms. During Levingston's brief tenure the aggressiveness of Pampean beef and grain producers began to reverse this process. Following the dismantling of the Ministry of Economy in mid-1971, agricultural prices far outstripped industrial prices. By the first quarter of 1973 the relation between agricultural and industrial wholesale prices had shifted roughly 30 percent in favor of rural producers. Thus, despite Lanusse's populist rhetoric, large transfers of wealth to agro-export interests were one of the prices the regime was obliged to pay in pursuit of a negotiated political solution.[26]

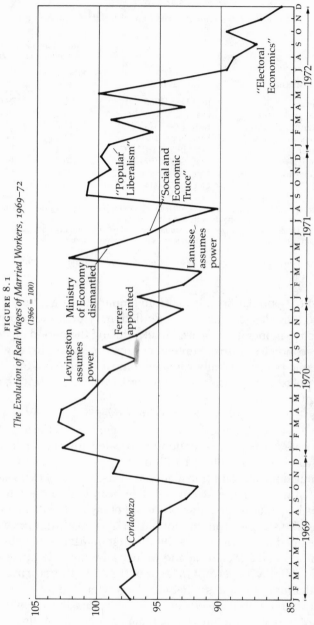

FIGURE 8.1
The Evolution of Real Wages of Married Workers, 1969–72
(1966 = 100)

SOURCE: Calculated from monthly data published by the *Instituto Nacional de Estadística*.

NOTE: Includes workers and salaried employees in all sectors of the economy.

The counterpart of high inflation and income transfers from the urban areas to rural producers was a decline in the real income received by wage earners. The sawtooth pattern depicted in Figure 8.1 shows that the recovery in real wages following the *cordobazo* was reversed under Levingston and Lanusse. The rise in real wages in the first months of the Lanusse regime quickly evaporated as price increases swamped the small raises accorded during the "truce." The decline continued in 1972, reflecting the orthodoxy of the "popular liberals." Except for a one-time jump corresponding to wage adjustments granted in May, real wages continued to fall through 1972, when labor's share of gross domestic product reached its lowest point (36.9 percent of GDP) since 1966.

The inflationary spiral generated by the Gran Acuerdo not only hurt urban industry and wage earners. The state faced a mounting fiscal crisis as it failed to conciliate the accumulation needs of the Argentine economy with the legitimation requirements of a retreating authoritarian regime. As indicated in Table 8.2, state revenues declined as a share of GDP as both Levingston and Lanusse used public spending to prop up flagging aggregate demand while attempting to respond to social needs.

In 1972, when the full impact of the Gran Acuerdo was felt, state spending actually declined, but revenues dipped even more sharply. As a result, the deficit remained at the same high level reached in 1971. Moreover, the 1967–70 trend toward increasing capital expenditure in productive investments was reversed. In 1971 and 1972 current expenses increased in response to labor militancy in the public sector. Therefore public investment, required to maintain aggregate demand, could only be sustained through deficit financing, a form of indirect inflation that benefited some sectors to the detriment of others.

The deterioration of Argentina's foreign exchange position provided a final indication of the economic costs of sustaining the GAN. From June 1966 until May 1970, Argentine economic growth had benefited from a steady rise in foreign exchange reserves. Under Levingston this trend was reversed by a surge in imports, lagging exports, and the erosion of business confidence: by the end of 1971, Argentina was in a net deficit position. Finally, in late 1972, lagging imports (due to the economic slowdown) and rising exports (boosted by favorable terms of

TABLE 8.2

The Fiscal Crisis of the State: Summary Indicators

(Millions of 1965 pesos)[a]

	1966	1967	1968	1969	1970	1971	1972	1973
I. *State expenditure*[b]								
Total	5,048	5,267	5,458	5,719	5,951	6,272	5,831	8,429
Pct. of GNP	15.4%	15.7%	15.5%	15.1%	15.1%	15.0%	13.4%	18.6%
II. *Treasury Revenue*[c]								
Total	2,699	3,336	3,598	3,821	3,930	3,578	3,260	3,385
Pct. of GNP	7.8%	9.4%	9.5%	9.8%	9.7%	8.6%	7.5%	7.5%
III. *Treasury Deficit*[d]								
Total	−2,683	−1,990	−2,360	−2,532	−2,476	−3,113	−2,763	−5,333
Pct. of GNP	7.8%	5.6%	6.2%	6.5%	6.1%	7.4%	6.3%	11.8%
Pct. of expenditure	53.1	37.8	43.2	44.3	41.6	49.6	47.4	63.3
Pct. of revenue	81.4	48.2	51.5	52.8	51.0	76.6	76.5	141.9

SOURCES: Expenditure data from unpublished worksheets made available by the Budget Department of the Ministry of Economy; revenue data calculated from the *Informe Económico*, I and II Quarter 1974, Table 39, pp. 66–67; GNP from *Sistema de cuentas del producto e ingreso de la Argentina* (Central Bank, 1975), Table 1, pp. 50–51.

[a]Deflated with the wholesale price index.

[b]Includes only the executive branch of the central government; excludes public enterprises, enterprises with state participation, provincial governments, and local governments.

[c]Includes only tax and non-tax revenues of the central government.

[d]Calculated with the following formula: the sum of (1) Treasury's "financial disequilibrium"; (2) capital income; (3) unpaid bills to creditors (*libramientos impagos*); minus (4) debt service payments.

trade) put an end to the hemorrhage of dollars leaving the country. But this came too late to ameliorate the effects of months of intense speculation against the peso by firms and individual savers made nervous by Lanusse's pursuit of the Gran Acuerdo.[27]

Realism and Illusion in Entrepreneurial Reaction to the GAN

Entrepreneurs did not immediately comprehend the significance of Lanusse's determination to confront the political crisis by extricating the military from the direct exercise of state power. Their initial reactions to Lanusse's overtures to the political parties, his rhetorical populism, and his constant zigzags in economic policy betrayed an evident nostalgia for Onganía and Krieger Vasena.[28] As the Gran Acuerdo gathered momentum and the 1973 election date neared, and as it became apparent that the military would not (or could not) countenance a return to rigid dictatorial rule, however, the more realistic business sectors began to adopt more flexible strategies.

Lanusse's earliest definitions of the Gran Acuerdo Nacional presaged the military's expanded autonomy from the dominant economic groups. In August 1971, the president challenged the most powerful economic groups to make strategic concessions in a "renunciation of sectorial interests." Lanusse warned that "There are economic and social problems whose solution permits of no postponement . . . [and] those solutions require a conciliatory attitude from all sectors of the country. . . . We all have something to give, but those who have more must shoulder the greatest responsibility."[29]

The GAN's challenge to "those who have more" was made even more explicit by Lanusse in May 1972. Lanusse argued that avoiding a "return to the past" required "all sectors to share a common minimum formula . . . that will facilitate social, economic, and political advancement." "To do otherwise," he averred, would "run the risk that everything will fall apart, even for those who—protected by a fortuitous economic comfort—consider that they can ride out the storm because they think that they are covered from all risk." He concluded by warning that "If each of us goes off in his own direction, that will be the best way to strangle the nation. But . . . the armed forces will not permit that to happen."[30]

Immediate reaction by the dominant groups was negative. During most of 1971 the free-enterprise ACIEL grouping combined public acceptance of the goal of "democratic institutionalization in a climate of liberty, progress, and justice" with a hard-line refusal to consider any economic concessions. This was made clear when the Unión Industrial, after a meeting with Interior Minister Mor Roig, declared itself in favor of "national unity," but warned that industrialists were not prepared to pay "any price" to see the GAN succeed.[31]

However, the UIA's reluctance to support the GAN began to change in response to the "social and economic truce" and the orthodox rhetoric from *quedantistas* in the Central Bank and the Finance Ministry. The UIA's about-face derived from big business's fear that continued obstinacy would play into the hands of the populist *institucionalistas*. The UIA leadership also faced internal conflicts spearheaded by powerful firms in key industries and provincial affiliates, who denounced the "centralism" of the *porteño* leadership and the "monopoly of the agro-industrial bloc."[32]

The UIA's shift toward a more flexible, conciliatory posture expressed a growing recognition that the regime's lack of legitimacy represented a fundamental threat to the political and economic interests of the UIA itself. According to the UIA leadership, the public was "skeptical and disbelieving" and had to be "induced to enthusiastic work" and greater "faith in their future." Therefore, the business community had to realize that the wealthy could no longer "impose sacrifices and privations on the popular sectors and make them pay the price of progress." Entrepreneurs were urged to "enter into the new political life" initiated by the GAN and to work to create a "climate of order and social harmony."[33]

The first concrete manifestation of this new stance came in May 1972, when the UIA joined the CGE and the CGT in agreeing to a wage and price pact. This departure from orthodoxy was seen by the UIA leadership as a "lesser evil" and a necessary "extra-economic" concession in support of the regime and the GAN. ACIEL free-enterprisers responded by roundly attacking both the UIA and the regime, vigorously arguing that a solution to the political crisis had to be subordinated to "sound" economic policies.[34]

The existence of two different strategies among the dominant economic groups became public in September 1972, just when the electoral campaign was beginning to heat up. The Unión Industrial broke with ACIEL by supporting wage increases in order to avoid a confrontation with the CGE and the CGT. This break sealed the UIA's commitment to the Gran Acuerdo. Given the extent of bourgeois disarray, the powerful domestic and transnational industrial firms that controlled the Unión Industrial evidently calculated that they had little to lose by abandoning the ineffectual ACIEL.[35]

The contrast between the UIA's flexibility and the rigid defense of sectorial interests by the Sociedad Rural, the Cámara de Comercio, the Bolsa de Comercio, and the other ACIEL affiliate organizations demonstrated a surprising lack of political vision on the part of the free-marketeers. The Sociedad Rural, for example, had in the past shown itself capable of effective resistance to industrialization projects that challenged its interests. But in the new political circumstances the SRA demonstrated that it lacked effectiveness and that much of its constituency continued to harbor dreams of returning to a pre-1930 agrarian utopia when agro-export interests had enjoyed unquestioned hegemony. The SRA's ability to play the new political game effectively was also constrained by the emergence of dissident groups within the organization. Unlike the UIA, however, the SRA's traditionalist sectors prevailed over reformist currents. The SRA also confronted challenges from other groups such as the Federación Agraria Argentina, representing smaller producers, and militant peasant leagues calling for an agrarian reform.[36]

The SRA blamed both the Lanusse regime's support for "disorderly industrialization" and those "parties and candidates who have formulated public declarations of marked statist and interventionist orientation" for the deepening political crisis. The SRA's denunciation of the regime's "superficial" policies, the parties, the CGE, and the CGT was complemented by reiterated demands for stronger controls over labor and a "return to law and order."[37] This hard-line position deepened the Sociedad Rural's political isolation. As the date for elections neared, the SRA's only alternatives were either to support right-wing parties with few electoral prospects or to encourage a coup by anti-GAN military officers.

The political posture assumed by the Confederación General Económica differed sharply from both the SRA's intransigence and the UIA's defensive posture. The CGE's political practice was based upon extreme tactical flexibility and an ability to maintain good relations with the Lanusse regime while also supporting Perón and the democratic opposition.

The CGE maintained generally good relations with the Lanusse regime throughout the middle months of 1971, supporting, for example, the creation of a Social and Economic Council. The CGE even proposed a "national unity" cabinet of politicians and Peronist and Radical party *técnicos*. The CGE also strongly backed Lanusse against "fascist" threats from nationalist hardliners within the military. By late 1971 and early 1972, however, CGE president Gelbard began to voice disillusionment over the ascendancy of the "popular liberals" within the regime. According to Gelbard, the regime was using "CGE language" to legitimate orthodox policies which violated the GAN itself. He also charged that a "non-national group" in the state, in collusion with its ACIEL allies, was consciously subverting the process of democratization.[38]

The CGE gradually moved to stake its claim to leadership within the rapidly expanding opposition front by broadening its populist discourse as the "authentic interpreter" of the demands of the middle sectors and the working class, including the demand for an end to authoritarianism and a rapid democratization of national life.[39] This bid for a major role in the democratic opposition produced a quick rebuke from Lanusse, who questioned the moral authority of its leaders. The CGE also confronted an attempt by the ACIEL and a dissident internal faction to oust Gelbard and his allies. In contrast to the UIA and the SRA, however, the CGE emerged from its period of internal strife more united than ever and with a clear vote of confidence in Gelbard's opposition strategy.[40]

By September-October 1972, Gelbard had maneuvered the CGE into an irrevocable alliance with the Peronist-led opposition front. Although the CGE did not directly endorse Peronist candidates, there was little doubt that it was an active, and indeed indispensable, participant in Perón's strategy to defeat Lanusse and the GAN.

War Games: "I Have Two Hands and I Use Both of Them"

The Gran Acuerdo confronted a thorny political dilemma. How could Lanusse and the military honor their promise of a *juego limpio*, with "neither vetoes nor proscriptions," while avoiding the "leap into the void" symbolized by a Perón candidacy for the presidency? The solution was to force Perón's voluntary "renunciation," making it appear that, in Mor Roig's words, Perón "can be, but does not want to be, a candidate."[41] This strategy's main drawback was that it required direct negotiations with Perón himself, as well as the risk that Perón might well decide "to kick over the negotiating table" and sabotage the entire transformist enterprise.

Both Lanusse and Perón were army generals by training and instinct, and both viewed their contest as a "war game." In making their moves, each adversary sought to maintain unity among his own forces while attempting to penetrate the enemy camp with as many beachheads and fifth columns as possible. The game also combined battlefield strategy with generous doses of the posturing, artifice, and bluffing more appropriate to high stakes poker.

Lanusse's initial efforts to "dominate the will of the enemy" began in Madrid, in April 1971, with highly secret talks between Juan Perón and Colonel Cornicelli, the president's trusted military aide. In a remarkable four-hour conversation, Perón and Cornicelli found some common ground. They agreed that a return to democracy was the best antidote to violent revolution in Argentina. But, while Cornicelli argued that the GAN (transformism) was the solution, Perón insisted that only far-reaching changes (reformism) under the Peronist banner had a chance of stemming the tide of revolution. The military, Perón said, was compromised because of its ties with "international synarchism" and susceptibility to imperialist pressures from the United States. Only Peronism, a "truly national and popular force," was capable of saving Argentina from Communism. Cornicelli countered with a warning that the "crazy left" within Peronism was merely using Perón's popularity to advance its own ambitions. Perón agreed, but asserted that only he, certainly not the military, was capable of blunting the revolutionary left's appeal among the working class and radicalized middle-class youth.[42]

Perón steadfastly refused to offer his "renunciation" or to distance himself from the Peronist youth's "revolutionary tendency" and the Peronist guerrilla groups, whom he referred to fondly as his *formaciones especiales.* Lanusse's offers of economic rewards, the dismissal of legal charges still pending against the exiled leader, and the return of Evita's cadaver were all equally unsuccessful in convincing Perón to support an "acceptable" candidate, i.e., Lanusse himself.[43]

Perón's masterful use of his famous "pendular strategy" of blowing hot then cold in negotiations with the regime responded to mutually reinforcing internal and external exigencies. Why should Perón gratuitously abandon the trump card represented by his candidacy? As he was fond of remarking: "I have two hands and I use both of them." Perón's carefully cultivated ambiguity kept his options open for any foreseeable contingency: a nationalist coup against Lanusse (a repeat of the October 1971 rebellion); an electoral alliance with the Hora del Pueblo; or even a "revolutionary war" based on his *formaciones especiales.* As Perón noted, these were not mutually exclusive tactics: "The path of armed struggle is indispensable. Each time the *muchachos* strike a blow for our side, they strengthen those at the negotiating table who search for a clean and clear electoral solution. Without the increasing attacks of the Vietcong guerrillas in the jungles, the Vietnamese delegation in Paris would have to pack their suitcases and return home."[44]

Perón's reliance on the pendular strategy was also influenced by the need to reinforce his uncontested leadership over the Peronist movement. The radicalization of Argentina's vast middle class following the *cordobazo* had contributed to the increasing heterogeneity of the Peronist movement. Perón responded by radicalizing his own discourse with favorable references to Marx, Lenin, Mao, and Fidel Castro, while tempering Peronism's traditional corporatist predilections (references to the "organized community" declined significantly) with ostensible approval of the utility of class struggle.[45]

Ironically, the most dangerous threat to Perón's leadership came from his own "personal delegate," Jorge Daniel Paladino. In hopes of sharing in state patronage in a future elected government, Paladino and his followers within the movement's "political wing" eagerly embraced the GAN, offering to "institutionalize" Peronism as a conventional party independent of Perón's control. When Perón became convinced that *paladinismo* was operating as an intermediary with the regime with its own agenda, he unceremoniously sacked Paladino and replaced him with Héctor J. Cámpora. The new "delegate," who was well known for his total subservience to Perón, then initiated a campaign of "unity, solidarity, and organization" to enforce greater "loyalty" in the movement's ranks.[46]

Perón also extended his pendular strategy beyond the confines of Peronism to win over those opposition sectors not affiliated with the Hora del Pueblo coalition. The most visible manifestation of Perón's hardening opposition stance was his courtship of Arturo Frondizi and a hodgepodge of nationalist groups belonging to the newly formed Frente Cívico de Liberación Nacional (FRECILINA). Responding to Perón's adroit orchestration, the FRECILINA, the Hora del Pueblo, the CGT, and the CGE were cajoled into rejecting the regime's demands for prior commitments concerning their candidates and platforms. If the military's "democratic vocation" was genuine—"without traps or exclusions"—there was nothing to negotiate; elections should be held as soon as possible. Naturally, these allies also rejected military demands for Perón's "self-proscription" as a candidate.[47]

Perón's political offensive against a "conditioned solution" forced a corresponding reaction from Lanusse. The regime tried to make Perón define himself once and for all by demanding that he condemn terrorism and "sit down at the negotiating table." Instead, Perón instructed Cámpora to issue mildly worded criticisms of the guerrillas, criticisms made all the more ambiguous by the praise heaped by more hard-line lieutenants on the Montoneros and smaller Peronist revolutionary groups. The *formaciones especiales*, these spokesmen explained, were "integral parts" of the movement; while they enjoyed "tactical autonomy" in their military operations, they operated under the overall "strategic command" located in Madrid.[48]

The cold war between Perón and Lanusse had heated up rapidly by May 1972. The president was under mounting pressures from his military colleagues to take drastic action to reverse the alarming erosion of popular support for the regime. "The country as a bloc was against the military government or indifferent," Lanusse noted in his memoirs. Some hard-line officers even spoke of the president's own "self-proscription" from the 1973 elections. This he refused to do, asserting that such a step would be a victory for Perón over the military. Lanusse warned: "If the Armed Forces disagree [with the GAN], they will also have to choose a new President." [49]

Perón skillfully parried Lanusse's thrust by publicly threatening his own candidacy. Perón's delegate, Héctor Cámpora, proclaimed: "About Perón's candidacy there is a reality: the *justicialistas*, the people, demand that Perón be a candidate and the General has always done what the people want." A month later, Perón himself went even further, saying "I will not self-proclaim myself nor will I self-proscribe myself. But if the people proclaim me and call me to elections, I cannot defraud them." [50]

Lanusse and Mor Roig were left with few options. After prolonged internal debate, the military leadership decided that in order to head off new coup threats, Lanusse had to confront Perón directly. This new attitude was revealed on 31 May 1972, when Lanusse publicly explained a series of decisions hammered out at the top level of military leadership: (1) the armed forces would retain the right of final approval of all candidates in the March 1973 elections; (2) the armed forces would also exercise the right to approve the economic and social policies of the future elected government; and (3) even after the elections, the armed forces intended to protect political and economic stability and would supervise the actions of the civilian government, which was described as a government of "transition and consolidation." The message was clear: if the parties (and Perón) refused to negotiate an accord accepting these conditions, the military might be forced to call off the elections and seek a "solution" without the parties. [51]

Lanusse's bid to regain the strategic initiative failed. The opposition was inflamed, and criticism of Lanusse within the military led to open discussion in the press of an imminent coup. Perón, in an attempt to further undermine Lanusse's military support, warned of a possible nationwide mass uprising—the much feared *argentinazo*—if the regime reneged on its promise of free elections: "Surely we want to avoid a civil war, but if we have no alternative, what can we do? We are not afraid of a civil war, although we do not want one." In a move calculated to enrage hard-line anti-Peronist officers, Perón also made public Colonel Cornicelli's heretofore secret mission to Madrid. Finally, early in July, the CGT, acting at Perón's direction, broke its truce with the regime. In a full-page statement in the major newspapers, the chieftains of the labor movement threatened that if "the people find the road to peaceful revolution closed," they will be forced to follow "the cruel road of violent revolution."[52]

On 7 July, the day the CGT issued its threat, Lanusse was scheduled to deliver his annual address to the armed forces. Buenos Aires breathed an atmosphere which the president himself described as one of an imminent coup. Lanusse had been "advised" by the highest ranking army generals to veto Perón's candidacy and to announce his own "self-proscription." Instead, Lanusse again repeated the military's conditions for elections, and startled the assemblage of army, navy, and air force officers by announcing that "the government will not proscribe Perón." A better solution had been found. To salvage the façade of *juego limpio*, the Junta had decided that all candidates for the March 1973 elections had to establish permanent residence in Argentina before 25 August 1972. All public officials (including Lanusse himself or other officers or civilians in high posts) intending to become candidates had to resign their posts by the same date.[53]

Believing that the elusive goal of preventing Perón's candidacy without resorting to a formal proscription had been assured, Lanusse and Mor Roig redoubled pressure on the parties to join the military at the bargaining table. The parties, however, countered with a "pact of guarantees" in defense of unfettered elections. Without interlocutors willing to join discussions in public, Mor Roig lamely called upon the political leaders to recognize the "urgencies of the hour" before it was too late.[54]

Lanusse and the military exhibited a curious mixture of overconfidence and desperation. Believing that Perón would be unable to recover from Lanusse's 7 July blow, they stepped up efforts to divide the Peronist movement through the "demystification" of the aging caudillo. Regime political operatives insinuated that Perón was "afraid" to return and that he had "betrayed" the Peronist masses. Speaking before 1,000 army officers at the Colegio Militar on 27 July, Lanusse, in a calculated exhibition of political *machismo*, challenged Perón to personal combat. Affirming that "nothing replaces the physical presence of the commander," Lanusse charged that the ex-president was a coward. Perón refused to come to Argentina because "he does not have the guts to return" (*"no le da el cuero para volver"*).[55]

The political conjuncture was thus extremely contradictory, providing ample terrain for maneuvers by both antagonists. Events initially seemed to evolve according to the regime's overall strategy, which assumed that as the campaign got under way the parties would reluctantly agree to the military's demands. Perón responded to this effort to limit his pendular strategy by trying to bypass Lanusse and Mor Roig. Perón intimated that he could not negotiate with a regime in crisis but was anxious to reach an accord with the armed forces, whom he said were a worthy interlocutor. Accordingly, in early October, Perón made public his Plan de Reconstrucción Nacional, which he presented as an alternative to the Gran Acuerdo. His plan, Perón said, was the "most generous and patriotic concession" that civilians could offer the military. The main concession was the promise to consider the "explicit determination of the future organic participation of the Armed Forces" in the future civilian government. This, Perón said, was the military's last chance to avoid "a future of anarchy, instability, and violence."[56]

Perón gave other indications that the regime had miscalculated in judging his strategy. On 17 October a date of important symbolic significance to the Peronist masses, Perón announced that he would soon return to Argentina, and called upon Peronists and the nation as a whole to accept his return as a "token of peace" and national reconciliation.[57] To the surprise and consternation of Lanusse, the military, and civilian anti-Peronists, Perón did return to Argentina as promised, on 17 November, after seventeen years of exile. Perón's arrival constituted a tremendous defeat for Lanusse, a defeat compounded by the tumultuous throng of 500,000 people anxious to meet their leader at Ezeiza International Airport outside Buenos Aires. Furthermore, the military blundered in blocking the crowd (approximately 20,000 troops were employed) and in keeping Perón a virtual prisoner at the airport hotel before letting him move to his house in a Buenos Aires suburb. Particularly galling was the highly visible presence of the Peronist Left chanting the slogans and waving the banners of the *formaciones especiales*.[58]

Perón had been forced to leave his self-described "golden cage" in Madrid, but his presence in Buenos Aires certainly did not imply submission to the GAN. On the contrary, "the physical presence of the commander" allowed Perón to regroup his forces in preparation for a final attack against a disoriented foe. In addition to defeating the military's demystification campaign, Perón's return confirmed his hegemony over a "combative" Peronism and consolidated his alliances with non-Peronist sectors, especially with the Radicals and the Hora del Pueblo. Perón's projection of the image of a united "civilian party" was cultivated in large, carefully orchestrated multiparty extravaganzas, exchanges of *abrazos* with old adversaries like Ricardo Balbín, the Radicals' presidential candidate, and gestures of reconciliation over national television. Perón's homecoming culminated in early December with the CGT and the CGE signing an Acta de Compromiso Nacional setting forth a platform for democracy and "national liberation."[59]

The choice of the presidential and vice presidential candidates of the recently formed Frente Justicialista de Liberación (FREJULI) was the most difficult challenge to face Perón during his stay in Buenos Aires. In addition to the top posts, the candidacies for provincial governors, deputies, senators, and thousands of minor positions were also at stake. Perón not only had to conciliate the demands of his non-Peronist allies, he also had to bring peace to the feuding factions of his own movement. Within Peronism, the main actors were the weak "political wing," which had no entrenched grass-roots organization, the radicalized Peronist Youth, which was able to mobilize a large popular following, and the powerful labor movement, which was resentful over attacks on its leaders by the Left as venal "labor bureaucrats" and "traitors."

These conflicts could only be resolved by fiat of the leader. On 14 December Perón unexpectedly left for Paraguay, leaving behind written instructions that were revealed in a turbulent session of the Congress of the Peronist party: Héctor J. Cámpora was tapped for the presidential nomination and Vicente Solano Lima, head of the Partido Conservador Popular, was named for the second spot.[60]

The Final Countdown

The electoral campaign began in earnest in early January 1973, with nine parties or coalitions competing for the presidency, with the following candidates: (1) Frente Justicialista de Liberación, Héctor J. Cámpora; (2) Unión Cívica Radical, Ricardo Balbín; (3) Alianza Popular Federalista, Francisco Manrique; (4) Alianza Popular Revolucionaria, Oscar Alende; (5) Alianza Republicana Federal, General (Ret.) Ezequiel Martínez; (6) Nueva Fuerza, Julio Chamizo; (7) Partido Socialista Democrático, Américo Ghioldi; (8) Partido Socialista de los Trabajadores, Juan Carlos Coral; and (9) Frente de Izquierda Popular, Jorge Abelardo Ramos.

The real contest shaped up between the center-left forces of party reformism—Cámpora and Balbín—and the right-wing groups identified with the Gran Acuerdo: Manrique, Martínez, and Chamizo. The only real challenge from the left came from Alende, who was supported by the vestiges of the old *intransigente* wing of Radicalism, the progressive wing of Christian Democracy, and the still-illegal Communist party.[61]

The early stages of the campaign were marked by optimism on the part of the regime and the dominant groups, who were buoyed by a plethora of scarcely sophisticated "pop surveys" conducted by the intelligence services and the mass media. Underlying this veritable "sociological war" was the expectation that the FREJULI would be limited to 35–40 percent of the vote, and that in the runoff election required by the reformed electoral code imposed by the regime all of the anti-Peronist forces would unite behind either Manrique, Martínez, or Balbín.[62]

This optimism, however, quickly waned when the combination of guerrilla violence, Perón's soft line toward the *formaciones especiales*, and military repression generated fresh demands for drastic action by military and civilian hard-liners. Some called for the veto of Cámpora's candidacy and the proscription of the FREJULI, while the more extreme advocated a coup to depose Lanusse and to return the country to full-blown dictatorial rule. Anything, it seemed, was preferable to the dreaded "leap into the void."

New repressive measures were instituted in response to an upsurge of guerrilla violence following the escape of top Montonero and ERP leaders from Trelew Military Prison in Patagonia. Simultaneously, Lanusse and other high-ranking officers attacked the FREJULI, charging Perón and his lieutenants with "complicity with terrorism."[63] Perón answered with a rhetorical escalation of his own. Commenting on the ERP's assassination of Admiral Emilio Berisso in late December, Perón remarked: "If I were fifty years younger, it would not be hard to understand if I went around planting bombs and taking justice into my own hands." Cámpora's benevolence toward the highly visible presence of the "revolutionary tendency" in his campaign only exacerbated matters. The civilian and military anti-Peronists' worst fears seemed confirmed by the popular slogan of the FREJULI campaign, *"Cámpora al gobierno, Perón al poder,"* which was clearly meant to imply that it would be Perón himself who would be calling the shots in the future government, not a domesticated "Peronism without Perón."[64]

Lanusse made a last desperate plea to the parties for an accord to guarantee the realization of elections on terms acceptable to the military. Both Perón and Balbín, however, stood fast by the earlier agreement hammered out by the Hora del Pueblo. Perón said that "everything is all arranged" between Peronism and Radicalism, the two major parties. Balbín and Cámpora met with the U.S. ambassador and publicly rejected the military's claim that the elections would only give birth to a "transition" government.[65]

The Gran Acuerdo and military transformism had come to a dead end. What else was left to be negotiated? Confronted with this somber prospect, support for the elections among powerful economic groups and even among right-wing Peronist unions eroded sharply. An insistent rumor campaign hinted that Lanusse himself might be sacrificed and that the elections themselves could be "indefinitely" postponed. The crucial question was the military's attitude in the face of a Peronist victory. Some hard-liners even argued that a Radical victory would be equally unacceptable; after all, didn't the party's tacit alliance with Perón demonstrate the "unreliability" of a Balbín government?[66]

As the crisis reverberated throughout the military, Lanusse found himself increasingly bereft of support from the officer corps. Symptomatic of the disarray was the ironic fact that Generals Sánchez de Bustamante and López Aufranc, who had earlier been stalwart supporters of the GAN, now represented antagonistic factions, both of which acted independently of La-nusse.[67] Lanusse responded by reasserting his dwindling authority with the presentation of two virtually identical documents, one signed by 53 active-duty army generals and the other by the Junta itself. These documents set forth "Five Points" which the military saw as crucial for protecting their cohesion and fundamental corporate interests under the soon-to-be elected government:

1. Respect for the Constitution and all existing laws and decrees issued since 1966 [i.e., no modification in either the "anti-subversion" legislation or the "reforms" regulating the political parties and the electoral process].

2. Full military support for the maintenance of "authentic democracy," "republican institutions," and the "full enjoyment of liberty" [i.e., a prohibition of Peronist "totalitarianism"].

3. Military insistence on the "independence and permanence of Judicial Powers" [i.e., no removal of judges named since 1966 to the Supreme Court or lesser courts].

4. A military veto of "indiscriminate amnesty" for those convicted or charged with subversion and terrorism or acts related to such activities [i.e., continuation of limits on free speech and abridgment of rights of association].

5. Military insistence that in the future "transition government," the commanders of the army, navy, and air force be accorded full ministerial rank, be allowed a free hand in managing the armed forces' internal affairs free from "political" interference, and be given full authority to protect the nation's internal and external security.[68]

Again the major parties refused to negotiate. In spite of the regime's last-ditch efforts to influence the vote, the FREJULI campaign took on an air of invincibility. Héctor Cámpora's pledge that with his victory "the Argentine people will return . . . as the protagonist of their own history"[69] was powerful medicine for a population suffering from nearly seven years of military dictatorship.

On 11 March 1973, in the country's freest elections since 1946, the FREJULI ticket received almost 6 million votes of the nearly 12 million votes cast. Cámpora's 49.6 percent total fell just short of the "50 percent plus one" vote required to avoid a runoff. The military ran up the white flag, however, and the day after the

TABLE 8.3

The 11 March 1973 Election Results

Candidate and party	Votes	Pct.
Cámpora (FREJULI)	5,907,464	49.6%
Balbín (UCR)	2,537,605	21.3
Manrique (APF)	1,775,876	14.9
Alende (APR)	885,201	7.4
Martínez (ARF)	347,215	2.9
Chamizo (NF)	234,188	2.0
Ghioldi (PSD)	109,068	0.9
Coral (PST)	73,796	0.6
Ramos (FIP)	48,571	0.4
Votes invalidated	7,152	–
Total valid votes	11,911,832	100.0%
Total registered voters	14,337,427	turnout 83.1%

SOURCE: Calculated from *La Nación*, 31 Mar. 1973.

voting Lanusse declared Cámpora and Solano Lima the winners. FREJULI candidates also won an overwhelming victory in
the lesser races, a victory that was confirmed in the 15 April
runoff for offices where no candidate had initially received a majority. The FREJULI won 20 out of 22 provincial governorships,
including victories for candidates close to the "revolutionary
tendency" in Buenos Aires, Córdoba, Mendoza, San Luis, Salta,
and Chubut. The FREJULI also won 45 of the 69 Senate seats
and 146 of the 243 seats in the Chamber of Deputies. The sec-
ond-place Radicals elected 12 senators and 51 deputies in the
national legislature.

Table 8.3 sheds additional light on the military's defeat at the
polls. Roughly 80 percent of the voters (summing the votes for
the FREJULI, the Radicals, Alende, and the three small left parties) roundly rejected seven years of military tutelage. Only
about 20 percent of the voters supported candidates identified
with the Argentine Revolution's policies. Brigadier Martínez,
the candidate closest to the regime, received only 2.9 percent of
the popular vote, while the candidate of the Nueva Fuerza, a
party committed to neo-liberal business-oriented policies, was
rewarded with only 2.0 percent of the vote. Together, these parties fell short of Oscar Alende, the major option on the Left, who
garnered 7.4 percent. Only Francisco Manrique, who espoused
a conservative brand of paternalistic populism, was able to make

a respectable showing, with a third-place finish of 14.9 percent. As had been the case in every free election since 1916, the dominant sectors of Argentine society had failed to convert their economic and social domination into an effective conservative presence in the electoral arena.[70]

The agony for the military was not yet over; nearly eleven weeks remained until Cámpora's inauguration on 25 May. Sullenly, the military began to accept the inevitability of a transfer of power. The military's preparation for its retreat to the barracks was eased during this interlude by Perón's and Cámpora's conciliatory posture. Public and private messages from both men let the military know that the future authorities would not tolerate further guerrilla activity. Perón also made self-effacing remarks to the effect that he was "just a soldier in the ranks" and did not intend to share power with Cámpora. The promise that Perón would wield effective power was "just a slogan invented by the *muchachos*."[71]

Héctor Cámpora assumed the presidency on 25 May 1973, ending seven years of military rule and seventeen years of Peronism's proscription from political participation through legal channels. Hundreds of thousands of citizens in Buenos Aires and throughout the interior exuberantly paraded through the streets hurling insults against Lanusse and the military and hailing Juan Domingo Perón as a hero and savior of the country. Prominent among the numerous foreign delegations in attendance at the Casa Rosada when Lanusse turned over the presidential baton to Cámpora were presidents Salvador Allende of Chile and Osvaldo Dorticós of Cuba, who stood at their colleague's side throughout the ceremony. In contrast, U.S. Secretary of State William Rogers, fearing the risk of a motorcade down Avenida 25 de Mayo, stayed away from the ceremonies. The victory was further symbolized by the epithets hurled at Lanusse and the commanders of the navy and air force when they departed from the presidential palace. The populace chanted "*¡Se van, se van y nunca volverán!*" ("They've gone, they've gone, and they won't be back again!").

Cámpora's three-hour inaugural address before Congress set forth the new regime's national-populist platform. On domestic issues, the new president stressed economic "reconstruction" and social welfare. On international issues, Cámpora pledged himself to "national liberation" in accord with Peronism's "Third Position" in the struggle against "both imperialisms."[72] The new president soon made it clear that he intended to exercise the powers of the commander-in-chief as mandated by the 1853 Constitution. In his first address to the military, Cámpora rejected the military's doctrine of apolitical military professionalism—which he criticized as "aristocratic and anachronistic." In its place, Cámpora praised the Peronist doctrine of an "alliance between the People and the Armed Forces." "You are not a movement or a political party at the service of [privileged] sectors," Cámpora reminded the assembled officers: "If the People and the Armed Services are the same entity, both should be united in the struggle for the national interests as they were defined on 11 March 1973."[73]

The Legacy of the "Argentine Revolution"

An Argentine sociologist has written that "Argentina has been built like a palimpsest of half-concluded projects."[74] No project in Argentine history was ever more "half-concluded" than Lanusse's attempt to extricate the military from direct responsibility for state power through the Gran Acuerdo Nacional. This chapter has sought to underscore and recapture the autonomy of the political sphere and struggles for power during this confused period, rejecting those interpretations which would reduce these complex events to an abstract economic logic. A brief recapitulation will serve to place this analysis in perspective.

The armed forces' assumption of a more direct political role in a regime in crisis was shaped by the top leadership's perception of the steps necessary to protect the military's basic corporate interests as an institution (i.e., internal cohesion, autonomy from external political forces, respect for professional norms, etc.). These corporate interests were threatened by class conflicts and political struggles that were reproduced, albeit in mediated fashion, within the armed forces themselves. This confluence of external and internal pressures crystallized in the emergence of a distinct "state interest" which redefined the strategic thrust of the military's traditional political managerialism.

In the case of Lanusse's military transformism, the unfolding of this statist logic had manifestly contradictory consequences. On the one hand, the armed forces largely succeeded in reinforcing their professionalism and safeguarding their internal cohesion. On the other hand, the rest of the state apparatus, especially the agencies responsible for economic policy, experienced progressive disaggregation in the face of a virtual invasion by a reactivated civil society. The state thereby was stripped of most of the remaining vestiges of its relative autonomy, rapidly becoming an arena for intense bureaucratic struggles involving shifting coalitions of state elites and their private-sector allies and clients. In short, the armed forces, seeking to implement a defensive strategy for reconstructing the political system on a more "liberal"—but not more democratic—basis, partially unhinged the "superior" interests of the state apparatus from the logic of capital accumulation that had informed the authoritarian project. For the rest of the state, however, the conventional boundaries normally insulating state elites from society were seriously undermined.

In a final irony, the armed forces' commitment to the protection of the system as a whole (and as distinguished from the specific economic-corporate interests of the dominant classes) paradoxically undermined the state's capacity to assure compliance with the basic functional requisites of capitalist accumulation. This paradox was exemplified by Lanusse's forced reliance on inflation to create the political maneuvering room needed for an elite-controlled liberalization of the authoritarian regime.

Similarly, Lanusse and Mor Roig attempted to co-opt the more pliant union leaders and absorb their reformist interlocutors in the Hora del Pueblo front while simultaneously conducting an implacable politico-military campaign to prevent Juan Perón from playing a decisive role in the elections and in a future "transition" government. Furthermore, the Gran Acuerdo's combination of liberalization and repression exacerbated the processes of radicalization and polarization that were sweeping large portions of Argentina's middle-class and working-class youth into militant and in some cases extremely violent opposition to the military regime and the existing social and economic order.

Notwithstanding Lanusse's skillful leadership and his deployment of all of the impressive powers of the state on behalf of the transformist project, once the electoral logic gained momentum there was no turning back. The FREJULI's campaign slogan of *"Cámpora al gobierno, Perón al poder"* captured faithfully, at least for a moment, Peronism's mounting strength. This popular challenge to authoritarian rule was the cause of the fears of the military and the dominant classes as well as the long-repressed hopes of the majority in Argentine society.

Now it was the turn of civilians to solve the riddle of reconciling the imperative of capitalist modernization with the demands of a stable, and legitimate, political order.

NINE

The "Proceso" and The Apotheosis of Authoritarianism

THE ARGENTINE Revolution's exit from power, accompanied by the overwhelming popular repudiation of Onganía, Levingston, and Lanusse meant that Peronism not only had returned to center-stage, but had also assumed at least nominal control of state power. Throughout the country there was a palpable optimism that, after nearly two decades, the popular majority once again had a legitimate voice in deciding Argentina's future. In the brief span of only three years, however, the triumphant Peronism of May 1973 underwent a crisis marked by uncontrollable political polarization, mismanagement of the economy, and severely damaging international economic trends, that led, in March 1976, to Argentina's second experiment in authoritarianism, the so-called Proceso de Reorganización Nacional ("Process of National Reorganization"), which the new president, General Jorge Rafael Videla, termed "the final chapter of one historical cycle and the beginning of another." In this Videla would be proven correct, though scarcely as he intended.

Faced with civil disorder and economic collapse, the new military regime engaged in a massive campaign of state terror aimed at reducing the populace to a quiescent citizenry incapable of opposing a new scheme of economic restructuring conceived in terms of strict liberal orthodoxy. But the attempted "capitalist revolution" failed to control inflation and threatened or destroyed numerous national industries. Amid various changes of leadership and personnel, the military's attempt to reverse its own policy failures merely continued to transfer the costs of its strategy to the working class and the middle sectors, while clearing the field for a new breed of financial speculators that profited from the enactment of monetarist-inspired economic reforms.

The desperate foray into the Malvinas Islands in April 1982 and the subsequent defeat at the hands of Great Britain further undermined the economy and brought the military to the end of its rope. Interservice finger-pointing within the military in the wake of the Malvinas fiasco made clear the bankruptcy of military rule and paved the way for a rapid transition to a civilian regime. But despite the new hopes associated with democracy's return, questions about Argentina's governability lingered on.

The Self-Destruction of the "Second Peronism"

"Cámpora to the government, Perón to power" was a marvelously effective slogan in melding together Peronism's warring factions, but what did it mean? Virtually the only agreement among these factions involved the transitional character of Cámpora's government. But how long was this transition to last? And who was to determine what came next?

Cámpora's government represented an extremely fragile compromise forged among the Peronist movement's "political branch," the powerful organized labor movement, and the "revolutionary tendency" based on the Peronist Youth and the guerrilla "special formations." These groups not only competed for control over the Peronist movement, they also represented widely divergent, indeed contradictory, politico-economic projects.

Cámpora and the leaders of the "political branch" were the weakest contenders for power. These professional politicians had no strong party organization and their only real force stemmed from their claim to represent Perón's wishes. The "union bureaucracy," in contrast, controlled a vast institutional empire, with rich pension funds and social-welfare services, and could call upon the loyalty of hundreds of thousands of rank-and-file workers. The leaders of organized labor were thus essential interlocutors; no Peronist government was possible without their participation and consent. Although the politicians and the labor sector were rivals, they also needed each other.

The Peronist left stood outside this convergence of interests. Opposed to the corruption and "betrayal" of the labor leaders and the timid "reformism" of the politicians, the left wing of Peronism saw itself as a revolutionary force. The Peronist Youth's favorite slogan, *"Cámpora leal, socialismo nacional"* ("Cámpora loyal, national socialism"), captured well the challenge that the "revolutionary tendency" represented for the traditional sectors of Peronism. Perón's pendular strategy during the electoral campaign had led the *muchachos* to believe that the aging *caudillo* was on their side. After all, it had been Perón himself who had promoted the close identification between the Peronist left and Cámpora, who the radicalized youth fondly referred to as *el tío*, their kindly "uncle."

Once in the presidency, Cámpora could not orchestrate a workable compromise among these rival interests. The prominence of politicians and appointees identified with the revolutionary tendency, and the constant mass mobilizations spearheaded by the Juventud Peronista, were very much at odds with the project of class conciliation espoused by Perón, by the Confederación General Económica, and by the labor bureaucrats controlling the CGT. When the press began to report on a "power vacuum" in the government, it became clear that Cámpora's days were numbered.[1]

Perón's return to Argentina, on 21 June, accelerated the pace of events. The Peronist left had prepared a huge rally at Buenos Aires' Ezeiza International Airport to receive "an old Montonero." In their chants, the most radical sectors at Ezeiza pledged: *"Vamos a hacer la patria peronista, pero la haremos montonera y socialista"* ("We are going to make the Peronista fatherland, but we'll make it Montonero and socialist"). The climate of a popular fiesta was turned into the "Massacre of Ezeiza" by actions initiated by armed thugs fielded by the Peronist movement's extreme right-wing sectors; hundreds of those in attendance were gunned down and others were hung from trees in the parks surrounding Ezeiza.

Perón's speech to the nation the next day did not even mention the word "socialism." Instead, Perón condemned all forms of revolutionary violence, while issuing a call for a return to Peronist orthodoxy and an end to popular mobilizations.[2] Several weeks later, Perón met with General Jorge Carcagno, commander of the army, for a "soldier to soldier" talk. Similar conversations with the chiefs of the navy and the air force followed. The vice governor of the province of Buenos Aires, Victorio Calabró, a leader of the powerful metalworkers union, declared: "With Perón in the country, no one else can be the president of the Argentines except him."[3]

On 13 July, less than two months after assuming office, Cámpora and his vice president presented their resignations, thus opening the way for Perón to become a presidential candidate for the third time in his life. And no sector of Peronism, not even the Montoneros, could object when the moderates and the right wing of the movement engineered the proclamation of the formula "Perón-Perón," on 2 August, with María Estela Martínez de Perón named as the vice presidential candidate. To no one's surprise, on 23 September 1973 Perón was elected president with a commanding 62 percent of the popular vote.[4]

Upon returning to the Casa Rosada he had abandoned in 1955, Perón's aspiration was to transform his impressive electoral mandate into a broad-based consensual system of legitimate authority. Perón's preferred label for this project was "integrated democracy," a more palatable term than the vaguely fascist *comunidad organizada* of the first Peronist epoch. The "Argentine Model" defended by Perón was to be based on a Social Pact harnessing labor and capital together in a joint effort of "national reconstruction." Combining institutions of parliamentary democracy with notions of corporatist representation, Perón interpreted his 1973 electoral victory as a mandate to create a modern variant of the populist class compromise as it existed prior to 1955. This compromise was embodied in a social pact, signed by the national government, the Confederación General Económica, and the Confederación General del Trabajo, that set forth the regime's priorities of economic growth, social justice, and national sovereignty.[5]

The structural conditions of Argentine society and economy in the 1940s had favored a program of industrialization based on the national market and a broad-based alliance between the nascent industrial bourgeoisie and the working class, under the tutelage of the state apparatus. The situation in the mid-1970s was vastly different. The intervening 30 years had resulted in a highly differentiated class structure rent by multiple cleavages giving rise to intensified conflicts between organized labor and capital, on the one hand, and rivalries among agrarian and industrial entrepreneurs and financial interests, on the other. Naturally, these conflicts were exacerbated by the different sectors' contradictory forms of accumulation and insertion into the world-economy.

Consequent upon these social and economic transformations and concomitant changes in the social composition of Peronism itself, a complex inversion took place which dramatically altered traditional manifestations of political struggle and class conflict in Argentine society. In the past, such struggles had been expressed in the highly charged polarization between Peronism and anti-Peronism. But, given Peronism's return to power, the main axis of political conflict and class struggle was now internalized within the heterogeneous Peronist movement itself. The political scene under the new regime thus resembled an open battleground of all the diverse, unresolved conflicts inherited from the previous military regime, plus new contradictions generated by the attempt to reenact the populist compromise in a highly inhospitable environment.

These contradictions played themselves out with considerable violence. The union bureaucracy countered the pro-Montonero sympathies of the Peronist Youth by fielding its own "youth" group dedicated to enforcing Peronist orthodoxy in the ranks of organized labor. José López Rega, Perón's private secretary and the confidant of Isabel Perón, who became known as *el brujo* ("sorcerer"), used his position as Minister of Social Welfare to form a neo-fascist paramilitary group, the Argentine Anti-Communist Alliance. The "AAA" declared open warfare against the revolutionary tendency, progressive politicians, and intellectuals suspected of leftist leanings. The stated goal of this internecine violence was an "ideological cleansing" (*depuración ideológica*) to eliminate *zurdos* (literally, left-handed persons) and Marxist "infiltrators" who had entered the Peronist Movement during the struggle against the dictatorship.

Against this backdrop, Perón's vision of a stable democracy based upon a broad consensus among the major parties and social groups seemed hopelessly utopian. The rightist violence of López Rega's "AAA" and the leftist violence of the Montoneros and the Marxist Ejército Revolucionario del Pueblo seemed to justify and feed on each other. The prospects for compromise began to fade rapidly.

Finally, in 1974, the social pact among organized labor, the national bourgeoisie, and the state fell victim to the *coup de grâce* delivered by the Arab-Israeli war of the previous year. Argentina's favorable terms of trade were suddenly reversed as OPEC oil prices (and the price of exports from the industrial countries) sharply outdistanced the price of primary exports in international markets. Industrialists abandoned the price freeze, followed immediately by the CGT and the unions, who demanded large wage increases. Inflation, which had declined greatly in 1973, rebounded sharply upward. And just when a strong hand at the helm was most needed, Perón's precarious health gave way. Perón's death, in July 1974, was a major blow to the Peronist regime's fragile stability. The resignation of the former CGE president José Gelbard as Minister of Economy several months after Perón's death made the social pact into a moot issue.[6]

The political mismanagement of the Isabel Perón regime accelerated Peronism's unraveling. Her government adopted an essentially passive attitude toward management of the economy. The government responded first to union demands for wage increases, then ratified entrepreneurs' and rural producers' demands for price increases. Meanwhile, the regime continued to print money at full speed to finance massive deficit spending. During the first five months of 1975, inflation rose at an average monthly rate of 6 percent, the fiscal deficit grew geometrically, and imports increased while exports declined, thus provoking growing balance-of-payments difficulties. By midyear the economy was out of control.

The climax came in June 1975 with the so-called *rodrigazo*, named for Economy Minister Celestino Rodrigo. In a dramatic and certainly unexpected policy shift for a self-styled "popular government," Rodrigo announced an IMF-style shock treatment (i.e. a 50-percent devaluation of the peso coupled with equivalent increases in public-sector prices, etc.) in a desperate attempt to stabilize the economy. Lacking sufficient authority to enforce its policies, however, the government quickly capitulated before coordinated labor strikes led by the Peronist CGT and massive demonstrations of popular opposition. Acting under pressure, the regime authorized a 140-percent adjustment in nominal wages and made reluctant attempts to rein in Peronism's extreme right-wing, fascist sectors led by José López Rega, the regime's Rasputin.

Organized labor's impressive display of militant economism and political independence from Isabel Perón's weak and vacillating leadership,[7] together with mounting destabilization efforts led by various entrepreneurial and military groups, pushed the economy into hyperinflation and deep recession. From June to August consumer prices jumped 102 percent. Production fell off sharply, and financial speculation reached astronomic levels. The state itself was one of the principal losers, facing an unprecedented fiscal crisis: the fiscal deficit for 1975 reached 17 percent of the country's gross domestic product.[8]

This chaotic situation deteriorated even further in the first three months of 1976. In a last frantic move, the Peronist government again turned to a stringent stabilization plan. The peso was devalued another 100 percent, and publicly controlled prices were hiked 90 percent; in contrast, the government only approved a meager 20-percent increase in nominal wages. In March, consumer prices shot up 38 percent, while wholesale prices rose 58 percent. Inflation in the previous twelve months had thus increased 738 percent. But that was only the beginning: some idea of the incredibly rapid "Weimarization" of Argentine politics can be gleaned by extrapolating from there, for the first quarter's inflation would yield a 3,000 percent annual rate, and the March figure alone would yield a fantastic 17,000 percent annual rate.[9] Moreover, 1976 began with a current account balance-of-payments deficit of almost $1.3 billion dollars and foreign reserves adequate for only two months of imports. Argentina was thus on the brink of ceasing payments on its foreign obligations, thereby seriously endangering its ties to the international economy. The government's abdication was complete. Peronism was leaderless.

Following a long period of internal negotiations, the military, together with powerful entrepreneurial and financial interests, accelerated their plans to restore order. To no one's great surprise, and to the undisguised relief of many ordinary Argentines (including Peronists), the armed forces intervened on 24 March 1976 and deposed the now thoroughly discredited Peronist regime. There was no resistance; the Plaza de Mayo was completely empty. Populism had succumbed to the cross fire between society's demands for greater democratization and the exigencies of the Argentine political economy.

The "New Political Economy" and State Terror

Under General Jorge Rafael Videla's leadership, the new military regime displayed two prominent characteristics: first, a logic of reaction, repression, and counterrevolution; and second, a foundational logic positing the establishment of a "New Order"[10] that soon was given the title Proceso de Reorganización Nacional. Repression was at first an emergency response to widespread popular mobilization, ideological polarization, and demands for the grass-roots democratization of politics and the economy that had exploded since the *cordobazo*. These developments engendered a perception by the military, the dominant classes, and many in the middle class of an impending threat to the survival of the state and even capitalist society itself. Proposals for a sharp rupture with the past, therefore, sought a long-range response to the perceived crisis of the normal functioning of the capitalist system. Pressures gathered for the implementation of a radical restructuring of the productive system aimed at a more dynamic reinsertion into the world-economy.

The state terrorism and repression unleashed by the military regime are too well known to require much discussion. Official statistics place the number of *desaparecidos* at 8,960, although many human rights groups mention figures of 15,000 to 25,000.[11] According to the Argentine military, from the point of view of its strategic national security doctrine, the very real crisis generated by Peronism's collapse, and the general perception of a swelling wave of insidious subversion, the "dirty war" against its fellow citizens was fully justified. There was much more at stake than a strictly military operation against domestic revolutionaries. According to their ideologues, the armed forces were locked in a true crusade as the lonely and misunderstood guardians of one of the most vulnerable outposts of "Western Civilization." This mentality not only served to rationalize and legitimate atrocious human rights violations to the regime's "internal public," but also reassured those in the United States and Western Europe who so enthusiastically endorsed the announced shifts in economic policy.

Military leaders were remarkably candid in explaining the rationale of state terrorism. General Luciano Menéndez, then head of the strategic Third Army Region in Córdoba, offered a particularly blunt explanation. He observed that there existed a division of labor within the regime: "While Videla governs, I kill." He also acknowledged that "We are going to have to kill 50,000 people: 25,000 subversives, 20,000 sympathizers, and we will make 5,000 mistakes."[12]

Commando groups were active during this period, allegedly acting "out of control." But harsh repression must be seen as a deliberate policy carried out under the responsibility of the top leaders of the regime and the military hierarchy. General Santiago Omar Riveros, the head of Argentina's delegation to the Inter-American Defense Board, headquartered in Washington, D.C., gave this explanation of the "dirty war":

We waged the war with a doctrine in hand, with written orders from the Superior Commands, we never needed paramilitary organizations, despite accusations to the contrary, we had a surplus of our own strength and legal organization for combat against irregular forces in an unconventional war. . . . It is a simple matter of not knowing or being aware that this war of ours was conducted by the Generals, Admirals, or Brigadiers of each force. It was not conducted by a dictator or any dictatorship, as world opinion is being led to believe. The war was conducted by the Military Junta of my country through the Chiefs of the Armed Forces.[13]

By the end of 1977 or early 1978, the ostensible cause of the military's harsh repression—revolutionary guerrilla groups and their "sympathizers"—had been made to "disappear," both literally and figuratively.

Continued high levels of state repression after 1978—albeit gradually shifting from indiscriminate to more focused violence against selected groups and individuals—served a dual purpose. First, state violence against real and imagined opponents reminded the dominant groups and fearful members of the middle class that they still needed the military to crush the subversive threat. Second, repression came to constitute an inherent structural characteristic of the regime's declared mission to enforce political demobilization and to destroy the autonomy of opposition political forces.

This structural aspect helps explains the transition from a preponderance of direct, physical manifestations of state terrorism to more ambitious efforts to control and disarticulate forms of ideological expression rooted both in the "high culture" of elite sectors as well as in mass culture and in the daily lives of ordinary citizens. This mission impelled authoritarian elites to force a retreat into civic privatism, to encourage self-censorship by both individuals and the mass media and, above all, to instill fear of exercising the most basic aspects of citizenship. Continuing repression, therefore, was less a product of the counterrevolutionary logic of the regime's initial installation period than a consequence of the foundational logic and the long-range project to impose a vast reorganization of Argentine society and political economy.

The basic orientation of post-1976 economic policies was actually of quite old vintage, dating back to the "free trade" doctrine of classical liberal orthodoxy and the halcyon days of the pre-1930 agro-export economy. Espousing Argentina's further integration into the world-economy, variants of the same ideas reemerged during every economic crisis since the Great Depression. A slightly different version of this doctrine also had long been defended by the International Monetary Fund and by the central bankers of the advanced countries. What was new about this thesis in the 1970s, however, was the prestige of scientific-technocratic legitimacy resulting from its association with the concept of "social market economy," so ably propagated in the Southern Cone countries by economists and technocrats educated at the University of Chicago and consequently known as the "Chicago boys." [14]

According to orthodox theorists, in previous economic crises this doctrine had never been given a "full test." The unparalleled severity of the 1975–76 economic and political crisis was the principal factor which led the armed forces, for the first time, to fully and explicitly adopt an extreme version (or versions, as we shall discover below) of this brand of liberal orthodoxy.

Strict adherence to the postulates of this new liberal orthodoxy was a crucial factor differentiating Argentina's second experience in military-sponsored capitalist reorganization from its first. The new economic team, led by Economy Minister José Martínez de Hoz, rejected the economic project implemented by the Onganía regime.[15] The Martínez de Hoz team regarded Krieger's policies as insufficiently orthodox, labeling them as only a more coherent, statist version of the Keynesian-inspired strategy of import-substitution industrialization advocated by Peronists, Radicals, *desarrollistas,* and military nationalists since the 1940s and 1950s.

According to the "free market" critique, Krieger's project necessarily implied excessive state intervention in the economy, an intervention, moreover, that was responsible for an unduly large and diversified industrial park protected by high tariff walls. The orthodox theorists also argued that Argentina's industrialization had been fueled by artificially high wages, unrealistically low public sector prices, exorbitant public spending (especially on social welfare and education), and systematic discrimination against Pampean agrarian producers in favor of subsidies to urban industries catering to mass consumption. The results, according to this diagnosis, were inevitable: high-cost and non-competitive domestic industries, a bloated and inefficient public sector, and recurring foreign-exchange bottlenecks.

Based on this radical rejection of earlier growth strategies, the Martínez de Hoz team proposed a so-called "New Political Economy." This approach to Argentina's chronic economic malaise explicitly defended the need to go beyond earlier policy initiatives, which, like Krieger's measures, had left intact the fundamental structures of the economy. It proposed, in effect, to carry out wholesale modifications in the basic parameters of the Argentine political economy. Such a transformation was to be implemented by means of forced "liberalization," including the dismantling of many of the administrative controls and public enterprises that had provided the state with instruments for regulating the economy.

The centerpiece of the "New Political Economy" was a far-reaching "opening" and reinsertion of Argentina's domestic economy into the world-economy according to strict criteria of efficiency and the law of comparative advantages. Only by making the economy as a whole more internationally competitive, it was argued, could the conditions be created for a more stable and dynamic model of accumulation, thereby eventually eliminating the deeply rooted causes of Argentina's slow growth and periodic crises.[16]

The radical departure from past strategies of accumulation this set of policies represented can be seen from the following seven key points. First, there would be a reduction of real wages to an "equilibrium" level about 40 percent below the average of the previous five years. (This would signify massive income transfers in favor of those sectors catering to high-income earners and agrarian producers, conversely reducing demand in those sectors producing mass-consumption goods. Pursuit of this goal was at least partially responsible for high levels of "structurally necessary" repression of the working class, unions, and political parties.) Second, export taxes on agricultural and livestock products would be eliminated, thus allowing the Pampean bourgeoisie to appropriate a significantly higher share of the differential rents which it realized on the world-market. Third, the domestic market would be opened up by a progressive reduction in import tariffs (from an average of over 80 percent to about 40 percent) in order to end "artificial" protection of domestic industries, increase overall efficiency and competitiveness in the industrial sector, and curb and control inflationary price hikes by local producers. Fourth, many of the subsidies that previous governments (military and civilian) had instituted to promote non-traditional manufactured export goods would be abolished, thus ending what was considered a violation of the law of comparative advantage. Fifth, foreign-exchange markets would be liberalized and the financial sector reformed, and this would be coupled with policies designed to finance public-sector deficits and investments by selling government bonds in the local capital market. Sixth, public-sector prices would be raised (a measured referred to as "*sinceramiento*"), and other parallel measures designed to promote greater efficiency and stimulate a more entrepreneurial style of administration in state enterprises would be adopted. Seventh, state activities would be cut back, especially by reducing public expenditure for social welfare (i.e., health, education, housing, etc.), rationalizing public-sector employment practices, raising taxes to cut the public deficit, and promoting the privatization of some public enterprises.

The Videla Regime and the "Capitalist Revolution"

Keeping in mind these basic points, we will now turn to a discussion of the implementation of the Martínez de Hoz strategy in the period from April 1976 to March 1981. The latter date is chosen not only because it marked the exit of the strategy's principal architect, but also because the subsequent regime headed by General Roberto Viola largely abandoned the original grand design to carry out a veritable "capitalist revolution."[17]

It will be recalled that the Martínez de Hoz team came to power in the midst of recession and hyperinflation that began with the *rodrigazo* of June 1975. The policies implemented over the next five years in response to this crisis evolved through four distinct phases, with short-run shifts in direction and in the choice of policy instruments, but with a continued adherence to the original long-range principles and goals of the "New Political Economy."[18]

1. Traditional Orthodox Stabilization (April 1976–May 1977).

The economic authorities attributed hyperinflation to excess demand, and the remedy they prescribed adhered closely to orthodox IMF-type stabilization formulas. The resulting policy package sought to manipulate relative prices and impose drastic deflation. Along with greater reliance on "free market" mechanisms and a reduction of state intervention, the authorities immediately announced their intention to open the economy to the outside in pursuit of comparative advantages. Argentina's foreign debt was renegotiated with the International Monetary Fund, and a new, extremely liberal foreign investment law was enacted to attract international capital. Price controls were generally eliminated, but control over wages was strictly enforced. In an effort to reduce state intervention and to deal with the galloping fiscal crisis, government spending was curtailed, taxes were raised, and a crackdown on tax evasion was announced.

Once the IMF's stamp of approval had been obtained, the international banking community enthusiastically responded to the regime's stabilization efforts with loans intended to help Argentina straighten out its economy.[19] The foreign-trade balance improved somewhat in response to bumper harvests and favorable prices for agricultural products. The drastic reduction of real wages further deepened the recession, but without appreciably curbing inflation. After slowing briefly in mid-1976, inflation once again accelerated, reaching a level about 50 percent higher than the norm of the pre-1975 period.

By early 1977, it became apparent that the initial stabilization measures had been ineffective. While retaining their initial diagnosis, the Martínez de Hoz team in March 1977 implemented a series of unorthodox "emergency" measures. The principal innovation obliged some 800 of the largest companies to agree to a six-month "price truce" to be implemented by a combination of administrative controls and voluntary compliance.

2. Orthodox Monetarist Stabilization (June 1977–April 1978).

The second phase represented the predominance of monetary orthodoxy in the overall management of the economy. It was characterized by one of the most ambitious structural objectives of the Martínez de Hoz project: a major "financial reform" instituted in June 1977. This reform, consisting of the freeing of interest rates, the decentralization of bank deposits, and a new law regulating financial institutions, was a new approach to the long-term goal of freeing the economy by linking the banking system to short-term capital markets (while lifting most controls over interest rates) and forcing state enterprises to turn to new capital markets to satisfy their financial needs.[20] These policies precipitated a boom in interest rates, thus further feeding inflation, while simultaneously discouraging investment in productive activities and stimulating all forms of financial speculation geared to maximum short-term profits.

Largely as a consequence of these reforms, the weak economic recovery registered during the first part of 1977 began to falter. Ironically, the success of policies designed to attract loans and foreign capital, though they built up foreign-exchange reserves, also had a highly inflationary impact on the domestic money supply. In September 1977, the authorities responded by announcing a renewed commitment to monetary orthodoxy through the imposition of additional controls over the future expansion of the money supply. They were frustrated, however, because the equally desirable goals of attracting foreign capital,

on the one hand, and adhering to domestic monetarist orthodoxy, on the other, counteracted and partially canceled each
other.

The resounding failure of monetarism was never admitted officially, as most orthodox "Chicago boys" struggled valiantly to
retain their hard-won positions within the regime. But in any
case, by early 1978 the extreme monetarist vision was gradually
abandoned in practice, if not in official discourse. This change
was dictated by the authorities' inability to "sanitize" and control foreign capital movements and by their need to moderate
the exorbitant interest rates responsible for continued recession
with hyperinflation. During these months, the more sophisticated technocrats of the "new" Chicago school began to replace
the less flexible representatives of the "old" Chicago school.[21]

3. Desindexación *and Imported Inflation* *(May–November 1978).*

In line with the economic team's now more pragmatic thrust,
Martínez de Hoz once again switched gears, introducing a third
phase of policymaking in May 1978. The original analysis of ex-
cess-demand inflation was abandoned and replaced by an emphasis on the role of costs and on the need to impose greater
market discipline on Argentine entrepreneurs. This was to be
accomplished by forcing modifications in expectations regarding
the future behavior of the economy. The central element of this
new policy orientation was referred to as *desindexación*, meaning
that future exchange-rate devaluations and changes in public-
sector prices would systematically be adjusted below the rate of
private-sector price increases. In theory, at least, this was to
force inflation downward.

Implementation of *desindexación* created a difficult dilemma for
Martínez de Hoz. As mentioned above, the priority placed on
reducing the fiscal deficit was counteracted by the inflow of foreign capital and loans, which became a principal exogenous factor in inflating the domestic money supply. The policy of *desindexación* could only be effective in modifying entrepreneurial
expectations and private-sector pricing policies to the extent that
the authorities were able to generate greater confidence regarding future exchange-rate policies. Success in restoring such con-

fidence, however, made recourse to foreign loans even more attractive, thus aggravating the difficulties of enforcing orthodox monetary policies.

In an attempt to escape this vicious circle, the authorities were forced to enact several, partially contradictory policies. First, restrictions were placed on the future inflow of new foreign capital, taking advantage of an exceptionally favorable external sector occasioned by high and rising international reserves. The existing rule that incoming funds had to remain in the country for at least two years—an effort to deal with flows of so-called "hot money"—was strengthened further by a requirement that 20 percent of any foreign loan must be deposited with the Central Bank without earning interest.

This new orientation had scarcely any visible impact on inflation. The failure of the *desindexación* policy, nevertheless, did have significant consequences for relative prices, especially for the prices of wage-goods and those goods Argentina traded on the international market. A reduction in the real exchange rate of the peso in relation to the U.S. dollar negatively affected meat and grain exports during 1978 and 1979, producing a decline of approximately 25 percent in their real prices, when compared with the average for the 1970–73 period. This counteracted the 1976–77 boom in the export of traditional agricultural and livestock products, thus attenuating the earlier massive income transfers in favor of the Pampean bourgeoisie. Despite these consequences, a continued increase in exports and a parallel decline in imports (due to domestic recession), plus large inflows of external capital, made it possible for Argentina to rebuild its foreign-exchange reserves to nearly $6 billion by the end of 1978 and $10.4 billion by the end of 1979. (See Table 9.1.) The real effects of these policies on the economy, however, were very transitory. During 1978, the recession deepened and inflation remained at its previous high levels.

4. The Convergencia Model
(December 1978–February 1981).

The fourth and final policy phase of the Martínez de Hoz reign was both the longest and by far the most controversial. This phase, which retained certain key elements of previous

TABLE 9.1

Balance of Payments, 1976–82

(*In millions of U.S. dollars*)

	1976	1977	1978	1979	1980	1981	1982
I. Current account	650	1,286	2,087	–550	–4,768	–3,771	–2,241
Trade balance	883	1,490	2,550	1,098	–2,519	–20	2,584
Exports	3,916	5,652	6,400	7,810	8,021	9,150	7,157
Imports	–3,033	–4,162	–3,850	–6,712	–10,541	–9,170	–4,573
Net services	–234	–244	–463	–1,649	–2,249	–3,751	–4,857
II. Capital account	543	941	–89	4,726	2,270	174	1,979
III. Variations in international reserves (III = I + II)	1,193	2,227	1,998	4,442	–2,796	–3,807	–641
IV. Total international reserves	1,772	3,999	5,997	10,439	7,643	3,836	3,195

SOURCE: Banco Central, *Boletín Estadístico*, various numbers.

policies, was guided by the apparently simple and logical theory of *convergencia*. Using a *tablita* establishing a schedule of predetermined devaluations, the authorities announced that the value of the peso would continue to be held substantially below the general level of price increases, thus forcing a decline in inflation. In this way, so the argument went, the exchange rate would cease to be a reflection or "validation" of the inflationary spiral and would become a true instrument of anti-inflationary policy. Theoretically, the rate of inflation would be forced to "converge" toward a level equivalent to international inflation plus domestic devaluation. The policy of *convergencia*—because it was premised on the overriding necessity to create a relative price structure to provide the "correct" signals required to direct local and foreign investment into priority areas enjoying comparative advantages—constituted a fundamental element in the regime's long-term policy of the structural transformation of Argentine capitalism.

The policy of *convergencia* had differential effects across the economy. Few problems were encountered in the agricultural sector, which, because of its firm export orientation, tended to closely follow price movements on the international market. The industrial sector was the most severely affected by the shift in policy. Protective tariffs were further reduced, thus forcing traditionally high-cost firms to face the effects of stiff competition from cheap imported goods. The magnitude of this foreign competition can be gauged by the dramatic jump in total imports: 73 percent in 1979 and 56 percent in 1980.

The Martínez de Hoz team clearly knew that this policy would force many nationally owned firms and local subsidiaries of transnational corporations producing for the domestic market into serious financial straits, if not outright bankruptcy. They faced this prospect with great equanimity, steadfastly believing that this was the necessary price to pay in order to redimension, and in some cases actually to dismantle, Argentina's overgrown industrial park. If one held to the view that the industrial sector was responsible for the worst inflationary excesses distorting and crippling the economy, this seemed to be the only logical policy.[22]

A third sector of the economy—that producing goods and services which did not enter into the foreign-trade circuit—was less affected by the authorities' attack on inflation via import competition. This sector was a major obstacle to the success of the regime's policies because it accounted for approximately 50 percent of Argentina's gross national product.[23] To meet this problem, the economic authorities resorted to more traditional anti-inflationary measures, including management of demand through wage controls and credit restrictions. They also stepped up efforts to contain prices by means of discretionary fiscal policies designed to provide incentives to those sectors and firms which collaborated by containing price increases. Such policies, however, were neither very effective nor consistently enforced.

The economy not only failed to respond to Martínez de Hoz's orthodox medicine, it actually entered into a new and deeper crisis. In April 1980, a large private bank, the Banco de Intercambio Regional (BIR), failed. Covering the BIR's liabilities cost the Central Bank two billion dollars. Panic spread, and by March 1981, 72 institutions had folded. In January 1981, Sasetru, an industrial conglomerate and Argentina's largest agricultural exporter, collapsed, leaving debts of over a billion dollars. Real wages declined sharply and unemployment doubled in only six months, with perhaps 15 percent of the urban labor force out of work. Mounting political tensions and growing uncertainty fed intense speculation against the peso and precipitated a massive wave of capital flight in early 1981. The "New Political Economy" had finally collapsed.[24]

Coping with Economic Disaster

On taking power in 1976, the military issued a "Statute of the Revolution" that stipulated a single, five-year mandate for the occupant of the presidency. Accordingly, a presidential succession was scheduled for 1981. General Roberto Viola's inauguration took place on 29 March 1981, amid the worst financial crisis since the advent of military rule five years earlier. In the prior two months, massive capital flight had reduced foreign-exchange reserves by more than $2 billion, interest rates had risen to an annual rate of more than 200 percent, and the public-sector deficit had soared out of control.[25]

Viola's first response to these mounting tensions was to dismantle the Ministry of Economy and to create five new ministries, each tied to a different sector of the entrepreneurial class. Lorenzo Sigaut, the new Finance Minister, quickly announced a new package of measures designed to regain control over the economy and to forge the semblance of consensus among the members of the new economic team. A major devaluation of approximately 23 percent was the most notable new initiative. Including this latest adjustment, peso devaluation in the first quarter of 1981 totaled 54 percent, more than for the entire year of 1980.

In a move to contain the devaluation's inflationary effects, it was partially offset by a 12-percent export tax on agricultural products. In contrast, since the maximum export subsidy for manufactured goods remained unchanged at 25 percent, industry received the full benefit of the new exchange rate. In an attempt to demonstrate continuity with his predecessor's orthodox policies, Sigaut also announced further tariff reductions. Although these policies met with guarded optimism, they promised only a temporary breathing space for the Viola regime.[26]

Yet another series of financial crises, between April and June of 1981, soon returned the country to an atmosphere of generalized collapse. In mid-June, the already weakened Viola regime initiated an ineffectual counteroffensive. Finance Minister Sigaut issued repeated warnings to those responsible for capital flight overseas and to those buying dollars in expectation of large new devaluations. The pace of events, however, immediately swamped his timid remonstrations, as panic buying of dollars soared to new heights. In the midst of mounting pressure from all sectors, the authorities were forced to permit a free float of the peso for financial transactions. They also agreed to a costly scheme whereby the government would assume responsibility for private-sector debts on very favorable terms. This scheme caused domestic entrepreneurs to create fictitious "paper loans" worth an estimated $5 billion, most of which left the country in the form of capital flight.

In the face of destabilization efforts spearheaded by financial interests,[27] Viola and Sigaut were unable to reverse the economy's downward slide. During the critical July-August period, their previously muted criticism of the post-1976 economic model was voiced in increasingly open fashion. This was accompanied by redoubled efforts to impose order in the chaotic exchange market, deal with the trade deficit, and improve the profile of future payments on Argentina's foreign debt. Plans were also announced to attack the sources of the financial speculation corroding the economy and to provide new incentives for productive investment in industry and agriculture.[28]

Sigaut's brief reign over the economy came to an abrupt end in December 1981 with the military crisis that led to Viola's ouster by the military junta. The palace coup against Viola and the subsequent assumption of the presidency by General Leopoldo Fortunato Galtieri represented a regrouping of various right-wing military sectors in a new and complex realignment with the economic and financial interests associated with the Martínez de Hoz group. Galtieri immediately moved to create an image of efficiency and boldness ("the period of words and promises is over; now is the time for firmness and action") and attempted to draw a sharp line between the incompetence of the Viola regime and the new departure he claimed to offer the nation.[29]

Galtieri's efforts to project a semi-populist style of leadership collided almost immediately with the general skepticism of most civilian sectors. This response was due, in large part, to the appointment of Roberto Alemann as the regime's "super-minister" charged with centralizing economic policymaking. Alemann strongly argued that the military's plans to reorganize Argentine society had run aground not because the original project was flawed, but because policies had not been applied with sufficient rigor (presumably by Martínez de Hoz himself) and because they had been abandoned under Viola and Sigaut.[30]

The economic conjuncture facing the Alemann team was not very propitious for a return to strict monetarist orthodoxy: the gross national product fell a record 11.4 percent in the final quarter of 1981, industrial production declined by nearly 23 percent, and real wages declined by almost 20 percent. Alemann's response, which local critics immediately compared with the "Reaganomics" in vogue in the United States, was a continued advocacy of classical liberal recipes, particularly the privatization of state enterprises and the dismantling of measures protecting local industry.

Moving quickly, Alemann promised to begin immediate shutdowns of "non-essential" public agencies and to sell public companies to the private sector. He thereby reinforced his image as a rigid ideologue and stuck to his trinity of desiderata: "deflate, deregulate, and denationalize." Emphasis on the privatization of state enterprises represented a return to the original post-1976 project. But in the new conjuncture, denationalization and privatization were also designed to fulfill important short-run objectives, such as acquiring badly needed cash from the sale of assets and attracting foreign investors.[31]

Alemann's fidelity to the original principles of the Proceso was reiterated in his first package of measures announced on Christmas Eve of 1981. Beginning with the decision to end the two-tier exchange rate and to introduce a general 10-percent export tax, he also instituted measures freezing state employees' wages (responsible for approximately 50 percent of government expenditures), raising taxes, and hiking public-sector prices. Alemann insisted that 1982 would be "difficult at the beginning, but later we'll have a slow recovery."[32]

Thus the basic outlines of the overall strategy were clear enough: drastic compression of domestic demand and radical cuts in public spending to reduce inflation and further open the economy to the international market. Traditional exports were to be stimulated through the exchange rate in an (ultimately futile) effort to compensate for the heavy burden of servicing the foreign debt (see Table 9.1 above). The already deep recession affecting industry and commerce was to be prolonged deliberately as a means of achieving the elusive goal of rationalizing the productive structure. In the context of these objectives, Alemann's assertion that it would be "unrealistic" to think of a return to democracy until the economy had recovered was both completely coherent and a tacit admission that political liberalization would be postponed into the distant future.[33]

The context of economic policymaking changed radically on 2 April 1982. In an incredible gamble, Argentina invaded the Malvinas Islands, igniting an international crisis with major diplomatic, political, and military ramifications. The military conflict in the South Atlantic had immediate and drastic repercussions on monetarist orthodoxy. These consequences were twofold: on the international front, Argentina was estranged from the United States, its principal strategic ally, and faced the imposition of economic sanctions by Great Britain and her allies in the European Economic Community; on the domestic front, the economy was placed on an urgent war footing.[34] By the end of 1982 Argentina was tottering dangerously on the precipice of international financial insolvency. At the time of Galtieri's unilateral move in the Malvinas, the foreign debt was already nearing the unofficial mark of $40 billion, or over 60 percent of the gross national product.

The domestic economic and political impact of the Malvinas crisis was hardly less devastating. The first casualties, of course, were Roberto Alemann and any lingering hopes for reorganization of the economy along orthodox lines. Moreover, the conflict rapidly subordinated all economic objectives to the political and strategic exigencies of running a war economy. These considerations went directly against the grain of the neo-liberalism pursued so tenaciously since 1976. Even if Argentina somehow had managed to avoid defeat, it would have been impossible to return to orthodox economic policymaking. Neo-liberal economic policies had become anathema to the majority of the population and were no longer palatable to important sectors within the armed forces.

Because of the Malvinas crisis, the financial system suffered a very significant loss of deposits. In April 1982 alone, the equivalent of more than $500 million was withdrawn, generally to buy dollars in neighboring Montevideo. This situation, plus fears of *dirigiste* statism spurred by emergency controls over the war economy, badly frightened the previously all-powerful financial sector. By May and June, many banking institutions were forced to close their doors, unable to weather massive withdrawals of deposits and a sharp rise in interest rates.

By contrast, the Malvinas war gave new political muscle to domestic industrial capital. The military demonstrated considerably more sympathy for the industrialists. National security considerations—including concern with protecting the country's badly deteriorated industrial base—took precedence over restructuring the economy according to the tenets of liberal orthodoxy. It was none too soon, since private business sectors were suffocating under indebtedness totaling $15 billion, over 60 percent of which was due for repayment within ninety days.[35]

The dramatic change in the political and economic climate was evident immediately following Galtieri's ouster and the Junta's appointment of General Reynaldo Bignone as the new president on 1 July 1982. The economic team appointed by Bignone was unable to reach a consensus on future policy. The ensuing conflict pitted Economy Minister José Dagnino Pastore against Domingo Cavallo, the president of the Central Bank. Cavallo was an ardent defender of national industry and a long-standing opponent of post-1976 policies. Dagnino Pastore, while basically a pragmatic technocrat, was identified more closely with economic liberalism, having served briefly as Onganía's Economy Minister. Dagnino Pastore resigned after only 53 days in office, but before leaving he admitted that the Argentine economy was in a "state of destruction without precedent, a situation which can be classified as a national emergency." He also made the regime uneasy when he proclaimed that "the time has come to explain without hypocrisy" how the huge foreign debt had been incurred.[36]

Cavallo soon left also, but not before winning several partial policy victories favorable to financially strapped companies. Cavallo's main achievement was a drastic financial reform that in only six months resulted in the liquidation of about 40 percent of the private sector's debt.[37] Instead of reassuring the private sector, however, the Bignone regime's emergency economic plan touched off a wave of panic: inflation continued to soar (from 105 percent in 1981 to 165 percent in 1982 and 344 percent in 1983) and fixed investment continued to fall sharply in the midst of a desperate stampede of speculation against the peso and a headlong rush to buy shares, property, household goods, or virtually anything that might retain some of its value. Such behavior appeared to be the only rational response to the latest turn in the inflationary spiral. Tax evasion and the state's fiscal imbalance grew apace. Table 9.2 shows the consequences.

Argentina's difficulties in meeting its international obligations began as early as July 1982 when the economic authorities first admitted the necessity of renegotiating the foreign debt. The subsequent negotiations with the International Monetary Fund witnessed an ironic and telling turnabout. Rather than insisting on a traditional recessionary shock treatment, IMF negotiators reportedly advised their local colleagues to reactivate the ailing

TABLE 9.2
Selected Economic Indicators, 1974–82

	1974	1975	1976	1977	1978	1979	1980	1981	1982
1. Gross domestic product (% variation)	6.5	−1.4	−3.1	4.8	−5.4	6.8	1.1	−6.1	−5.2
2. Industrial production (% variation)	6.1	−3.0	−4.6	4.0	−10.5	9.1	−3.7	−15.2	−4.7
3. Inflation (% variation in consumer prices)	24.2	182.7	443.0	176.2	175.4	159.5	100.8	104.5	164.8
4. Public deficit (% of GDP)	8.2	16.2	11.2	5.2	7.2	8.0	8.5	9.0	8.0
5. Real per capita GDP (% variation)	4.0	−1.8	−2.1	4.8	−4.7	5.4	−0.5	−7.3	−6.9

SOURCE: Banco Central, *Boletín Estadístico*, various numbers.

Argentine economy. The reasons were not hard to see—rising unemployment, large general strikes and political protests, and domestic industry's continuing decline.[38]

Already sticky negotiations with the IMF and international banks were made even more difficult by Argentina's mounting political instability. IMF representatives and foreign bankers frequently seemed not to know which of their interlocutors actually had decision-making power. Conversely, Argentine authorities were unable to arrive at common positions or even to provide the necessary technical data required for proper negotiations.

One revealing incident—which left IMF representatives (and many Argentines, no doubt) quite perplexed—occurred in the preparations for a standby agreement to roll over Argentina's debt payments: $10 billion of the total foreign debt of approximately $40 billion had simply vanished without any proper recording of where it went. One World Bank official aptly referred to Argentina's economic troubles as a "financial Hiroshima."[39]

Neo-Liberalism and the Restructuring of the Entrepreneurial Class

The original counterrevolutionary political agenda and monetarist-inspired strategy of accumulation gave the post-1976 form of authoritarian state power both a pronounced militaristic cast and a blatantly class character. This combination had a serious negative impact not only on the great majority of the population but also on a significant portion of the Argentine bourgeoisie.[40] Two fundamental questions need to be answered. First, what kind of capitalist reorganization was implied by the post-1976 project? Second, what were this project's implications for Argentina's relations with the changing world-economy?

The prospects for endogenously determined growth were not very promising for Argentina during these years. In contrast to most other newly industrializing countries, however, Argentina seemed well-positioned to make the most of externally oriented development based on the one area in which it enjoyed a notable comparative advantage: the production of meat and grains. The technocrats, bankers, and entrepreneurs responsible for policy during the Proceso were quick to recognize the promise of "food power."[41] One high-ranking member of the economic team offered the following succinct analysis of Argentina's possibilities: "We are aware that one sector of our industry—agro-industry—is where Argentina has noteworthy advantages which put it in a privileged position in the concert of nations. Therefore, the country should make a formidable effort to develop that industrial sector which will situate us . . . in the vanguard and which will be a fundamental factor in the take-off we are looking for."[42]

This definition of the agrarian sector's potential strategic role recalls the questions raised in our opening discussion of the cycles of crisis in the post-1930 political economy. Two clarifications are needed to dispel some common misconceptions. First, the proposals to open Argentina to the international market did not mean a restoration of the pre-1930 agro-export economy. The fact that the first stage of the project of economic reorganization placed the rural sector in a privileged position did not imply a utopian vision based on "reagrarianization" or "pastoralization." While it is true that Pampean producers were allowed the more complete usufruct of their differential land rents, this was for the purpose of converting the more aggressive rural entrepreneurs into a modern and dynamic, export-oriented, agro-industrial complex.

Second, the unstated objective of the proposed restructuring of the economy was the establishment of conditions for sustained modernization of the entire productive system by overcoming, or at least attenuating, the contradictory, bi-polar pattern of accumulation which had emerged since the 1930s. This more "homogeneous" productive system was to be founded upon those sectors—both agrarian and industrial—capable of producing at internationally competitive prices.

Despite the nostalgia these policies initially evoked among certain agrarian interests, this was an eminently forward-looking project. It was based on the thesis that further import substitution in certain sectors of domestic industry was not only possible, but absolutely necessary. Only in this limited sense was the rural sector seen as a basic pillar of the project of economic reorganization.[43]

Turning to the industrial sector, we find that the Proceso followed a highly selective strategy of incentives focused on the

TABLE 9.3

Composition of Capital Goods, 1975–80

	I Total capital goods (1975 = 100)	II Pct. of capital goods of nat'l origin	III Pct. of capital goods imported	IV Physical volume of capital goods imports (1973 = 100)	V Capital goods as pct. of total imports
1975	100.0	74.6%	25.4%	107.4	–
1976	106.8	78.5	21.5	91.1	16.6%
1977	129.1	72.2	27.8	184.7	–
1978	102.0	65.7	34.3	155.4	–
1979	120.1	62.9	37.1	191.1	–
1980	111.4	49.8	50.2	204.3	21.4

SOURCES: Columns I, II, and III calculated from Central Bank data cited in *El Cronista Comercial*, 24 Nov. 1980. Columns IV and V taken from Canitrot, "Teoría y práctica del liberalismo," Table A.7, p. 176.

expansion of basic infrastructure. From 1976 to 1978, fully 75 percent of state incentives for industry went for modernization of the petrochemical, steel, and paper and cellulose sectors. This concentration of investments was based on a coherent program to redimension local industry and a logic that looked to substitute imports of those goods that still had a decisive weight in the total import bill.[44]

This strategy was designed to clear the way for tariff reductions and intended to free foreign exchange for other imports (thus dismantling inefficient sectors and firms), while also permitting a renegotiation of the terms of trade for Argentina's traditional exports. The growing reliance on imported capital goods was aimed at reducing the cost of inputs consumed by the rural sectors and other industrial sectors of basic industry. As Table 9.3 demonstrates, nearly three-quarters of capital goods were domestically produced in 1975. By 1980, imports accounted for one-half of all capital goods consumed by the Argentine economy.

The corollary of promoting the expansion of basic infrastructure was a deliberate effort to dismantle those industries incapable of surviving the cold blast of import competition. The consequent "de-industrialization" resulted in a general process of contraction, concentration, and centralization of capital in the manufacturing sector. In 1974, manufacturing industry ac-

TABLE 9.4
Production in the Manufacturing Industry, 1975–80
(1970 = 100)

	1975	1976	1977	1978	1979	1980	Pct. growth, 1975–80
Food, beverages, and tobacco	111.1	114.4	107.2	101.5	103.1	102.5	−7.7%
Textiles, clothing, and leather	112.1	106.0	110.0	94.4	104.6	92.3	−17.7
Wood and furniture	111.4	91.1	95.4	94.3	104.8	104.1	−6.6
Paper, printing, and publications	120.2	105.2	105.3	108.7	110.6	101.9	−15.2
Chemicals, rubber, and plastic	119.0	121.0	122.8	113.1	127.0	128.0	7.6
Glass and nonferrous metals	114.4	110.4	108.9	109.4	117.1	112.9	−1.3
Basic metals	123.4	111.5	128.1	121.1	141.7	128.0	3.7
Machinery and equipment	124.0	121.7	148.7	118.5	134.6	130.8	5.5
Total industry	117.1	114.8	121.6	108.3	118.2	114.1	−2.6%
Annual growth rates, in pct.	−2.0%	5.9%	−10.9%	9.1%	−3.5%		

SOURCE: Canitrot, "Teoría y práctica del liberalismo," Table A.24, p. 185.

counted for over 29 percent of gross domestic production; after 1976, industry's share fell to 26.6 percent in 1979, to 25.4 percent in 1980, and to only 22.1 percent in 1981.[45]

By 1981 total industrial production was 17 percent less than in 1975. In the important metallurgical sector, total physical output declined 25 percent in 1980 and an additional 45 percent in 1981 when the full impact of previous policies began to be felt. Even the sectors originally selected to play a strategic role were in full crisis by 1981. The petrochemical sector was operating at only 50 percent of installed capacity, chemicals at 45 percent, steel at 54 percent, and even the once dynamic automotive sector limped along at a mere 25 percent of installed capacity.[46]

The full extent of de-industrialization is reflected in the fact that the average annual growth rate of the industrial sector from 1977 to 1981 was −4.7 percent; the figure was −15.2 percent in 1981 and −4.7 percent in 1982. More disaggregated data, presented in Table 9.4, reveal the extent of industrial decline.

How were the costs and benefits of this de-industrialization distributed? It comes as no surprise that workers and sectors of the middle classes were made to bear the heaviest burden of the neo-liberal strategy. As the data in Table 9.5 show, salary earners experienced a dramatic decline in their share of gross domestic production.

How income transferred to firms and wealthy individuals was distributed is a difficult question. However, contrary to some simplistic interpretations, foreign capital was not the sole or even the principal beneficiary. Here we can only give some very fragmentary answers. Looking at the industrial sector, there is evidence that the ability to survive the restructuring of that sector probably depended less on the size of the firm or on the nationality of its capital than on its efficiency in adjusting to the new strategy through technological modernization or through shifting into commercial and importing activities. Along with international banks, the sectors of foreign capital that benefited most from Argentina's closer integration with the world market were the grain giants that monopolized the commercialization of wheat and many other primary exports.

While the picture remains unclear, the real beneficiaries of post-1976 policies were probably a small number of large nationally owned firms. These firms, taking advantage of state subsi-

TABLE 9.5

Income Transfers from Salaried Workers to Other Sectors, 1974–80

(*Billions of 1976 U.S. dollars*)

Year	Gross Domestic Product	Participation of salaried workers in GDP (percent)	Transfer to other sectors in relation to 1976
1974	44.5	49.8%	–
1975	44.3	47.5	–
1976	43.0	34.6	5.5
1977	44.8	29.0	8.3
1978	42.9	27.1	8.8
1979	46.3	29.1	8.5
1980	46.5	28.9	8.6
Total transfer			39.7

SOURCE: José Miguel Candia, "Cambios en el mercado de trabajo en el periodo 1976–1981 y perspectivas," in *Argentina: políticas económicas alternativas* (Mexico City: CIDE, Estudios de Caso Num. 1, Serie Instituto de Estudios Económicos de América Latina, Septiembre de 1982), Table 3, p. 68.

dies and/or easy access to foreign loans, were able to diversify their investments in the agribusiness sector, in areas of basic infrastructure, and in the lucrative construction business. Many firms also branched out into the rapidly expanding import business and, above all, into financial activities of all types. These firms not only consolidated their leading positions in their respective original spheres but began to form the core of a new dominant entrepreneurial group.[47]

The key to this new dominant group's emergence was the reorientation of relative prices and transfer mechanisms geared to orthodox monetarist principles. This reorientation substantially reversed the previous pattern of subsidizing urban industrial activities to the detriment of rural producers. All the surplus was not invested in agrarian modernization, however. A significant portion was invested in the new capital market created by the 1977 financial reform. Herein lay the explanation of the strange logic that made financial speculation the dynamic axis of the new economic model. According to one influential analysis,

the passage of the management of intersectoral transfers of income from the state to the financial sector signified . . . a transfer of power. In the philosophy of liberalism, the financing sector is the vital center of the functioning of a free enterprise system. It theoretically guarantees an appropriate neutrality that is the condition of efficiency and that the state, due to its own political nature, is unable to offer. In fact, the transfer of power places the industrial sector, as a net debtor, in a situation of dependence with respect to the financial sector. . . . In the few years that have passed since 1975, there have emerged rapidly in the Argentine economy various financial giants which have extended their control to the most important industrial groups and even to some entire branches of production.[48]

The power thus acquired by the so-called *patria financiera* (literally, the "financial fatherland") was reflected in the financial sector's rapid growth between 1976 and 1981: its relative share of gross domestic product more than doubled, increasing from around 4 percent to over 9 percent.

Industrial capital, in contrast, was caught between fear of losing the protection of an all-powerful regime (i.e., state repression of working-class militancy and policies for wage compression) and meager opportunities for accumulation. In fact, as the crisis deepened, many entrepreneurs in the manufacturing sector faced real threats to their very existence, and some failed to survive.

Transition After Political Collapse

Any "progress" achieved on the political front during the five years of the Videla regime was quickly dissipated during Viola's nine-month reign. This brief period witnessed the reemergence of political discontent, open expressions of unrest from organized labor, and the first stirrings from new social movements among the popular sectors. Viola also confronted the ever more strident demands of industrial and rural entrepreneurs, who were battered by the economic crisis but still fearful of what the end of military rule might mean.

The Viola regime expressed an interest in reaching a consensus with the civilian opposition through a "political opening," but its efforts were to no avail. The *Multipartidaria*, a grouping formed in July 1981 of the five largest parties, led by the Peronists and Radicals, rejected the regime's timid offers of political "dialogue" and the "concertation" of economic policy.[49]

Viola's authority on major political and economic questions was severely limited by the active role assumed by the Junta.

Consequently, Viola found himself caught in the pincer movement formed by military factional disputes and conspiracies and
by the financial sector's repeated attacks, which reflected a coordinated destabilization plan directed against the regime. In
early December 1981, Viola finally fell victim to this dual opposition in a palace coup led by General Galtieri and other military
hard-liners who were anxious to "deepen the revolution" by returning to unabashed dictatorial methods.[50]

Taking a leaf from Lanusse's manual of politico-military strategy, Galtieri sought to avoid his predecessor's fate by retaining
his army post. He simultaneously pursued a neo-liberal economic strategy and unsuccessfully attempted to project a populist image, all the while attacking the political parties. However,
the regime's failure to generate any significant popular support
was graphically demonstrated by the mass mobilization and
rally organized by the CGT on 30 March 1982.[51]

On 2 April, three days after the labor rally, Galtieri and the
Junta embarked upon the ill-fated Malvinas adventure. Driven
primarily by factional struggles within the regime, the decision
to invade the British-controlled archipelago resulted from a massive error in the regime's interpretation of the contradictory signals emitted by military leaders and neo-conservative civilian
strategists within the Reagan administration. Galtieri and his
top civilian and military strategists apparently expected that, in
exchange for the "practical support" the military had provided
against alleged Soviet-Cuban influence in Central America, Argentina could count on U.S. passivity in the conflict with Great
Britain. A second, and decidedly secondary, factor may have
been Galtieri's hope that popular enthusiasm for the recovery of
Argentina's sovereignty over the Malvinas would somehow rub
off on his regime.[52]

Galtieri had not completely misread the potential for popular
support of the war, although he erred if he thought that such
enthusiasm expressed any sympathy for the military regime
(crowds in the Plaza de Mayo chanted that "The Malvinas are
Argentine, so are the disappeared!"). But the failure to comprehend the subordinate role allocated to Argentina in Washington's global strategy proved fatal to Galtieri's gamble. Inept
diplomacy and poor performance on the battlefield by the Argentine military led in mid-June to surrender in Port Stanley.[53]
Galtieri's ouster inevitably followed.

The political liquidation of the Proceso became evident in the wake of the Malvinas disaster. In fact, the Malvinas conflict fundamentally transformed the relation of political forces in Argentine society. Argentina's defeat, and the mounting wave of disillusionment and popular frustration it engendered, served as a catalyst for the regime's subsequent political breakdown. The military humiliation in a "major political undertaking for which it had requested, or forcibly extracted, the consent of the broad masses"[54] of the population, focused attention on the "other war," the internal war, which had ripped apart the basic fabric of Argentine society.

General Reynaldo Bignone's caretaker government assumed power in July 1982. Bignone's administration was constantly buffeted by conflicts among the army, navy, and air force over the apportionment of blame for the recent military defeat. Internal differences within the military overlapped with differences over how to respond to the upsurge of business and labor protests and the unearthing of hundreds of unmarked graves of *desaparecidos*. The military's pleas for "conciliation" and guarantees of immunity from prosecution for human rights abuses fell on the deaf ears of the *Multipartidaria* and the civilian opposition.

By the end of 1982 the regime's political bankruptcy left no option but to announce plans for civilian rule. The decision to hold elections, however, was not a concession wrenched from a defeated military establishment by a strong party opposition. On the contrary, it was the weakness of the political parties that allowed the military to unilaterally conduct the political transition. In the Argentine case, a "liberalizing coalition" of military and civilian moderates did not emerge to lead the transition process. Nevertheless, it was no longer a question of whether the military would leave power, but when they would make their exit.[55]

After protracted negotiations, Bignone and the Junta finally announced that elections would be held on 30 October 1983. When the presidential campaign got under way few Argentines doubted that the Peronists would triumph. As Table 9.6 reveals, however, changes of opinion among undecided voters during 1983 gradually shifted the balance in favor of the Radicals.

Raúl Alfonsín, the Radicals' standard-bearer, projected an image of honesty and civility that was symbolized by his cam-

TABLE 9.6

Changes in Voter Attitudes and Intentions During the 1983 Presidential Election Campaign

(*Percentages*)

	Electoral results on 3/11/73	Electoral Preferences					Electoral results on 10/3/83
		9/82	3/83	8/83	9/83	10/83	
Radical	21%	11%	14%	22%	36%	36%	50%
Peronist	49	21	21	25	25	28	39
Others	28	2	4	6	5	5	8
Undecided	–	66	61	47	34	31	–
Blank/Null	2	–	–	–	–	–	3

SOURCE: Mora y Araujo, "La naturaleza de la coalición alfonsinista," Table 2, p. 40.

paign slogan of "Democracy or Anti-Democracy." After seven years of brutal dictatorship, few Argentines disagreed. Alfonsín's denunciation of a secret *pacto militar-sindical* between military hard-liners and Peronism's union bureaucrats further mobilized widespread sentiment for democracy in the Radicals' favor. According to the Radicals, the pact rested on an agreement between Lorenzo Miguel, head of the powerful 62 Organizaciones, the political arm of the Peronist unions, and army commander General Cristino Nicolaides. In exchange for the army's support in winning the elections, the Peronists were alleged to have agreed not to push for the investigation and prosecution of human rights violations during the "dirty war."[56]

On 10 October, Alfonsín received 52 percent of the valid votes; 40 percent went to Italo Luder, the Peronist candidate. The Unión Cívica Radical won control of most provincial governments. The Radicals also captured an outright majority in the Chamber of Deputies, and narrowly failed to gain control of the Senate. The Peronists ran well only in the poorest and least populous provinces. In contrast, the Radicals scored strong victories in the urban areas, where they won the overwhelming vote of the middle classes and did remarkably well among women and young voters, while making significant inroads among the working class, long the electoral bastion of Peronism. For the first time in 38 years, head-to-head competition between Radicals and Peronists had given the nod to the non-Peronist candidate.[57]

The Acceleration of Argentina's Relative Decline in the World-Economy

Alfonsín's election and the massive repudiation of military rule demonstrated, once again, that the failure of authoritarian regimes has been inextricably tied to successive failures to restructure the Argentine political economy. It will be recalled that vis-à-vis 28 nations, fully 25 percent of Argentina's relative decline since 1930 took place during the Proceso (see Tables 2.1 and 2.2). Thus it will be useful to examine Argentina's insertion in the world-economy in order to place the military's project in a broader comparative context.

Comparison of the international economic strategies of Argentina, Brazil, and Mexico helps to identify two different modes of insertion into the world-economy.[58] In one mode, countries rapidly expanded their foreign debt as part of a deliberate strategy of industrialization geared toward deepening their productive structures; this strategy entailed protection of the domestic manufacturing sector from foreign imports. In the second mode, breaking sharply with past strategies of import-substitution industrialization, countries deliberately opened their economies to the vagaries of the international marketplace in pursuit of comparative advantages. It should be stressed that *both* strategies sought greater integration with transnational capitalism, but their consequences were very different. The first strategy was followed by Brazil and Mexico and the second by the Southern Cone countries: Chile, Uruguay, and Argentina.

Prior to the 1982 debt crisis, both Mexico and Brazil maintained a very rapid pace of economic growth: between 1975 and 1981, the Brazilian economy expanded by 37 percent and the Mexican economy by 57 percent. Subsequently, of course, both Mexico and Brazil plunged into their deepest economic crises in the last fifty years, and both were burdened with huge foreign debts of over $100 billion. Policymakers in Mexico and Brazil pursued this strategy of foreign indebtedness to finance a process of industrial accumulation, to create large and sophisticated agro-industrial complexes, and to generate new jobs in the urban labor force. As mentioned above, Brazilian and Mexican policymakers deliberately sought to integrate their productive structures with the world-economy. Both countries fell into crisis, but a crisis induced by growth and expansion.

Argentina (along with Chile and Uruguay) pursued under the Proceso a very different strategy and, like Brazil and Mexico, came to experience severe economic turmoil. The difference was, of course, that Argentina's crisis was one resulting not from debt-led expansion but from the paradoxical combination of debt and de-industrialization. Argentina's was a crisis of shrinkage.

The dilemma facing the architects of the new strategy during the Proceso was how to take advantage of the rapid expansion in international liquidity that took place in the 1970s. Given the recessionary consequences of their strategy, it was impossible to look to internal demand to absorb external loans, credit, and investment. The economy's general contraction, plus the rise in foreign-exchange reserves, meant that the only way to attract external capital was through expansion of the foreign debt. This was accomplished by reducing import duties, by financing public expenditures and infrastructure projects with external credit, and by setting exchange-rate policies that led to an overvalued peso and a middle- and upper-class boom of consumerism fueled by so-called *plata dulce* or "sweet money."

In response to these policies, Argentina's foreign debt jumped from less than $10 billion in 1976 to nearly $45 billion by 1982. (See Table 9.7.) According to World Bank estimates, 37 percent of this debt resulted from the service of the foreign debt itself. Of the rest, 28.5 percent went to "unregistered" imports— basically arms and military equipment—and 7.4 percent corresponded to the growth of Central Bank reserves.[59] From 1975 to 1981, Mexico's debt to private international banks increased 4 times, Brazil's 3.5 times, and Argentina's 4.5 times. In contrast with the rapid expansion of the other two countries, however, Argentina's stagnation meant that per capita gross domestic product declined by 9 percent from 1975 to 1982.

Rapid economic expansion in Mexico and Brazil was fueled primarily by internal savings, despite the phenomenal increase in foreign indebtedness. In Argentina, the opposite took place. According to calculations from the 1976–81 period, the gap between potential internal savings (if past trends had continued) and actual savings registered in these years implied a contrac-

TABLE 9.7

Argentina's Foreign Debt

(*Millions of U.S. dollars*)

Year	Public	Private	Total
1962	2,169	685	2,854
1963	2,327	503	2,830
1964	2,034	882	2,916
1965	1,956	684	2,650
1966	1,959	704	2,663
1967	1,999	645	2,644
1968	1,754	1,051	2,805
1969	1,996	1,234	3,230
1970	2,143	1,732	3,875
1971	2,527	1,998	4,525
1972	3,046	2,046	5,092
1973	3,316	1,670	4,986
1974	3,878	1,636	5,514
1975	4,941	3,144	8,085
1976	6,648	3,090	9,738
1977	8,127	3,634	11,761
1978	9,453	4,210	13,663
1979	9,960	9,074	19,034
1980	14,459	12,703	27,162
1981	20,024	15,647	35,671
1982	28,616	15,018	43,634
1983	32,230	14,270	46,500

SOURCE: Banco Central de la República Argentina.

tion of capital accumulation of approximately $20 billion. The dismantling of roughly 30 percent of Argentina's industrial park in the same period resulted in a total "dis-accumulation" of industrial capital of approximately $30 billion. The sum of these figures implies a total loss of approximately $50 billion in a five-year period.[60]

The "Proceso" in Perspective: The Logic of State Power in Checkmate

The Proceso was a variant of the so-called "new authoritarianism" and shared certain family traits with the earlier Argentine Revolution and other dictatorial regimes in the Southern Cone. The initial, partially successful phases of both the Argentine Revolution and the Proceso were similar projects of military transformism based on offensive strategies to carry out profound changes in the polity, society, and economy. A comparison of the failure and collapse of the two projects points to some interesting contrasts. Lanusse's Gran Acuerdo Nacional was a defensive strategy designed to protect the armed forces, the interests of the state, and the dominant social groups from the radical revolutionary and democratic forces that emerged in the wake of the *cordobazo*. In contrast, the collapse of the Proceso failed to produce a military politician of the caliber, strategic vision, and tactical skills of Lanusse. Certainly neither Galtieri nor Bignone measured up to this role.

The Videla regime had many factors working in its favor, especially compared to the Onganía regime. First, state terrorism and neo-liberal economic policies had inflicted a major political and economic defeat on the popular sectors and the subordinate fractions of industrial capital. As a result, second, policymakers were remarkably unencumbered by political obstacles and thus enjoyed a large degree of freedom to confront Argentina's contradictory, bi-polar pattern of accumulation through a program of radical economic restructuring. Third, authoritarian elites presided over state institutions characterized by considerable internal unity, coherence, and relative autonomy vis-à-vis civil society. And, fourth, the armed forces had achieved a relatively high degree of internal cohesion, professionalism, and consensus in support of a radical project seeking a new order.[61] On each count, the situation facing the Onganía regime had been less favorable. Contrasting the two periods thus highlights the immensely greater power of the post-1976 regime and, conversely, the serious weakening of civil society. This clear combination of superior state power and a debilitated society placed the post-1976 regime on a different evolutionary path from the one traveled by Onganía, Levingston, and Lanusse.

The architects of the political strategy of the Proceso sought to extend the political institutionalization of the authoritarian regime over a period long enough to make the neo-liberal policies irreversible. Mindful of what followed Perón's victory over Lanusse, these strategists hoped to make it impossible for any future civilian or military regime to embark on a dangerous "return to the past."[62]

This logic necessarily implied a wholesale redistribution of social power in Argentine society, particularly the destruction of the economic bases that had, in the past, made possible the cyclical reemergence of defensive alliances between organized labor and the subordinate fractions of capital. In 1973, the Unión Industrial had joined the CGE and had given half-hearted support to Perón's call for a Social Pact. Such compromises were no longer necessary. One of the first steps the Videla regime took in 1976 was to dissolve the Confederación General Económica and to establish the UIA as its sole interlocutor for the industrial sector. But even the transnational and large domestic firms could not escape state-imposed *gleichschaltung* when the UIA was placed under intervention to assure support for Martínez de Hoz's policies. Only in 1979 was the UIA allowed to select its own leaders. The CGE remained outlawed.[63]

Deprived of an autonomous voice, industrialists resorted to speculation and capital flight to register their discontent. Typically, Martínez de Hoz responded to these challenges by reminding businessmen of his great prestige in the international financial community and the military's support for his policies. He frequently exhorted entrepreneurs "to believe once and for all in the continuity of the program that is being carried out. . . . This program is not the program of President Jorge R. Videla or the program of Minister Martínez de Hoz, it is the program approved by the Armed Forces."[64]

The neo-liberal economic strategy undermined the power of organized labor through policies that widened wage differentials across and within economic sectors. This tended to create a segmented labor market and deepened the working class's structural heterogeneity, while a growing stratification of life-styles and consumption patterns tended to make collective action across class boundaries more difficult. The contrast between the sharp gains in labor productivity and the negative trends in manufacturing employment depicted in Table 9.8 gives an idea of the magnitude of the changes in labor's position in the Argentine economy.

Important steps were also taken to weaken the working class's organizational base. The goal was to abolish "political unionism" by attacking the CGT's role in coordinating Argentina's hundreds of unions and by drastically curtailing the economic

TABLE 9.8
Industrial Employment, 1975–80
(1970 = 100)

	1975	1976	1977	1978	1979	1980	Pct. growth, 1975–80
Food, beverages, and tobacco	121.9	122.7	117.5	105.6	105.8	108.0	−11.4%
Textiles, clothing, and leather	111.7	107.2	98.4	87.4	79.9	64.1	−42.6
Wood and furniture	126.1	119.2	112.2	99.5	91.6	85.4	−32.3
Paper, printing, and publications	103.7	94.3	84.8	82.7	81.2	81.4	−21.5
Chemicals, rubber, and plastic	124.1	125.7	119.0	108.1	105.6	73.9	−40.5
Glass and nonferrous metals	107.3	104.1	94.5	90.6	92.5	86.9	−19.0
Basic metals	136.2	130.4	127.7	119.0	119.0	114.7	−15.8
Machinery and equipment	123.4	116.5	108.9	96.9	96.7	88.8	−28.0
Total industry	119.2	115.3	108.1	97.7	95.6	88.2	−26.0%
Pct. change in total employment		−3.3%	−6.2%	−9.6%	−2.2%	−7.7%	
Product per man, total industry	98.2	99.6	112.5	110.8	123.6	129.4	31.8%
Labor costs, total industry	103.2	64.2	58.2	58.5	62.5	73.2	

SOURCE: Canitrot, "Teoría y práctica del liberalismo," Tables A.25, A.26, on p. 186; Table A.28 on p. 188.

power of the unions. These measures were seen as integral aspects of the overarching project to restructure the economy and depoliticize society.[65]

These social transformations also involved efforts to create a "culture of fear." Consonant with the regime's initial counter-revolutionary logic, policies in this area responded first to the need to demobilize and disarticulate possible sources of resistance and opposition. When, by 1978, "order" and "discipline" had been restored, a more ambitious effort was undertaken. This effort was geared toward the coordination of state power over the mass media and cultural and educational institutions with an eye toward modifying the society's basic values.[66]

The implicit goal was to extend state penetration of civil society by creating a climate of "social authoritarianism" and intolerance parallel to the political authoritarianism imposed by the state. In this way, authoritarian elites in the state and private sectors were groping toward the creation of a kind of de facto legitimacy. Such an ersatz legitimacy would not be based on consensus and compromises established through party competition in the parliament and the electoral arena, but rather would be crystallized in a new "common sense" functioning at the level of the normal repertoire of social practices in the ostensibly "non-political" realms of everyday life. While the Proceso may have failed to create an alternative legitimacy, there is no doubt that state repression, pervasive anomie, and widespread speculative behavior by individuals from all social classes did have extremely serious consequences for Argentine political culture.[67]

It would be comforting to believe that the mobilization and reactivation of Argentine civil society in 1982 and 1983 had been heroically responsible for authoritarianism's collapse. But this was not exactly true. In fact, the weakening of Argentine society wrought by the Proceso went hand-in-hand with the shrinkage and de-industrialization of the economy. In fact, it was primarily the military's own political incompetence and internal contradictions that finally brought the regime to its knees, not irresistible pressure from an aroused citizenry. It is conjecture, of course, but had the Malvinas debacle not occurred the outcome probably would have been quite different. Although the prospects for dramatic success were few, the efforts begun in 1976 to revamp the economy and to achieve a more dynamic place for

Argentina in the world-economy, all the while backed by a highly coercive authoritarian state, might well have continued for years. Ultimately, however, politics took command and the Malvinas war and the armed forces' inability to govern themselves, much less a reawakening civil society, dictated a rapid and unseemly retreat from the direct exercise of state power.

Argentina's tragic experience under the Proceso offered at least two optimistic lessons. First, while democratic regimes have failed in meeting the challenge of reconciling legitimate rule with economic growth, military regimes have generally fared even worse. Second, the failure of military-inspired attempts to create a new society along authoritarian lines showed that even apparently overwhelming coercive force, allied to powerful social and economic interests, may well be insufficient to assure the triumph of a seemingly invincible logic of power. Civil society in Argentina, perhaps to a greater extent than elsewhere in Latin America, possessed its own superior logic, a logic which repeatedly demonstrated a remarkable capacity to resist and defeat attempts to impose authoritarian rule and to reorder society. But could this logic of resistance serve as the foundation for a viable project of democratization?

TEN

Alfonsín and the Unfinished Agenda of Democratic Class Compromise

FROM 1930 to 10 December 1983, when Raúl Alfonsín assumed the presidency, Argentina had 24 presidents, sixteen of whom were army generals. The period witnessed 26 successful military coups, and hundreds of attempted coups. Only two elected presidents, Justo and Perón, both generals, successfully completed their constitutionally mandated terms of office. Military regimes, of course, had proven as unstable as civilian regimes; of the presidents imposed by armed fiat, only General Jorge Rafael Videla completed the term in office previously stipulated by the military. Raúl Alfonsín was only the third president to occupy the Casa Rosada by means of free elections unmarred by proscriptions, the other two untainted contests being those of 1946 and 1973. If Argentina's past democratic transitions had miscarried, would the latest experiment in civilian rule turn out any differently?

The inglorious dénouement of the Proceso was certainly a positive sign for the democratic transition begun in December 1983. But in view of the weaknesses and mistakes of previous civilian regimes, there was reason for concern that there might be an irreconcilable structural incompatibility between liberal democracy and capitalist development in Argentina. Moreover, the collapse of the Proceso understandably caused some troubled observers to conclude that the real contradiction was that between the Argentine political economy and *any* kind of stable political order, democratic or dictatorial.[1] Whether the Argentines' well-demonstrated capacity to resist authoritarianism could form the basis of a viable alternative project of democratization remained to be seen.

The situation confronting Alfonsín was suffused with highly contradictory prospects. The contrast between the democratic transitions experienced in Brazil, Spain, and Uruguay and that of Argentina is instructive. In cases of liberalization and democratization "from above," authoritarian elites retained considerable control over the state apparatus and capacity to dictate the political agenda to the civilian opposition. But in Argentina the Malvinas debacle made possible a "transition after collapse" leading quickly to a less constricted and more open and competitive political democracy. Also, the simultaneity of liberalization and democratization meant that Argentina faced fewer obstacles to significant social and economic reforms than Brazil, for example.[2]

Yet, because the armed forces and the dominant classes were partially deprived of their heretofore privileged access to and control over the state apparatus, they posed a serious challenge to the new democracy. Military hard-liners constituted the kernel of a disloyal opposition, while recalcitrant sectors of the entrepreneurial class, at best lukewarm converts to democracy, acted as semiloyal participants giving only contingent support to the new civilian rulers. Thus, the same factors that made for a rapid transition to a relatively liberal polity also meant that the possibility of a dramatic authoritarian reversal remained a real threat to Argentina's fragile democracy.

This chapter does not offer a painstaking reconstruction of Alfonsín's tenure or an exhaustive analysis of the prospects for democracy in Argentina. To do so would require another, equally long book. The role of the armed forces, electoral politics, and institutional questions in general, while certainly crucial, are not our central focus. Instead, we will examine Argentina's democratic transition, albeit somewhat obliquely, by raising some perennial questions in the political sociology and political economy of capitalist societies: How is it possible for liberal democracy to coexist with a market economy? How can the logic of citizenship, implying a commitment to political equality and the progressive removal of barriers to political participation, be reconciled with a system of production and a class structure that generate profound inequalities of wealth, income, and life-chances?

Previous discussion of the unraveling of the Peronist variant of populist reformism, the failures of restricted democracy under Frondizi and Illia, the miscarriage of the Argentine Revolution, and, finally, the collapse of the extremely violent attempt to impose a capitalist utopia during the Proceso bears witness to the deeply rooted difficulties of trying to fashion a viable class compromise in Argentina. Has Alfonsín's government nudged Argentina closer to the type of class compromise characteristic of the developmental path followed by the capitalist democracies of Western Europe and North America? Could Alfonsín succeed where others failed?

Alfonsín's Challenge:
Democracy with Economic Stabilization

Following his assumption of the reins of government in December 1983, Raúl Alfonsín moved rapidly and successfully to consummate the "first transition" to liberal democracy. Respect for the rights of citizenship, freedom of association and political activity, and adherence to regularly scheduled elections have been unequivocal during the Alfonsín years. Relations with the military have been stormy, as one might have expected, but the principle of civilian control over the armed forces has made significant progress. This principle was forcefully asserted in the Radical party's 1983 election manifesto, which declared: "Democracy cannot live in this country while the Armed Forces set themselves as the arbiters of sovereignty, and with Armed Forces that place their own corporate interests above their professional obligations."[3] Moreover, during his first week in office, Alfonsín proposed legislation to revoke the amnesty the military had given themselves just three months earlier, and soon thereafter named a commission (the Comisión Nacional sobre la Desaparición de las Personas, or CONADEP), headed by the novelist Ernesto Sábato, to investigate the crimes of the "dirty war."[4]

Trials for the leaders of the Proceso began in April 1985 and had significant results. General Videla and Admiral Emilio Massera received life sentences; General Viola was given a seventeen-year sentence; and General Galtieri was acquitted on repression charges. (However, Galtieri was condemned to twelve years in prison for his role in the Malvinas war.) Admiral Jorge

Anaya received a fourteen-year sentence, and Brigadier General Basilio Lami Dozo was sentenced to eight years.

But pressure to try additional officers under the *Punto Final* law (the government's first concession to limit prosecutions for human rights violations) sparked a major rebellion by the so-called *carapintadas* (because of their use of camouflage paint) during Easter week of 1987. And dissatisfaction with the *Obediencia Debida* law, passed by Congress to protect officers judged to have "duly obeyed" their superiors during the repression, again fomented significant uprisings in January and December 1988.[5] In recognition of these ominous rumblings Alfonsín was forced to tread carefully, but he continued to assert civilian ascendancy. As part of Alfonsín's military reform program, a new defense law was passed in April 1988 that explicitly barred the military intelligence services from intervention in domestic civil conflicts.[6]

Yet the "second transition," involving the consolidation of a broad-based popular legitimacy, the institutionalization of an effective system of representation and accountability through the electoral and parliamentary arenas, and the promotion of a more tolerant and participatory democratic political culture, was an even more difficult problem, as was dealing with the calamitous economic crisis. In fact, management of the economy and the tasks of consolidation were inextricably interconnected.

The regime change of December 1983 occurred when the Argentine economy was in the midst of an unprecedented crisis. While population growth continued, gross domestic production in 1983 was roughly equivalent to that of 1970, leading to a large deterioration in per capita income. By the end of the Proceso fixed investment had fallen more than 30 percent compared to the average of the previous decade, the purchasing power of wage earners was below that of the decade of the 1960s, and the public-sector deficit in 1983 was conservatively estimated at 11.1 percent of GDP. The fiscal crisis of the state thus interacted with and compounded a long-term accumulation crisis. A general overview of the economic situation of this period is provided in Table 10.1.

Looming over all else in 1983 was the foreign debt of some $46 billion, which represented nearly 80 percent of GDP. Not only was the international financial community wary about making

TABLE 10.1

Principal Economic Indicators, 1983–87

	1983	1984	1985	1986	1987
Growth rate of GDP[a]					
Total GDP	2.8	2.6	−4.7	5.4	1.6
Manufacturing	10.8	4.0	−11.2	12.9	−0.6
Agriculture	1.9	3.6	−1.7	−2.8	1.8
Construction	−13.1	−20.0	−6.7	9.0	14.8
Public-sector percentage of GDP[b]					
Current revenues	23.6	22.9	27.5	25.9	24.4
Current expenditures	26.8	25.2	25.4	23.2	24.4
Current savings	−3.2	−2.3	2.1	2.7	0.0
Capital expenditures	7.9	6.1	5.6	5.4	6.3
Deficit or surplus	−11.1	−8.4	−3.5	−2.7	−6.3
Growth rates of money, prices, and wages					
Domestic credit	400.8	565.7	356.1	86.8	151.7
Money supply (M1)	362.0	546.7	697.9	70.7	106.6
Consumer prices	343.8	626.7	672.2	90.1	131.3
Real wages[c]	24.1	27.1	−12.2	−5.7	−7.6
Terms of trade					
(1980 = 100)	86.4	99.9	87.0	75.0	68.7
Balance of payments[d]					
Current account	−2.44	−2.54	−0.96	−2.86	−4.70
Trade balance	3.71	3.94	4.90	2.46	0.56
Exports	7.83	8.07	8.42	6.85	6.20
Imports	4.12	4.13	3.52	4.39	5.64
Net services	−6.17	−6.49	−5.86	−5.32	−5.25
Caital account (net)	.41	2.74	2.25	1.68	1.85
Change in net reserves	−2.47	0.14	0.98	−0.87	−2.21

SOURCE: Inter-American Development Bank, *Economic and Social Progress in Latin America, 1988 Report* (Washington, D.C., 1988), p. 328.

[a]GDP at market prices, sector of origin at factor cost.

[b]Non-financial public sector, cash flow basis, includes Central Government revenues and expenditures, Social Security, and local governments, plus the net result of operations of non-financial public enterprises.

[c]In the manufacturing sector.

[d]Billions of current dollars.

new loans, but, to make matters worse, the hemorrhage of capital flight overseas by wealthy Argentines continued unabated. From 1971 to 1985, Argentina's external debt had increased nearly $41 billion; capital flight alone accounted for 63.3 percent of the increase in the debt burden.[7]

Although sobered by the crisis, the Alfonsín government felt that its electoral majority gave it the necessary political legitimacy to confront the economic situation without concessions to its opponents. In fact, during this initial period, the Alfonsín administration acted to distance the state from the powerful domestic and transnational forces, both seen as potentially disloyal, anti-democratic, or simply oriented toward their own narrow economic-corporate interests. Significantly, the Radicals felt relatively unconstrained by Peronism, whose leadership was divided and disoriented by its electoral defeat. Not only had many rank-and-file Peronists abandoned their own presidential candidate, many had joined Radicals in enthusiastically chanting "*Alfonsín y Perón, un solo corazón*" ("Alfonsín and Perón, one heart").[8]

This sense of national unity gave rise to an optimistic voluntarism that led Alfonsín's more euphoric partisans (and perhaps the president himself) to imagine that *alfonsinismo* could become a "third historical movement" destined to supersede both Radicalism and Peronism, thereby creating a permanent electoral majority. The ideological discourse emanating from the regime accorded the triumphant *alfonsinistas* a virtual monopoly on civic virtue and ethical principles. The Peronist-controlled labor movement and the armed forces, the key components of the so-called *patria corporativa*, were portrayed as unfit for the new democracy.

The *alfonsinistas* immediately took a number of initiatives to consolidate their position and to assert the regime's capacity to rule autonomously. This desire to act boldly was particularly evidenced in a unilateral style of macroeconomic policymaking that placed little priority on consultations with interests in civil society. Alfonsín and Bernardo Grinspun, the Economy Minister, assumed power promising to "reinvigorate the economy and establish an equitable distribution of income. We shall not seek growth first and redistribution later. That approach is not viable."[9] This pledge clearly meant not knuckling under to the IMF's calls for economic orthodoxy in confronting the external debt.

Consequently, Alfonsín and Grinspun adopted a strategy of brinkmanship by suspending all debt payments on the principal and by systematically delaying interest payments in a game of financial "chicken," forcing the IMF, creditor banks, and foreign governments to come to the rescue with a combination of bridge loans and rescheduling. Typical of Alfonsín's verbal confrontation with the IMF and creditor banks was a famous speech in mid-May 1984 in which the president declared: "It is as if the [financial] centers have gone mad, but we will not pay usury. . . . It seems as if the developing countries were being attacked with a neutron bomb in reverse, which leaves men, women and other creatures alive, while destroying the nations' productive apparatus. This madness must be ended once and for all."[10]

In June 1984, the Argentine economic authorities defiantly submitted a letter of intent to the IMF that was not the product of the usual lengthy negotiations. This unilateral plan called for a 6- to 8-percent raise in real wages, an increase in the money supply beyond IMF-imposed guidelines, and limits on interest payments so as not to require drastic cuts in imports. This was unacceptable to the international financial community.[11]

Finally, in early September 1984, following extremely tense and chaotic negotiations, Grinspun and Central Bank President Enrique García Vásquez succumbed to international pressure and reached an agreement with the IMF. The resulting austerity package called for a sharp reduction in inflation (from the current annual rate of 1,200 percent to 150 percent), the elimination of price controls, a reduction of the public-sector deficit (to 5.4 percent of GDP by the end of 1985), and a liberalization of foreign trade restrictions.[12] The acceleration of price hikes to an average monthly figure of 24.1 percent during the first quarter of 1985 made evident the Alfonsín administration's total failure to adhere to IMF austerity. Consequently, in March 1985, the IMF and the banks suspended new loans.

The strategy advanced by Grinspun was premised upon the mistaken assumption that the Keynesian, pump-priming policies implemented by the Radicals twenty years earlier, during the brief Illia government, were still viable. This nostalgic strategy did not take into consideration the profound disarticulation of the productive structure wrought by the neo-liberal project implemented by Martínez de Hoz. Runaway inflation and the difficulties in reactivating the ravaged economy were eloquent testimony to this mistaken vision. Grinspun paid the price in February 1985 by resigning as Economy Minister.

Dreams of a "third historical movement" began to evaporate

in the face of evidence that exemplary dedication to good government alone was not sufficient to resolve the deepening economic crisis. The government's economic strategy led to mounting confrontations with the class organizations representing local and transnational entrepreneurial interests, who were increasingly disenchanted with both the Radicals' style of economic management and the content of their policies. Agrarian capital, with the Sociedad Rural Argentina in the vanguard, aggressively rejected all measures that challenged its usufruct over the surplus generated by the countryside, such as levies on agricultural exports and limitations on domestic meat sales. The Unión Industrial Argentina also strongly criticized state intervention in the economy, especially price controls, and resisted efforts to increase tax revenues. The banking sector objected to the government's monetary and credit policies and opposed all efforts to reduce financial speculation and reorient capital toward productive endeavors.[13]

Government initiatives, such as a sweeping legislative proposal to restructure and democratize the unions, also clashed with the Peronist leadership of the labor movement. In February 1984, this centerpiece of the Alfonsín government's political agenda went down to defeat in the Senate, where the Peronists and several small parties had a majority.[14] Similarly, in June 1984, efforts by the Radicals to forge a political pact with the other major parties (through a so-called *Acta de Coincidencias*) failed to produce a broad consensus giving the government a free hand to pursue its policies without partisan opposition. In short, in confronting the economic crisis, the Alfonsín government could not count on either the acquiescence of rival political parties in Congress or the support of the "organized interests" such as the CGT, the UIA, or the SRA.[15]

Following the suspension of new loans by the IMF and the banks, and Grinspun's exit, a new political and economic strategy was sorely needed. The appointment of Juan Sourrouille, a Harvard-trained economist with impeccable academic credentials and considerable professional experience, as Economy Minister, signaled that a departure from previous policies was in the offing. No one, however, could have predicted the depth of the future changes in the regime's economic strategy or their implications for Argentine democracy.

According to Alfonsín's second economic team, major structural changes in the Argentine economy, to overcome both
chronic economic instability and long-term stagnation, were urgently required.[16] Although the strategy of brinkmanship vis-à-
vis the international financial community had failed, Sourrouille
continued to reject the orthodox adjustment policies espoused
by the IMF. Economic stabilization was a necessity, Sourrouille
readily acknowledged, but the new minister chose to implement
a risky anti-inflationary program calling for the application of a
sudden "heterodox shock" to jerk the economy back from the
precipice.

This novel stabilization plan promised to strengthen democratic rule by bringing inflation under control without either recession or a politically dangerous reduction in living standards.
Many analysts have in effect suggested an elective affinity between heterodox shock policies and fragile democratic governments. As Albert Hirschman put it:

To be sure, the new democratic governments, especially when they
take over from greatly detested or despised authoritarian regimes, will
have to cope with a burst of combativeness of social groups. But at the
same time they can call upon a special reserve of good will and trust
which stands to their credit as a result of the political liberties and human rights they have restored or established. It is this considerable as-
set of the new Argentinian and Brazilian governments that was a basic
factor in the success of the monetary reforms, for if the inflationary tug-
of-war, in which the various social groups have engaged for so long, is
suddenly to be replaced by cooperation and willingness to believe in
the success of the new policy, some basic trust must exist in the government that is enunciating the new program.[17]

If the affinity postulated by Hirschman were borne out, then one
could expect that Alfonsín and the Radicals should have been
poised to make progress toward a class compromise reconciling
democracy with Argentine capitalism. But has the Argentine experience since June 1985 warranted this prediction of a seren-
dipitous affinity between heterodox policies and democracy? In
order to address this question we must first discuss orthodox
stabilization programs and identify the political reasons for their
failure.

Despite considerable diversity, it is possible to speak of a general orthodox paradigm. As advocated by the IMF, orthodoxy is

premised on a commitment to market-based solutions and the rolling back of "excessive" state intervention in the economy. IMF orthodoxy also prescribes closer integration of peripheral economies into international financial circuits and trade and capital regimes. Accordingly, the principal policies of IMF adjustment programs aim to (1) correct the external trade deficit and stabilize international reserves at safe levels; (2) curtail and eventually eliminate the public-sector deficits; and (3) bring inflation under control. Generally, orthodox policies have had far more success in meeting the external payments objective than in reducing inflation. Some critics argue, in fact, that guaranteeing external solvency is really the only objective pursued by orthodox programs.[18]

Sharply heightened social and distributional conflicts have usually been equally as important as, if not more important than, technical economic factors in the failure of IMF orthodoxy. As we have seen, such underlying sociopolitical conflicts have been endemic in Argentina. These conflicts exemplify basic "coordination problems" in the logic of collective action.

The strategic interaction between labor and capital in the context of high inflation provides a classic example of a "prisoners' dilemma" in which the structure of payoffs is strongly analogous to a negative-sum game. Regardless of labor's response to high inflation (wage restraint or militant economism), the best strategy for individual capitalists will be to raise prices as high and as rapidly as possible, thereby reducing real wages and increasing real profits. This intensifies sociopolitical conflict, and deteriorates the position of both labor and capital to a greater extent than if they had agreed to maintain wages and profits constant, but with a lower rate of inflation.[19]

Similarly, because of the pronounced asymmetry between receiving the benefits and sharing the costs, stabilization programs are extremely susceptible to breakdown due to "free-rider" defections. There are strong incentives for all actors— capital, labor, and the state—to refuse to share the burden of austerity. Since the benefits of reduced inflation are inherently collective, "attempts to transfer the costs of stabilization onto others will be the norm rather than the exception."[20]

This perspective underscores the rationality of the actors' refusal to share in the costs of austerity. But it is not merely a question of rationality. We know that in Argentina distributional struggles leading to the breakdown of stabilization programs are deeply embedded in issues involving class and power. What the liberal-pluralist tradition refers to as the "privileged position of business" is rooted in capital's indispensable role in the process of accumulation, and its control over wealth, production, and investment decisions.[21] Workers and unions, in contrast, do not control productive assets and consequently cannot exercise the same leverage in distributional conflicts. (By the same token, labor's capacity to disrupt production can lead entrepreneurs to shift investments toward speculative activities or to engage in capital flight, thereby aggravating inflation and furthering de-industrialization.) Therefore, as the Argentine case amply demonstrates, labor has frequently been forced to shoulder a disproportionate decline in its real income during periods of high inflation, while sustaining a disproportionate burden of the sacrifices imposed by anti-inflationary programs.

This asymmetry in costs explains why organized labor in Argentina (along with unprotected strata of the middle classes and competitive sectors of manufacturing) has always been strongly opposed to stabilization efforts. While it is necessary to distinguish carefully between actual practice and ideological discourse, it is nevertheless also true that the dominant sectors of industrial, agrarian, and financial capital have generally supported stabilization, confident of their capacity to free-ride to their own benefit. Austerity and recession, while hurting many (perhaps even a majority of) individual capitalists and firms, play a functional role for capital as a whole by recreating the conditions (via Schumpeter's "creative destruction" of less efficient firms and technologies and restoration of a positive balance of payments) for a new cycle of accumulation. In addition, because of their superior material resources, entrepreneurs wield immense leverage vis-à-vis state elites in shaping stabilization policies in accord with business interests.[22]

Mindful of the political tug-of-war that had undermined previous anti-inflation efforts, Sourrouille and his heterodox team believed that their novel proposals could sever the Gordian knot by making possible effective stabilization without undermining democratic legitimacy. They believed that sharp distributional conflicts, in which capital gains the upper hand (and authoritarian solutions become more probable), would be less likely if the regressive impacts on income distribution associated with conventional stabilization could be avoided. The *heterodoxos* did not reject the necessity of painful external adjustment or the efficacy of tight control over monetary variables in curbing runaway inflation. They did, however, object to the high social costs involved, and denied that a sharp recession was inevitable in order to cure inflation.[23]

The *heterodoxos* based their policy prescriptions on a key characteristic of the Argentine economy: the pervasive indexation of virtually all types of monetary contracts, rents, wages, and bonds to official price indexes. In a highly inflationary environment, formal indexation, or "monetary correction," enables economic agents (particularly capital) to partially avoid the erosion of their wages and rents. Indexation, in effect, creates a built-in "memory system" perpetuating inflation indefinitely; future inflation is simply a function of past inflation.[24]

The *heterodoxos* made this memory system the cornerstone of their critique of IMF-style stabilization. They argued that there is a significant, and frequently overlooked, "inertial" component in inflations of 100 percent, 200 percent, and higher. Inertial inflation, in their view, was the reason that orthodox policies designed to reduce aggregate demand had little impact on inflation. Orthodox shocks as well as orthodox gradualism were, therefore, doomed to failure. Effective stabilization mandates the sudden elimination of the effects of past inflation. Consequently, heterodox shock policies seek to eradicate this memory system by means of the wholesale de-indexation of public- and private-sector prices and a sweeping monetary reform, including the creation of a new currency with a fixed parity in relation to the dollar.

The efficacy of these policies depended on a temporary freeze on wages and prices; in fact, wage and price controls were the cornerstone, the *sine qua non*, of the heterodox paradigm. The *heterodoxos* favored temporary controls to cool off distributional struggles and to help avoid the negative-sum payoffs common to conventional stabilization programs. Moreover, some *heterodoxos* argued that temporary wage and price controls would help to bolster liberal democratic politics. How?

The *heterodoxos* respected the role of price mechanisms in competitive markets and argued that stringent controls were necessary to assure price stability only until the inertial component of inflation had been eliminated. Unlike the negative-sum game under hyperinflation, once price equilibrium had been attained and inertial factors purged, continued state intervention in markets would be made unnecessary. The "visible hand" of the state was supposed to move the economy from a high-inflation equilibrium to a low-inflation equilibrium. Then, barring external shocks, and if the government maintained a moderate wage policy, competition and the self-interest of individual capitalists would allow the market's "invisible hand" to reproduce a low-inflation equilibrium. If transitory coordination of labor and capital through wage and price controls was combined with a concerted attack on the "deep" structural causes of inflation stressed by conventional orthodoxy (protectionism, subsidies, overvalued exchange rates, etc.), then price stability and renewed economic growth would be possible, and without authoritarianism.

The Implementation of the Austral Plan

The unveiling of the new strategy could hardly have come at a less propitious moment. Argentina's relations with the IMF, the U.S. Treasury, and the creditor banks were at an impasse. Foreign-exchange reserves were depleted, and manufacturing was still reeling from the shrinkage of the industrial sector promoted by the preceding military regime.[25] But the threat of hyperinflation (consumer prices rising at a monthly rate of 30 percent and wholesale prices zooming upward at 50 percent) finally spurred Juan Sourrouille to implement untried, emergency measures.

Sourrouille unveiled the Austral Plan on 14 June 1985. The Austral Plan's chief policy instruments consisted of (1) a new currency—the Austral—to replace the peso at a rate of 1 austral per 1,000 pesos, with the exchange rate devalued 18 percent in terms of the dollar; (2) the imposition of a wage and price freeze, with citizens urged to denounce violators; (3) a combination of policies to reduce the budget deficit, including large increases in

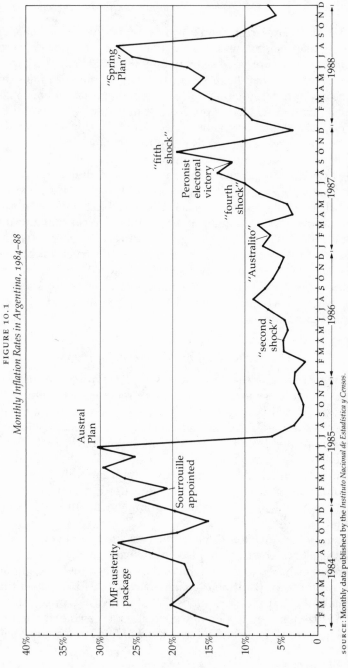

FIGURE 10.1
Monthly Inflation Rates in Argentina, 1984–88

SOURCE: Monthly data published by the *Instituto Nacional de Estadística y Censos*.
NOTE: Data for inflation in early 1989 became available after this figure was prepared: January, 8.9 percent; February, 9.6 percent; and March, 17.0 percent.

charges for government-produced services (electricity, petro-leum products, transportation, etc.); and (4) a pledge not to print inflationary quantities of money—this commitment to be carried out by separating the Central Bank's acquisition of do-mestic assets from the financing needs of the Treasury.[26]

Initial reactions to the Austral Plan exceeded expectations. As Figure 10.1 illustrates, wage and price controls succeeded in lim-iting inflation to only 20.2 percent during the six months follow-ing the Plan's inauguration (as opposed to price hikes for the 1985 calendar year totaling 385.4 percent), as monthly rates plummeted to approximately 3 percent by the end of 1985. After a small dip immediately following the announcement of the new policies, industrial output rebounded a strong 13 percent in the last quarter of 1985.[27]

Despite these triumphs, the private sector became increas-ingly critical of Alfonsín's policies. Agricultural producers, led by the Sociedad Rural Argentina, complained of low prices and protested against taxes on commodity exports. Backed by the Unión Industrial, manufacturers responded with renewed capi-tal flight, reductions in planned investments, and the withhold-ing of their products from the market, thereby contributing to widespread shortages of consumer goods and industrial inputs. Organized labor, led by the Confederación General de Trabajo, became more militant in demanding wage increases to reverse a decline in purchasing power. By February 1986, there were pow-erful political forces pushing for a revision of the Austral's freeze on wages and prices.

Reacting to these pressures, in early April 1986 Sourrouille announced a second phase of the Austral Plan. Along with moderate wage increases, Sourrouille replaced the system of rigid price controls with a new scheme of "administered prices" designed to satisfy entrepreneurs' demands for price hikes to accompany the increased costs of inputs. Also, the policy of fixed exchange rates was abandoned in favor of a return to the crawling-peg system of periodic devaluations.

The loosening of controls immediately sparked an acceleration of inflation. By the third quarter of 1986, the average of con-sumer and wholesale price indexes grew at a monthly rate of 7.6 percent. The budget deficit also increased, while the trade bal-ance deteriorated. Much of the blame for this was attributed to the Central Bank, which had resisted the tight monetary policies insisted on by the IMF. Economy Minister Sourrouille and the Central Bank also fought over the pace and scope of reforms of the financial system. These disputes testify to the political constraints that made it virtually impossible to mount a frontal attack on the underlying causes of inflation. The resulting impasse placed an enormous, and increasingly unsustainable, burden on wage and price controls.

Sourrouille responded by shifting to a progressively more restrictive monetary policy, by stepping up tax collection efforts, and by pledging to expand the privatization of state enterprises, while reintroducing direct controls over wages and prices. An attempt was made to maintain purchasing power by allowing wages to rise in line with inflation.

Despite the stops and starts, reliance on flexible controls scored some successes: following a period of stagnation, GDP expanded by 11 percent and industrial output by over 26 percent in the twelve months ending September 1986. Investment in machinery and equipment jumped nearly 35 percent in the same period. Inflation from June 1985 to June 1986 was only 50.1 percent; and at 86.8 percent, inflation in 1986 was the lowest since 1974.[28] But these figures are misleading because the Alfonsín administration failed to control the inflationary pressures generated by economic recovery.

This failure was admitted in September 1986, when Sourrouille imposed a monetary crunch to maintain price stability while limiting economic expansion. But by January 1987, when inflation jumped 7.6 percent, it was clear that the policy of monetary squeeze was not working, forcing Sourrouille to announce yet another round of heterodox shocks in February, including another "temporary" freeze on wages and prices. When the "Australito," as the reimposition of controls was dubbed, failed to stem the resurgence of inflation, the economic team was obliged to sign a new letter of intent with the IMF promising to carry out a much more stringent "structural adjustment." Official discourse identified three major objectives: to accelerate integration with the world-economy; to carry out a sweeping reform of capital markets; and to restructure and privatize public enterprises (including a pledge to lay off 20 percent of all public-sector employees over three years).[29]

With the Australito, Alfonsín and Sourrouille shifted to more orthodox and increasingly draconian measures, including extremely high positive interest rates, which rekindled inflationary pressures while simultaneously causing unemployment to rise and threatening to plunge the weakened economy into deep recession. In July 1987 a fourth shock was administered, but labor and entrepreneurial resistance torpedoed wage and price controls as inflation accelerated significantly in the second half of the year.

A palpable loss of credibility in the government's economic management plus a general sense of weariness and political disenchantment led to the Radicals' defeat in the September 1987 elections. The Peronists, in contrast to their poor showing in 1985 (when they received only 34 percent of the vote to the Radicals' 43 percent), staged an impressive political comeback in Congress, receiving 41 percent of the vote to 37 percent for the Radicals. The Peronists also took control of sixteen of 22 provincial governorships, including that of the populous Province of Buenos Aires; the Radicals retained control only in two provinces, including Córdoba. Alfonsín responded with a cabinet reshuffle and a fifth shock designed to reduce the budget deficit through large increases in tax revenues and higher charges for public services, which produced a sharp decline in real wages and strengthened already strong recessionary tendencies. Growth for 1987 was a meager 1.6 percent, with inflation nearing 180 percent and rising.

The logic of the debt crisis—payments on interest and principal exceeding new loans, resulting in a net transfer of capital to foreign creditors—continued to drive economic policy in 1988. The relevant data are presented in Table 10.2. The virtual exhaustion of foreign-exchange reserves (the trade surplus for 1987 was less than $1 billion), together with the Peronists' demands for new policies, forced Alfonsín to repeatedly stake his personal prestige in defense of his Economy Minister's policies. Sourrouille, in turn, adopted a tougher bargaining posture vis-à-vis the IMF and the creditor banks. Notwithstanding the rhetoric, however, a letter of intent specifying stringent austerity goals was agreed to with the IMF in February 1988. The failure of these measures was soon evident, however, as inflation continued to skyrocket at an annual rate of nearly 400 percent.

TABLE 10.2

Selected Indicators of Argentina's Foreign Debt Burden

(*Millions of U.S. dollars*)

	Foreign debt	New loans	Principal repaid	Interest repaid	Net transfer[a]
1970[b]	$5,171	$907	$772	$338	−$203
1975[b]	6,581	920	1,422	723	−1,225
1980	27,157	4,708	1,853	1,337	1,518
1981	35,657	8,346	1,950	2,045	4,352
1982	43,634	7,054	1,294	2,435	3,325
1983	45,925	2,833	1,364	2,417	−948
1984	48,856	802	812	3,277	−3,268
1985	49,324	3,790	1,018	4,389	−1,617
1986	49,715	2,602	2,043	3,707	−3,147
1987	56,813	3,116	695	3,775	−1,354
1988[c]	60,200	2,600	1,759	2,757	−1,916

SOURCE: Bartlett, "A Vicious Circle Keeps Latin America in Debt," based upon data from the World Bank, the Institute of International Finance, and J. P. Morgan and Company.

[a] Difference between new loans and payments on old loans.
[b] Excludes short-term debt.
[c] Estimate.

Inflation rates above 25 percent in both July and August, together with the IMF's cancellation of undrawn loans from previous negotiations and the continuing net drain of capital abroad, left the government with precious little maneuvering room. To make matters worse, polls favoring the Peronist candidate in the upcoming May 1989 presidential elections led to a sense of desperation in the Radical party, which clamored for the government to do something, anything, to bring the economy under control. In response, the economic authorities resorted to yet another application of shock therapy. In early August 1988, Alfonsín and Sourrouille announced the so-called Plan Primavera (Spring Plan), consisting of a temporary price "truce" negotiated with the Unión Industrial, a 30-percent hike in public tariffs, and a 12-percent devaluation of the Austral. Inflation did fall, although the benefits were not distributed evenly; the big losers were the agricultural sector and wage earners, with oligopoly industrial firms and the financial sector the main beneficiaries.[30] As in the past, however, the exacerbation of distributional conflict caused by large income shifts from one group to another made for a highly volatile situation in which, with the exception of the speculators, almost everyone would eventually incur losses. This occurred sooner than expected. In March 1989 inflation exploded, reaching 80 percent in May and continuing to rise. The Austral, which had exchanged at 17 to the dollar in February, declined to almost 200 to the dollar in only four months. Panic speculation and massive capital flight fed fears that price hikes for the year might surpass 10,000 percent. By the eve of the May presidential election the Alfonsín government was virtually helpless, without any coherent economic strategy, heterodox or orthodox.

Social Pacts: A Surrogate for Class Compromise?

Alfonsín's commitment to democratic consolidation gave a particular urgency to the search for new mechanisms by which the relevant collective actors could be brought into the decision-making process. Proposals for *concertación* through "social and economic pacts" gained considerable cachet as the best way to guarantee and deepen the democratization process. Many saw in *concertación* virtues analogous to those manifested by democratic class compromises in an earlier period in the advanced capitalist world.[31]

What exactly is *concertación*, and could it serve as an effective surrogate for, or precursor to, democratic class compromise? *Concertación* is essentially a social democratic variant of familiar neo-corporatist arrangements to facilitate bargaining among labor organizations, business groups, and state elites. However, as in Western Europe, the objectives of *concertación* go beyond the regulation of distributive conflicts to proposals for the establishment of rules or norms to guide the functioning of the global economic system.[32]

Understandably, the allure of stabilization via pact-making lies in the possibility of counteracting negative-sum payoffs in situations of high inflation and low institutionalization of socio-political conflict. (Class compromises had similarly emerged in Europe in the troubled economic times of the 1930s.) Through pact-making, relevant social and economic actors are called upon to cooperate actively in making stabilization work, rather than shifting the burdens of austerity onto other groups in pursuit of short-term advantages. In addition to facilitating a more equitable sharing of the costs of stabilization, social pacts were believed to foster a more democratic political culture in which confrontation and veto politics were replaced by a new logic of positive-sum outcomes based upon compromise and bargaining. Theoretically, all groups and sectors would be better off in this democratic class struggle.

It should be made clear, however, that several demanding conditions must be fulfilled for a social pact between business, organized labor, and the state to succeed. First, *concertación* requires that the government and the regime be accepted as legitimate by the relevant social actors. Second, there must be a reasonable convergence in the overall strategies followed by capital, labor, and the state. Third, notwithstanding their contradictory interests, labor and capital must have clear incentives (usually in the context of economic crisis) to retreat from their maximalist goals and must reach an implicit agreement regarding a minimum policy agenda and the appropriate format to conduct their bargaining. Fourth, state elites must be willing to delegate at least part of their authority over economic matters to organized labor and associations representing entrepreneurial interests, thereby attributing public status to private interests. Finally, in exchange, business and labor leaders must be convinced to risk their own political power by mobilizing their ideological and organizational resources to assure the legitimation of state policies among their followers and within civil society as a whole. In Argentina, the fragmentation of interests on the part of both labor and capital (the absence of bilateral representational monopoly) means that fulfilling these conditions will prove no easy task.[33]

Prior to the Austral Plan the Alfonsín government had frequently proclaimed its interest in forging a social pact, but little progress was made.[34] In July 1984, Interior Minister Antonio Troccoli, a leading Radical politician, called for *concertación*, saying that the government wanted "much more than a simple agreement on prices and salaries"; what was at stake, he said, was nothing less than the definition of the "nation that we want." However, Economy Minister Grinspun showed little inclination to share responsibility for economic matters with representatives of labor and entrepreneurs.

In late September 1984, following a general strike against official policies, the CGT, the UIA, the SRA, and five other business organizations presented the government with a joint document calling for economic reactivation and a greater role for private initiative. With Grinspun and Troccoli continuing to emit contradictory signals, the government was unable to make the concessions required to reach an agreement. It continued to conduct on-again, off-again negotiations with the CGT and the business groups until January 1985, when the CGT finally broke off the talks.

At that point, Alfonsín called the CGT hierarchy to a secret meeting to iron out differences. The president presented a so-called "Pacto de Olivos" calling for a social and economic accord to be agreed to by labor and business. In addition to a pledge to maintain the level of real wages, the pact also called for the creation of an advisory commission consisting of government officials and union and business representatives.

The Pacto de Olivos represented a fleeting high point in attempts at *concertación*. As inflation mounted and Grinspun appeared on the way out, the so-called "Group of Eleven," consisting of the CGT and ten leading business organizations, conducted their own parallel *concertación*. This led to proposals for an alternative version of a social pact and an economic program substantially at odds with that of the government.

Relations between the state and representatives of labor and entrepreneurial interests deteriorated rapidly following the appointment of the new economic team headed by Sourrouille. In April, the president issued a dramatic call for a "war economy" from the balcony of the Casa Rosada. Saúl Ubaldini, one of the CGT's top leaders, responded with a virtual ultimatum: "either the government changes its policies or it [must] go." [35]

In this atmosphere of inflamed rhetoric and waning hopes for a social pact, it was not surprising that neither entrepreneurs nor organized labor played a role in formulating the new heterodox policies. The initial success of the Austral Plan in containing inflation allowed the government new autonomy in its negotiations with representatives of the different social forces. In effect, the macroeconomic logic of the Austral Plan relegated plans for a social pact to a decidedly secondary plane. This was bolstered by Radicalism's success in the by-elections for the Chamber of Deputies in November, and by Alfonsín's call for a "democratic convergence" in December 1985. [36]

Impelled by the failure of the Peronist party apparatus to regain the political initiative in the electoral arena, organized labor moved to radicalize its opposition to Alfonsín's economic policies. The CGT leadership went beyond criticism of the government's wage policies to call for a fundamental revision of the Austral Plan, including suspension of negotiations with the IMF and a moratorium on debt payments. At the same time, direct bilateral discussions, without state participation, between the CGT and the representative organizations of industry, agriculture, and commerce, which had advanced in the pre-Austral period, broke down almost completely.

The economic authorities were able to get much of the Austral Plan implemented over the opposition of the CGT by winning the tacit acceptance of individual unions crucial to its policies. The government took advantage of, and often promoted, serious divisions within the labor movement. When the CGT was "normalized" in November 1986 (it had been under government intervention since 1976), there existed three rival factions, all proclaiming their allegiance to Peronism: the 62 Organizaciones, the oldest grouping, was led by Lorenzo Miguel and defended its role as the guardian of Peronist orthodoxy in the labor movement; the Movimiento de Renovación Sindical Peronista, an independent, "renovating" faction, had emerged in opposition to the Proceso (when it was known as the Comisión de los 25); and *ubaldinismo*, a new faction, was defined by loyalty to the personalistic leadership of Saúl Ubaldini, the new secretary-general of the CGT. Subsequently, there emerged a fourth faction known as the Grupo de los 15, whose principal figure was Carlos Alderete, leader of the powerful Luz y Fuerza electrical workers union. Alfonsín's political strategists succeeded in co-opting this last grouping (and further dividing the labor movement) by naming Alderete to head the Labor Ministry in April.[37]

The deterioration in real wages, shown in Table 10.3, strongly conditioned organized labor's relations with the government. The plight of workers and the salaried middle class—marked by the sharp decline in real wages registered in 1985 and the failure to recover wage levels of 1983–84—interacted with the failure of the social pact, the onset of recession, and conflicts among rival currents to produce the fluctuations in strike behavior revealed in Figure 10.2.[38]

TABLE 10.3

The Evolution of Real Wages

(*Dec. 1983 = 100*)

	Manufacturing		Public administration		State enterprises	
	Level	Percent variation	Level	Percent variation	Level	Percent variation
1982	73.5	−5.2%	82.3	−25.4%	70.6	−22.4%
1983	93.4	27.0	90.3	9.8	94.7	34.1
1984	112.4	20.4	91.9	1.7	97.9	3.4
1985	90.3	−19.7	71.1	−22.6	86.5	−11.6
1986	92.2	2.1	67.1	−5.6	92.9	7.4
1987	86.7	−5.9	66.3	−1.3	86.0	−7.4
1988	74.5	−12.5	78.7	33.2	90.0	−0.4

SOURCE: *Clarín Económico*, 7 Aug. 1988, p. 2. Based upon data from FIEL and the Ministry of Economy.

NOTE: Wage data refer to wages actually received; variations are calculated on an annual basis; data for the public administration refer to "category 16" employees; 1988 data are estimates for August.

For Alfonsín and Sourrouille, deepening conflicts with organized labor did not mean cozy relations with the entrepreneurial class. The failure to incorporate the business community into an institutionalized social pact stemmed in part from capital's own political and organizational fragmentation. Contradictory interests pitted urban capital against rural producers. Industrial firms frequently had different interests from the commercial and financial sectors. In the key industrial sector, longstanding antagonisms also existed between smaller firms producing for the mass consumption market and large national and transnational firms producing for the affluent and for export to the world market. For example, large Argentine and transnational firms generally supported the Austral Plan's anti-inflation achievements, and strongly opposed wage concessions to labor. After all, why agree to concessions to labor or rely on the uncertainties of *concertación* when the government's incomes policy guaranteed wage restraint? Why not let Alfonsín, Sourrouille, and the Radicals pay the political price of antagonizing labor?

Even though the *concertación* framework did not give capital a direct role in shaping macroeconomic policy, there existed an implicit pact between certain entrepreneurial groups and the Alfonsín regime. Informal contacts and negotiations *a título per-*

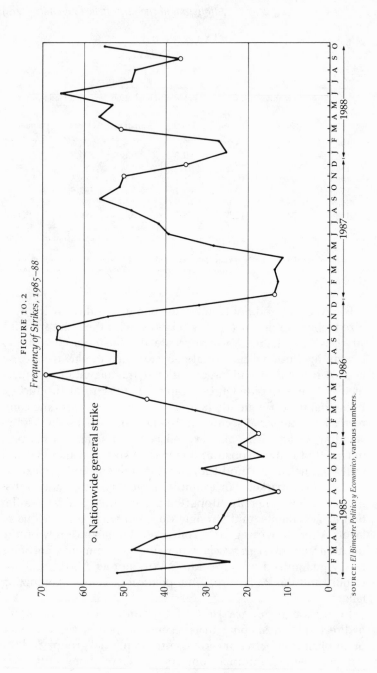

FIGURE 10.2
Frequency of Strikes, 1985–88

○ Nationwide general strike

SOURCE: *El Bimestre Político y Economico*, various numbers.

sonal between leading figures known as the "captains of industry" and Alfonsín and the economic authorities took place regularly. These "captains" represented a diverse array of economic
groups, ranging from modern agro-industrial enterprises, large
construction companies, and other firms dependent on public-
sector spending to the most modern and dynamic manufacturing firms, many capable of competing in world markets.[39]

The Alfonsín government's project for industrial reconversion
and reinsertion in the world-economy, and the imperative to
generate large trade surpluses to service the debt, essentially
coincided with the interests of specific "captains" and economic
groups as well as with those of the largest and most dynamic
firms, thereby making a formal social pact unnecessary. For Alfonsín and Sourrouille, it made better sense to avoid the cum-
bersome formalities of *concertación* and, instead, to try to gain
private-sector compliance by granting the top elite of the Argentine entrepreneurial class and specific transnational firms special access to policymakers.[40] It may be questioned, however,
whether the privileged treatment accorded entrepreneurs who,
in the recent past, had benefited handsomely from their support
of military rule served the cause of democratic consolidation.

Even entrepreneurial support for Alfonsín from the "captains" evaporated in the rarefied environment preceding the
presidential elections. Economic chaos in the wake of the collapse of the Plan Primavera was the primary factor responsible
for the victory of the Peronist candidate on 14 May 1989. Carlos
Saúl Menem, the governor of the poor province of La Rioja, garnered a convincing 47 percent of the vote to defeat Eduardo
Angeloz, the Radical standard-bearer and governor of Córdoba,
who received 37 percent of the vote. Despite his popular support, Menem's vague promise of a "productive revolution" offered precious few ideas about how the Peronists intended to
tackle the intractable problems of foreign debt, fiscal crisis, and
uncontrollable inflation. Few Argentines, including fervent *justicialistas*, believed that the country's precipitous economic decline would soon be reversed.

The Unfinished Agenda of Class Compromise

The legacy of heterodox policymaking leaves lingering questions. Heterodox policies helped to avoid disaster, but did they

lead to economic stabilization? Have they contributed to the emergence of a class compromise furthering democratic consolidation? The Austral Plan demonstrated that heterodox programs can, for a while at least, successfully control high inflation. The Austral performed better than past orthodox stabilization policies in curbing inflation and maintaining positive growth rates. By the same token, one major failure was that entrepreneurs' expectations were destabilized, thereby stimulating even more massive speculation and discouraging investment of a long-term nature. Again compared to the probable effects of more orthodox policies, the Austral Plan was partially successful in cushioning the effects of austerity and in moderating regressive impacts on labor and the poor.[41]

Despite these achievements, the Argentine experience also makes clear that heterodox programs face severe challenges when wage and price controls are loosened. It remains unclear how the "invisible hand" of the market is to take over without the danger of reigniting inflation and renewing the distributive struggles that undermine fragile democracies. The answer, as orthodox critics correctly point out, depends in part on the audacity with which state elites take advantage of disinflation to attack the "deep" causes of endemic inflation.

Paradoxically, success in reducing inertial inflation (and the "inflationary tax" charged by state and private agents such as banks and oligopoly price setters) may have actually exacerbated conflicts over income distribution. However, greater transparency in the functioning of the economy, combined with the ability to calculate costs more precisely, led labor and capital to act more aggressively to defend and, if possible, to increase their relative shares of national income.

Are heterodox policies more supportive of democracy than orthodox alternatives? What if IMF-style stabilization programs had been adopted by the Alfonsín government in June 1985? Perhaps a positive trade balance would have been achieved, thus pleasing the IMF and the creditor banks. However, the fate of orthodox experiments in other countries leads one to believe that the implementation of a conventional "structural adjustment" strategy probably would have caused a much more drastic fall in aggregate demand.

By postponing recession and partially cushioning social conflict, heterodox policies bought time and badly needed maneuvering room for the beleaguered Alfonsín government. However, civilian sectors of uncertain loyalty, many of whom were never attracted to heterodox policies in any event, tended to view Alfonsín's and Sourrouille's refusal to adopt "tough" (i.e., orthodox) measures as tantamount to "populism" and a harbinger of uncontrollable unrest and economic collapse. This perception held the risk of setting in motion a profoundly reactionary logic leading to demands for an authoritarian "restoration of order."

In postauthoritarian situations, political legitimacy is very fragile and is at least in part contingent on material payoffs. A less equivocal loyalty to democratic institutions and norms requires time to develop. Heterodox policies alone cannot guarantee success, of course, but the Austral Plan did help the Alfonsín government survive trying circumstances. Of perhaps greater importance than economic payoffs was the fact that there is a greater commitment to democracy than ever before, and a somewhat greater awareness of the immense difficulties of promoting growth.

The implementation of the heterodox shocks in Argentina calls attention to a real danger. If heterodox stabilization merely attacks the inertial component of inflation, leaving underlying causes of high inflation and price disequilibrium untouched, policymakers will face a strong temptation to reimpose controls. But a succession of heterodox shocks will undermine the credibility of official policies, provoke a new eruption of runaway inflation, and seriously weaken the popularity of elected officials. Although the legitimacy of democratic institutions remained largely intact, the Radicals' 1987 electoral setback caused Alfonsín to propose a "pact of governability" to ensure legislative support for government policies. The Peronists were lukewarm,[42] and the CGT immediately rejected the pact, clearly preferring to maintain their distance from the government in anticipation of the May 1989 presidential elections.

The use by policymakers of the "heterodox breathing space" raises additional questions about the interactions of democracy and stabilization. Heterodox policies initially acted on politicians and policymakers like a powerful aphrodisiac. The easy popularity generated by the magical "quick fix" generated a sense of euphoric complacency that obscured the need to broaden and deepen the democratization process. At the outset of the transition from authoritarianism, social pacts in the framework of *concertación* were seen as ideal institutional arrangements for combating inflation while consolidating democracy. The evidence is ambiguous, but the Argentine experience is not encouraging on this score. For the most part, business and labor merely observed the unfolding of the Austral Plan from the sidelines. They protested vociferously when their interests were affected, but had little or no say in policy implementation.

Several of the reasons for the marginal role played by *concertación* are evident. First, business associations and labor organizations were hardly capable of disciplining their heterogeneous memberships. Organized labor, in particular, was plagued by internecine struggles that made it difficult for the unions to mobilize the legitimacy and resources required of interlocutors in a workable social pact. Second, by pursuing particularistic strategies to maximize nominal wages or profits, labor and especially capital operated as textbook examples of free-riders hell-bent on transferring the costs of stabilization onto each other or onto consumers and the state. Third, the Alfonsín administration was constantly plagued by bureaucratic struggles within the policymaking apparatus. These intra-regime struggles undercut the ability of state elites to bargain and compromise with organized labor and business organizations. Rather than showing a willingness to cede part of its decision-making authority to private groups—a prerequisite for successful macroeconomic policymaking through social pacts—the Alfonsín government, particularly the economic teams under both Grinspun and Sourrouille, usually attempted to insulate themselves from the political arena and sought to follow familiar technobureaucratic modes of decision-making and policy implementation. In effect, the Alfonsín government demanded passive acquiescence to official policies while refusing effective consultation with the very parties on whose cooperation successful stabilization depended.

By the close of the Alfonsín years, heterodox policies were little more than a memory. The Austral Plan's audacity in setting forth new instruments to confront the economic crisis had been progressively diluted by moves toward more orthodox policies, including a greater opening to world markets, "rolling back the state," and accommodation with external creditors.[43]

A question of political leadership arises. Why did the initial popular enthusiasm for the Austral Plan turn into despair? The Alfonsín government can be faulted for its timidity in attempting to build new political coalitions and institutions to channel popular support on behalf of a program of social and economic reform. Consequently, the famous Argentine *mufa*, that combination of collective frustration, desperation, and cynicism, became widespread, feeding a dangerous demobilization and retreat into civic privatism. Moreover, the initial successes of heterodox policies could not make up for a similar political timidity in reforming inefficient and unjust financial systems and revising fiscal and tax policies. If attempted soon enough, a concerted attempt to parlay the initial euphoria produced by the Austral Plan into measures such as exchange reforms, elimination of public-sector "sacred cows," and progressive taxation might have provided the underpinnings for long-term success.

Finally, the initial success in controlling inflation could not be sustained in view of the failure to resolve the debt crisis. Alfonsín and the economic authorities share only part of the blame, however. Primary responsibility falls elsewhere, on the IMF, the international bankers, and the Reagan administration. Still, the essentially political failures by Argentine leaders make sober judgments unavoidable. Alfonsín and his *heterodoxo* advisers not only hesitated in eliciting popular support for their policies through *concertación* and the expansion of participation, they also shrank back from the unpalatable, but strategically necessary, task of expanding their base of political support. When distributional conflicts make it inevitable that there will be winners and losers, democrats must take the offensive or run the risk of conceding the political and ideological leadership to the enemies of democracy.

The conundrum was a real one. In effect, rather than risk civilian rule (and its own power) by extending democratization beyond the politico-institutional sphere to address the transformation of the political economy, the Alfonsín government opted to manage the economy and the structures of economic power inherited from the days of authoritarian rule. Alfonsín and his strategists probably felt that they had no choice, and they may have been correct. But their chosen course was very dangerous, because by reaffirming the existing order they risked losing popular support and legitimacy. And without that mobilization of active popular support, state elites in fragile democracies face virtually irresistible pressures from powerful domestic and transnational interests to abandon alternative policies, like the Austral Plan, in favor of unadorned IMF orthodoxy.

Are there any options? Economic mismanagement under authoritarianism bequeathed the Radicals a disastrous legacy. But, after more than six years of civilian rule, the failures of the half-measures like the Austral Plan are also apparent. Perhaps the lesson to be learned is that if stabilization and external adjustment programs are to succeed, the making of macroeconomic policy can no longer remain the exclusive preserve of technocratic elites, even those of a heterodox persuasion. In Argentina, legitimation through elections is not sufficient to guarantee popular acceptance of painful stabilization policies. Given the powerful corporatist logic that pervades Argentine society, good government and competent economic management are not enough. Stabilization must be negotiated directly through bargaining and compromise with relevant social and economic actors.

Attempts to forge a viable class compromise should not be limited to the confines of *concertación*, however. Social pacts may play a useful role, but only a limited one. Particularly if recession and inflation worsen, there is a real danger that without the political will to extend representation—and real influence—to a broad array of collective actors, social pacts may actually undermine fragile democracies. Moreover, the rhetoric of social pacts may actually serve to mask the absence of effective consultation and obscure the largely decorative role of political parties and parliamentary bodies in macroeconomic policymaking and implementation. In this regard, the reliance on executive decrees to implement heterodox stabilization is a clear brake on the democratization process. Without broader participation by politicians and the major political actors not represented by the powerful corporate interests, social pacts may become little more than a façade behind which the aggrandizement of executive prerogative and the privatization of state power can coexist undisturbed by accountability to elected representatives.

This raises a fundamental question about democracy and effective economic strategies. It is tempting to conclude that economic success requires more democratic decision-making processes. However, there probably is little necessary correlation between the two spheres except in the kind of extreme case Argentina lived between 1976 and 1980, in which there was almost no penetration by civil society in the decision-making process. The irony nevertheless remains that the centralization of power in the executive probably holds less promise for democratic consolidation than a "riskier" strategy based on the empowerment of elected politicians and other actors in civil society who have been long excluded from meaningful participation in national politics. This interpretation no doubt goes against the grain of more conventional views. Many analysts and practitioners of an orthodox as well as a heterodox persuasion will no doubt feel that the effective representation of the political parties and major collective actors—more democracy, in other words—can only intensify an already contentious environment, thereby working against rational and consistent economic policymaking. But the failures of technocratic modes of policymaking under both civilian and military regimes in Argentina and elsewhere provide little support for this position. In fact, at least in Argentina, heterodox policies probably did not fare better precisely because democratization was not carried far enough.

The preference for democracy is not merely normative, but stems from practical concerns as well. In the end, there are no easy recipes for economic stabilization with social justice and without authoritarianism. At the risk of sounding utopian, it may be that if viable solutions are to be found for restructuring the Argentine political economy, their implementation will require a more far-reaching democratization of the state and social and economic life. And in this we find the principal lesson of the drama of Argentine politics in the late twentieth century.

Reference Matter

Notes

For full forms of citation of works given in short form in the Notes, see the Bibliography following.

Chapter One

1. See the discussion of alternative conceptions of political economy in Tozze, "Perspectives and Theory: A Consumer's Guide"; and Gilpin, *The Political Economy of International Relations*.

2. O'Donnell's most complete statement of the bureaucratic-authoritarian model can be found in his *Modernization and Bureaucratic-Authoritarianism*, and in "Reflections on the Patterns of Change in the Bureaucratic-Authoritarian State." In terms of the sociology of knowledge, O'Donnell's contribution—combining as it did elements from the modernization school as well the then-emerging dependency perspective, interwoven with strands of analysis belonging to classical Marxism (e.g., the analysis of dictatorial "regimes of exception")—was advanced at a very propitious moment of intellectual crisis. See Klarén, "Lost Promise: Explaining Latin American Underdevelopment"; and, for the Argentine case, Verón, *Imperialismo, lucha de clases y conocimiento: 25 años de sociología en la Argentina*.

3. For the most extensive critique of the BA model, see Cammack, "The Political Economy of Contemporary Military Regimes in Latin America: From Bureaucratic-Authoritarianism to Restructuring." Many of the criticisms advanced by Cammack were foreshadowed in earlier, less harsh evaluations. See, for example, Kaufman, "Industrial Change and Authoritarian Rule in Latin America: A Concrete Review of the Bureaucratic Authoritarian Model"; Cardoso, "On the Characterization of Authoritarian Regimes in Latin America"; Serra, "Three Mistaken Theses Regarding the Connection between Industrialization and Authoritarian Regimes"; Hirschman, "The Turn to Authoritarianism in Latin America and the Search for Its Economic Determinants"; and Remmer and Merkx, "Bureaucratic-Authoritarianism Revisited."

4. For a persuasive argument in favor of a diversity of historical paths, see Cardoso and Faletto, *Dependency and Development in Latin America*. Also see Roxborough, "Unity and Diversity in Latin American History," which makes explicit the Cardoso/Faletto insistence on diversity in criticizing the BA model and other "modal pattern" paradigms. O'Donnell is aware that there are fundamental differences between the military regimes of the 1960s and those of the 1970s. For instance, in his later work he no longer discusses the imperative of "deepening" and instead mentions "transnationalization" as the underlying economic project of these regimes. See O'Donnell, "Las fuerzas armadas y el estado autoritario del Cono Sur de América Latina." In fact, attempts to find a close correlation between regime types and economic performance have not been particularly convincing. See Hartlyn and Morley, "Political Regimes and Economic Performance in Latin America." Variables other than regime type, such as the class composition of governing coalitions, prevailing ideologies, or the international context, seem equally if not more significant.

5. Cammack, p. 4. Some of the difficulties are immediately apparent from Collier's attempt to offer "an inventory of alternative explanations of the rise of authoritarianism and its non-appearance in certain countries," which lists sixteen factors broad enough to cover almost any situation. See Collier, "The Bureaucratic-Authoritarian Model: Synthesis and Priorities for Future Research," p. 388.

6. See Daniel Levine's essay "Paradigm Lost: Dependence to Democracy," for a critical review of O'Donnell, Schmitter, and Whitehead, eds., *Transitions from Authoritarian Rule: Prospects for Democracy*.

7. See Cammack, and also Rouquié and Sidicaro, "Etats autoritaires et liberalisme économique en Amérique Latine: une approche hétérodoxe." In an essay published in the same volume as Cammack's article, I offered an interpretation of post-1976 Argentina based on the restructuring perspective: "Reflections on the Political Economy of Authoritarian Rule and Capitalist Reorganization in Contemporary Argentina." A revised and expanded version appears as Chapter 9 of this book.

8. Cammack, p. 25. While a strong critic of the BA model, Cammack calls attention to one of O'Donnell's articles as offering suggestive insights compatible with the restructuring perspectives. See Guillermo O'Donnell, "State and Alliances in Argentina, 1956–1976."

9. See the methodological distinctions between "lumpers" and "splitters" made by Cammack. Also see Roxborough in "Unity and Diversity in Latin American History." In this context, the BA model is preeminently "lumper" in orientation, while the restructuring perspective exemplifies a "splitter" approach to comparative analysis. Among Latin Americanists, the possibilities of the latter approach have been best re-

alized in Charles Bergquist's excellent study of the working class in the export sector. See his *Labor in Latin America*. For a stimulating discussion of alternative approaches to the logic of comparison, see Skocpol and Somers, "The Uses of Comparative History in Macro-Social Inquiry."

10. See Garretón, "Em Torno da Discussão sobre os Novos Regimes Autoritários na América Latina."

11. See the comments on relations between the state and class in William Canak, "The Peripheral State Debate: State Capitalist and Bureaucratic-Authoritarian Regimes in Latin America"; and Esping-Andersen, Friedland, and Wright, "Modes of Class Struggle and the Capitalist State."

12. For surveys of recent theoretical work on the state, see Jessop, *The Capitalist State*; and Carnoy, *The State and Political Theory*. For my own critique of this literature, see William C. Smith, "Crisis of the State and Military-Authoritarian Rule in Argentina, 1966–1973," chap. 1.

13. For a pioneering discussion of why authoritarian regimes find it so difficult to consolidate their rule, see Linz, "The Future of an Authoritarian Situation or the Institutionalization of an Authoritarian Regime: The Case of Brazil."

14. As Skocpol notes, "State organizations necessarily compete with the dominant class(es) in appropriating resources from the economy and society." As state elites seek to increase the size and autonomy of state institutions, their attempts "merely to perform the state's 'own' functions may create conflicts of interest with the dominant class." Finally, she explains that "Although both the state and the dominant class(es) share a broad interest in keeping the subordinate classes in place in society and at work in the existing economy, the state's own fundamental interest in maintaining sheer physical order and political peace may lead it—especially in times of crisis—to enforce concessions to subordinate-class demands. These concessions may be at the expense of the interests of the dominant class, but not contrary to the state's own interests in controlling the population and collecting taxes and military recruits." See Skocpol, *States and Social Revolutions: A Comparative Analysis of France, Russia, and China*, p. 30.

15. See O'Donnell and Schmitter, eds., *Transitions from Authoritarian Rule: Tentative Conclusions*; and William C. Smith, "The Political Transition in Brazil: From Authoritarian Liberalization and Elite Conciliation to Democratization."

16. See Therborn, "The Rule of Capital and the Rise of Democracy"; and Offe, "Competitive Party Democracy and the Keynesian Welfare State."

17. In addition to the essays by Therborn and Offe, see Bowles and

Gintis, *Democracy and Capitalism: Property, Community, and the Contradictions of Modern Social Thought.*

18. The following discussion draws heavily on the work of Przeworski. See especially his *Capitalism and Social Democracy*, and "The Structure of Class Conflict in Democratic Capitalist Societies," co-authored with Michael Wallerstein.

19. Przeworski, "Compromiso de clases y Estado: Europa Occidental y América Latina," p. 249.

20. On the frequently overlooked role of the middle class, see Fuentes Muñoz-Ledo, *The Middle Class and Democracy in Latin America: Argentina, Brazil, and Mexico.*

21. Gramsci, *Selections from the Prison Notebooks*, p. 210 and *passim*; and Huntington, *Political Order in Changing Societies*, chap. 4.

22. For a provocative exploration of these questions, see Korzeniewicz, "Labor in the Semiperiphery: Argentina, Australia and Brazil"; Arrighi and Drangel, "The Stratification of the World-Economy: An Exploration of the Semiperipheral Zone"; and Arrighi, Korzeniewicz, and Martin, "Three Crises, Three Zones: Core-Periphery Relations in the Long Twentieth Century."

Chapter Two

1. Díaz Alejandro, *Essays on the Economic History of the Argentine Republic*, pp. 54–58.

2. Llach, *Reconstrucción o estancamiento*, pp. 25–35. Llach's provocative analysis of the reasons for Argentina's decline is that of an economist. For an excellent analysis focusing on questions central to the sociology of development, see Waisman, *Reversal of Development in Argentina: Postwar Counterrevolutionary Policies and Their Structural Consequences*, especially chaps. 1, 2, and 7.

3. Sábato, "Notas sobre la formación de la clase dominante en la Argentina moderna (1880–1914)." Also see Oszlak, *La formación del estado argentino.*

4. Cortés Conde and Gallo, *La formación de la Argentina moderna*, pp. 25–26; Sunkel and Paz, *El subdesarrollo latinoamericano y la teoría del desarrollo*, pp. 50–62; Furtado, *Economic Development of Latin America: A Survey from Colonial Times to the Cuban Revolution*, pp. 27–34; and Ferrer, *The Argentine Economy*, pp. 75–132.

5. See the classic studies by Germani, *Estructura social de la Argentina* and *Política y sociedad en una época de transición*. Also see Murmis, Pérsico, and Cepeda, *Tipos de capitalismo y estructura de clases.*

6. Sábato, "Notas sobre la formación de la clase dominante," pp. 139–40. Also see Cavarozzi, "Elementos para una caracterización

del capitalismo oligárquico"; Flishman, *La renta del suelo y el desarrollo agrario argentino*; and Balán, "Una cuestión regional en la Argentina: burguesías provinciales y el mercado nacional en el desarrollo agro-exportador."

7. Gallo and Sigal, "La formación de los partidos políticos contemporáneos: La U.C.R. (1890–1916)"; and Rock, *Politics in Argentina, 1890–1930: The Rise and Fall of Radicalism*, pp. 34–40.

8. Peter Smith, *Argentina and the Failure of Democracy: Conflict Among Political Elites, 1904–1955*, pp. 92–93.

9. Smith notes that because non-citizen immigrants were excluded, "the suffrage was effectively extended *from the upper class to selected segments of the middle class, to the distinct disadvantage of the lower class, especially the urban working class*," ibid., p. 11 (emphasis in original).

10. Cornbilt, "La opción conservadora en la política argentina," p. 620 (emphasis in original).

11. Peter Smith, "The Breakdown of Democracy in Argentina, 1916–1930"; and Rock, *Politics in Argentina*, pp. 241–51.

12. For interpretations stressing the centrality of politics over economic factors in the 1930 coup, see Rock, *Politics in Argentina*, and Potter, *Political Institutions, Political Decay and the Argentine Crisis of 1930*.

13. Potash, *El éjercito y la política en la Argentina, 1928–1945: De Yrigoyen a Perón*, pp. 53–87.

14. Ibid., pp. 88–154, and Goldwert, *Democracy, Militarism, and Nationalism in Argentina, 1930–1966*, pp. 35–50.

15. By late 1933 Justo's economic team explicitly recognized that the previous phase of prodigious growth under the direct stimulus of the European economy had come to an end. See Murmis and Portantiero, *Estudios sobre los orígenes del peronismo/1*, p. 21. Also see Díaz Alejandro, *Essays*, pp. 98, 103; Villanueva, "Economic Development," pp. 62–66; and Jorge, *Industria y concentración económica*, pp. 107–8.

16. See Jorge, *Industria*, Table 5, p. 77, and Table 13, p. 133.

17. On the notion of a specific "state interest," see Skocpol, *States and Social Revolutions: A Comparative Analysis of France, Russia, and China*, chap. 1.

18. Murmis and Portantiero, *Estudios*, pp. 44–45, and Llach, "Dependencia, procesos sociales y control del estado en la década del treinta."

19. On conflicts between these two groups in the post–World War I era, see Ortiz, *Historia económica de la Argentina*, and Peter Smith, *Carne y política en la Argentina*, especially chap. 6.

20. Llach, "El Plan Pinedo, su significado histórico y los orígenes de la economía política del peronismo," pp. 23, 92.

21. For the parliamentary debates and the positions of the parties and economic groups, see *ibid.*, and Murmis and Portantiero, *Estudios*, pp. 35–42.

22. Spalding, *Organized Labor in Latin America*, pp. 157–62; Bergquist, *Labor in Latin America*, pp. 139–48; Doyon, "El crecimiento sindical bajo el peronismo"; and Peralta Ramos, *Acumulación del capital y crisis política en Argentina (1930–1974)*, pp. 56–62.

23. Luna, *Ortiz: Reportaje a la Argentina opulenta*.

24. See the statements by General Luis Perlinger, the Interior Minister of the new regime, and other figures active in the coup quoted by Potash, *El éjercito*, pp. 197, 225–26.

25. Vilas, "Política y conflictos sociales de la industrialización periférica: El primer peronismo." Also see Panaia and Lesser, "Las estrategías militares frente al proceso de industrialización (1943–1947)."

26. Ciria, *Partidos y poder en la Argentina moderna (1930–1946)*, pp. 319–24.

27. Díaz Alejandro, *Essays*, p. 110; and Mallon and Sourrouille, *Economic Policymaking in a Conflict Society: The Argentine Case*, p. 9.

28. Skupch, "Nacionalización, libras bloqueadas y sustitución de importaciones"; Díaz Alejandro, *Essays*, pp. 106–26; Mallon and Sourrouille, *Economic Policymaking*, pp. 5–14 and Table 2–1, p. 38; and Fodor, "Perón's Policies for Agricultural Exports, 1946–1948: Dogmatism or Commonsense?"

29. Notwithstanding frequent analogies to Bonapartism, Caesarism, or other variants of "bourgeois revolution from above," studies suggest that industrialists played little or no role in the emergence of Peronism prior to 1948. See Kenworthy, "Did the 'New Industrialists' Play a Significant Role in the Formation of the Peronist Coalition?," pp. 15–28. For assertions that industrialists did support Perón, see Cuneo, *Crisis y comportamiento de la clase empresaria*, pp. 180–90; and Niosi, *Los empresarios y el Estado argentino*, pp. 18–19.

30. Cuneo, *Crisis y comportamiento*, pp. 191–214.

31. Mainwaring, "The State, Political Crisis, and Regime Breakdown: Peronism, 1952–1955," p. 122.

32. Deconcentration occurred in the slower growing light industrial sectors (textiles, food and beverages, clothing, etc.), while concentration proceeded in the more dynamic intermediate and heavy industrial sectors (basic metals, vehicles, petrochemicals, etc.), which increased both their proportion of industrial GDP and share of industrial employment. See Goetz, "Concentración y desconcentración en la industria argentina desde la década de 1930 a la de 1960"; and Santu, "Poder económico y burguesía industrial en la Argentina, 1930–1954."

33. See Cardoso and Faletto, *Dependency and Development in Latin*

America, pp. 137–38, for the political and ideological consequences of this for the populist compromise.

34. On Peronist ideology, see Ciria, *Perón y el justicialismo*, and Corradi, "Between Corporatism and Insurgency: The Sources of Ambiguity in Peronist Ideology."

35. Speech by Perón before the Buenos Aires Stock Exchange in August 1944, in Perón, *El pueblo quiere saber de qué se trata*. Also see Perón's *La comunidad organizada*.

36. Quoted by Vilas, "Política y conflictos sociales," p. 60.

37. Doyon, "El crecimiento sindical," Table 3, p. 158.

38. Little, "Party and State in Peronist Argentina."

39. Doyon, "Conflictos obreros durante el régimen peronista (1946–1955)."

40. Godio, *La caída de Perón*, and Peña, ed., *El peronismo: Selección de documentos*, pp. 146–47.

41. F. H. Cardoso, "Associated-Dependent Development: Theoretical and Practical Implications." Also see Gerchunoff and Llach, "Capitalismo industrial, desarrollo asociado y distribución del ingreso entre los dos gobiernos peronistas: 1950–1972."

42. This jump of 243 percent compares with an increase of only 32 percent for Latin America as a whole in the same period. See Sourrouille, "La presencia y comportamiento de las empresas extranjeras en el sector industrial argentino," for a survey of the transnational presence in Argentina.

43. Khavise and Piotskowski, "La consolidación hegemónica de los factores extranacionales: El caso de 'las cien empresas industriales más grandes'"; Cimillo et al., *Acumulación y centralización del capital en la industria argentina*; Skupch, "Concentración industrial en la Argentina: 1955–1966."

44. Fracchia and Altimir, "Income Distribution in Argentina," p. 114.

45. Braun and Joy, "A Model of Economic Stagnation: A Case Study of the Argentine Economy." On the failure of producers to make improvements in agricultural productivity, see Martínez de Hoz, *La agricultura y la ganadería argentina en el período 1930–1960*, chap. 6; and Díaz Alejandro, *Essays*, chap. 3.

46. See Brodersohn, "Políticas económicas de corto plazo, crecimiento con inflación en la Argentina, 1950–1972." For an exploration of the pendular movements of the different fractions of capital, see O'Donnell, "State and Alliances in Argentina, 1956–1976"; and Portantiero, "Economía y política en la crisis argentina: 1958–1973."

47. See F. H. Cardoso, *Ideologías de la burguesía industrial en las sociedades dependientes (Argentina y Brasil)*, chap. 5.

48. O'Donnell, "State and Alliances in Argentina."

49. Mallon and Sourrouille, *Economic Policymaking*, pp. 14–19; and Wynia, *Argentina in the Postwar Era: Politics and Economic Policymaking in a Divided Society*, chap. 6.

50. Hodges, *Argentina, 1943–1976: The National Revolution and Resistance*, chap. 3.

51. Data on sociopolitical protest used in this and subsequent chapters—to be referred to as the "Archive on Sociopolitical Protest in Argentina, 1956–1974"—was compiled from the daily newspaper *La Razón*. Each event (e.g., strike, bombing, attempted assassination) was recorded separately and then aggregated on a monthly, quarterly, or yearly basis, as appropriate. This project was carried out under the direction of Guillermo O'Donnell, with the participation of Lila Milutín and Ricardo Milutín. Lila Milutín and the author completed the data set for the 1973–74 period. I thank Guillermo O'Donnell for sharing this valuable data and Lila Milutín for her help in its analysis.

52. Snow, *Political Forces in Argentina*, p. 29.

53. Mallon and Sourrouille, *Economic Policymaking*, p. 21.

54. Goldwert, *Democracy, Militarism, and Nationalism*, pp. 188–202; and Springer, "Disunity and Disorder: Factional Politics in the Argentine Military."

55. O'Donnell, "Modernization and Military Coups: Theory, Comparisons, and the Argentine Case," and William Smith, "The Armed Forces and the Bureaucratic-Authoritarian State in Argentina."

56. Snow, "Parties and Politics in Argentina: The Elections of 1962 and 1963."

57. Niosi, *Los empresarios*, chap. 5.

58. Astiz, "The Argentine Armed Forces: Their Role and Political Involvement."

59. For an analysis of military thinking in the immediate pre-coup period, see William Smith, "The Armed Forces and the Bureaucratic-Authoritarian State."

60. See the excellent essay by Korzeniewicz, "Labor in the Semiperiphery: Argentina, Australia and Brazil in the Long Twentieth Century." Also see Arrighi and Drangel, "The Stratification of the World-Economy: An Exploration of the Semiperipheral Zone," and Arrighi, Korzeniewicz, and Martin, "Three Crises, Three Zones: Core-Periphery Relations in the Long Twentieth Century."

61. See Vilas, "Política y conflictos sociales," Table 11, and Kaplan, "El estado empresario en la Argentina," for a detailed discussion of state enterprises during this period.

62. Díaz Alejandro, *Essays*, pp. 111–12; Mallon and Sourrouille, *Economic Policymaking*, pp. 54–55; and Eshag and Thorp, "Las políticas económicas ortodoxas de Perón a Guido (1953–1963)," p. 71.

63. Mallon and Sourrouille, *Economic Policymaking*, p. 13; and Ferrer, *Crisis y alternativas de la política económica argentina*, pp. 27–33.

Chapter Three

1. A capitalist state (as opposed to a state in a capitalist society) employs positive, negative, and disguising selective mechanisms in formulating public policy. Positive selective mechanisms serve to distill a "collective interest of capital" from the narrow, more parochial interests of specific entrepreneurial groups divided by competition. Negative mechanisms exclude anti-system interests from the state's policy agenda. Disguising mechanisms operate to maintain the appearance of neutrality and technical rationality in the implementation of class-specific policies in a market economy. These mechanisms operate through a hierarchy of processes, consisting of institutional structures, ideology, and repression. See Offe, "Structural Problems of the Capitalist State," and "The Theory of the State and the Problem of Policy Formation."

2. The "language of the state," as Poulantzas labels it (noting that "not everyone can talk the language of the state, nor can it come from just anywhere"), consists of interconnected discourses directed toward diverse sectors within the state apparatus and civil society. The ideological composition of this discourse fluctuates according to the group addressed. In exclusionary regimes, in particular, the "truth of power often escapes the popular masses . . . the masses do not manage to hear the state discourse directed to the dominant classes." See Poulantzas, *State, Power, Socialism*, pp. 32–33.

3. See Stepan, "The New Professionalism of Internal Warfare and Military Role Expansion"; Garretón, "De la seguridad nacional a la nueva institucionalidad: Notas sobre la trayectoria ideológica del nuevo Estado Autoritario."

4. The *Acta*, the complementary addenda, and Onganía's key speeches are reprinted in Villegas, *Políticas y estrategias para el desarrollo y la seguridad nacional*, pp. 257–68, and in Selser, *El onganiato: La espada y el hisopo*, Vol. 1, pp. 297–316.

5. "Mensaje de la Junta Revolucionaria al Pueblo Argentino," in Villegas, *Políticas y estrategías*, p. 257.

6. *Ibid.*, pp. 258–59.

7. "Acta de la Revolución Argentina," in Selser, *El onganiato*, Vol. 1, p. 300.

8. "Objectivos Políticos (Fines de la Revolución)," in *ibid.*, p. 305. Also see *Polémica*, No. 11 (1972), p. 280.

9. See "Políticas del Gobierno Nacional," in Selser, *El onganiato*, p. 308.

10. *Ibid.*, pp. 309–10.

11. For details on censorship, purges, and attacks on the press and the university, see Fayt, *El político armado: Dinámica del proceso político argentino (1960/1971)*, pp. 147–52, and also Selser, *El onganiato*, pp. 117–28.

12. See *La Nación*, 7 Mar. 1967, for the text of this law. Also see Botana, Braun, and Floria, *El régimen militar, 1966–1973*, pp. 247–51.

13. Botana, Braun, and Floria, *El régimen militar*, pp. 252–60; and *Confirmado*, 31 Aug. 1967, pp. 8–9.

14. For a complete description of the reorganized executive branch, see Fayt, *El político armado*, p. 153.

15. Also operating as part of the augmented presidential bureaucracy was the Secretaría de Informaciones del Estado (SIDE), a powerful intelligence agency independent of the secret services of the three branches of the armed services.

16. General Villegas's book, *Políticas y estrategías*, is an essential source on the official thinking behind the reorganization of the state which gave rise to the *Sistema*.

17. See Gracía Lupo, *Mercenarios y monopolios en la Argentina de Onganía a Lanusse: 1966–1973*, pp. 116–21. On the ideology of pre-Keynesian orthodoxy in Argentina, see Diamand, *Doctrinas económicas, desarrollo e independencia*, pp. 313–44; and Kesselman, *Las estrategias de desarrollo como ideologías*.

18. On the background of Salimei and his collaborators, see Selser, *El onganiato*, vol. 1, pp. 71–82. Like Onganía, Salimei had been formed in the *cursillista* tradition of right-wing Catholic nationalism.

19. Niosi, *Los empresarios y el Estado Argentino*, p. 172.

20. On Salimei's policies, see *Polémica*, no. 11 (1972), pp. 261–68, and the international edition of *La Nación* for the period Aug.-Dec. 1966.

21. Many members on the Tami team had served in the National Development Council and the Harvard University Development Advisory Service during the Illia government. See Selser, *El onganiato*, Vol. 2, pp. 197–204, and Mallon and Sourrouille, *Economic Policymaking in a Conflict Society*, pp. 25–29.

22. The objections to orthodox policies are spelled out in a memo entitled "Algunas ideas básicas en materia de política económica" submitted to President Onganía and Minister Salimei in early July 1966. Large portions of this document are reproduced in Selser, *El onganiato*, Vol. 1, pp. 199–203.

23. The opposition of the *técnicos* emerged in August 1966 in the context of negotiations with the International Monetary Fund. See Selser, *El onganiato*, Vol. 1, pp. 219–26, for the relevant text.

24. Statements by Eduardo Zalduendo, vice-president of the Central Bank, quoted in *ibid.*, p. 220.

25. See Mariano Grondona, "¿Esto es una Revolución?," *Primera Plana*, 4 Oct. 1966, p. 10.

26. See Navarro Gerassi, *Los nacionalistas*, for useful background.

27. Selser, "El Ateneo como grupo de presión," in *El onganiato*, Vol. 1, pp. 25–42, and Gracía Lupo, "Los Cursillos de Cristianidad, partido secreto de Onganía," in *Mercenarios y monopolios en la Argentina de Onganía a Lanusse*, pp. 9–24.

28. The Ateneo was formed in 1962 and was first known as the "Cursos de Cultura Católica." For a partial listing of the Ateneo members in the Onganía government, see "El Ateneo de la República en el poder," *Análisis*, 16 Jan. 1967, pp. 12–15. See Navarro Gerassi, *Los nacionalistas*, pp. 215–34, for a discussion of the group's ideology.

29. *Primera Plana*, 10 Jan. 1967, p. 12.

30. Text in *La Nación*, 29 Mar. 1967. Also see Mariano Grondona, "La trampa del tiempo," *Primera Plana*, 27 June 1967, pp. 11–12.

31. As Díaz Colodrero explained: "Timing is the frontline protagonist of politics, therefore this political pause [i.e., the "economic" period] is already policy. . . . If having a political plan means having a concept of politics, the government does have a political plan; if it means having an electoral calendar, the government does not have a political plan. The important thing is to prevent premature politicization from stalling the realization of such an ambitious revolutionary process. . . ." See the interview in *Primera Plana*, 22 May 1967, p. 10.

32. See the public discussion in August and September of 1967 in *La Nación*, and "Gobierno: ¿ha nacido un plan político?," in *Primera Plana*, 19 Sept. 1967, pp. 12–14.

33. "¿Hacia una definición ideológica?," *Primera Plana*, 26 Sept. 1967, pp. 12–14.

34. See "Corporativismo para cordobeses," in *Primera Plana*, 14 Nov. 1967, p. 18, and "¿Qué hacer con las provincias?," in *Primera Plana*, 12 Dec. 1967, p. 13.

35. See the editorial in *Análisis*, 22 Apr. 1968, for a summary of the contacts with parties during this period.

36. The quoted statement was made by General Borda during a press conference with foreign correspondents. See the text in *La Nación*, 25 Apr. 1967. See also "Gobierno: el juego de palabras," *Primera Plana*, 30 Apr. 1967, p. 12. The decline in public support is verified by comparing polls from June 1967 and June 1968; see *Primera Plana*, 27 June 1967, p. 13, and 25 June 1968, pp. 14–15.

37. The first hint of their decision came in late June 1968 with the announcement by the right-wing nationalist governor of Córdoba, Carlos Caballero, of a "pilot project" of "communitarianism in action." Onganía himself promoted such policies in a tour through Tucumán, Ju-

juy, and Catamarca, three of the poorest provinces. See the following articles in *Primera Plana*: "El gobierno en apuros," 2 July 1968, pp. 13–14; "Gobierno: el plan de Calamuchita," 6 Aug. 1968, pp. 13–15; and "El tiempo: económico y levemente social," 24 Sept. 1968, pp. 13–15.

38. For one of the most polished statements reflecting a liberal Catholic view, see Brown and Floria, "Del gobierno revolucionario al orden constitucional." For the right-wing nationalist view, see "Ateneo: política, esa mala palabra," *Análisis*, 4 Nov. 1968, p. 17.

39. The key event was a "summit meeting" with 200 high-ranking functionaries held in late March 1969 in which Onganía demanded greater productivity and commitment to revolutionary transformations. See the text of this speech in *La Nación*, 27 Mar. 1969, and the negative public reaction in "Gobierno: la campana de cristal," *Primera Plana*, 8 Apr. 1969, pp. 8–9, and "Didáctica para funcionarios" and "Repercusiones, autoridad y futuro," in *Panorama*, 1 Apr. 1969, pp. 6–7, and 8 Apr. 1969, pp. 8–9, respectively.

40. See the text of Onganía's speech in *La Nación*, 7 May 1969. The plan called for the formation of 2,000 "advisory councils" composed of 40,000 members appointed by muncipal, provincial, and national authorities. See "Onganía: la caza de aliados," *Primera Plana*, 13 May 1969, pp. 8–10.

41. See "Trémula, participación, dureza económica," *Panorama*, 13 May 1969, pp. 6–8.

42. See Frondizi's declarations in *Los Principios*, 18 July 1966, and in *Polémica*, no. 11 (1972), p. 4.

43. Cited in *Polémica*, no. 10 (1972), p. 278. Perón's hard line was expressed in a letter sent to the Peronist movement's "high command" in November 1966. See "El Pacto Illia-Perón," *Primera Plana*, 8 July 1967, pp. 13–15.

44. For useful surveys of leaders and platforms, see Castagno, *Tendencias y grupos políticos en la realidad argentina*, and Andino and Paredes, *Breve historia de los partidos políticos argentinos, 1874–1974*.

45. On the *golpistas*, see the following articles in *Primera Plana*: "El avance de los golpistas," 23 Apr. 1968, pp. 12–14; "Entre los bobos anda el juego," 16 July 1968, pp. 17–18; "Aramburu propone una salida," 22 Apr. 1968, pp. 14–17; "Aramburu: otra vez presidente," 14 May 1968, pp. 17–18; and "El plan político de Alsogaray," 2 July 1968, pp. 21–22.

46. See *Primera Plana*: "El Pacto Illia-Perón," 8 July 1967; "Calma, calma radicales," 1 Aug. 1967, p. 14; "El cerco se cierra," 23 July 1968, pp. 21–22; "Peronismo: el giro a la derecha," 22 Oct. 1968, p. 12. Also

see "Radiografía de las izquierdas," *Análisis*, 7 Feb. 1967, pp. 30–34, and excerpts from a five-hour interview with Perón in *Panorama*, 1 Apr. 1969, pp. 13–18.

47. See *Primera Plana*: "¿El fin de la aventura?" 8 Aug. 1967, pp. 18–19; "Frondizi-Frigerio: ¿qué buscan ahora?" 28 Mar. 1967, pp. 12–14; "El pleito militar," 4 June 1968, p. 16; and "El gobierno en apuros," 2 July 1968, pp. 13–14. Also see "Frondizi propone una salida," *Panorama*, 8 Apr. 1969, pp. 15–16.

48. Onganía's personality reinforced his view of authority. He was "a soldier's soldier, 'uncontaminated' by the connections that most important men have with the country's political and other elites. This uncommitted quality and his aloofness have no doubt enhanced the legendary character of his authority, but the plain fact is that Onganía assumed the presidency with very little known about his political ideas or his skill at convincing—as distinct from commanding." Rowe, "Onganía's Argentina: The First Four Months," p. 2. For Onganía's view of the military's role, see "Lo que nunca se contó," *Extra*, June 1969, p. 12, and the special edition of *Panorama*, 10 June 1970, published after his ouster.

49. When General Alsogaray assumed command of the army he carefully defended the "delegate" theory, saying that the army would do whatever was necessary to "prevent anyone or anything from deviating" from the path chosen in June 1966. Onganía answered demanding "total obedience." On the repercussions of these speeches in the military, see *Primera Plana*, 17 Jan. 1967.

50. Lanusse, *Mi testimonio*, p. xv.

51. On General Alsogaray, see Gracía Lupo, "Los Alsogaray: biografía de una dinastia military," in *Mercenarios y monopolios*, pp. 116–21.

52. See *Primera Plana*, "Historia de ascensos y conspiraciones," 14 Nov. 1967, p. 14, and "Gobierno: fasten seat belts," 29 Aug. 1967, pp. 12–13. Generals Juan Enrique Guglialmelli and Juan Iavicoli, two well-known military *desarrollistas*, went even further, linking economic orthodoxy and the penetration of the multinational firms to threats to national security. See "¿Quien representa a quien?," *Análisis*, 4 Sept. 1967, pp. 8–9.

53. See "La proclama que López no firmó," *Primera Plana*, 20 Feb. 1968, pp. 13–14, and the collection of General López's speeches, statements, and interviews, *Ideas políticas del General Cándido López*.

54. On the impact in the officer corps, see *Primera Plana*, "Oposición: para López no hay verano," 16 Jan. 1968, pp. 12–13, and "Lopizmo (I): un frente opositor," 5 Mar. 1968, pp. 14–17.

55. General Alsogaray informed the top 48 army generals that On-

ganía had recognized his "mistakes" but had also affirmed that while the armed forced did not "govern or co-govern," they did "constitute the support of the Revolution." See "Gobierno: el difícil tiempo nuevo," *Primera Plana*, 26 Mar. 1968, pp. 12–13.

56. For details, see *La Nación*, 23 May 1968, and "Gobierno, 1— Ejército, 1," *Primera Plana*, 28 May 1968, pp. 13–15.

57. See General Alsogaray's speech in *La Nación*, 30 May 1968. Subsequently General Alsogaray reportedly said that General Borda, the Interior Minister, was "little less than a Nazi."

58. *La Nación*, 30 May 1968.

59. In addition to replacing Alsogaray with General Lanusse, Onganía also replaced Admiral Benigno Varela with Admiral Pedro Gnavi and Brigadier General Jorge Zuviria with Brigadier General Adolfo Alvarez. Onganía also ousted Generals Villegas, Guglialmelli, and Iavicoli from their posts. See "Gobierno: la crisis militar," *Primera Plana*, 27 Aug. 1968, pp. 13–15.

60. In the annual promotions, General Lanusse took the opportunity to support officers who shared his liberal outlook and distrust of Onganía. See *Primera Plana*, "Las designaciones en el ejército," 17 Sept. 1968, pp. 14–15.

61. The principal conspiracy was led by General Enrique Rauch, the so-called "first *azul*," who had been retired by Onganía in 1964. Rauch accused the regime of a "shameful sell-out of our national patrimony to international finance, which lacks morals, a country, and a flag." He also called upon the military to "react with great virility" to throw out the "usurpers and despots." On the conspirators and their civilian allies, see *Primera Plana*, "Ejército: el golpe de Rauch," 19 Nov. 1968, pp. 13–14, and "Oposición: Año Nuevo, ¿vida nueva?" 7 Jan. 1969, pp. 13–14.

Chapter Four

1. Editorial in *Primera Plana*, 31 Jan. 1967, p. 14. On Krieger Vasena's background and the events surrounding his appointment, see Gracía Lupo, *Mercenarios y monopolios en la Argentina*, pp. 118–21; and Selser, *El onganiato*, Vol. 1, pp. 283–91.

2. Krieger's project went beyond the "deepening" discussed by Guillermo O'Donnell, although industrial integration certainly stood at the heart of his strategy. O'Donnell and his critics agree, however, that strategies involving a break with conventional import-substitution policies are incompatible with the "non-hegemonic coalitions" that characterized the earlier populist and developmentalist periods. To be successful, alternative strategies such as Krieger's do not necessarily require authoritarian rule, but they do seem to require either substan-

tial economic resources (e.g., Venezuela) or strict limitations on popular participation and party competition (e.g., Colombia or Mexico.) See O'Donnell, "Reflections on the Patterns of Change in the Bureaucratic-Authoritarian State," and Kaufman, "Industrial Change and Authoritarian Rule in Latin America: A Concrete Review of the Bureaucratic-Authoritarian Model."

3. Quoted in Ministerio de Economía y Trabajo, *Política económica argentina*, Vol. 1, p. 35.

4. Banco Central, *Sistema de cuentas del producto e ingreso de la Argentina*, Vol. 2, pp. 182–89, and Ministerio de Economía y Trabajo, *Informe Económico*, II Quarter 1974, p. 46.

5. *Primera Plana*, 14 Mar. 1967, pp. 49–50; also see *La Prensa*'s editorial of 24 Jan. 1967.

6. See *Primera Plana*, "Gobierno: La oposición interna," 11 Apr. 1967, pp. 12–13.

7. See William C. Smith, "Heterodox Shocks and the Political Economy of Democratic Transition in Argentina and Brazil."

8. The exchange rate remained fixed for the next two years. See de Pablo, *Política antiinflacionaria en la Argentina*, pp. 24–27; and Diamand, *Doctrinas económicas, desarrollo e independencia*, pp. 185–91.

9. Only 4 million dollars in long-term investment arrived in 1967, following a net outflow of 104 million dollars in 1966. De Pablo, *Política antiinflacionaria en la Argentina*, pp. 43–44.

10. For details of the tax reforms, see Banco Central, *Memoria Anual*, 1967, p. 3; *La Nación*, 9 May 1967, p. 1; and de Pablo, *Política antiinflacionaria*, pp. 27–29.

11. See de Pablo, "La Ley 17.224 y la distribución inter-gremial del peso de la política antiinflacionaria."

12. *Primera Plana*, "Empresarios: hora de comprometerse," 18 Apr. 1967, pp. 20–23, and "Empresarios: apoyo condicionado," 6 June 1967, pp. 20–22. By late 1968, some 3,500 firms were participants in this agreement. *La Nación*, 24 Jan. 1969.

13. De Pablo, *Política antiinflacionaria*, p. 49.

14. See *La Nación* (international edition), 5 August 1967.

15. On the shift to pump-priming policies, see *Primera Plana*, "Dr. K.V.: como aprendí a cebar la bomba," 8 Aug. 1967, p. 17; and Ministerio de Economía y Trabajo, *Política económica*, Vol. 1, p. 47.

16. Typical of Krieger's use of the vote of international confidence to generate domestic credibility was a speech before a meeting of the Bolsa de Comercio, the UIA, the SRA, and the Consejo Interamericano de Comercio y Producción in November 1968. After citing the number of foreign visitors as proof of interest in investing in Argentina, Krieger said this resulted from the country's "special conditions," including the

"reign of law and order" and Argentina's location "far from the zone of conflict." The text of Krieger's speech is found in Ministerio de Economía y Trabajo, *Política económica*, Vol. 2, pp. 88–90.

17. Calculations from unpublished data furnished to the author by the budget office of the Ministry of Economy.

18. See Krieger's exposition of his policies for 1969 before leading multinational and domestic business executives in Ministerio de Economía y Trabajo, *Política económica*, Vol. 2, pp. 125–26.

19. These concerns were by no means new. See Niosi's analysis of anti-labor proposals put forward by business, *Los empresarios y el Estado argentino*, pp. 160–63.

20. See, for example, the interview with Horacio García Belsunce, president of the Chamber of Commerce and a prestigious entrepreneur with links to both local and foreign industrial firms and banks. *Primera Plana*, 6 June 1967, p. 24.

21. See, for instance, the SRA's letter to Krieger of 22 Mar. 1967, in SRA, *Memoria Anual*, 1966/67, pp. 65–66.

22. Speech by SRA president Faustino Alberto Fano in *ibid.*, pp. 66–67.

23. Rural organizations had lobbied hard for a new law (*Ley de Arrendamientos y Aparcerías*) that eliminated legal protections for sharecroppers and strengthened the hand of rural property owners. They also had actively campaigned to close the less efficient sugar mills in the province of Tucumán. On these activities see CAC, *Memoria Anual*, 1967, p. 6.

24. *La Nación*, 19 May 1968. See the SRA's reply of 23 May 1968 in SRA, *Memoria Anual*, 1967/68, p. 79.

25. A key source on responses to policies designed to promote agrarian modernization is Margenat, "Las organizaciones corporativas del sector agrario." For discussion of the profitability and microeconomic rationality of land use and production techniques, see Flishman, "Modelo de asignación de recursos en el sector agropecuario," and Braun, "La renta absoluta y el uso ineficiente de la tierra en la Argentina."

26. Statement to the press on 11 Nov. 1968, reprinted in SRA, *Memoria Anual*, 1968/69, p. 48.

27. See *ibid.*, pp. 53–54, for the flavor of the Assembly's debates. Also see Margenat, "Las organizaciones corporativas," pp. 19–20.

28. Letter from CARBAP leaders to President Onganía dated 19 Nov. 1968, cited in Margenat, "Las organizaciones corporativas," p. 19.

29. See Margenat, "Las organizaciones corporativas," pp. 24–25, 43, for an analysis of the FAA's positions.

30. Letter sent by FAA leaders to President Onganía in April 1969,

cited in *ibid.*, pp. 25–26. In response to the polarization among rural producer organizations, the FAA joined the CGE, making the CGE the "authentic and sole organization of the small and medium bourgeoisie, industrial . . . as well as agrarian and commercial." Niosi, *Los empresarios*, p. 170.

31. On this new cleavage, see Cardoso and Faletto, *Dependency and Development in Latin America*, chap. 6, as well as Cardoso's *Ideologías de la burguesía industrial en las sociedades dependientes*.

32. Gelbard, *Democracia y participación*, pp. 7–8. UIA data are cited in Niosi, *Los empresarios*, p. 170.

33. See the data presented in Niosi, *Los empresarios*, Table 22, p. 219, and Table 42, p. 234.

34. See, for example, the interview of a delegation of top rural producers with Onganía in SRA, *Memoria Anual*, 1966/67, pp. 54–55. Also see UIA, *Memoria Anual*, 1966/67, p. 32; and BC, *Memoria Anual*, 1967, p. 6.

35. CAC, *Memoria Anual*, 1968, pp. 73–74.

36. See the CGE's criticism in CGE, *Memoria Anual*, 1967, pp. 11–14.

37. See the CGE's note sent to Krieger Vasena on 9 Sept. 1967, cited by Niosi, *Los empresarios*, p. 169, and a statement by Pedro J. Cristia, the CGE's president, cited in *Polémica*, "El relevo de los comandantes," No. 14 (1972), p. 102.

38. UIA, *Memoria Anual*, 1968/69, pp. 29–30; *Primera Plana*, "Economía: la diversión se acabó," 30 July 1968, pp. 12–14; and *La Nación*, 5 Dec. 1968.

39. CGE, *Memoria Anual*, 1968, p. 4.

40. See Altimir, "Evaluación de la política económica actual." This article appeared in a publication of the CGE's research arm.

41. For a useful discussion of this opposition, see *Primera Plana*, "Krieger Vasena: ¿qué pasa si se va?" 20 May 1969, pp. 14–16.

42. See O'Donnell, "Reflections on the Patterns of Change in the Bureaucratic-Authoritarian State," pp. 17–18.

43. For data on investment, see Ministerio de Economía y Trabajo, *Informe Económico* (I and II Quarter 1974), Table 34, pp. 56–57.

Chapter Five

1. According to Poulantzas, the allegiance given by a "support class" is "generally not based on any real political sacrifice" of dominant class interests. Rather, support is based on a "process of ideological illusion." He further notes that support is not generally manifested in "immediate class relations but operates through the intermediary of the state," which manipulates the "power fetishism" of many subordinate groups seeking a neutral state above class conflict to protect them from

dominant groups. See Poulantzas, *Political Power and Social Classes*, pp. 243–44.

2. For comparative analyses, see Spalding, *Organized Labor in Latin America*, and Bergquist, *Labor in Latin America*.

3. On the question of "threat," see O'Donnell, "Reflections on the Patterns of Change in the Bureaucratic-Authoritarian State," and Stepan, *The State and Society: Peru in Comparative Perspective*, chap. 3.

4. Good overviews of transformations in occupational structure and labor markets are found in Altimir, "La distribución del ingreso y el empleo en el sector manufacturero argentino"; Llach, "Estructura ocupacional y dinámica del empleo en la Argentina: sus peculiaridades, 1947–1970"; Gerchunoff and Llach, "Capitalismo industrial, desarrollo asociado y distribución del ingreso entre los dos gobiernos peronistas: 1950–1972"; and Marshall, "Mercado de trabajo y crecimiento de los salarios en la Argentina."

5. The distinction between dynamic and static sectors follows standard usage employed by the Central Bank and CONADE. On the correlation between dynamic sectors and large firms, and between foreign ownership (capital-intensive technology) and stagnant growth, competitiveness, and local ownership (labor-intensive technology), see Sourrouille, "La presencia y el comportamiento de la empresas extranjeras en el sector industrial argentino."

6. Cavarozzi, "Unions and Politics in Argentina, 1955–1962," pp. 8–9.

7. For details, see Cavarozzi, "Sindicatos y política en Argentina, 1955–1958," and Potash, *The Army and Politics in Argentina, 1945–1962*, pp. 225–31.

8. On the Resistencia, see Vigo, *Crónicas de la resistencia*, and Hodges, *Argentina, 1943–1976: The National Revolution and Resistance*.

9. Torre, "El movimiento sindical en la Argentina," p. 19. On labor resistance to rationalization efforts, see James, "Rationalization and Working Class Response."

10. On Frondizi's policies, see Wynia, *Argentina in the Postwar Era*, chap. 4.

11. See Brodersohn, ed., *Estrategias de industrialización para la Argentina*, and Ferrer, "Devaluación, redistribución de ingresos y el proceso de desarticulación industrial en la Argentina." On Frondizi's reliance on repression, see Rouquié, *Poder militar y sociedad política en la Argentina*, vol. 2, pp. 153–74.

12. James, *Unions and Politics: The Development of Peronist Trade Unions, 1955–1966*, p. 183, cited in Munck et al., *Argentina: From Anarchism to Peronism*, p. 153.

13. See the account of a one-time *vandorista* turned critic in Miguel Gazzera, "Nosotros los dirigentes."

14. For Greater Buenos Aires, in the 1960–65 period the number of strikes averaged 38 per year, with an average of 161,000 strikers involved and an average of 855,000 working days lost. This compares with the 45 strikes, 1.4 million strikers, and 10 million days lost in 1959. Calculated from Rotondaro, *Realidad y cambio en el sindicalismo*, p. 241. For data on strikes in the nation as a whole, see Table 2.7 above.

15. For an account of bureaucratization and corruption, see Correa, *Los jerarcas sindicales*.

16. On the La Falda and Huerta Grande programs, see Cerro, *De Perón al Cordobazo*, pp. 210–11, and Munck et al., *Argentina: From Anarchism to Peronism*, p. 156.

17. According to one account, "the objective of the mobilizations was to cancel out rank-and-file action, to continue wearing them down, and at the same time to create the appropriate climate for a coup d'état. . . ." Echague, *Las grandes huelgas*, p. 102.

18. On the factional struggles, see Munck et al., *Argentina: From Anarchism to Peronism*, pp. 159–60.

19. Peralta Ramos, *Acumulación del capital y crisis política en Argentina (1930–1974)*, pp. 96 and 140.

20. Eiegelbaum, "The First Year of the 'Argentine Revolution': A New Experiment in Corporatism?," p. 248.

21. As we saw in Chapter 3, the Catholic-nationalist discourse was present alongside expressions of free-enterprise liberalism and developmentalist-interventionism in the regime's founding ideology.

22. Zorrilla, *Estructura y dinámica del sindicalismo argentino*, p. 142, and Carri, *Sindicatos y poder en la Argentina*, p. 185.

23. For a comparison of the positions of Vandor and Alonso on this point, see Balve et al., *Lucha de calles, lucha de clases*, p. 172.

24. "La Confederación General del Trabajo de la República Argentina," dated 29 June 1966, reprinted in Senén González, *El sindicalismo después de Perón*, pp. 95–98.

25. DIL, *Estudios Sindicales*, 3 (1966), p. 207.

26. See *Polémica*, 10 (1972), pp. 265, 268, and 274; and Senén González, *El sindicalismo después de Perón*, pp. 101–2.

27. *La Nación*, coverage on 14 and 15 Dec. 1966.

28. On the wave of strikes and Vandor's role, see *Primera Plana*, 27 Feb. 1967, pp. 8–10. Also see Rotondaro, *Realidad y cambio en el sindicalismo*, pp. 325–29; and Carri, *Sindicatos y poder en la Argentina*, pp. 162–64.

29. On the sequence of events, see *Polémica*, 11 (1972), p. 7.

30. Balve et al., *Lucha de calles, lucha de clases*, p. 173.

31. "Gobierno-gremios: la guerra de nervios," *Primera Plana*, 2 May 1967, pp. 12–13.

32. "Gobierno: la lucha por el poder," *Primera Plana*, 12 Sept. 1967,

p. 13. Also see Buchanan, "State Corporatism in Argentina: Labor Administration under Perón and Onganía."

33. See Torre, "El proceso político interno de los sindicatos en Argentina."

34. See the analysis in Balve et al., *Lucha de calles, lucha de clases*, pp. 173–74.

35. While Vandor was reluctant to subordinate his faction to the designs of the nationalists, the *vandoristas* and Vandor himself frequently entered into alliances of convenience with entrepreneurs to defend their "common interests," for example, trading wage increases for opposition to denationalization. See Balve et al., *Lucha de calles, lucha de clases*, pp. 172–74.

36. Taccone made this statement on 1 Oct. 1967 in a public meeting with San Sebastián present. See Senén González, *El sindicalismo después de Perón*, p. 94. Taccone also explained the unions' support for the Onganía regime by noting that "the political parties were no longer representative of the totality and needed the complementary action of the dynamic groups of society." He also stated that he believed in "a statist society [*sociedad estatal*], that is, in the possibility that social development will occur within the state." N. Dominguez, *Conversaciones con Juan José Taccone*, as cited by Munck et al., *Argentina: From Anarchism to Peronism*, pp. 160–61.

37. During this period San Sebastián repeatedly offered "participation" to the *colaboracionistas* in the drafting of legal measures relating to the new union statutes. See "El ocaso de la CGT?," *Primera Plana*, 30 Oct. 1967, pp. 12–14; and "Gremios: ¿la hora del gobierno?," *Primera Plana*, 21 Nov. 1967, pp. 12–13.

38. "Documento del Consejo Ejecutivo de la Federación de Asociaciones de Trabajadores de la Sanidad Argentina," dated July 1967, as quoted in Peralta Ramos, *Acumulación del capital y crisis política*, pp. 142–43. Also see "En Defensa de las Empresas y Riquezas Nacionales y la Independencia y Soberanía de Nuestra Patria," *La Razón*, 20 Nov. 1967, and Senén González, *El sindicalismo después de Perón*, pp. 95, 105–7.

39. The CGT de los Argentinos was also known as the CGT de Paseo Colón after the street on which its headquarters was located. Likewise, the CGT de Azopardo was named after its street location.

40. Ongaro soon proved correct: the headquarters of the CGT de los Argentinos was taken over by an armed gang and the occupation ratified by the government. For Ongaro's remarks, see *Polémica*, 13 (1972), p. 65. The new organization's first declaration, "CGT con la Patria y el Pueblo Argentino," is reprinted in Senén González, *El sindicalismo después de Perón*, pp. 113–17.

41. "Mensaje a los Trabajadores y al Pueblo Argentino," reprinted in Senén González, pp. 118–25.

42. *Ibid.* Also see *Primera Plana*, 14 May 1967, p. 13, for Ongaro's rejection of corporatist proposals.

43. Ongaro, "Habla Ongaro," p. 20. Also see Ongaro, *Sólo el pueblo salvará al pueblo.*

44. Declaration of 1 May 1968 reprinted in Senén González, *El sindicalismo después de Perón*, pp. 118–25.

45. See the CGT de Azopardo's statement of 1 May 1968, "Manifesto de 1 de Mayo," and its document of 1 June 1968, "Declaración y Resolución sobre el Momento Actual Argentino," both in Senén González, pp. 125–28 and 136, respectively.

46. See Balve et al., *Lucha de calles, lucha de clases*, pp. 174–75; and Peralta Ramos, *Acumulación del capital y crisis política*, p. 143.

47. See Zorrilla, *Estructura y dinámica del sindicalismo argentino*, chap. 3, for analysis of organizational and structural characteristics of Argentine unions in this period. See DIL, *Nucleamientos Sindicales*, for a complete listing of the unions belonging to the rival CGTs.

48. Quoted in *Panorama*, 10 Sept. 1968, p. 6.

49. For details of intervention on behalf of "friendly" leaders, see "Gobierno-gremios: mi general, cuánto valés," *Primera Plana*, 4 Feb. 1969, pp. 8–10.

50. See *ibid.*, and *La Nación*, 1 Feb. 1969, for details on Onganía's new overtures to the *colaboracionistas.*

51. On the rapprochement between Vandor and Perón, see "Oposición: Año Nuevo, ¿vida nueva?," *Primera Plana*, 7 Jan. 1969, pp. 13–14.

52. See *Polémica*, 14 (1972), p. 90.

53. "Alianzas: los idus de junio," *Primera Plana*, 2 July 1969, pp. 14–15.

54. See *Polémica*, 14 (1972), p. 90.

55. Vandor's speech is cited in Balve et al., *Lucha de calles, lucha de clases*, p. 176. For details on Vandor's overtures to *clasista* leaders in Buenos Aires, Rosario, and Córdoba, see "La batalla por los gremios," *Panorama*, 3 June 1969, pp. 12–13.

Chapter Six

1. Major studies of the *cordobazo* include Balve et al., *Lucha de calles, lucha de clases*; Delich, *Crisis y protesta social: Córdoba, 1969–1973*; and Agulla, *Diagnóstico social de una crisis: Córdoba, mayo de 1969.*

2. Useful sources on the events leading up to the *cordobazo* include Graham-Yool, ed., *Tiempo de tragedia: Cronología de la Revolución Argentina*, pp. 70–72; and González Trejo, *Argentina: Tiempo de violencia.* Also see "Córdoba, después del estrajo," *Primera Plana*, 10 June 1969,

pp. 17–21; and "La violencia asistio a la cita," *Panorama*, 3 June 1969, pp. 6–8.

3. Delich, *Crisis y protesta social*, pp. 91–93; Agulla, *Diagnóstico de una crisis*, p. 79; and "Trémula social, participación y dureza económica," *Panorama*, 13 May 1969, pp. 6–8.

4. Balve et al., *Lucha de calles, lucha de clases*, p. 185.

5. Delich, *Crisis y protesta social*, pp. 153–66; and "Los fantasmas de mayo," *Panorama*, 2 Dec. 1969, pp. 12–13.

6. Balve et al., *Lucha de calles, lucha de clases*, p. 158.

7. These data and those following are found in a study by the research department of the CGE and published in "Estructura económica de Córdoba," *Estudios de la Economía Argentina*, No. 7 (Aug. 1979). Also see Delich, *Crisis y protesta social*, pp. 26–31; and Delich, "Córdoba: la movilización permanente."

8. See Nun, "La industria automotriz argentina: Estudio de un caso de superpoblación flotante"; Balve et al., *Lucha de calles*, pp. 163–64 and 172–77; and Delich, *Crisis y protesta social*, pp. 39–48.

9. On the origins of the auto industry in Argentina, see "Car Wars" in *NACLA Report on the Americas*, 13, No. 4 (1979); and Jenkins, *Transnational Corporations and the Latin American Automobile Industry*.

10. Delich, *Crisis y protesta social*, p. 98.

11. Huntington, *Political Order in Changing Societies*, p. 196.

12. These data form part of the Archive on Sociopolitical Protest in Argentina, based on the Buenos Aires daily *La Razón*.

13. See Milutín, "Changing Patterns of Worker Protest in Argentina, 1956–1974," and "Algunas características de los movimientos huelguísticos en la Argentina, 1956–1974." Also see Jelin, "Conflictos laborales en la Argentina, 1973–1976."

14. Data collected by the Ministry of Labor.

15. A key figure in this convergence was John William Cooke, who had been Perón's "personal delegate" for a period after 1955 and who later spent some time in Cuba. See his book *La Revolución y el peronismo* for an analysis of the 1966 coup and the new regime from the perspective of the Peronist revolutionary left.

16. See Gillespie, *Soldados de Perón: Los Montoneros*, for an excellent study of this group. Also see Hodges, *Argentina, 1943–1976: The National Revolution and Resistance*; Giussani, *Montoneros: La soberbia armada*; Russell, Schenkel, and Miller, "Urban Guerrillas in Argentina: A Select Bibliography"; and Geze and Labrousse, *Argentine: Révolution et Contre-Révolution*.

17. De Pablo, *Política antiinflacionaria en la Argentina*, pp. 99–100; and Ministerio de Economía y Trabajo, *Informe Económico* (I and II Quarters of 1974), Table 46, pp. 78–79.

18. "Blanqueo: Haz el bien sin mirar a quien," *Panorama*, 17 Mar. 1970, pp. 16–17.

19. See "Dagnino Pastore en la picota," *Panorama*, 4 Feb. 1970, pp. 68–69.

20. For the flavor of financial irregularities and excessive speculation on the part of many firms and financial institutions, see *La Nación*, 15 Feb. 1970.

21. "Agro: todo puede arreglarse," *Primera Plana*, 22 Apr.1969, p. 15; and "Grandeza y miseria del campo," *Análisis*, 29 July 1969, pp. 10–11.

22. "Mensaje del Agro," dated 29 July 1969 in SRA, *Memoria Anual* (1968/70), pp. 67–69; and "Agro: todos a una Fuenteovejuna," *Primera Plana*, 29 July 1969, pp. 20–21.

23. The following discussion of the "meat crisis" generally follows the analysis in Duejo, *El capital monopolista y las contradicciones secundarias en la sociedad argentina*, pp. 79–98.

24. Interview in *El Economista*, 24 Apr. 1970. Anchorena particularly denounced Krieger Vasena's involvement in Deltec International, a firm involved in the international beef trade. For many nationalists Deltec symbolized a virtual international conspiracy against Argentine producers.

25. See "El agro dice que no," *Panorama*, 2 June 1970, pp. 16–17, for the positions taken at the annual assembly of the Federación Argentina de Cooperativas Agrarias (FACA).

26. *Ibid.*

27. Diamand, *Doctrinas económicas, desarrollo e independencia*, p. 186.

28. *Ibid.*, p. 188.

29. For examples of this rhetoric, see the Interior Minister's comments and the transcript of President Onganía's TV speech in *La Nación*, 2 and 5 July 1969, respectively.

30. These charges are found throughout the CGE's *Memorias Anuales* for 1968–69 and 1969–70.

31. Ongaro was imprisoned after the *cordobazo* and the CGT de los Argentinos forced to go underground. There was an effort to organize a new resistance around the slogan "Unite from Below, Organize through Combat." See Hodges, *Argentina, 1943–1976*, pp. 61–62.

32. On the impact of Vandor's assassination, see Gazzera, "Nosotros, los dirigentes," pp. 169–83; "La sombra de Vandor," *Panorama*, 3 Feb. 1970, pp. 6–7; and "La herencia de Vandor," *Análisis*, 24 Mar. 1970, pp. 12–13.

33. "Otra semana violenta," *Panorama*, 23 Sept. 1969, pp. 6–10; and "La cuenta regresiva," *Análisis*, 30 Sept. 1969, pp. 7–9.

34. See "Onganía: mes 40, hora cero," *Panorama*, 30 Sept. 1969, pp. 6–9, on the divisions within the National Security Council and the

threat to "wipe out" the labor movement. On the panicky response of the labor leaders, see Gazzera, "Nosotros, los dirigentes," pp. 179–80.

35. For San Sebastián's threat to "organize" the entrepreneurs and their reaction, see "El dar que no es dar," *Análisis*, 7 Oct. 1969, pp. 6–10.

36. Many military officers did not accept the official explanation of the *cordobazo* and attempted to press for changes from within the National Security Council. See "Los cambios en el gobierno," *Primera Plana*, 10 June 1969, pp. 12–13.

37. Lanusse, *Mi testimonio*, p. 5. Lanusse's memoirs are a valuable source on the military's worsening relations with Onganía. Although at times self-serving (they were published in part to defend Lanusse from right-wing critics following the 1976 military coup), they identify the positions held by many key military and civilian participants and quote extensively from military documents that have never been published.

38. See the text in *La Nación*, 30 May 1969. Also see Lanusse, *Mi testimonio*, pp. xviii–xix, 4, 6, and 59.

39. "Córdoba: el ejército en el poder," *Panorama*, 1 July 1969, pp. 9–10. Also see Lanusse, *Mi testimonio*, pp. 3–19. Lanusse cites a poll commissioned by CONASE following the *cordobazo* showing overwhelming rejection of the regime's policies.

40. See the text in *La Nación*, 8 July 1969.

41. On Labanca's conspiracy and the parallel plots by other right-wing nationalist officers, see "La tormenta militar," *Análisis*, 5 Aug. 1969, pp. 6–8; "El extraño retiro del General Labanca," *Primera Plana*, 29 July 1969, pp. 10–11; "Ejército: la ofensiva de Lanusse," *Primera Plana*, 5 Aug. 1969, pp. 11–12; and "Definiciones en la cumbre," *Panorama*, 30 Dec. 1969, pp. 6–7. Also see Colonel Guevara, *Argentina y su sombra*.

42. For an interesting analysis of the political orientations of 24 out of 52 army generals with command of troops, see "Los dueños de la Revolución: ¿qué piensan los generales?" *Panorama*, 15 July 1969, pp. 8–10. The press played an important role in building up Lanusse's image; see, for example, "Actos de conducción," *Análisis*, 12 Aug. 1969, p. 10.

43. Lanusse quotes from tape records of these meetings in *Mi testimonio*, pp. 57–58. Also see "Futuro con constitución, parlamento y partidos," *Panorama*, 9 Sept. 1969, pp. 6–9.

44. This plan, dated 18 Nov. 1969, also mentioned the possibility of leaving Onganía in office but giving effective power to a prime minister named by the military. See *Mi testimonio*, pp. 55–56.

45. "Retornos, nombramientos, precisiones," *Panorama*, 3 Mar. 1970,

pp. 6–8; "Gremios: la huelga de las naranjas," *Panorama,* 28 Apr. 1970, pp. 10–11; "Los cambios en la Aeronaútica," *Panorama,* 17 Mar. 1970, p.10; and "La crisis larvada," *Análisis,* 28 Apr. 1970, pp. 8–10.

46. Text in *La Nación,* 22 Apr. 1970. Also see "Onganía versus Frondizi," *Análisis,* 28 Apr. 1970, pp. 12–13; and Lanusse, *Mi testimonio,* pp. 85–86.

47. For details of this key document, see Fayt, *El político armado,* p. 198; Lanusse, *Mi testimonio,* pp. 87–90; and "De cómo empezó la cruzada militar contra los monopolios," *Panorama,* 9 Feb. 1971, pp. 8–9.

48. Lanusse quotes from a reconstruction of this meeting based on notes taken by various participants in *Mi testimonio,* pp. 91–103.

49. Text in *La Nación,* 30 May 1970. Also see "Todos los odios," *Análisis,* 2 June 1970, pp. 7–9.

50. Indicative of this perception was the new-found aggressiveness of the Radicals. Ricardo Balbín, in a speech before 500 people, called for Radicalism to "launch its call for a struggle for national liberation. . . . Down with the Dictatorship." "A la ocasión la pintan calva," *Panorama,* 2 June 1970, p. 14.

51. Many of Aramburu's military and civilian supporters believed (as some continue to believe) that Onganía and his nationalist staff were involved in the assassination. See, for example, former vice president Admiral Isaac Rojas' graveside speech in *La Prensa,* 19 July 1970; and "El caso Aramburu: la eclosión de un Tercer Frente," *Panorama,* 7 Aug. 1970, pp. 10–13.

52. *La Prensa,* 10 June 1970. For the text of Onganía's resignation, see *La Nación,* 9 June 1970.

53. Text of the Junta's declaration in *La Nación,* 10 June 1970.

Chapter Seven

1. Gramsci, *Selections from the Prison Notebooks,* p. 210.

2. *Ibid.,* pp. 210–18.

3. *Ibid.,* pp. 106–13, 118–22. Also see Macciocchi, *Gramsci y la revolución de occidente,* pp. 103–24.

4. Gramsci, *Selections,* pp. 58–59. In the context of severe crisis, the state itself acts as a "party" by setting itself "above the parties . . . so as to disintegrate them, to detach them from the broad masses and obtain a force of non-party men linked to the government" (p. 227).

5. Lanusse, *Mi testimonio,* pp. 138–39; and "General Levingston: otra manera de pasar al frente," *Panorama,* 16 June 1970, pp. 8–10.

6. Levingston was a cavalry officer who had participated in the creation of the SIDE intelligence service in 1956. He subsequently had been a professor at the Escuela Superior de Guerra and had served as

the head of the army's own intelligence service. He was very active in the *azul-colorado* conflicts of the early 1960s. See *La Nación*, 14–18 June 1970, for details.

7. "Coyuntura: prudencia ante los cambios en el gobierno," *Panorama*, 16 June 1970, pp. 16–17; and Braun and Kesselman, "Argentina 1971: Estancamiento estructural y crisis de coyuntura," p. 46.

8. See *La Nación*, 19 June 1970; and "El debut de Moyano Llerena," *Panorama*, 23 June 1970, p. 12. See Guglialmelli, *120 días en el gobierno*, pp. 13–55, for the full text of policy discussions among government and private-sector economists.

9. Guglialmelli, *120 días en el gobierno*, pp. 13–55.

10. See the joint declaration issued by the UIA, the Bolsa de Comercio, and the Cámara Argentina de Comercio in BC, *Memoria Anual* (1970), pp. 223–24; and the UIA statement in *La Prensa*, 4 July 1970.

11. See the text of a speech by the UIA's president in the *Revista de la Unión Industrial*, No. 46 (July-Sept. 1970), pp. 36–40.

12. See the numerous notes and declarations during the Moyano Llerena period in the SRA's *Memoria Anual* for 1969/70.

13. For examples of Levingston's nationalist rhetoric, see the speeches in *La Nación*, 24 June 1970 and 24 Dec. 1970. Also see his interview in *Confirmado*, 14 Sept. 1970.

14. Guglialmelli's appointment to head CONADE represented the Junta's attempt at rapprochement with military nationalists and *desarrollistas*. Upon his forced retirement by Onganía, Guglialmelli had founded *Estrategía*, a journal of geo-political thought with a pronounced nationalist tilt. For an example of Guglialmelli's positions, see "Responsibilidad de la Fuerzas Armadas en la Revolución Nacional." Guglialmelli's book, *120 días en el gobierno*, reproduces several valuable documents illustrating policy disputes during this period.

15. See "4 + 5 = 9," *Análisis*, 15 Sept. 1970, pp. 8–10.

16. "Los cuatro meses de Moyano Llerena," *Panorama*, 20 Oct. 1970, pp. 20–22.

17. For the text of Guglialmelli's resignation and a flurry of acrimonious exchanges between Guglialmelli and Levingston, see *120 días en el gobierno*, pp. 82–94.

18. Text in *La Nación*, 27 Oct. 1970. Ferrer was well-known to a generation of Argentine students and intellectuals for his structuralist critique of economic orthodoxy in his book *The Argentine Economy*, published in Spanish in 1963. On the response to Ferrer's appointment, see "Cambio de guarda: cómo salir del pantano," *Panorama*, 27 Oct. 1970, pp. 16–17; and "En la chancha se ven los pingos," *Primera Plana*, 27 Oct. 1970, pp. 19–20.

19. A comparison of Ferrer's policies with those advocated in two CONADE development plans produced during the Levingston period shows striking similarities. See CONADE, *Plan Nacional de Desarrollo, 1970–1974*, and *Plan Nacional de Desarrollo y Seguridad, 1971–1975*.

20. See the texts of Ferrer's speeches and press conferences in *La Nación*, 30 Dec. 1970 and 14 Jan. 1971. Also see the introduction to the *Informe Económico* (I Quarter 1971) published by the Ministerio de Economía y Trabajo.

21. See Ferrer's speech in *La Nación*, 27 Oct. 1970; "Coraje no le falta," *Análisis*, 3 Nov. 1970, pp. 8–9; and Braun and Kesselman, "Argentina 1971," pp. 51–52.

22. See the text of Ferrer's television address explaining the *Compre Nacional* law in *La Nación*, 30 Dec. 1970.

23. "El despegue de Ferrer," *Análisis*, 5 Jan. 1971, pp. 8–9; and "Rentabiliad y salarios: sube y baja para empresarios y sindicalistas," *Panorama*, 16 Feb. 1971, pp. 16–17.

24. See "Carnes por televisión: tres actos para un problema muy trajinado," *Panorama*, 2 Mar. 1971, pp. 16–17.

25. For business reactions, see Ribas, "La viabilidad de la metas económicas," pp. 23–26; Bolsa de Comercio, *Memoria Anual* (1970), pp. 7, 19–22, 26.

26. See the paid advertisements in *La Nación*, 30 Dec. 1970 and 12 Mar. 1971.

27. See *Primera Plana*, 27 Oct. 1970, pp. 25–26, for a discussion of CGE policies and statements by Gelbard.

28. *Ibid.*

29. For the Junta's official position, see Presidencia de la Nación, *Políticas Nacionales*, issued in June 1970. Also see Lanusse, *Mi testimonio*, p. 104; and "Cheque a cierto plazo," *Análisis*, 16 June 1970, pp. 8–10.

30. On the cabinet's selection, see Lanusse, *Mi testimonio*, pp. 148, 157; and "Gobierno: el gabinete del Doctor Caligari," *Panorama*, 23 June 1970, pp. 6–7.

31. According to Lanusse, each decree law of "transcendent significance" passed through a maze of bureaucratic steps: from the ministry or secretariat level to the presidency; then to the three services; and finally to the Junta. If the Junta and the president could not come to unanimous agreement in a stipulated time, the president could break the stalemate. See *Mi testimonio*, pp. 166–67.

32. *La Nación*, 24 June 1970. Also see "Los objetivos y los plazos," *Análisis*, 14 July 1970, pp. 8–10; and Lanusse, *Mi testimonio*, p. 151.

33. For Levingston's declarations, see *La Nación*, 30 Sept.1970 and 1 Oct. 1970. These statements came in the midst of a series of meetings,

at Levingston's initiative, with ex-presidents Frondizi, Guido, and O'Farrell. Onganía and Illia refused to attend, and of course Perón was in Spain.

34. "Interior: en busca del Gran Khan," *Primera Plana*, 27 Oct. 1970, pp. 17–18; and "Gobierno: el parto de los montes," *Análisis*, 3 Nov. 1970, pp. 8–9.

35. "El presidente y los oficiales," *Panorama*, 24 Nov. 1970, p. 16; and "Las rebeliones increibles," *Análisis*, 24 Nov. 1970, pp. 8–10.

36. See the text of the "political plan" in *La Nación*, 30 Dec. 1970. For details of Levingston's meetings with supporters, see "Ulises: ¡cuántos días para volver a Itaca!," *Panorama*, 5 Jan. 1971, pp. 8–9; and "Los alquimistas de la política," *Panorama*, 12 Jan. 1971, pp. 10–12.

37. Text in *La Nación*, 27 Jan. 1971. This statement was followed a week later by Levingston's attack on the grain monopolies and attacks on foreign oil companies. See "De cómo empezó la cruzada nacionalista contra los monopolios," *Panorama*, 9 Feb. 1971, pp. 8–10.

38. Quoted in *Polémica*, 19 (1972), p. 234.

39. "Igual que antes pero distinto," *Panorama*, 13 Oct. 1970, p. 12.

40. Interview in *Panorama*, 4 Aug. 1970, pp. 12–13.

41. *La Nación*, 11 Nov. 1970. For background on the Hora del Pueblo, see Castagno, *Tendencias y grupos políticos en la realidad argentina*, pp. 37–41.

42. Hora del Pueblo document dated 16 Feb. 1971 as quoted in Castagno, *Tendencias y grupos*, p. 40.

43. *Ibid.*; and "La caída de un intocable y la supremacia nacionalista," *Panorama*, 16 Feb. 1971, pp. 8–9.

44. Letter from Perón to Paladino, quoted in "Gobierno: entre los consejos de Alende y los fuegos opositores," *Panorama*, 26 Jan. 1971, pp. 8–9.

45. Castagno, *Tendencias y grupos políticos*, pp. 41–45.

46. For documents setting forth the CGT's position, see Senén González, *El sindicalismo después de Perón*, pp. 148–62. The possibility of conciliation with the regime suffered a reverse with the assassination of José Alonso in late August. See "Alonso asesinado: otro puente que cae," *Panorama*, 1 Sept. 1970, pp. 8–11.

47. For details on these strikes, see "Las huelgas del 12 y 13: algo más que un largo fin de semana," *Panorama*, 18 Nov. 1970, pp. 8–9.

48. See Duval, "Argentina: sindicatos y movimientos de masas"; Delich, *Crisis y protesta social*, pp. 119–36; and Torre, "Una nueva oposición social," and "El programa de STIRAC-STIRAM."

49. Quoted in Balve et al., *Lucha de calles, lucha de clases*, pp. 23–24.

50. For extensive documentation on the *vivorazo*, see *ibid.*, pp. 310–13; "El volcán político: temblor en Buenos Aires, llamas en

Córdoba," *Panorama*, 16 Mar. 1971, pp. 8–10; and "Política: sube y baja," *Primera Plana*, 23 Mar. 1971, pp. 10–11.

51. Examples of "armed propaganda" included the occupation of several small towns in the provinces of Córdoba and Buenos Aires by the Montoneros and other smaller Peronist groups, a spectacular plane skyjacking and leafletting of the industrial city of Rosario by the Fuerzas Armadas de Liberación, a raid by the Montoneros on the Córdoba Jockey Club, and an attack by the Fuerzas Armadas Peronistas on the homes of U.S. military personnel. There also were repeated coordinated bombings of military and civilian targets and the well-publicized exploits of so-called "Hunger Commandos," who distributed food, milk, clothes, school supplies, appliances, and other items of mass consumption in poor and working-class neighborhoods. See Hodges, *Argentina, 1943–1976*, and the chronology and sources in Russell, Schenkel, and Miller, "Urban Guerrillas in Argentina."

52. The Junta's control was strengthened by the forced retirement of officers and Lanusse's use of personal visits to and constant surveillance of suspected dissidents. See "Organigramas: a paso redoblado," *Panorama*, 30 June 1970, pp. 12–13; and "Un plan y cinco convocatorias," *Análisis*, 8 Sept. 1970, pp. 8–10.

53. Lanusse, *Mi testimonio*, pp. 173–74.

54. *Ibid.*, pp. 157–58.

55. Lanusse cites these options in *Mi testimonio*, p. 156. See *La Nación*, 3 Mar. 1971, for Lanusse's speech upon assuming command of the Junta. Also see "Gobierno: la disputa de los dos nacionalismos," *Panorama*, 9 Mar. 1971, pp. 9–10.

56. General Aufranc as quoted in Lanusse, *Mi testimonio*, p. 199.

57. For Levingston's version of these events, see "Comunicado del General Levingston al pueblo de la República," quoted in *Polémica*, 19 (1972), p. 242. Lanusse's version, including the Junta's offer to establish co-rule with Levingston, is given in *Mi testimonio*, pp. 199–210.

58. Text of the Junta's communiqué in *La Nación*, 24 Mar. 1971.

Chapter Eight

1. Text in *La Nación*, 2 May 1971. Similar ideas were expressed in Lanusse's speech at the Escuela de Aviación in Córdoba on 28 Apr. 1971. See "Fragores: entre el bombo de Perón y la metralleta guerrillera," *Panorama*, 4 May 1971, pp. 8–9.

2. On Mor Roig's selection and promises to legalize the parties, see Lanusse, *Mi testimonio*, pp. 217–18, and Ministerio del Interior, *Proyectos y bases elaborados por la Comisión Coordinadora del Plan Político*, pp. 15–18.

3. "Líderes políticos: ¿ha llegado la hora del pueblo con voz y

voto?," *Panorama*, 30 Mar. 1971, pp. 8–9; "De la cautela de Perón al sigilo de Sulzberger," *Panorama*, 13 Apr. 1971, pp. 8–9; "La tercera es la vencida," *Análisis*, 6 Apr. 1971, pp. 8–10; and "Políticos: la piedra en el estanque," *Confirmado*, 31 Mar. 1971, pp. 8–9.

4. See the UIA's statement in *La Nación*, 16 Apr. 1971, and "Economía: todos a opinar," *Análisis*, 11 May 1971, pp. 14–15.

5. "Economía: todos a opinar," *Análisis*, 11 May 1971, pp. 14–15. Also see the CGE's 1971 *Memoria Anual* for the text of letters sent by the CGE to Lanusse before he was officially named to the presidency.

6. See "Discusión sobre el Consejo Económico y Social," *La Opinión*, 21 Aug. 1971; "Los frentes del acuerdo," *Análisis*, 20 July 1971, pp. 11–13; and "Los secretos del 'acuerdo,'" *Confirmado*, 14 July 1971, pp. 10–13. Conservative sectors charged that Lanusse was creating a "dictatorial tripod" joining the CGT, the CGE, and the Peronist party in a policy of "appeasement." Lanusse's definition of his government as "center-left" and his rejection of the thesis of "ideological frontiers" during trips to Chile and Peru also antagonized the Right. See the editorials in *La Prensa* and *La Nación* on 28 and 29 July 1971. Also see "El viaje de Lanusse, que inquieta a la derecha, fue un proyección externa de la política acuerdista," *La Opinión*, 19 Oct. 1971.

7. These two commissions included jurists, social scientists, and military officers. See Mor Roig's statements in Ministerio del Interior, *Proyectos y bases*, pp. 19–24, and "Dictamenes: once a media tarde," *Primera Plana*, 8 June 1971, pp. 12–13.

8. See *Proyectos y bases*, pp. 91–109; Botana et al., *El régimen militar*, pp. 328–33; and "La Comisión Coordinadora reduciría a cuatro años el mandato presidencial," *La Opinión*, 24 Sept. 1971.

9. See *La Nación*, 18 Sept. 1971. The date for elections was subsequently moved up to 11 Mar. 1973.

10. For details, see "¡Largaron!," *Análisis*, 6 July 1971, pp. 8–9, and "¿Qué se está cocinando?," *Primera Plana*, 6 July 1971, pp. 10–11. For an analysis of the ideology of the posters and other mass media publicity, see "Carteles y avisos optimistas promocionaron el Acuerdo Nacional," *La Opinión*, 26 June 1971.

11. See Lanusse's attack on the *golpistas* in *La Nación*, 9 Oct. 1971. Also see "Lanusse logró consolidar su proyecto político y demonstrar su hegemonía en el campo militar," *La Opinión*, 10 Oct. 1971, and "El país se opone al fascismo en todos los ámbitos," *La Opinión*, 13 Oct. 1971. Lanusse's version is given in *Mi testimonio*, pp. 249–52.

12. Lanusse defended the position that "economic stability" depends on an "authentic, representative, modern, and efficient democracy." See *La Nación*, 11 Mar. 1971.

13. For details on the nationalist opposition, including the support

given by Onganía and Levingston, and factionalism in the navy and air force, see "Informe especial: que piensan las bayonetas," *Panorama*, 25 May 1971, pp. 12–16; "El frente interno," *Análisis*, 18 May 1971, pp. 8–10; "La lucha por el acuerdo," *Análisis*, 8 Oct. 1971, pp. 12–13; "La doctrina del Gatopardo," *Panorama*, 23 Nov. 1971, pp. 20–21. For analyses of the rebellion's failure, see "Cercados por las fuerzas leales, se rindieron ayer por la mañana los sublevados," *La Opinión*, 12 Oct. 1971.

14. Quoted in Balve et al., *Lucha de calles, lucha de clases*, pp. 23–24. Also see "El comandante del Tercer Ejército cree necesario re-educar al pueblo," *La Opinión*, 2 Nov. 1971.

15. The text of the new law can be found in *La Nación*, 19 June 1971. Also see "Imponen su posición los camaristas del nuevo fuero anti-subversivo," *La Opinión*, 13 July 1971.

16. See Graham-Yool, ed., *Tiempo de tragedia*, pp. 108–19, for a partial list of protests. Also see "STIRAC y STIRAM representan una nueva forma de organización," *La Opinión*, 27 Oct. 1971.

17. Journalist Horacio Eichelbaum noted that "teachers in the provinces still retain a halo as representatives of culture, and they have a decisive influence in the midst of the vast middle class partial to conservatism. When they are hosed down and beaten with sticks and walked on by horses, an injury is committed against the entire community." "Los errores de Gabrielli y la crisis de la clase media, causas del conflicto mendocino," *La Opinión*, 7 Apr. 1971.

18. By 1971, assassination attempts had vastly increased and total occurrences of revolutionary direct action had almost doubled since 1969. See Table 6.6.

19. See "Coyuntura sin política económica," *Análisis*, 6 Apr. 1971, pp. 14–16; "Planes: La Hora del Pueblo versus Ferrer," *Confirmado*, 31 Mar. 1971, pp. 22–24; "Gabinete: cifras, futuro y muchas expectativas," *Panorama*, 18 May 1971; and "El peso se hunde: De Discépolo a Aldo Ferrer ¿dónde hay un mango?," *Panorama*, 1 June 1971, pp. 18–21.

20. "El Gran Acuerdo Nacional obliga al gobierno a paliativos populistas en Economía," *La Opinión*, 5 June 1971.

21. The labels are more useful than the usual distinction between "liberals" and "populists." See Eduardo Crawley, "La reacción pública puso fin a la impunidad del liberalismo," *La Opinión*, 27 Nov. 1971.

22. The terms were borrowed by critics of regime policies from neighboring Chile, then in the midst of a destabilization campaign against Salvador Allende. See Jacobo Timmerman, "Con el retorno del presidente sería implementado un nuevo plan económico," *La Opinión*, 12 Dec. 1971.

23. For the general policy orientations of the *institucionalistas*, see

"Directivas económicas del CONADE para 1971," *La Opinión*, 27 June 1971. Differences between the two camps surfaced publicly in a joint news conference of the "economic cabinet." See *La Nación*, 4 Aug. 1971.

24. Hirschman, *Journeys Toward Progress*, p. 221. Also see O'Connor, *The Fiscal Crisis of the State*, and Hirsch and Goldthorpe, eds., *The Political Economy of Inflation*.

25. See the analysis by Braun and Gambarotta, "1972. Crisis económica y política: Los límites del reformismo."

26. Agriculture Minister Di Rocco calculated that by late 1971 approximately 1 billion dollars were added to the income of rural producers due to the shift in relative prices. See "Di Rocco explicó su política a la Escuela Superior de Guerra," *La Opinión*, 16 Sept. 1971.

27. From June 1972 to May 1973 the peso was overvalued at a fixed rate of 10 pesos to 1 U.S. dollar. On the black market the peso's value averaged 25–30 percent above the official rate. See the *Boletín Informativo*, No. 25 (1973), published by Organización Technint.

28. See the UIA statement in *La Nación*, 20 Oct. 1971, criticizing the "application of demagogic and aggressive criteria on economic and social questions."

29. Text in *La Nación*, 21 Aug. 1971.

30. Text in *La Nación*, 5 May 1972.

31. *La Nación*, 24 Mar. 1971. For similar positions by other ACIEL affiliates, see "Advierte al gobierno sobre la socialización de la producción," *La Opinión*, 3 June 1971, and "Entidades empresarias liberales critican acciones del Estado," *La Opinión*, 30 June 1971.

32. See "Subversión provinciana," *Análisis*, 10 Dec. 1971, p. 26, and the following articles in *La Opinión*: "La UIA y una entidad empresaria santafesina se intercambiaron severas acusaciones" (22 Mar. 1972), "Los empresarios cordobeses presentaron su propio proyecto de promoción fabril" (10 June 1972), "El empresariado del interior del país formó dos nuevas entidades" (7 July 1972), and "Aumenta el poder y la influencia del empresariado del interior del país" (11 July 1972).

33. For the text of the "Industry Day" speech by the UIA president, see *La Nación*, 3 Sept. 1971. Also see "Coelho fue reelecto por segunda vez presidente de la Unión Industrial," *La Opinión*, 28 Oct. 1971.

34. See the following articles in *La Opinión*: "Compromiso de 123 empresas para evitar la caída del salario real" (16 May 1972), "La gran empresa toma el acuerdo de precios como un mal menor" (18 May 1972), and "ACIEL reindivica el Acta de la Revolución Argentina" (29 June 1972).

35. On the break, see "Política y salarios," *Análisis*, 22 Sept. 1972, pp. 14–15. At roughly the same time there occurred a parallel division within the ranks of the largest financial institutions. Previously, both foreign and domestic banks had been joined in the Asociación de Ban-

cos de la República Argentina, but now the ten largest national banks left the ABRA to form the Asociación de Bancos Argentinos (ADEBA), which proceeded to adopt a position similar to that of the UIA. See "Sesionó por primera vez la Asociación de Bancos Argentinos," *La Opinión*, 31 Mar. 1972, and "Siete bancos conedieron al Estado un crédito de 30 miliones de dólares," *La Opinión*, 29 Mar. 1972.

36. Bolsa de Comercio, *Memoria Anual* (1971), pp. 3–6, 19–26, 295–96. For conflicts involving the SRA, other rural producers, and the Peasant Leagues, see the following articles in *La Opinión*: "Marcha sobre Resistencia" (31 Dec. 1971), "La Marcha sobre Resistencia congregó a 10.000 campesinos del Nordeste" (1 Jan. 1972), "La Federación Agraria resolvió acción de protesta sin fecha," (8 Apr. 1972), "El Congreso del Campo ofrecerá al P.E. un programa agropecuario" (31 May 1972), "Una entidad cooperativista elevó un plan de reforma agraria sin expropriaciones" (6 July 1972), and "La Federación Agraria precisa sus objetivos de transformación rural" (22 July 1972).

37. See the SRA's 1972 *Memoria Anual*, pp. 84–87, and the 1973 *Memoria Anual*, pp. 55–57, 67–71, and 75–76.

38. See the following articles in *La Opinión*: "La CGE la aprueba y reclama un régimen de reactivación" (18 June 1971), "La CGE y la HDP creen que nacionalizando los depósitos haberá créditos para empresas del país" (22 June 1971), and "La reunió plenaria propone la gran salida nacional y un plan económico" (7 July 1971).

39. The evolution of the CGE's position can be traced in *La Opinión*: "Gelbard explicó la posición de la CGE frente al gobierno ACIEL" (24 July 1971), "ACIEL y CGE derivan una lucha ideológica al ataque personal" (29 July 1971), "Un documento de la CGE analiza la actual crisis económica" (19 Sept. 1971), "La CGE y la CGT difundieron un documento con sus coincidencias" (27 Oct. 1971), "La CGE se pronunció explicitamente contra la conducción económica" (16 Nov. 1971), and "La Confederación General Económica y la Unión Cívica Radical emitieron declaraciones sobre la actualidad" (11 Feb. 1972).

40. "El proceso político gravita en la lucha interna por el control de una gran central empresaria," *La Opinión*, 8 Apr. 1972, and "El empresariado nacional se convierte en un importante factor de poder político," *La Opinión*, 26 Apr. 1972.

41. Mor Roig's remarks at a 23 May 1971 meeting of the army high command as reported by Lanusse, *Mi testimonio*, p. 280.

42. The Perón-Cornicelli interview took place on 22 Apr. 1971. The full text was published by Perón in "Perón-Cornicelli: versión completa de la entrevista," *Las Bases*, 18 July 1972, pp. 34–47. Also see "Lanusse dio a publicidad la entrevista del colonel Cornicelli con Juan Perón," *La Opinión*, 4 June 1972.

43. Following up on Cornicelli's mission, Lanusse sent other emis-

saries to Madrid, including Air Force General Martínez (whom Lanusse referred to as his "Argentine Kissinger"), Argentina's ambassador to Spain, General Jorge Rojas Silveyra, and neo-Peronist leader Elias Sapag. See three articles in *La Opinión*: "Ha sido modificada la situación de Juan Perón en España, y gozará ahora de toda libertad de acción" (19 Apr. 1971), "Rojas Silveyra tendrá a su cargo tratativas con Perón" (17 July 1971), and "El viaje a Europa de Eszquiel Martínez incluye una importante entrevista con Juan Perón" (30 Dec. 1972).

44. In a letter to the hard-line faction of the Peronist Youth, Perón explained that he would employ three parallel tactics: (1) "revolutionary war"; (2) "military popular conspiracy"; and (3) "surface-level political struggle." Text in *La Opinión*, 21 May 1971. Throughout 1971 and 1972 the press published similar letters to Perón's lieutenants in Argentina.

45. This period witnessed a huge outpouring of books, articles, and even a film exalting Perón's "Third Position" and commitment to "national socialism." For a sampling, see the film and book by Gettino and Solanas, *Actualización política y doctrinaria para la toma del poder*; Carpani, *Nacionalismo, peronismo y socialismo nacional*; and the interesting review of (and contribution to) this ideological confusion by Ferla, *La tercera posición ideológica*. Also see James, "The Peronist Left, 1955–1975," especially pp. 282–85, and Dodson, "Priests and Peronism: Radical Clergy in Argentine Politics."

46. For Perón's view of Lanusse's courting of neo-Peronist groups and the details of Paladino's ouster, see the following articles in *Las Bases*: "El 'juego pendular' del oficialismo" (23 Nov. 1971), pp. 28–30; "Algunas observaciones sobre el compañero Paladino" (2 May 1972), pp. 11–14; "Unidad, solidaridad y organización" (23 Nov. 1971), pp. 6–7; and "A los dirigentes peronistas" (21 Dec. 1971), pp. 8–10.

47. On the FRECILINA and Perón's relations with Frondizi, see Prieto, *De Perón 1955 a Perón 1973*, pp. 193–97; "La única verdad es la realidad," *Las Bases*, 15 Feb. 1972, p. 8; "Perón-Frondizi: el acuerdo de Madrid," *Panorama*, 21 Mar. 1972, pp. 14–17; "Arturo Frondizi: el Frente Cívico, contracara del GAN," *Panorama*, 8 Apr. 1972, pp. 18–19; "La caldera del diablo," *Confirmado*, 14 Mar. 1972, pp. 8–10; and Perón's "ecumenical" message to the UN General Secretary and heads of state, in *La Opinión*, 25 Mar. 1972.

48. See "Violencia en la Argentina: los políticos se definen," *Panorama*, 20 Apr. 1972, pp. 16–21; "Los voceros de Perón en Madrid desmienten anteriores declaraciones contra la violencia y los asesinatos," *La Opinión*, 12 Apr. 1972; and "Las tácticas de Lanusse y los extremos de la política," *La Opinión*, 4 Apr. 1972.

49. See Lanusse, *Mi testimonio*, pp. 271 and 279; "Peronismo una negociación con dignidad," *Panorama*, 25 May 1972, pp. 8–9; and "El

ministro Mor Roig enfoca el tema de las candidaturas presidenciales," *Panorama*, 25 Apr. 1972.

50. Perón's statement was made in his first televised press conference since 1955. See "Perón dio una conferencia de prensa referida a la actualidad argentina," *La Opinión*, 21 May 1972. Shortly afterward, José Rucci, the head of the CGT, stated that "the only alternative is elections with Perón's candidacy or civil war." *La Nación*, 27 May 1972.

51. See text in *La Nación*, 1 June 1972, and Lanusse, *Mi testimonio*, pp. 281–83. Lanusse's statement reflected a widespread view in the military. See "La solución electoral depende del logro de una fórmula de concordancia política," *La Opinión*, 13 May 1972.

52. "Perón sostuvo que, de no cumplirse sus exigencias, la Argentina podría precipitarse en una guerra civil," *La Opinión*, 29 June 1972. The CGT's statement can be found in *La Nación*, 9 July 1972.

53. Presidencia de la Nación, "Mensaje del Presidente de la Nación a las Fuerzas Armadas" (7 July 1972). Also see *Mi testimonio*, p. 288.

54. See the text of the "pact of guarantees" in *La Nación*, 20 July 1972. Also see "Mor Roig afirmó que el proceso de institucionalización seguirá adelante," *La Opinión*, 26 July 1972, and "El punto de no retorno," *Análisis*, 28 July 1972, pp. 12–13.

55. Text in *La Nación*, 28 July 1972. Lanusse's fixation with Perón was described as "almost obsessive," with 2,000 words out of 7,300 dedicated to Perón. See "Acotaciones del discurso de 27 de julio," *Panorama*, 3 Aug. 1972, p. 14. Lanusse's strong attack may have been motivated in part by Perón's statements to *La Vanguardia* of Barcelona in which he said that he would not return to Argentina at that time because "in leadership I am a professional. I have dedicated all my life to the study of leadership and it is not to be expected that I could fail in the use of its instruments." See Terragno, *Los 400 días de Perón*, p. 81.

56. "Mensaje desde Madrid acerca del acuerdo para la Reconstrucción Nacional, incluidos los 10 puntos mínimos para el acuerdo," in Perón, *Juan Perón, 1973–1974: todos sus discursos, mensajes y conferencias*, Vol. 1, pp. 11–14.

57. "Mensaje desde Madrid al pueblo argentino y a los compañeros peronistas," in *ibid.*, pp. 15–17. Also see "Las dificultades del 'acuerdo chico,'" *Panorama*, 9 Oct. 1972, pp. 12–13.

58. For descriptions of Perón's arrival and his move to his house in Vicente López, see *La Nación* for the period 17–19 Nov. 1972.

59. See descriptions of these events in *La Nación*, 21 and 22 Nov. 1972; Perón, *Juan Perón, 1973–1974*, Vol. 1, pp. 21–30; and "Plan Perón: libretos y cortinas de humo," *Confirmado*, 28 Nov. 1972, pp. 12–13. For Lanusse's frustration with Perón's masterful performance, see *Mi testimonio*, p. 302.

60. "Cámpora-Lima la fórmula de la discordia," *Panorama*, 21 Dec.

1972, pp. 14–16; and "Fórmulas para perder y estrategías para ganar," *Análisis/Confirmado*, 19 Dec. 1972, pp. 8–10.

61. See Andino and Paredes, *Breve historia de los partidos políticos argentinos*, pp. 193–213; and "El voto de las izquierdas," *Panorama*, 1 Feb. 1973, pp. 20–22. For background on the military's "request" that Brigadier Martínez retire and run for the presidency, see Lanusse, *Mi testimonio*, pp. 303–4, 308.

62. See "Encuesta: Ganan Cámpora, Balbín y Manrique," *Panorama*, 8 Feb. 1973, pp. 22–27; and "Encuesta: los resultados del ballotage," *Análisis/Confirmado*, 15 Feb. 1973, pp. 24–27.

63. For the charges against the FREJULI, see *La Nación*, 6 Feb. 1973.

64. Perón gave credence to this belief in remarks to *Le Monde*, in which he praised Cámpora for his "loyalty," while stressing "I am still the strategist, the leader." He added that "it is one thing to reach the government and another to take power. That is why I say, first the government and a month later power." *Facts on File 1973*, p. 19. For the FREJULI's "programmatic platform," see Cámpora, *La revolución peronista*, pp. 7–67.

65. See "Estrategía de Perón," *Análisis/Confirmado*, 28 Feb. 1973, pp. 8–9; and "La UCR, Perón y los militares," and the interview with Balbín, both in *Panorama*, 6 Feb. 1973, pp. 15, 18, and 16–17, respectively.

66. On the rumor campaigns, see "Pacto de guarantías: tormenta de verano," *Panorama*, 25 Jan. 1973, pp. 12–13; "Las condiciones militares," *Panorama*, 1 Feb. 1973, pp. 8–9; and "Civiles y militares: carta de situación," *Análisis/Confirmado*, 6 Feb. 1973, pp. 6–8.

67. See "La encrucijada de los militares," *Panorama*, 8 Feb. 1973, pp. 12–13; and "La situación militar," *Panorama*, 22 Feb. 1973, pp. 12–13.

68. Lanusse explained to the Junta that these two documents were necessary because if the military did not act, "the subversion that we are combating is going to assume power via the electoral route." See *Mi testimonio*, pp. 317–19, with the full texts on pp. 319–22. For an analysis of divisions within the army at this point, see "Radiografía de la cúpula," *Panorama*, 26 Apr. 1973, pp. 18–20.

69. See denunciations of government harassment by Cámpora and Frondizi in *La Nación*, 24 and 25 Feb. 1973.

70. For analyses of the March 11 vote, see Mora y Araujo, "La estructura social del peronismo: un análisis electoral interprovincial," and Jorrat, "Algunas notas sobre la correlación negativa entre el voto del FREJULI y clase obrera."

71. "Mensaje de la Victoria," in Perón, *Juan Perón, 1973–1974*, Vol. 1, pp. 42–43. During this period Cámpora met with Lanusse and the navy and air force commanders and with the Pope in the Vatican giving

reassurances of his moderation. The moderate and right-wing sectors of Peronism were also asserting themselves, eclipsing somewhat the radicalized sectors. See "Peronismo: la lucha por el poder," *Análisis/ Confirmado*, 27 Mar. 1973, pp. 10–14; and "Vicente Solano Lima: ¿amigo o enemigo?," *Nuevo Confirmado*, 15 May 1973, pp. 10–12. In response to a plea from Cámpora, the Montoneros ceased most operations, but the ERP continued to carry out assassinations, kidnappings, and bombings. For details on ERP activities, including the assassination of Admiral Hermes Quijada, and on Ford Motor Company's announcement of a 1 million dollar donation of food and medical equipment to the poor, see Russell, Schenkel, and Miller, "Urban Guerrillas in Argentina," pp. 84–85.

72. "Mensaje ante la Asamblea Legislativa," in Cámpora, *La revolución peronista*, pp. 76–190. That same night 50,000 Peronists and leftists threatened to storm Villa Devoto Prison, forcing Cámpora to issue an executive pardon for all political prisoners.

73. "A las Fuerzas Armadas," delivered 6 July 1973, in Cámpora, *La revolución peronista*, pp. 191–202. Also see "El camino de la consolidación," *Nuevo Confirmado*, 10 July 1973, pp. 6–8.

74. Corradi, *The Fitful Republic: Economy, Society, and Politics in Argentina*, p. 111.

Chapter Nine

1. Commenting on the government's internal divisions, the editors of *Pasado y Presente* said that "Cámpora represented a methodology of political action more than an alternative program." See "Del gobierno de Cámpora a Perón en el poder," p. 181. Also see Maceyra, *Cámpora/ Perón/Isabel*, pp. 70–86; De Ris, *Retorno y derrumbe: el último gobierno de Perón*, pp. 55–70; and Torre, *Los sindicatos en el gobierno, 1973–1976*, pp. 41–66.

2. Text in *La Opinión*, 22 June 1973.

3. Quoted in de Ris, *Retorno y derrumbe*, p. 66.

4. See the essays on the 1973 election in Mora y Araujo and Llorente, eds., *El voto peronista: ensayos de sociología electoral argentina*.

5. Landi, "La tercera presidencia de Perón: gobierno de emergencia y crisis política"; Braun, *El plan económico del gobierno popular;* and Ayers, "The 'Social Pact' as Anti-Inflationary Policy: The Argentine Experience Since 1973." Also see the text of the Social Pact in Poder Ejecutivo, *Plan Trienal para la Reconstrucción y Liberación Nacional*.

6. On Perón's last year, see Godio, *El último año de Perón*. On economic policy, see Di Tella, *Perón-Perón, 1973–1976*.

7. Cavarozzi, "Algunas consideraciones sobre la crisis política en la Argentina y el rol del movimiento obrero"; Maceyra, *Cámpora/Perón/*

Isabel, pp. 114–35; Torre, *Los sindicatos en el gobierno, 1973–1976*, pp. 105–45; and De Ris, *Retorno y derrumbe*, 131–44.

8. In 1975 revenues covered only 22.8 percent of public expenditures, compared to 88.4 percent in 1970 and 46.5 percent in 1974. Calculated from Ministerio de Economía y Trabajo, *Informe Económico* (I and II Quarters of 1974), and unpublished data furnished by the Ministry's Oficina del Presupuesto.

9. See Frenkel, "Inflación y política antiinflacionaria en la Argentina, 1975–1978," and Canitrot, "La viabilidad de la democracia: un análisis de la experiencia peronista, 1973–1976."

10. See Garretón's important essay, "Em Torno da Discussão sobre os Novos Regimes Autoritários na América Latina."

11. According to a report presented to President Raúl Alfonsín, of the 8,960 "disappeared," 30.2 percent were workers; 21 percent students; 17.9 percent white-collar employees; 10.7 percent professionals; 5.7 percent teachers; 3.8 percent housewives; 2.5 percent military personnel; 1.6 percent journalists; 1.3 percent actors and artists; 0.3 percent priests and nuns; and 5 percent other. Comisión Nacional sobre la Desaparición de las Personas, *Nunca Más*, p. 480.

12. *Argentina Outreach*, various numbers in 1976. General Ibérico St. Jean, military governor of the Province of Buenos Aires, echoed these sentiments: "First we will kill all the subversives, and then all their collaborators; then, their sympathizers; then, those who are indifferent to us; and finally those who show any fear." Cited in Camps, "Los desaparecidos están muertos."

13. Quoted in OAS, *Report on the Situation of Human Rights in Argentina*, p. 135n. In his introduction to *Nunca Más*, the novelist Ernesto Sábato writes: "From the voluminous documentation we have gathered, we deduce that human rights were violated by organs of the state through the repression of the Armed Forces. . . . From our information, it appears that this technology of hell was carried out by sadistic but controlled agents."

14. For a lucid explanation of the influence of the "Chicago boys" in the Southern Cone, see O'Brien, "Authoritarianism and the New Orthodoxy: The Political Economy of the Chilean Regime, 1973–1982."

15. Martínez de Hoz's own ideas are spelled out in *Bases para una economía moderna* and in his numerous speeches. Also see Schvarzer, *La política económica de Martínez de Hoz*; Deheza, *El plan de Martínez de Hoz y la economía argentina*; and Beccaria and Carciofi, "The Recent Experience of Stabilising and Opening Up the Argentine Economy." For broader, comparative analyses, see Foxley, *Latin American Experiments in Neoconservative Economics*, and Ramos, *Neoconservative Economics in the Southern Cone of Latin America*.

16. For the best summary, see Canitrot, "La disciplina como objetivo de la política económica: un ensayo sobre el programa económico del gobierno argentino desde 1976."

17. For the notion of a "capitalist revolution" applied to neo-liberal policies, see Vergara, "Transformaciones en las funciones del Estado bajo el régimen militar."

18. With a few minor variations, the following analysis follows the chronology proposed by Frenkel in "Inflación y política antiinflacionaria en la Argentina" and "Las recientes políticas de estabilización en Argentina: de la vieja a la nueva ortodoxia."

19. For details of Argentina's negotiations with the IMF, see Martel, "Domination by Debt: Finance Capital in Argentina."

20. On the 1977 reform, see Feldman and Sommer, *Crisis financiera y endeudamiento externo en la Argentina*, pp. 38–48.

21. Frenkel, "Las recientes políticas de estabilización," p. 34.

22. See Martínez de Hoz, "A New Stage in the Application of the Economic Programme Was Started."

23. "Argentina: The Wizard's Postmortem," *Latin America Regional Report: Southern Cone*, 6 Mar. 1981, pp. 5–6.

24. Roque Fernández, "La crisis financiera argentina: 1980–1982"; FIEL, *Indicadores de Coyuntura*, Feb. 1982; and *El Cronista Comercial*, 19 Jan. 1981.

25. See Gambetta, "Los militares argentinos en búsqueda de una normalización"; and "Apertura y política económica," *El Cronista Comercial*, 19 Mar. 1981.

26. For the text of Sigaut's announcement, see *El Cronista Comercial*, 2 Apr. 1981. On the repercussions, see "Una aproximación al nuevo equipo económico," *Clarín*, 6 Apr. 1981.

27. For example, Juan Alemann (finance minister under Martínez de Hoz) commented that Sigaut's policy, "with uncontrolled money supply, growing inflation, and heavy foreign debt, is looking more and more like Germany in 1923." Quoted in "Argentine Army Quarrels while the Peso Burns," *Latin America Regional Reports: Southern Cone*, 26 June 1981, pp. 1–2.

28. Text in *El Cronista Comercial*, 20 Aug. 1981.

29. *La Nación*, 23 Dec. 1981.

30. See Alemann's statement in Ministry of Economy, *Economic Information on Argentina*, 121 (Nov.-Dec. 1981), pp. 6–7.

31. The regime claimed to have completely privatized 342 companies (and partially privatized 63 additional firms) worth some $300 million by March 1980. See "The Subsidiary Role of the State: Numerous Enterprises Return to the Private Domain," *Economic Information on Argentina*, 108 (July-Aug. 1980), pp. 44–45. However, the state assumed control

of firms valued at approximately $3 billion during the same period. See Ferrer, "El monetarismo en Argentina y Chile."

32. See "Alemann's Austerity Plan Brings Reaganomics to Buenos Aires," *Latin American Weekly Report*, 8 Jan. 1982, pp. 1–2.

33. See "Alemann Seeks Denationalization," in *Latin America Weekly Report*, 5 Feb. 1982, p. 5.

34. See Spagnolo, "Costo económico del conflicto de la Malvinas."

35. On shifts in economic policy during the war, see "Malvinas Occupation Gives Alemann a New Problem," *Latin America Regional Reports: Southern Cone*, 9 Apr. 1982, p. 1, and "Economic Team Fights It Out," *Latin America Weekly Report*, 4 June 1982, p. 1.

36. Text in *El Cronista Comercial*, 6 July 1982.

37. See "Difundieron la concertación de precios," *Clarín*, 17 July 1982, and Peralta Ramos, "Toward an Analysis of the Structural Basis of Coercion in Argentina: The Behavior of the Major Fractions of the Bourgeoisie, 1976–1983," p. 60.

38. Rossi, "FMI Pede que o Governo Argentino Reative Economia."

39. *Latin American Weekly Report*, 26 Nov. 1982.

40. Marcelo Cavarozzi notes that the regime's economic policies represented a "bourgeois revolution against the bourgeoisie . . . and the proletarians." *Autoritarismo y democracia (1955–1983)*, p. 60. Also see Frenkel and O'Donnell, "The 'Stabilization Programs' of the International Monetary Fund and Their Internal Impacts."

41. See Teubal, "La crisis alimenticia y el Tercer Mundo: Una perspectiva latinoamericana," and Nudelman, "Argentina en el conflicto de las hegemonías." See also Sidicaro, "Poder y crisis de la gran burguesía agraria argentina," pp. 89–100, for an analysis of Pampean producers during this period.

42. Statement by the Secretary of Agriculture, cited in Geller, "Argentina: la ofensiva del 76," p. 57.

43. For an argument that these policies were not anti-industrial, but geared toward industrial reconversion, see Rímez, "Las experiencias de apertura externa y desprotección industrial en el Cono Sur," pp. 103–24.

44. Schvarzer, "Estrategia industrial y grandes empresas: el caso argentino."

45. Calculated from Banco Central, *Boletín Estadístico*, various numbers.

46. Cited in the *Folha de São Paulo*, 23 Feb. 1982.

47. See Schvarzer, "Las empresas industriales más grandes de la Argentina: Una evaluación," and "Cambios en el liderazgo industrial argentino en el periódo Martínez de Hoz."

48. Canitrot, "La disciplina como objetivo," p. 29n.

49. See Andrés Fontana's analysis of Viola's overtures in "Fuerzas Armadas, partidos políticos y transición a la democracia en Argentina," pp. 12–13.

50. According to an editorial in *La Nación* on 6 Dec. 1981, "civilian forces, those close as well as those distanced from the armed forces, followed events [of the coup] as simple spectators." Cited in Fontana, "Fuerzas Armadas, partidos políticos y transición a la democracia," p. 27.

51. See the Junta's message on the sixth anniversary of the 1976 coup in *Clarín*, 25 Mar. 1982. The events of the CGT's protest are covered in *Clarín*, 31 Mar. 1982.

52. See Fontana, "Fuerzas Armadas, partidos políticos y transición a la democracia," p. 30; and Feldman, "The U.S. Role in the Malvinas Crisis, 1982: Misguidance and Misperception in the Argentine Decision to Go to War." Also see Galtieri's interview with Oriana Fallaci in *El Bimestre Político y Económico*, No. 3 (1982), pp. 123–29.

53. See the preliminary report of the "Rattenbach Commission" (headed by Lt. General Benjamín Rattenbach) published in *La Nación*, 24 Aug. 1983. For details on morale and abuses committed by superior officers, see Kon, *Los chicos de la guerra*, and Túrolo, *Así lucharon*.

54. See Gramsci's essay "Observations on Certain Aspects of the Structure of Political Parties in Periods of Organic Crisis," in *Selections from the Prison Notebooks*, pp. 210–33.

55. Fontana, "Fuerzas Armadas, partidos políticos y transición a la democracia," pp. 25–26; and Fontana, "De la crisis de las Malvinas a la subordinación condicionada: Conflictos intramilitares y transición política en Argentina."

56. See Alfonsín's press conference published in *La Nación*, 3 May 1983.

57. On the transformations of the party system, see Cavarozzi, "Peronistas y radicales: Diez años después." For analyses of the elections, see Cattenberg, "Las elecciones del 30 de octubre de 1983: El surgimiento de una nueva convergencia electoral"; Mora y Araujo, "La naturaleza de la coalición alfonsinista"; and Jorrat, "Las elecciones de 1983: ¿Desviación o realineamiento?"

58. The following analysis draws upon Ferrer, *La posguerra* and *¿Puede Argentina pagar su deuda externa?* Also see Furtado, *A Nova Dependência*, chap. 7.

59. World Bank, *Economic Memorandum on Argentina* (1984), p. 17. From 1976 to 1979, military expenditures averaged about $1.5 billion annually, but then increased: $3.1 billion in 1980, $10.1 billion in 1981, $14.7 billion in 1982, and $12.7 billion in 1983. See the 1984 edition of International Institute for Strategic Studies, *The Military Balance*. From

1979 to 1983, Argentina ranked ninth among all Third World arms importers, with 3.1 percent of total expenditures. In Latin America, only Cuba ranked above Argentina, accounting for 3.7 percent of the Third World total. See SIPRI, *World Armaments and Disarmament Yearbook* for 1984.

60. See Ferrer, *¿Puede Argentina pagar su deuda externa?*, pp. 93–105.

61. This is not to say there was complete harmony. In fact, the decision in 1976 to divide power between the president and the Junta, together with the practice of dividing national, provincial, and parastatal appointments on the basis of a one-third allocation to each of the three branches of the armed forces, resulted in significant friction and fragmentation of organizational power. Nevertheless, internal conflicts on matters of a radical restructuring of polity, society, and economy probably were less severe than in the past. On the division of posts, see "La cúpula cívico-militar," *Carta Política*, May 1976, pp. 32–35, and Vanossi, "Reflexiones sobre el nuevo régimen institucional argentino."

62. The military's thinking about institutionalization was set forth in a 1979 document, "Bases Políticas de las Fuerzas Armadas para el Proceso de Reorganización Nacional." For an analysis, see Portantiero, "Bases políticas, ley sindical y el plan del capital," pp. 2–3. As part of this effort to build support, the regime also supported mothers' centers, neighborhood councils, and other "apolitical" organizations, particularly in urban shantytowns. After the Malvinas conflict, many of these *villas miserias* erupted in so-called *vecinazos* in opposition to the regime, led by the same community organizations. See Jelin, ed., *Los nuevos movimientos sociales*, and Silva and Schuurman, "Neighborhood Associations in Buenos Aires: Contradictions within Contradictions."

63. See the studies ("Estructura, carácter y comportamiento de las principales corporaciones empresarias de la Argentina") of the UIA, the SRA, the Cámara de Comercio, etc. conducted at the Centro de Investigaciones Sociales sobre el Estado y la Administración (CISEA). Also see Ester Fernández, "Comportamiento de los organismos empresarios en la Argentina (1976–1983)."

64. Quoted in Peralta Ramos, "Toward an Analysis of the Structural Basis of Coercion in Argentina," p. 55. The same message was used to convince the international community. For example, in early 1978, Martínez de Hoz told a seminar of 100 international bankers and executives that his plans would be carried out regardless of popular opposition because they were backed by the military, "the only possible source of political support." *Latin America Economic Report*, 14 Apr. 1978.

65. For analyses of the extent of these changes, see Dieguéz and Gerchunoff, "La dinámica del mercado laboral en la Argentina, 1976–1981," pp. 4–40; Mann and Sánchez, "Monetarism, Economic

Reform and Socio-Economic Consequences: Argentina, 1976–1982";
and Delich, *Metáforas de la sociedad argentina*, pp. 71–148.

66. See Corradi, "The Culture of Fear in Civil Society," and "The
Mode of Destruction: Terror in Argentina." Also see O'Donnell, "La
cosecha del miedo," and "Democracia en la Argentina: micro y macro."

67. For some provocative speculation about the impact of state policies on political culture, see Landi, "Conjeturas políticas sobre la Argentina post Malvinas." Also see Brunner, *La cultura autoritaria en Chile*.

Chapter Ten

1. For a sophisticated statement of this position, see Sábato and
Schvarzer, "Funcionamento da Economia e Poder Político na Argentina: Empecilhos para a Democracia."

2. For a recent survey of transitions to democracy, see O'Donnell,
Schmitter, and Whitehead, eds., *Transitions from Authoritarian Rule:
Prospects for Democracy*. Also see Viola and Mainwaring, "Transitions
to Democracy: Brazil and Argentina in the 1980s"; Share and Mainwaring, "Transitions through Transaction: Democratization in Brazil
and Spain"; William C. Smith, "The Political Transition in Brazil: From
Authoritarian Liberalization and Elite Conciliation to Democratization";
and O'Donnell, "Challenges to Democratization in Brazil: The Threat
of a Slow Death."

3. Cited in Rock, *Argentina 1516–1987: From Spanish Colonization to
Alfonsín*, p. 394.

4. See CONADEP, *Nunca más*.

5. See Mignone, "The Military: What Is to Be Done?"; the essays in
Unidos, 4, no. 15 (Aug. 1987); Ubertalli et al., *El complot militar: un país
en obediencia debida*; and López, *El último levantamiento*.

6. For a provocative discussion of the problems of demilitarization
in democratic transitions, see Stepan, *Rethinking Military Politics: Brazil
and the Southern Cone*.

7. In comparison, only 11.6 percent of the increase in Brazil's debt
during the same period can be traced to capital flight; the Argentine
situation more closely resembled that of Mexico, where the corresponding figure was 60.3 percent. In 1985 Argentines had total stock of foreign assets valued at $43.2 billion, or 93.6 percent of the country's for-
eign debt of $46.1 billion. World Bank, *World Debt Tables, 1986–87*. For
other estimates of Argentine assests abroad, see Christian, "Argentina's Dollar-Based Economy."

8. *La Nación*, 31 Oct. 1983.

9. See Alfonsín's speech to the nation, *Clarín*, 17 Dec. 1983, and
Grinspun's economic message, *La Nación*, 25 Jan. 1984.

10. Cited by Monteón, "Can Argentina's Democracy Survive Economic Disaster?," p. 21. Argentina's bargaining strategy carried an implicit threat to form a debtors' cartel. On the difficulties of forming such a cartel to counterbalance the creditors' cartel, see O'Donnell, "External Debt: Why Don't Our Governments Do the Obvious," and "Brazil's Failure: What Future for Debtors' Cartels?"

11. Stiles, "Argentina's Bargaining with the IMF," p. 68.

12. *Ibid.*, pp. 69–70.

13. See Schvarzer and Sidicaro, "Empresarios y el Estado en la reconstrucción de la democracia en la Argentina."

14. Alfonsín's far-reaching proposal to democratize the unions by proposing new rules for internal elections was presented during the new government's first week in power. For details, see *Clarín*, 18 Dec. 1983. After its defeat in the Senate, the government retreated from this touchy issue. Finally, in early 1988, a much less stringent law was approved by Congress. See "Ley de Asociaciones Sindicales: Normas nuevas y presiones antiguas," *El Bimestre Político y Económico*, no. 38 (1988), pp. 14–16.

15. See the excellent analysis by de Ris, Cavarozzi, and Feldman, "Concertación, estado y sindicatos en la Argentina contemporánea," pp. 39–40.

16. For an idea of Sourrouille's general analysis of the Argentine economy of the mid-1980s, see Sourrouille, Kosacoff, and Lucangeli, *Transnacionalización y política económica en la Argentina.*

17. Hirschman, "The Political Economy of Latin American Development: Seven Exercises in Retrospection," pp. 28–29.

18. Pastor, *The International Monetary Fund and Latin America: Economic Stabilization and Class Conflict.*

19. Maital and Benjamini, "Inflation as a Prisoners' Dilemma," and Maital and Lipnowski, eds., *Macroeconomic Conflict and Social Institutions.*

20. Kaufman, "Democratic and Authoritarian Responses to the Debt Issue: Argentina, Brazil, and Mexico," p. 479.

21. Lindblom, *Politics and Markets: The World's Political Economic Systems.* Also see Block, "The Ruling Class Does Not Rule: Notes on the Marxist Theory of the State," and "Beyond Relative Autonomy: State Managers as Historical Subjects."

22. Kaufman, "Democratic and Authoritarian Responses," pp. 480–81.

23. For a comparison of orthodox and heterodox paradigms, see Dornbusch and Simonsen, *Inflation Stabilization with Incomes Policy Support.*

24. The Brazilian literature on heterodox shocks stresses this point.

See Arida and Lara-Resende, "Inflação Inercial e Reforma Monetária: Brasil"; Lopes, *O Choque Heterodoxo: Combate à Inflação e Reforma Monetária*; and Bresser Pereira and Nakano, *The Theory of Inertial Inflation: The Foundation of Economic Reform in Brazil and Argentina*, chap. 3.

25. The contrast with Brazil on the eve of the launching of the Cruzado Plan, in February 1986, reveals why the Austral Plan was more orthodox than the Cruzado Plan (critics say an "IMF mimic"). While the Sarney government faced an acceleration of inflation and was out of compliance with its agreement with the IMF, Brazil enjoyed a comfortable foreign-exchange position and was in the midst of a strong cyclical recovery, with growth rates of 4.5 percent and 8.3 percent in 1984 and 1985, respectively. See William C. Smith, "Heterodox Shocks and the Political Economy of Democratic Transition in Argentina and Brazil."

26. For details, see Ministerio de Economía de la República Argentina, *Mensajes del Ministro de Economía Dr. Juan V. Sourrouille*, pp. 18–28; Inter-American Development Bank, *Economic and Social Progress in Latin America*, p. 191; and Frenkel and Fanelli, "El Plan Austral: un año y medio después."

27. Central Bank of Argentina, *Argentine Economic Memorandum 1986, Second Quarter*.

28. Frenkel and Fanelli, "El Plan Austral: un año y medio después."

29. Central Bank, *Argentine Economic Memorandum 1987*, p. 2; and Ministerio de Economía, "Un nuevo impulso al Plan de Reforma Económica."

30. For details of the Plan Primavera and analysis of its impacts, see the articles in *Clarín* (int'l ed.), 1–7 Aug. 1988, and in *Clarín Económico*, 7 Aug. 1988.

31. For an early and widely cited example of this enthusiasm, see Grossi and dos Santos, "La concertación social: una perspectiva sobre instrumentos de regulación económico-social en procesos de democratización."

32. In Western Europe, where it has been practiced for decades in a number of countries, *concertación* has served to consolidate representative democracy by contributing to the emergence of more sharply crystallized collective identities of key societal actors. In the European context, *concertación* has not replaced parliament and the party system as the principal means of interest mediation; rather it has been an additional arena contributing to a pluralist society by redefining the mode of action of the principal protagonists in civil society and in the polity. On the compatibility of neo-corporatism with liberal democracy, see Offe, "Societal Preconditions of Corporatism and Some Current Dilemmas in Democratic Theory."

33. De Ris, Cavarozzi, and Feldman, "El contexto y los dilemas de la concertación en la Argentina actual," pp. 192–93; Lange, "The Institutionalization of Concertation."

34. The following discussion of the period prior to the announcement of the Austral Plan follows the description in De Ris, Cavarozzi, and Feldman, "Concertación, estado y sindicatos," pp. 40–50.

35. See *Clarín*, 27 Apr. 1985.

36. For the text of Alfonsín's so-called "Parque Norte" speech and essays analyzing the president's new ideological discourse, see Aznar et al., *Alfonsín: Discursos sobre el discurso*.

37. Lorenzo Miguel's faction had nearly 40 percent of the delegates to the CGT, the *renovadores* 26 percent, and the *ubaldinistas* 23 percent. The rest were non-Peronists. See Palomino, "La normalización de la CGT: ¿Diez años no es nada?," pp. 5–10. Also see Godio, "Lazzaretistas, desestabilizadores y renovadores," and Gaudio and Domeniconi, "Las primeras elecciones sindicales en la transición democrática." Alderete resigned in September 1987, when his position became untenable following the Peronist electoral victory.

38. See Héctor Palomino, "Los conflictos laborales bajo el gobierno constitucional: Del Plan Austral al Ministro de Trabajo Carlos Alderete (1985–1987)."

39. Conversations with economists, sociologists, and several "political operators" linked to them indicate that the "captains" represent firms that were able to delink themselves substantially from domestic mass consumption, thus making them less interested in broad cross-class alliances. Many of the firms involved either have access to international capital markets or have considerable internal capacity to finance their operations. Consequently, the "captains" could live with the Austral's wage and price controls as long as interest rates were kept high. The "captains" were not "credit takers" but "investors" who were able to compensate losses on sales due to price controls by financial speculation through their so-called *mesas de dinero*, or "money tables."

40. For example, beginning in 1986, many owners or managers from the largest firms were courted to assume key administrative posts in a variety of public enterprises and/or to oversee the government's plans for privatization, rationalization, and "de-monopolization" of the public sector. See Schvarzer and Sidicaro, "Empresarios y el Estado en la recontrucción de la democracia en la Argentina," p. 13.

41. For a discussion of austerity and labor's wage losses, see Marshall, "The Fall of Labor's Share in Income and Consumption: A New 'Growth Model' for Argentina?" See Christian, "Argentina's Dollar-Based Economy," for details on capital flight.

42. For details of this proposed pact and responses to it, see *Clarín*, 30 Oct. 1987 and 1 Nov. 1987.

43. A major ideological realignment concerning the role of the state was under way in both the Radical and, more ambiguously, the Peronist parties. At pains to distinguish his plan to roll back the state from Martínez de Hoz's slogan *"achicar el estado para agrandar la nación,"* Alfonsín proclaimed that "The state does not have the right to repress the supply of essential services to the community when it is not in a position to provide them itself." *Latin American Regional Reports: Southern Cone Report*, 26 May 1988, p. 1.

Bibliography

This Bibliography is arranged in five sections, as follows: Argentine Government Documents; Newspapers; Periodicals; Publications of Entrepreneurial Organizations; and Books, Articles, and Manuscripts.

Argentine Government Documents

Banco Central de la República Argentina. *Argentine Economic Memorandum 1987: I/II Quarters*. Buenos Aires, 1987.
——. *Boletín Estadístico*. Buenos Aires, Monthly, 1966–87.
——. *Memorias Anuales*. Buenos Aires, 1966–85.
——. *Sistema de cuentas del producto e ingreso de la Argentina*, 2 vols. Buenos Aires, 1975.
Consejo Federal de Inversiones. *Desarrollo económico y planificación en la República Argentina: Selección bibliográfica, 1930–1972*. Buenos Aires, 1972.
Consejo Nacional de Desarrollo (CONADE). *Plan Nacional de Desarrollo, 1965–1969*. Buenos Aires, 1965.
——. *Plan Nacional de Desarrollo, 1970–1974*. Buenos Aires, 1970.
——. *Plan Nacional de Desarrollo y Seguridad, 1971–1975*. Buenos Aires, 1971.
Instituto Nacional de Estadística y Censos (INDEC). *Boletín estadístico trimestral*. Quarterly, 1970–74.
Junta Militar. *Documentos básicos y bases políticas de la Fuerzas Armadas para el Proceso de Reorganización Nacional*. Buenos Aires, 1980.
Ministerio de Economía. *Argentine Economic Memorandum 1986: Second Quarter*. Buenos Aires, 1986.
——. *Memorandum of Understanding on Economic Policy*. Buenos Aires, 12 Jan. 1987.
——. *Mensajes del Ministro de Economía Dr. Juan V. Sourrouille*. Buenos Aires, 1986.
——. *Mensajes del Ministro de Economía Dr. Juan V. Sourrouille*. Buenos Aires, 1987.
——. "Un nuevo impulso al Plan de Reforma Económica." 25 Feb. 1987.

Ministerio de Economía y Trabajo. *Argentine Economic Development.* Buenos Aires, 1976–78.

————. *Argentine Economic Policy (Speeches of Dr. José María Dagnino Pastore While in Office as Minister of Economy and Labour).* Buenos Aires, 1970.

————. *Eighteen Months of Argentine Economic Development: (April–September 1976–1977).* Buenos Aires, 1977.

————. *Informe Económico.* Buenos Aires: Quarterly, 1968–74.

————. *Política económica argentina: Discursos del Ministro de Economía y Trabajo.* Buenos Aires: vol. I (1968) and vol. II (1969).

————. *Speeches by the Minister of Economy and Labour, Dr. José María Dagnino Pastore.* Buenos Aires, 1969.

————. Unpublished national budget expenditure worksheets, 1963–74.

Ministerio de Interior. *Proyectos y bases elaborados por la Comisión Coordinadora del Plan Político.* Buenos Aires, June 1971.

Poder Ejecutivo Nacional. *Plan Trienal para la Reconstrucción y Liberación Nacional.* Buenos Aires, 1973.

Presidencia de la Nación. *Documento de trabajo sobre la bases políticas de la Reorganización Nacional.* Buenos Aires, Aug. 1978.

————. "Mensaje de Presidente de la Nación a las Fuerzas Armadas." Buenos Aires, 7 July 1972.

————. "Mensaje del Presidente de la Nación General de Brigada (R.E.) Roberto Marcelo Levingston." 23 June 1970.

————. *Políticas Nacionales.* Buenos Aires, June 1970.

Newspapers

Ambito Financiero. Buenos Aires. Daily, various dates, 1983, 1987.

Clarín. Buenos Aires. Weekly International Edition. 1982–88.

Clarín Económico. Buenos Aires. Sunday Economic Supplement. 1982–88.

El Cronista Comercial. Buenos Aires. Daily, various dates, 1970–82.

El Economista. Buenos Aires. Daily, various dates, 1970–82, 1987.

La Nación. Buenos Aires. Daily, 1966–75; Weekly International Edition, 1982–87.

La Opinión. Buenos Aires. Daily, various dates, 1971–75.

La Prensa. Buenos Aires. Daily, various dates, 1966–73.

La Razón. Buenos Aires. Daily, various dates, 1956–74.

Le Monde Diplomatique en Español. México, D.F. 1982–84.

Página 12. Buenos Aires. Daily, various dates, 1987.

Periodicals

Análisis. Buenos Aires. Weekly, 1966–73.

Análisis/Confirmado. Buenos Aires. Weekly, 1973.

Argentina Outreach. Berkeley, Calif.: Argentine Information and Service Center. Bimonthly, 1976–80.

Carta Política. Buenos Aires. Weekly, 1973–76.
Competencia. Buenos Aires. Weekly, 1970–73.
Confirmado. Buenos Aires. Weekly, 1966–73.
El Bimestre Político y Económico. Bimonthly, 1982–88.
El Descamisado. Buenos Aires. Weekly, 1973–74.
Extra. Buenos Aires. Weekly, 1967–68.
La Ciudad Futura. Buenos Aires. Monthly, 1987–88.
Las Bases. Buenos Aires. Weekly, 1972–73.
Latin American Political Report. London. Weekly, 1973–80.
Latin American Regional Reports: Southern Cone Report. London. Monthly, 1982–88.
Mercado. Buenos Aires. Weekly, 1970–74.
Militancia. Buenos Aires. Weekly, 1973–74.
Nuevo Confirmado. Buenos Aires. Weekly, 1973.
Panorama. Buenos Aires. Weekly, 1962–75.
Panorama de la Economía Argentina. Buenos Aires. Quarterly, 1965–73.
Polémica (1962–1972: los hechos, los hombres). Nos. 1–18 (1972).
Primera Plana. Buenos Aires. Weekly, 1962–73.
Redacción. Buenos Aires: Monthly, 1973–75, 1983.
Semana Política. Buenos Aires. Weekly, 1975–76.

Publications of Entrepreneurial Organizations

Bolsa de Comercio (BC). *Memorias Anuales*. Buenos Aires, 1966–75.
Cámara Argentina de Comercio (CAC). *Memorias Anuales*. Buenos Aires, 1967–75.
Confederación General Económica (CGE). *Estudios sobre la Economía Argentina*. Buenos Aires, 1968–74.
———. *Historia de la CGE*. Buenos Aires, 1969.
———. *La etapa reinvindicatoria*. Buenos Aires, 1969.
———. *Lineamientos para un programa global de transformación nacional*. Buenos Aires, 1971.
———. *Memorias Anuales*. Buenos Aires, 1966–76.
———. *Sugerencias del empresariado nacional para un programa de gobierno*. Buenos Aires, Mar. 1973.
Fundación de Investigaciones Económicas Latinoamericanas (FIEL). *Indicadores de Coyuntura*. Buenos Aires, 1973–87.
———. *Las inversiones extranjeras en la Argentina*. Buenos Aires, 1973.
Organización Technint. *Boletín Informativo*. Various issues, 1966– 74.
Sociedad Rural Argentina (SRA). *Memorias Anuales*. Buenos Aires, 1966–76.
Unión Industrial Argentina (UIA). *Memorias Anuales*. Buenos Aires, 1966–76, 1985–86.
———. *Revista de la Unión Industrial*. Buenos Aires, 1966–73.

Books, Articles, and Manuscripts

Abalo, Carlos. "La discusión sobre la política económica del gobierno militar." *Controversia*, no. 1 (Oct. 1979): 25–27.

———. "Notas sobre el carácter acual del capitalismo argentino." *Cuadernos de Marcha*, no. 2 (July-Aug. 1979): 29–38.

Abós, Alvaro. *Las organizaciones sindicales y poder militar*. Buenos Aires: CEAL, 1984.

Agulla, Juan Carlos. *Diagnóstico social de una crisis: Córdoba, mayo de 1969*. Buenos Aires: Editel, 1970.

Alchouron, Guillermo, et al. *¿Podrá sobrevivir el Plan Austral?* Buenos Aires: Editorial de Belgrano, 1987.

Allub, Leopoldo. "Estado y sociedad civil en Argentina: Patrones de emergencia, desarrollo y estabilidad del Estado argentino." *Revista Mexicana de Sociología*, 37, no. 3 (1975): 655–96.

Altimir, Oscar. "Estimaciones del distribución del ingreso en la Argentina, 1953–1980." *Desarrollo Económico*, no. 100 (1986): 521–66.

———. "Evaluación de la política económica actual." *Estudios sobre la Economía Argentina*, no. 1 (May 1968).

———. "La distribución del ingreso y el empleo en el sector manufacturero argentino." *Desarrollo Económico*, no. 51 (1973): 583–89.

Altimir, Oscar, Oscar Santamaría, and Juan Sourrouille. "Los instrumentos de promoción industrial en la posguerra." *Desarrollo Económico*, no. 27 (1967): 362–76.

Andersen, Perry. "The Antinomies of Antonio Gramsci." *New Left Review*, no. 100 (Nov. 1976–Jan. 1977): 5–80.

Andino, Ramón, and Eduardo J. Paredes. *Breve historia de los partidos políticos argentinos, 1874–1974*. Buenos Aires: Alzamor Editores, 1974.

Arida, Pérsio, and André Lara-Resende. "Inflação Inercial e Reforma Monetária: Brasil." In Pérsio Arida, ed., *Inflação Zero: Brasil, Argentina, Israel* (Rio de Janeiro: Paz e Terra, 1986), pp. 9–37.

Arrighi, Giovanni, and Jessica Drangel. "The Stratification of the World-Economy: An Exploration of the Semiperipheral Zone." Paper presented at the Colloquium on the Present Downturn of the World-Economy Compared to Previous Downturns. Binghamton, N.Y. 7–9 Nov. 1985.

Arrighi, Giovanni, Roberto P. Korzeniewicz, and William G. Martin. "Three Crises, Three Zones: Core-Periphery Relations in the Long Twentieth Century." *Cahier du GIS Economie Mundiale, Tiers Monde, Development*, no. 6 (Mar. 1986): 125–62.

Astiz, Carlos. "The Argentine Armed Forces: Their Role and Political Involvement." *The Western Political Quarterly*, 22, no. 4 (1969): 862–78.

Ayers, Robert L. "The 'Social Pact' as Anti-Inflationary Policy: The Argentine Experience Since 1973." *World Politics*, 28, no. 4 (1976): 473–501.

Aznar, L., et al. *Alfonsín: Discursos sobre el discurso*. Buenos Aires: FUCADE/EUDEBA, 1986.

Azpiazu, Daniel, et al. "Acerca del desarrollo industrial argentino: Un comentario crítico." *Desarrollo Económico*, no. 60 (1976): 581–612.

Azpiazu, Daniel, Eduardo M. Basualdo, and Miguel Khavisse. *El nuevo poder económico en la Argentina de los años 80*. Buenos Aires: Legasa, 1986.

Baily, Samuel. *Labor, Nationalism, and Politics in Argentina*. New Brunswick, N.J.: Rutgers University Press, 1967.

Balán, Jorge. "Una cuestión regional en la Argentina: Burguesías provinciales y el mercado nacional en el desarrollo agroexportador." *Desarrollo Económico*, no. 69 (1978): 49–88.

Balve, Beba, et al. *Lucha de calles, lucha de clases: Elementos para su análisis (Córdoba 1969–1971)*. Buenos Aires: Editorial La Rosa Blindada, 1973.

Bartlett, Sarah. "A Vicious Circle in the Latin American Debt Crisis." *New York Times*, 15 Jan. 1989.

Beccaria, L., and R. Carciofi. "The Recent Experience of Stabilising and Opening Up the Argentine Economy." *Cambridge Journal of Economics*, no. 6 (1982): 145–65.

Bergquist, Charles. *Labor in Latin America: Comparative Essays on Chile, Argentina, Venuezuela, and Colombia*. Stanford, Calif.: Stanford University Press, 1986.

Bernetti, Jorge. "Argentina: La moderada opocisión partidaria." *Cuadernos del Tercer Mundo*, no. 31 (July 1979).

Block, Fred. "Beyond Relative Autonomy: State Managers as Historical Subjects." In Ralph Miliband and John Saville, eds., *Socialist Register 1980* (London: The Merlin Press, 1980), pp. 227–42.

———. "The Ruling Class Does Not Rule: Notes on the Marxist Theory of the State." In Thomas Ferguson and Joel Rogers, eds., *The Political Economy: Readings in the Politics and Economics of American Public Policy* (Armonk, N.Y.: M.E. Sharpe, 1984), pp. 32–46.

Bobbio, Norberto. "Gramsci y la concepción de la sociedad civil." In Alessandro Pizzorno et al., ed., *Gramsci y las ciencias sociales* (Córdoba: Cuadernos de Pasado y Presente, 1974).

Borón, Atilio. "El estudio de la movilización política en América Latina: Movilización electoral en la Argentina y Chile." *Desarrollo Económico*, no. 46 (1972): 211–44.

———. "New Forms of Capitalist State in Latin America: An Exploration." *Race and Class*, 20, no. 5 (1979).

Botana, Natalio, et al. *El orden conservador: La política argentina entre 1880 y 1916*. Buenos Aires: Sudamericana, 1977.

Botana, Natalio, Rafael Braun, and Carlos Floria. *El régimen militar, 1966–1973.* Buenos Aires: Ediciones La Bastilla, 1973.

Botzman, Mirta, Edgardo Lifchitz, and María Renzi. "Argentina: Autoritarismo, 'librecambio' y crisis en el proceso actual." *Economía de América Latina*, no. 2 (1979): 127–54.

Bowles, Samuel, and Herbert Gintis. *Democracy and Capitalism: Property, Community, and the Contradictions of Modern Social Thought.* New York: Basic Books, 1987.

Braun, Oscar. *Comercio internacional e imperialismo.* Buenos Aires: Siglo Veintiuno Editores, 1973.

————. "Desarrollo del capital monopolista en la Argentina." In Oscar Braun, ed., *El capitalismo argentino en crisis* (Buenos Aires: Siglo Veintiuno Editores, 1973), pp. 11–44.

————. *El desarrollo del capitalismo monopolista en la Argentina.* Buenos Aires: Tiempo Contemporáneo, 1970.

————. *El plan económico del gobierno popular.* Buenos Aires: Editorial El Coloquio, 1974.

————. "La renta absoluta y el uso ineficiente de la tierra en la Argentina." *Desarrollo Económico*, no. 54 (1974): 399–404.

Braun, Oscar, and Héctor Gambarotta. "1972. Crisis económica y política: Los límites del reformismo." In Oscar Braun, ed., *El capitalismo argentino en crisis* (Buenos Aires: Siglo Veintiuno Editores, 1973), pp. 119–63.

Braun, Oscar, and J. L. Joy. "A Model of Economic Stagnation: A Case Study of the Argentine Economy." *Economic Journal*, 78, no. 312 (1968).

Braun, Oscar, and Ricardo Kesselman. "Argentina 1971: Estancamiento estructural y crisis de coyuntura." In Oscar Braun, ed., *El capitalismo argentino en crisis* (Buenos Aires: Siglo Veintiuno Editores, 1973), pp. 45–72.

Bresser Pereira, Luiz, and Yoshiaki Nakano. *The Theory of Inertial Inflation: The Foundation of Economic Reform in Brazil and Argentina.* Boulder, Colo.: Lynne Rienner, 1987.

Brodersohn, Mario. "Políticas económicas de corto plazo, crecimiento con inflación en la Argentina, 1950–1972." In Consejo Professional de Ciencias Económicas, eds., *Problemas económicos argentinos: Diagnóstico y política* (Buenos Aires: Ediciones Macchi, 1974), pp. 1–64.

————."Sobre 'Modernización y autoritarismo' y el estancamiento inflacionario argentino." *Desarrollo Económico*, no. 51 (1973): 591–605.

Brodersohn, Mario, ed. *Estrategias de industrialización para la Argentina.* Buenos Aires: Editorial del Instituto Di Tella, 1970.

Brown, Leopoldo, and Carlos Floria. "Del gobierno revolucionario al orden constitucional." *Criterio*, 13 June 1968.

Brunner, José Joaquín. *La cultura autoritaria en Chile.* Santiago: FLACSO, 1981.

Buchanan, Paul G. "State Corporatism in Argentina: Labor Administration under Perón and Onganía." *Latin American Research Review,* 20, no. 1 (1985): 61–95.

Buci-Glucksmann, Christine. *Gramsci y el Estado: Hacia una teoría materialista de la filosofía.* Mexico City: Siglo Veintiuno Editores, 1978.

Cammack, Paul. "The Political Economy of Contemporary Military Regimes in Latin America: From Bureaucratic-Authoritarianism to Restructuring." In Philip O'Brien and Paul Cammack, eds., *Generals in Retreat: The Crisis of Military Rule in Latin America* (Manchester: Manchester University Press, 1985), pp. 1–36.

Cámpora, Héctor. *El mandato de Perón.* Mexico City: author's edition, 1975.

———. *La revolución peronista.* Buenos Aires: EUDEBA, 1973.

Camps, Ramón J. "Los desaparecidos están muertos." *El Bimestre Político y Económico,* no. 7 (1983): 62–65.

Cándido López, Adolfo. *Ideas políticas del General Cándido López.* Buenos Aires: author's edition, 1969.

Canitrot, Adolfo. "La disciplina como objetivo de la política económica. Un ensayo sobre el programa económico del gobierno argentino desde 1976." *Estudios CEDES,* no. 6. Buenos Aires: Centro de Estudios de Estado y Sociedad, 1979.

———. "La viabilidad de la democracia: Un análisis de la experiencia peronista, 1973–1976," *Estudios Sociales,* no. 11. Buenos Aires: Centro de Estudios de Estado y Sociedad, 1978.

———. "Orden social y monetarismo." *Estudios CEDES,* no. 7. Buenos Aires: Centro de Estudios de Estado y Sociedad, 1982.

———. "Teoría y práctica del liberalismo. Política antiinflacionaria y apertura económica en la Argentina, 1976–1981." *Desarrollo Económico,* no. 82 (1981): 131–89.

Cantón, Darío. *Elecciones y partidos políticos en la Argentina (Historia, interpretacíon y balance: 1910–1966).* Buenos Aires: Siglo Veintiuno Editores, 1973.

———. *La política de los militares argentinos: 1900– 1971.* Buenos Aires: Siglo Veintiuno Editores, 1971.

Cardoso, Eliana A. "Seigniorage and Repression: Monetary Rhythms of Latin America." Paper presented at the 14th International Congress of the Latin American Studies Association. New Orleans. 17–19 Mar. 1988.

Cardoso, Fernando Henrique. "Associated-Dependent Development: Theoretical and Practical Implications." In Alfred Stepan, ed., *Authoritarian Brazil: Origins, Policies, Future* (New Haven, Conn: Yale University Press, 1973), pp. 142–78.

356   *Bibliography*

———. *Ideologías de la burguesía industrial en las sociedades dependientes (Argentina y Brasil)*. Mexico City: Siglo Veintiuno Editores, 1971.

———. "Las contradicciones del desarrollo asociado." *Desarrollo Económico*, no. 53 (1974): 3–32.

———. "On the Characterization of Authoritarian Regimes in Latin America." In David Collier, ed., *The New Authoritariansim in Latin America* (Princeton, N.J.: Princeton University Press, 1979), pp. 33–60.

Cardoso, Fernando Henrique, and Enzo Faletto. *Dependencia y desarrollo en América Latina*. Mexico City: Siglo Veintiuno Editores, 1969.

———. *Dependency and Development in Latin America*. Berkeley: University of California Press, 1979.

Carnoy, Martin. *The State and Political Theory*. Princeton, N.J.: Princeton University Press, 1984.

Carpani, Ricardo. *Nacionalismo, peronismo y socialismo nacional*. Buenos Aires: Cuadernos de Socialismo Nacional, Revolucionario y Latinoamericano, 1972.

———. *Poder imperialista y liberación nacional (las luchas del peronismo contra la dependencia)*. Buenos Aires: Efece Ediciones, 1973.

Carri, Roberto. *Sindicatos y poder en la Argentina*. Buenos Aires: Editorial Sudestada, 1967.

Carta Política. "La cúpula cívico-militar." *Carta Política*. May 1976: 32–35.

Castagno, Antonio. *Tendencias y grupos políticos en la realidad argentina*. Buenos Aires: EUDEBA, 1972.

Castex, Mariano. *Un año de Lanusse: Del acuerdo increíble al retorno imposible*. Buenos Aires: Achával Solo, 1973.

Cattenberg, Edgardo R. "Las elecciones del 30 de octubre de 1983: El surgimiento de una nueva convergencia electoral." *Desarrollo Económico*, no. 98 (1985): 259–69.

Cavarozzi, Marcelo. "Algunas consideraciones sobre la crisis política en la Argentina y el rol del movimiento obrero." Buenos Aires: Centro de Investigaciones en Administración Pública, Instituto Torcuato Di Tella, 1974.

———. *Autoritarismo y democracia, 1955–1983*. Buenos Aires: Centro Editor de América Latina, 1983.

———. "Elementos para un caracterización del capitalismo oligárquico." *Revista Mexicana de Sociología*, 40, no. 4 (1978): 1327–52.

———. "Peronismo, sindicatos y política en la Argentina (1943–1981)." In Pablo González Casanova, ed., *Historia del movimiento obrero en América Latina* (Mexico City: Siglo Veintiuno Editores, 1984), pp. 146–99.

———. "Peronistas y radicales: Diez años después." *Debates en la Sociedad y la Cultura*, 1 (1984): 50–53.

———. "Populismos y 'partidos de clase media' (notes comparativos)." Buenos Aires: Documento CEDES, June 1976.

———. "Sindicatos y política en Argentina, 1955–1958." *Estudios CEDES.* Buenos Aires, Centro de Estudios de Estado y Sociedad, 1979.

———. "Unions and Politics in Argentina, 1955–1962." Working Paper No. 63. Washington, D.C.: The Wilson Center, 1980.

Cerro, Francisco. *De Perón al Cordobazo.* Buenos Aires: Centro Editor de América Latina, 1974.

Child, John. "Geopolitical Thinking in Latin America." *Latin American Research Review,* 14, no. 2 (1979): 89–112.

Christian, Shirley. "Argentina's Dollar-Based Economy." *New York Times,* 23 Jan. 1989.

Cimillo, Elsa, et al. *Acumulacíon y centralización del capital en la industria argentina.* Buenos Aires: Editorial Tiempo Contemporáneo, 1973.

Ciria, Alberto. *Partidos y poder en la Argentina moderna (1930–1946).* Buenos Aires: Editorial Jorge Alvarez, 1969.

———. *Perón y el justicialismo.* Buenos Aires: Siglo Veintiuno Editores, 1971.

Collier, David. "The Bureaucratic-Authoritarian Model: Synthesis and Priorities for Future Research." In David Collier, ed., *The New Authoritarianism in Latin America* (Princeton, N.J.: Princeton University Press, 1979), pp. 363–98.

CONADEP. *Nunca más: Informe de la Comisión Nacional sobre la Desaparición de las Personas.* Buenos Aires: CONADEP, 1984.

Consejo Profesional de Ciencias Económicas. *Informe Económico de Coyuntura.* Buenos Aires, Monthly, 1985–88.

Cooke, John William. *La revolución y el peronismo.* Buenos Aires: Ediciones E.R.P., 1968.

Cornbilt, Oscar. "European Migrants in Argentine Industry and Politics." In Claudio Veliz, ed., *The Politics of Conformity in Latin America* (Oxford: Oxford University Press, 1967), pp. 221–48.

———. "La opción conservadora en la política argentina." *Desarrollo Económico,* no. 56 (1975): 599–640.

Corradi, Juan. "Between Corporatism and Insurgency: The Sources of Ambiguity in Peronist Ideology." In Morris Blackman and Ronald Hellman, eds., *Terms of Conflict: Ideology in Latin American Politics* (Philadelphia: Institute for the Study of Human Issues, 1977), pp. 97–128.

———. "The Culture of Fear in Civil Society." In Mónica Peralta Ramos and Carlos H. Waisman, eds., *From Military Rule to Liberal Democracy in Argentina* (Boulder, Colo: Westview Press, 1987), pp. 113–30.

———. *The Fitful Republic: Economy, Society, and Politics in Argentina.* Boulder, Colo.: Westview Press, 1985.

———. "The Mode of Destruction: Terror in Argentina." *Telos*, no. 54 (1982–83): 61–76.

Correa, Jorge. *Los jerarcas sindicales*. Buenos Aires: Editorial Obrados, 1974.

Cortés Conde, Roberto, and Ezequiel Gallo. *La formación de la Argentina moderna*. Buenos Aires: Paidós, 1973.

Cuneo, Dardo. *Crisis y comportamiento de la clase empresaria*. Buenos Aires: Pleamar, 1967.

Deheza, Carlos Palacio. *El plan de Martínez de Hoz y la economía argentina*. Buenos Aires: Ediciones Corregidor, 1981.

Delich, Francisco. "Córdoba: La movilización permanente." *Los Libros*, 21 (1971): 4–8.

———. *Crisis y protesta social: Córdoba 1969–1973*. Buenos Aires: Siglo Veintiuno Editores, 1974.

———. "Desmovilización social, reestructuración obrera y cambio sindical." In Peter Waldman and Ernesto Garzón Valdéz, eds., *El poder militar en la Argentina (1976–1981)* (Buenos Aires: Editorial Galerna, 1983), pp. 101–15.

———. *Metáforas de la sociedad argentina*. Buenos Aires: Sudamericana, 1986.

De Pablo, Juan Carlos. "La ley 17.224 y la distribución intergremial del peso de la política antiinflacionaria." *Libro de FIEL*, no. 4 (1967).

———. *Política antiinflacionaria en la Argentina*. Buenos Aires: Amorroutu Editores, 1972.

———. *Política económica argentina*. Buenos Aires: Ediciones Macchi, 1984.

———. "Precios relativos, distribución del ingreso y planes de estabilización: La experiencia argentina durante 1967–1970." *Desarrollo Económico*, no. 56 (1975): 55–84.

De Ris, Liliana. *Retorno y derrumbe: El último gobierno peronista*. Mexico City: Folios, 1981.

De Ris, Liliana, Marcelo Cavarozzi, and Jorge Feldman. "Concertación, estado y sindicatos en la Argentina contemporánea." *Estudios CEDES*. Buenos Aires: Centro de Estudios de Estado y Sociedad, 1987.

———. "El contexto y los dilemas de la concertación en la Argentina actual." In Mario dos Santos, ed., *Concertación político-social y democratización* (Buenos Aires: Biblioteca de Ciencias Sociales, 1987), pp. 189–223.

Diamand, Marcelo. *Doctrinas económicas, desarrollo e independencia: Economía para las estructuras productivas desequilibradas*. Buenos Aires: Paidós, 1973.

Diamand, Marcelo, and D. Naswesski. "Argentina's Foreign Debt: Its Origin and Consequences." In Miguel Wionczek, ed., *Politics and*

Economics of External Debt Crisis: The Latin American Experience (Boulder, Colo.: Westview Press, 1985), pp. 231–76.

Díaz Alejandro, Carlos F. *Essays on the Economic History of the Argentine Republic.* New Haven, Conn.: Yale University Press, 1970.

———. *Exchange-Rate Devaluation in a Semi-Industrialized Country: The Experience of Argentina.* Cambridge, Mass.: M.I.T Press, 1965.

Diéguez, Héctor, and Pablo Gerchunoff. "La dinámica del mercado laboral urbano en la Argentina, 1976–1981." *Desarrollo Económico*, no. 93 (1984): 3–40.

Diéguez, Héctor, and Alberto Petrecolla. "Crecimiento, distribución y bienestar: Una nota sobre el caso argentino." *Desarrollo Económico*, no. 61 (1976): 101–22.

———. "La distribución funcional del ingreso y el sistema previsional en la Argentina, 1950–1972." *Desarrollo Económico*, no. 55 (1974): 423–40.

DIL. *Nucleamientos Sindicales.* Buenos Aires: July 1972.

Di Tella, Guido. "Argentina's Most Recent Inflationary Cycle, 1975–85." In Rosemary Thorp and Laurence Whitehead, eds., *Latin American Debt and the Adjustment Crisis* (Pittsburgh: University of Pittsburgh Press, 1987), pp. 162–207.

———. *Perón-Perón, 1973–1976.* Buenos Aires: Sudamericana, 1983.

Di Tella, Guido, and D. C. M. Platt. *The Political Economy of Argentina, 1880–1930.* London: Macmillan, 1986.

Di Tella, Torcuato. *El sistema político argentino y la clase obrera.* Buenos Aires: EUDEBA, 1964.

Dodson, Michael. "Priests and Peronism: Radical Clergy in Argentine Politics." *Latin American Perspectives*, 1, no. 3 (1974): 58–72.

Dornbusch, Rudiger, and Mário Henrique Simonsen. *Inflation Stabilization with Incomes Policy Support.* New York: Group of Thirty, 1987.

Doyon, Louise. "Conflictos obreros durante el régimen peronista (1946–1955)." *Desarrollo Económico*, no. 67 (1977): 437–74.

———. "El crecimiento sindical bajo el peronismo." *Desarrollo Económico*, no. 57 (1975): 151–62.

Duejo, Gerardo. *El capital monopolista y las contradicciones secundarias en la sociedad argentina.* Buenos Aires: Siglo Veintiuno Editores, 1973.

Duval, Natalia. "Argentina: Sindicatos y movimiento de masas." *Historia del Movimiento Obrero*, no. 95 (1974).

Echague, Carlos. *Las grandes huelgas.* Buenos Aires: Centro Editor de América Latina, 1971.

Eiegelbaum, Claire H. "The First Year of the 'Argentine Revolution': A New Experiment in Corporatism?" Ph.D. diss., Harvard University, 1968.

El Bimestre Político y Económico. "Ley de Asociaciones Sindicales:

Normas nuevas y presiones antiguas." *El Bimestre Político y Económico*, 38 (1988): 14–16.

Epstein, Edward C. "Labor Populism and Hegemonic Crisis in Argentina." In Edward Epstein, ed., *Trade Unions and the State in Latin
America* (Winchester, Mass: Allen & Unwin, forthcoming).

———. "Politicization and Income Distribution in Argentina: The Case
of the Peronist Worker." *Economic Development and Cultural Change*,
23, no. 4 (1975): 615–31.

———. "What Difference Does Regime Type Make? Economic Auster-
ity Programs in Argentina." In Howard Handelman and Werner
Baer, eds., *Paying the Costs of Austerity in Latin America* (Boulder,
Colo.: Westview Press, forthcoming).

Eshag, Eprime, and Rosemary Thorp. "Las políticas económicas ortodoxas de Perón a Guido (1953–1963)." In Aldo Ferrer et al., *Los
planes de estabilización en la Argentina* (Buenos Aires: Paidós, 1969), pp.
63–132.

Esping-Andersen, Gosta, Roger Friedland, and Erik Olin Wright.
"Modes of Class Struggle and the Capitalist State." *Kapitalistate*, nos.
5/6 (1976): 186–220.

Evans, Peter. *Dependent Development: The Alliance of Multinational, State,
and Local Capital in Brazil*. Princeton, N.J.: Princeton University Press,
1979.

Fayt, Carlos. *El político armado: Dinámica del proceso político argentino
(1960/1971)*. Buenos Aires: Ediciones Pannedille, 1971.

Feinmann, José Pablo. *El peronismo y la primicia de la política*. Buenos
Aires: Cimarrón Librería Editorial, 1974.

Feldman, David Lewis. "The U.S. Role in the Malvinas Crisis, 1982:
Misguidance and Misperception in the Argentine Decision to Go to
War." *Journal of Interamerican Studies and World Affairs*, 27, no. 2
(1985): 1–22.

Feldman, Ernesto, and Juan Sommer. *Crisis financiera y endeudamiento
externo en la Argentina*. Buenos Aires: Centro de Economía Trans-
nacional/Centro Editor de América Latina, 1986.

Ferla, Salvador. *La tercera posición ideológica*. Buenos Aires: Ediciones
Meridiano, 1974.

Fernández, Arturo. *Las prácticas sociales del sindicalismo, 1976–1982*.
Buenos Aires: CEAL, 1985.

Fernández, Ester. "Comportamiento de los organismos empresarios en
la Argentina (1976–1983)." Buenos Aires: Centro de Estudios para el
Proyecto Nacional, 1985.

Fernández, Roque B. "La crisis financiera argentina: 1980–1982." *Desarrollo Económico*, no. 89 (1983): 79–98.

Ferrer, Aldo. *Crisis y alternativas de la política económica argentina*. Buenos
Aires: Fondo de Cultura Económica, 1977.

―――. "Devaluación, redistribución de ingresos y el proceso de desarticulación industrial en la Argentina." In Aldo Ferrer et al., *Los planes de estabilización en la Argentina* (Buenos Aires: Paidós, 1969), pp. 13–30.

―――. "El monetarismo en Argentina y Chile." *Ambito Financiero*, 13 June 1980.

―――. *La posguerra.* Buenos Aires: El Cid Editor, 1982.

―――. *¿Puede Argentina pagar su deuda externa?* Buenos Aires: El Cid Editor, 1982.

―――. *The Argentine Economy.* Berkeley: University of California Press, 1967.

Flishman, Guillermo. "Modelo de asignación de recursos en el sector agropecuario." *Desarrollo Económico*, nos. 39–40 (1970): 375–93.

―――. *La renta del suelo y el desarrollo agrario argentino.* Mexico City: Siglo Veintiuno Editores, 1977.

Fodor, Jorge. "Perón's Policies for Agricultural Exports, 1946–1948: Dogmatism or Commonsense?" In David Rock, ed., *Argentina in the Twentieth Century* (London: Duckworth, 1975), pp. 135–61.

Fodor, Jorge, and Arturo O'Connell. "La Argentina y la economía atlántica en la primera mitad del siglo XX." *Desarrollo Económico*, no. 49 (1973): 3–66.

Fontana, Andrés. "De la crisis de las Malvinas a la subordinación condicionada: Conflictos intramilitares y transición política en Argentina." Working Paper No. 74. Kellogg Institute, University of Notre Dame, Aug. 1986.

―――. "Forças Armadas e Ideologia Neoconservadora: O 'Encholhimento' do Estado na Argentina (1976–1981)." *Dados*, 27, no. 3 (1984): 347–59.

―――. "Fuerzas Armadas, partidos políticos y transición a la democracia en Argentina." *Estudios CEDES.* Buenos Aires: Centro de Estudios de Estado y Sociedad, 1984.

Foxley, Alejandro. *Latin American Experiments in Neoconservative Economics.* Berkeley: University of California Press, 1983.

Fracchia, Alberto, and Oscar Altimir. "Income Distribution in Argentina." *Economic Bulletin for Latin America*, no. 11 (1966).

Freels, John William, Jr. *El sector industrial en la política nacional.* Buenos Aires: EUDEBA, 1970.

Frenkel, Roberto. "Inflación y política antiinflacionaria en la Argentina, 1975–1978." *Estudios CEDES.* Buenos Aires: Centro de Estudios de Estado y Sociedad, 1979.

―――. "Las recientes políticas de estabilización en Argentina: de la vieja a la nueva ortodoxia." Rio de Janeiro: Instituto de Relações Internacionais, 1980.

Frenkel, Roberto, and José María Fanelli. "El Plan Austral: Un año y medio después." Manuscript, 1987.

Frenkel, Roberto, and Guillermo O'Donnell. "The 'Stabilization Programs' of the International Monetary Fund and Their Internal Impacts." In Richard Fagen, ed., *Capitalism and the State in U.S.–Latin American Relations* (Stanford, Calif.: Stanford University Press, 1979), pp. 171–216.

Frenkel, Roberto, José María Fanelli, and Carlos Winograd. "Stabilization and Adjustment Programmes in Argentina." Buenos Aires: Centro de Estudios de Estado y Sociedad, Dec. 1986.

Fuentes Muñoz-Ledo, Luisa (Lisa). "The Middle Class and Democracy in Latin America: Argentina, Brazil, and Mexico." Ph.D. diss., Stanford University, 1987.

Furtado, Celso. *A Nova Dependência*. Rio de Janeiro: Paz e Terra, 1982.

———. *Economic Development of Latin America: A Survey from Colonial Times to the Cuban Revolution*. London: Cambridge University Press, 1970.

Gallo, Ezequiel, and Silva Sigal. "La formación de los partidos políticos contemporáneos: La U.C.R. (1890–1916)." In Torcuato Di Tella, Gino Germani, and Jorge Graciarena, eds., *Argentina, sociedad de masas* (Buenos Aires: EUDEBA, 1971), pp. 41–66.

Gambetta, Carlos. "Los militares argentinos en búsqueda de una normalización." *Le Monde Diplomatique en Español*, Apr. 1981.

Garretón, Manuel Antonio. "De la seguridad nacional a la nueva institucionalidad: Notas sobre la trayectoria ideológica del nuevo Estado Autoritario." *Revista Mexicana de Sociología*, 40, no. 4 (1978): 1259–82.

———. *El proceso político chileno*. Santiago: Facultad Latinoamericana de Ciencias Sociales, 1983.

———. "Em Torno da Discussao sobre os Novos Regimes Autoritários na América Latina." *Dados*, 25, no. 2 (1982).

Gaudio, Ricardo, and Héctor Domeniconi. "Las primeras elecciones sindicales en la transición democrática." *Desarrollo Económico*, 26, no. 103 (1986): 423–53.

Gazzera, Miguel. "Nosotros los dirigentes." In Miguel Gazzera and Norberto Ceresole, *Peronismo: Autocrítica y perspectivas* (Buenos Aires: Editorial Descartes, 1970).

Gelbard, José Ber. *Democracia y participación*. Buenos Aires: Confederación General Económica, 1968.

Geller, Lucio. "Argentina: La ofensiva del 76." *Economía de América Latina*, no. 3 (1979): 147–70.

Gerchunoff, Pablo, and Juan Llach. "Capitalismo industrial, desarrollo asociado y distribución del ingreso entre los dos gobiernos peronistas: 1950–1972." *Desarrollo Económico*, no. 57 (1977): 3–54.

Germani, Gino. *Estructura social de Argentina*. Buenos Aires: Raigal, 1955.

————. *Política y sociedad en una época de transición*. Buenos Aires: Paidós, 1966.

Gettino, Octavio, and Fernando Solanas. *Actualización política y doctrinaria para la toma del poder*. Buenos Aires: Ediciones Pevuel, n.d.

Geze, François, and Alain Labrousse. *Argentine: Révolution et Contre-Révolution*. Paris: Editions du Seuil, 1975.

Giddens, Anthony. *Central Problems in Social Theory: Action, Structure and Contradiction in Social Analysis*. Berkeley: University of California Press, 1979.

Gillespie, Richard. *Soldados de Perón: Los Montoneros*. Buenos Aires: Grijalbo, 1987.

Gilpin, Robert. *The Political Economy of International Relations*. Princeton, N.J.: Princeton University Press, 1987.

Giussani, Pablo. *Los días de Alfonsín*. Buenos Aires: Legasa, 1986.

————. *Montoneros: La soberbia armada*. Buenos Aires: Sudamericana-Planeta, 1984.

Godio, Julio. *El último año de Perón*. Caracas: Universidad Simón Bolívar, 1981.

————. *La caída de Perón*. Buenos Aires: Granica, 1973.

————. "Lazzaretistas, desestabilizadores y renovadores." *La Ciudad Futura*, 1 (1986): 4–5.

Goetz, A. L. "Concentración y desconcentración en la industria argentina desde la década de 1930 a la de 1960." *Desarrollo Económico*, no. 60 (1976): 507–48.

Goldwert, Marvin. *Democracy, Militarism, and Nationalism in Argentina, 1930–1966*. Austin: University of Texas Press, 1972.

González Trejo, Horacio. *Argentina: Tiempo de violencia*. Buenos Aires: Carlos Pérez Editor, 1969.

Gracía Lupo, Rogelio. *Mercenarios y monopolios en la Argentina de Onganía a Lanusse: 1966–1973*. Buenos Aires: Achával Solo, 1973.

Graham-Yool, Andrew, ed., *Tiempo de tragedia: Cronología de la Revolución Argentina*. Buenos Aires: Ediciones de la Flor, 1972.

Gramsci, Antonio. *Selections from the Prison Notebooks*. New York: International Publishers, 1971.

Grossi, María, and Mario dos Santos. "La concertación social: Una perspectiva sobre instrumentos de regulación económico-social en procesos de democratización." *Crítica y Utopía*, no. 9 (1983): 127–50.

Guevara, Juan Francisco. *Argentina y su sombra*. Buenos Aires: author's edition, 1970.

Guglialmelli, Juan Enrique. *120 días en el gobierno*. Buenos Aires: author's edition, 1971.

————. "Responsibilidad de las Fuerzas Armadas en la Revolución Nacional." *Estrategia*, no. 4 (1969).

Halperín Donghi, Tulio. "Algunas observaciones sobre Germani, el surgimiento del peronismo y los migrantes internos." *Desarrollo Económico*, no. 56 (1975): 765–82.

———. "Argentina's Unmastered Past." *Latin American Research Review*, 23, no. 2 (1988): 2–25.

———. *Historia contemporánea de América Latina*. Madrid: Alianza Editorial, 1969.

Hartlyn, Jonathan, and Samuel A. Morley, "Political Regimes and Economic Performance in Latin America." In Jonathan Hartlyn and Samuel A. Morley, eds., *Latin American Political Economy: Financial Crisis and Political Change* (Boulder, Colo.: Westview Press, 1986), pp. 15–37.

Hirsch, Fred, and John H. Goldthorpe, eds. *The Political Economy of Inflation*. Cambridge, Mass.: Harvard University Press, 1978.

Hirschman, Albert. *Journeys Toward Progress: Studies of Economic Policy-Making in Latin America*. New York: Anchor Books, 1965.

———. "The Political Economy of Import-Substituting Industrialization in Latin America." *Quarterly Journal of Economics*, 82, no. 1 (1968): 2–32.

———. "The Political Economy of Latin American Development: Seven Exercises in Retrospection." *Latin American Research Review*, 22, no. 3 (1987): 7–36.

———. "The Turn to Authoritarianism in Latin America and the Search for Its Economic Determinants." In David Collier, ed., *The New Authoritarianism in Latin America* (Princeton of N.J.: Princeton University Press, 1979), pp. 61–98.

Hodges, Donald. *Argentina, 1943–1976: The National Revolution and Resistance*. Albuquerque: University of New Mexico Press, 1976.

———. *Argentina, 1943–1987: The National Revolution and Resistance*. Albuquerque: University of New Mexico Press, 1988.

Huntington, Samuel. *Political Order in Changing Societies*. New Haven, Conn.: Yale University Press, 1968.

Ianni, Otavio. *La formación del estado populista en América Latina*. Mexico City: Ediciones Era, 1975.

Inter-American Development Bank. *Economic and Social Progress in Latin America*. Washington, D.C.: IDB, various years.

International Institute for Strategic Studies. *The Military Balance*. London: 1984.

International Monetary Fund. *Government Financial Statistics Yearbook*. Washington, D.C.: IMF, various years.

———. *International Financial Statistics*. Washington, D.C.: IMF, various issues.

Itzocovitz, Victoria. "Organizaciones corporativas del empresariado argentino: La Cámara de Comercio." Buenos Aires: Centro de Investigaciones Sociales sobre el Estado y la Administración, 1985.

Itzocovitz, Victoria, and Jorge Schvarzer. "Organizaciones corporativas del empresariado argentino: ADEBA (Asociación de Bancos Argentinos)." Buenos Aires: Centro de Investigaciones Sociales sobre el Estado y la Administración, 1986.

James, Daniel. "Power and Politics in Peronist Trade Unions." *Journal of Interamerican Studies and World Affairs*, 20, no. 1 (1978): 3–36.

———. "Rationalization and Working Class Response: The Extent and Limits of Factory Floor Activity in Argentina." *Journal of Latin American Studies*, 13, no. 2 (1981): 375–402.

———. "The Peronist Left, 1955–1975." *Journal of Latin American Studies*, 8, no. 2 (1976).

Jelin, Elizabeth. "Conflictos laborales en la Argentina, 1973–1976." *Revista Mexicana de Sociología*, 40, no. 2 (1978): 421–66.

———. *La protesta obrera*. Buenos Aires: Nueva Visión, 1974.

Jelin, Elizabeth, ed., *Los nuevos movimientos sociales*. Buenos Aires: Centro Editor de América Latina, 1985.

———. *Movimientos sociales y democracia emergente*. Buenos Aires: Centro Editor de América Latina, 1987.

Jenkins, Rhys. *Transnational Corporations and the Latin American Automobile Industry*. Pittsburgh: University of Pittsburgh Press, 1987.

Jessop, Bob. *The Capitalist State*. London: Martin Robinson, 1982.

Jorge, Eduardo. *Industria y concentración económica (desde principios del siglo hasta el peronismo)*. Buenos Aires: Siglo Veintiuno Editores, 1971.

Jorrat, Jorge. "Algunas notas sobre la correlación negativa entre el voto del FREJULI y clase obrera." *Desarrollo Económico*, no. 59 (1975): 445–58.

———. "Las elecciones de 1983: ¿Desviación o realineamiento?" *Desarrollo Económico*, no. 101 (1986): 89–120.

Kaminsky, Gregorio. "Vigilar, sospechar y denunciar." *Controversia*, no. 4 (1980): 30.

Kaplan, Marcos. "El estado empresario en la Argentina." *Aportes*, no. 10 (1968): 33–69.

Kaufman, Robert. "Democratic and Authoritarian Responses to the Debt Issue: Argentina, Brazil, and México." *International Organization*, no. 39 (1985): 473–503.

———. "Industrial Change and Authoritarian Rule in Latin America: A Concrete Review of the Bureaucratic-Authoritarian Model." In David Collier, ed., *The New Authoritarianism in Latin America* (Princeton, N.J.: Princeton University Press, 1979), pp. 165–254.

Kenworthy, Eldon. "Did the 'New Industrialists' Play a Significant Role in the Formation of the Peronist Coalition, 1943–1946?" In Alberto

Ciria et al., *New Perspectives on Modern Argentina*. (Bloomington, Ind: Latin American Studies Program, 1972), pp. 15–28.

———. "The Function of the Little-Known Case Study in Theory Formation, or What Peronism Wasn't." *Comparative Politics*, 6, no. 1 (1973): 17–45.

Kesselman, Ricardo. *Las estrategias de desarrollo como ideologías*. Buenos Aires: Siglo Veintiuno Editores, 1973.

Khavise, Miguel, and Juan Piotskowski. "La consolidación hegemónica de los factores extranacionales: El caso de 'las cien empresas industriales más grandes.'" In *El poder económico en la Argentina* (Buenos Aires: Centro de Investigaciones en Ciencias Sociales, n.d.), pp. 77–98.

Klarén, Peter F. "Lost Promise: Explaining Latin American Underdevelopment." In Peter F. Klarén and Thomas J. Bossert, eds., *Promise of Development: Theories of Change in Latin America* (Boulder,Colo.: Westview Press, 1986), pp. 3–34.

Kohl, James, and John Litt. *Urban Guerrilla Warfare in Latin America*. Cambridge, Mass.: M.I.T. Press, 1974.

Kon, Daniel. *Los chicos de la guerra*. 7th ed.; Buenos Aires: Editorial Galerna, 1983.

Korzeniewicz, Roberto P. "Labor in the Semiperiphery: Argentina, Australia and Brazil in the Long Twentieth Century." Paper presented at the 82d Annual Meeting of the American Sociological Association. Chicago. Aug. 1987.

———. "The Labor Movement in Argentina, 1887–1973." Ph.D. diss., State University of New York, Binghamton, 1988.

Kvaternik, Eugenio. "¿Fórmula o fórmulas? Algo más sobre nuestro sistema de partidos." *Desarrollo Económico*, no. 47 (1972): 613–22.

———. "Sobre partidos y democracia en la Argentina entre 1955 y 1966." *Desarrollo Económico*, no. 71 (1978): 409–32.

Laclau, Ernesto. *Politics and Ideology in Marxist Theory*. London: New Left Books, 1977.

Laclau, Ernesto, and Chantal Mouffe. *Hegemony and Socialist Strategy: Toward a Radical Democratic Politics*. London: Verso, 1985.

Landi, Oscar. "Argentina 1985: Los sentidos del pacto democrático." Paper presented at a conference on "América Latina: ¿Cuál democracia?" Fundación Internacional Lelio Basso. Rome, Italy. Dec. 1985.

———. "Conjeturas políticas sobre la Argentina post Malvinas." *Revista Mexicana de Sociología*, 44, no. 4 (1982): 1225–49.

———. "La tercera presidencia de Perón: Gobierno de emergencia y crisis política." *Revista Mexicana de Sociología*, 40, no. 4 (1978): 1353–1410.

———. "Sobre lenguajes, identidades y ciudanías políticas." In Norbert

Lechner, ed., *Estado y política en América Latina* (Mexico City: Siglo Veintiuno Editores, 1981), pp. 172–98.

Lange, Peter. "The Institutionalization of Concertation." Working Paper Number 26, Duke University Program in International Political Economy, 1987.

Lanusse, Alejandro A. *Mi testimonio.* Buenos Aires: Lassere Editores, 1977.

Lechner, Norbert. "Poder y orden: La estrategia de la minoría consistente." *Revista Mexicana de Sociología,* 40, no. 4 (1978): 1201–58.

Lehmbruch, Gerhard. "Concertation and the Structure of Corporatist Networks." In John H. Goldthorpe, ed., *Order and Conflict in Contemporary Capitalism* (Oxford: Clarendon Press, 1984), pp. 60–79.

Levine, Daniel H. "Paradigm Lost: Dependence to Democracy." *World Politics,* 40, no. 3 (1988): 377–94.

Lifschitz, Edgardo. "Exitos y fracasos de la política económica de la Junta Militar." *Cuadernos de Marcha,* no. 2 (1979): 21–28.

Lindblom, Charles. *Politics and Markets: The World's Political Economic Systems.* New York: Harper and Row, 1977.

Lindenboim, Javier. "El empresariado industrial argentino y sus organizaciones gremiales entre 1930 y 1946." *Desarrollo Económico,* no. 62 (1976): 163–202.

Linz, Juan. "The Future of an Authoritarian Situation or the Institutionalization of an Authoritarian Regime: The Case of Brazil." In Alfred Stepan, ed., *Authoritarian Brazil: Origins, Policies, and Future* (New Haven, Conn.: Yale University Press, 1973), pp. 233–54.

Little, Walter. "Electoral Aspects of Peronism, 1946–1954." *Journal of Interamerican Studies and World Affairs,* 15, no. 3 (1973): 267–84.

———. "La tendencia peronista en el sindicalismo argentino: El caso de los obreros de la Carne." *Aportes,* no. 19 (1971): 107–24.

———. "Party and State in Peronist Argentina." *Hispanic American Historical Review,* 53, no. 4 (1975): 644–62.

———. "The Populist Origins of Peronism." In David Rock, ed., *Argentina in the Twentieth Century* (London: Duckworth, 1975), pp. 162–78.

Llach, Juan José. "Dependencia, procesos sociales y control del estado en la década del treinta." *Desarrollo Económico,* no. 45 (1972): 173–84.

———. "El Plan Pinedo de 1940: Su significado histórico y los orígenes de la economía política del peronismo." *Desarrollo Económico,* no. 92 (1984): 515–58.

———. "Estructura ocupacional y dinámica del empleo en la Argentina: Sus peculiaridades, 1947–1970." *Desarrollo Económico,* no. 68 (1978): 539–92.

———. "Intereses económicos dominantes y los orígines del peronismo." Manuscript, 1972.

————. Reconstrucción o estancamiento. Buenos Aires: Editorial Tésis, 1987.

Looney, Robert E. The Political Economy of Latin American Defense Expenditures: Case Studies of Venezuela and Argentina. Lexington, Mass.: D.C. Heath, 1986.

Lopes, Francisco. O Choque Heterodoxo: Combate à Inflação e Reforma Monetária. Rio de Janeiro: Editora Campus, 1986.

López, Ernesto. El último levantamiento. Buenos Aires: Legasa, 1988.

Luna, Felix. El 45: Crónica de un año decisivo. Buenos Aires: Sudamericana, 1970.

————. Ortiz: Reportaje a la Argentina opulenta. Buenos Aires: Sudamericana, 1978.

Macciocchi, María Antonietta. Gramsci y la revolución de occidente. Mexico City: Siglo Veintiuno Editores, 1975.

Maceyra, Horacio. Cámpora/Perón/Isabel. Buenos Aires: Centro Editor de América Latina, 1983.

Mainwaring, Scott. "El movimiento obrero y el peronismo, 1952–1955." Desarrollo Económico, no. 84 (1982): 515–30.

————. "The State, Political Crisis, and Regime Breakdown: Peronism, 1952–1955." Senior thesis, Yale University, 1978.

Maital, Shlomo, and Y. Benjamini. "Inflation as a Prisoners' Dilemma." Journal of Post-Keynesian Economics, 2, no. 4 (1980): 459–81.

Maital, Shlomo, and Irwin Lipnowski, eds. Macroeconomic Conflict and Social Institutions. Cambridge, Mass.: Ballinger, 1985.

Mallon, Richard, and Juan Sourrouille. Economic Policymaking in a Conflict Society: The Argentine Case. Cambridge, Mass.: Harvard University Press, 1975.

Mann, Arthur, and Carlos F. Sánchez. "Monetarism, Economic Reform and Socio-Economic Consequences: Argentina, 1976–1982." International Journal of Social Economics, 11, no. 3/4 (1984).

Margenat, Nidia. "Las organizaciones corporativas del sector agrario." Buenos Aires: Consejo Federal de Inversiones, n.d.

Marín, Eduardo. "El 25 de mayo de 1973: Cámpora al gobierno." Transformaciones en el Tercer Mundo, no. 24 (1973).

Marshall, Adriana. "Mercado de trabajo y crecimiento de los salarios en la Argentina." Desarrollo Económico, no. 59 (1978): 20–39.

————. "The Fall of Labor's Share in Income and Consumption: A New 'Growth Model' for Argentina?" In William Canak, ed., Lost Promises: Debt, Development, and Democracy in Latin America (Boulder, Colo.: Westview Press, 1988), pp. 47–65.

Martel, Julian (pseud.). "Domination by Debt: Finance Capital in Argentina." NACLA Report on the Americas, 12, no. 4 (1978): 20–39.

Martínez, Tomás Eloy. La novela de Perón. Buenos Aires: Legasa, 1987.

Martínez de Hoz, José. "A New Stage in the Application of the Economic Programme Was Started." *Economic Information on Argentina,* no. 109 (1980): 3–13.

———. *Bases para una economía moderna.* Buenos Aires: 1981.

———. *La agricultura y la ganadería argentina en el período 1930–1960.* Buenos Aires: 1967.

Merkx, Gilbert. "Sectoral Clashes and Political Change: The Argentine Case." *Latin American Research Review,* 4, no. 3 (1969): 89–114.

Mignone, Emilio F. "The Military: What Is to Be Done?" *NACLA Report on the Americas,* 21, no. 4 (1987): 15–24.

Milutín, Lila Felicitas. "Algunas características de los movimientos huelguísticos en la Argentina, 1956–1974." Manuscript, 1976.

———. "Changing Patterns of Worker Protest in Argentina: 1956–1974." Manuscript, 1976.

Moneta, Carlos J., Ernesto López, and Aníbal Romero. *La reforma militar.* Buenos Aires: Legasa, 1985.

Monteón, Miguel. "Can Argentina's Democracy Survive Economic Disaster?" In Mónica Peralta Ramos and Carlos H. Waisman, eds., *From Military Rule to Liberal Democracy in Argentina* (Boulder, Colo.: Westview Press, 1987), pp. 21–38.

Mora y Araujo, Manuel. "La estructura social del peronismo: Un análisis electoral interprovincial." *Desarrollo Económico,* no. 56 (1975): 699–718.

———. "La naturaleza de la coalición alfonsinista." In Natalio R. Botana et al., *La Argentina electoral* (Buenos Aires: Sudamericana, 1985), pp. 89–97.

Mora y Araujo, Manuel, and Ignacio Llorente, eds., *El voto peronista: Ensayos de sociolgogía electoral argentina.* Buenos Aires: Sudamericana, 1980.

Mora y Arajuo, Manuel, and Peter H. Smith. "Peronism and Economic Development: The 1973 Elections." In Fredrick C. Turner and José Enrique Miguens, eds., *Juan Perón and the Reshaping of Argentina* (Pittsburgh: University of Pittsburgh Press, 1983), pp. 171–88.

Most, Ben. "Authoritarianism and the Growth of the State in Latin America: An Assessment of Their Impacts on Argentine Public Policy, 1930–1970." *Comparative Political Studies,* 13, no. 2 (1980): 123–44.

Munck, Ronaldo, with Ricardo Falcón and Bernardo Galtelli. *Argentina: From Anarchism to Peronism—Workers, Unions and Politics, 1955–1985.* London: Zed, 1987.

Murmis, Miguel, and Juan Carlos Portantiero. *Estudios sobre los orígenes del peronismo/1.* Buenos Aires: Siglo Veintiuno Editores, 1972.

Murmis, Miguel, Mario Pérsico, and Carlos Ramil Cepeda. *Tipos de capitalismo y estructura de clases: La formación de la Sociedad Argentina, 1500–1800.* Buenos Aires: La Rosa Blindada, 1974.

Navarro Gerassi, Marysa. *Los nacionalistas.* Buenos Aires: Editorial Jorge Alvarez, 1968.

Niosi, Jorge. *Los empresarios y el Estado Argentino (1955–1969).* Buenos Aires: Siglo Veintiuno Editores, 1974.

Nudelman, Ricardo. "Argentina en el conflicto de las hegemonías." *Controversia,* no. 2/3 (1979): 15–16.

Nun, José. "La industria automotriz argentina: Estudio de un caso de superpoblación flotante." *Revista Mexicana de Sociología,* 40, no. 1 (1978): 55–106.

O'Brien, Philip. "Authoritarianism and the New Orthodoxy: The Political Economy of the Chilean Regime, 1973–1982." In Philip O'Brien and Paul Cammack, eds., *Generals in Retreat: The Crisis of Military Rule in Latin America* (Manchester: University of Manchester Press, 1985), pp. 144–83.

O'Connor, James. *The Fiscal Crisis of the State.* New York: St. Martins Press, 1973.

———. *Accumulation Crisis.* New York: Basil Blackwell, 1984.

O'Donnell, Guillermo. "Brazil's Failure: What Future for Debtors' Cartels?" *Third World Quarterly,* 9, no. 4 (1987): 1157–66.

———. "Challenges to Democratization in Brazil: The Threat of a Slow Death." *World Policy Journal,* 5, no. 2 (1988): 281–300.

———. "Corporatism and the Question of the State." In James Malloy, ed., *Authoritarianism and Corporatism in Latin America* (Pittsburgh: University of Pittsburgh Press, 1977), pp. 47–87.

———. "Democracia en la Argentina: Micro y macro." In Oscar Oszlak, ed., *'Proceso,' crisis y transición democrática* (Buenos Aires: Centro Editor de América Latina, 1987), pp. 13–30.

———. "External Debt: Why Don't Our Governments Do the Obvious?" *CEPAL Review,* no. 27 (1986): 27–33.

———. "La cosecha del miedo." *Nexos,* 6 (1983): 6–12.

———. "Las fuerzas armadas y el estado autoritario del Cono Sur de América Latina." In Norbert Lechner, ed., *Estado y política en América Latina* (Mexico City: Siglo Veintiuno, 1981), pp. 199–237.

———. *Modernization and Bureaucratic-Authoritarianism: Studies in South American Politics.* Berkeley, Calif.: Institute of International Studies, 1973.

———. "Modernization and Military Coups: Theory, Comparisons, and the Argentine Case." In Abraham Lowenthal, ed., *Armies and Politics in Latin America* (New York: Holmes & Meier, 1976), pp. 197–243.

————. "Reflections on the Patterns of Change in the Bureaucratic-Authoritarian State." *Latin American Research Review*, 13, no. 1 (1978): 3–38.

————. "Reply to Remmer and Merkx." *Latin American Research Review*, 17, no. 2 (1982): 41–50.

————. "State and Alliances in Argentina, 1956–1976." *Journal of Development Studies*, 15, no. 1 (1978): 3–33.

————. "Tensions in the Bureaucratic-Authoritarian State and the Question of Democracy." In David Collier, ed., *The New Authoritarianism in Latin America* (Princeton, N.J.: Princeton University Press, 1979), pp. 285–318.

O'Donnell, Guillermo, Phillipe C. Schmitter, and Laurence Whitehead, eds. *Transitions from Authoritarian Rule: Prospects for Democracy*. Baltimore, Md.: Johns Hopkins University Press, 1986.

Offe, Claus. "Competitive Party Democracy and the Keynesian Welfare State." In Claus Offe, *Contradictions of the Welfare State* (John Keane, ed.; Cambridge, Mass.: M.I.T. Press, 1984), pp. 179–206.

————. "Societal Preconditions of Corporatism and Some Current Dilemmas in Democratic Theory." Working Paper No. 44, Kellogg Institute, University of Notre Dame, 1984.

————. "Structural Problems of the Capitalist State." *German Political Studies*, no. 1 (1974): 31–56.

————. "The Theory of the State and the Problem of Policy Formation." In Leon Lindberg, ed., *Stress and Contradiction in Modern Capitalism: Public Policy and Theory of the State* (New York: D.C. Heath, 1975), pp. 124–44.

Offe, Claus, and Volker Ronge. "Theses on the Theory of the State." *New German Critique*, no. 6 (1975): 137–47.

Ongaro, Raimundo. "Habla Ongaro." *Cristianismo y Revolución*, 13 (Apr. 1969).

————. *Sólo el pueblo salvará al pueblo*. Buenos Aires: Editorial Las Bases, 1970.

Organization of American States, Inter-American Commission on Human Rights. *Report on the Situation of Human Rights in Argentina*. Washington, D.C.: OAS General Secretariat, 1980.

Ortiz, *Historia económica de la Argentina*. 2 vols. Buenos Aires: Pampa y Cielo, 1964.

Oszlak, Oscar. *La formación del estado argentino*. Buenos Aires: Editorial de Belgrano, 1982.

Palomino, Héctor. "La normalización de la CGT: ¿Diez años no es nada?" *El Bimestre Político y Económico*, no. 31 (1987): 5–10.

————. "Los conflictos laborales bajo el gobierno constitucional: Del Plan Austral al Ministro de Trabajo Carlos Alderete (1985–1987)." In *Debate Sindical*. Buenos Aires: Fundación Friedrich Ebert, 1987.

Palomino, Mirta L. de. "Tradición y poder: La Sociedad Rural Argentina, 1955–1983." Buenos Aires: Centro de Investigaciones Sociales sobre el Estado y la Administración, 1987.

Panaia, Marta, and Ricardo Lesser. "Las estrategias militares frente al proceso de industrialización (1943–1947)." In Marta Panaia, Pedro Skupch, and Ricardo Lesser, eds., *Los orígines del peronismo/2* (Buenos Aires: Siglo Veintiuno Editores, 1972), pp. 83–164.

Pasado y Presente. "Del gobierno de Cámpora a Perón en el poder: La crisis de julio y sus consecuencias políticas." *Pasado y Presente,* 4, no. 2/3 (1973): 271–83.

Pastor, Manuel, Jr. *The International Monetary Fund and Latin America: Economic Stabilization and Class Conflict.* Boulder, Colo.: Westview Press, 1987.

Peña, Milciades, ed. *El peronismo: Selección de documentos para la historia.* Buenos Aires: Ediciones Ficha, 1973.

Peralta Ramos, Mónica. *Acumulación del capital y crisis política en Argentina (1930–1974).* Mexico City: Siglo Veintiuno Editores, 1978.

———. *Estapas de acumulación y alianzas de clases en la Argentina (1930–1970).* Buenos Aires: Siglo Veintiuno Editores, 1973.

———. "Toward an Analysis of the Structural Basis of Coercion in Argentina: The Behavior of the Major Fractions of the Bourgeoisie, 1976–1983." In Mónica Peralta Ramos and Carlos H. Waisman, eds., *From Military Rule to Liberal Democracy in Argentina* (Boulder, Colo.: Westview Press, 1987), pp. 39–68.

Perón, Juan. *El pueblo quiere saber de qué se trata.* Buenos Aires: Editorial Freeland, 1973.

———. *Juan Perón, 1973–1974: Todos sus discursos, mensajes y conferencias, Tomos I y II.* Buenos Aires: Editorial de la Reconstrucción, 1974.

———. *La comunidad organizada.* Buenos Aires: Ediciones Cepe: 1973.

Portantiero, Juan Carlos. "Bases políticas, ley sindical y el plan del capital." *Controversia,* no. 4 (1980): 2–3.

———. "Clases dominantes y crisis política en la Argentina actual." In Oscar Braun, ed., *El capitalismo argentino en crisis* (Buenos Aires: Siglo Veintiuno Editores, 1973), pp. 73–118.

———. "De la crisis del país popular a la reorganización del país burgués." *Cuadernos de Marcha,* no. 2 (1979): 11–20.

———. "Economía y política en la crisis argentina: 1958–1973." *Revista Mexicana de Sociología,* 41, no. 1 (1979): 531–65.

Portelli, Hugues. *Gramsci y el bloque histórico.* Buenos Aires: Siglo Veintiuno Editores, 1973.

Porto, Alberto. "Un modelo simple sobre el comportamiento macroeconómico argentino en el corto plazo." *Desarrollo Económico,* no. 59 (1975): 353–72.

Potash, Robert. *El ejército y la política en la Argentina, 1928–1945: De Yrigoyen a Perón.* Buenos Aires: Sudamericana, 1971.

———. *The Army and Politics in Argentina, 1945–1962.* Stanford, Calif.: Stanford University Press, 1980.

Potter, Anne. "Political Institutions, Political Decay and the Argentine Crisis of 1930." Ph.D. diss., Stanford University, 1978.

Poulantzas, Nicos. *Las crisis de la dictaduras: Portugal, Grecia, España.* Mexico City: Siglo Veintiuno Editores, 1976.

———. *Political Power and Social Classes.* Trans. Timothy O'Hagan. London: New Left Books, 1973.

———. *State, Power, Socialism.* Trans. Patrick Camiller. London: New Left Books, 1978.

Prieto, Ramón. *De Perón 1955 a Perón 1973.* Buenos Aires: Ediciones Macacha Guemes, 1974.

———. *El pacto: Ocho años de la política argentina.* Buenos Aires: Ediciones en Marcha, 1963.

Przeworski, Adam. *Capitalism and Social Democracy.* Cambridge: Cambridge University Press, 1985.

———. "Compromiso de clases y Estado: Europa Occidental y América Latina." In Norbert Lechner, ed., *Estado y Política en América Latina* (Mexico City: Siglo Veintiuno Editores, 1981), pp. 236–71.

Przeworksi, Adam, and Michael Wallerstein. "The Structure of Class Conflict in Democratic Capitalist Societies." *American Political Science Review,* no. 76 (1982): 215–38.

Ramos, Jorge Abelardo. *La era del bonapartismo.* Buenos Aires: Plus Ultra, 1973.

Ramos, Joseph. *Neoconservative Economics in the Southern Cone of Latin America.* Baltimore, Md.: The Johns Hopkins University Press, 1986.

Ranis, Peter. "Early Peronism and the Post-Liberal Argentine State." *Journal of Interamerican Studies and World Affairs,* 21, no. 3 (1979): 313–38.

———. "Peronism Without Perón: Ten Years After the Fall (1955–1965)." *Journal of Interamerican Studies,* no. 8 (1966): 112–128.

Remmer, Karen. *Party Competition in Argentina and Chile: Political Recruitment and Public Policy, 1890–1930.* Lincoln: University of Nebraska Press, 1984.

Remmer, Karen, and Gilbert Merkx. "Bureaucratic-Authoritarianism Revisited." *Latin American Research Review,* 17, no. 2 (1982): 3–40.

Ribas, Armando. "La viabilidad de las metas económicas." *Revista de la UIA,* no. 47 (1970): 23–26.

Rímez, Marc. "Las experiencias de apertura externa y desprotección industrial en el Cono Sur." *Economía de América Latina,* no. 2 (1979): 103–24.

Rock, David. *Argentina 1516–1987: From Spanish Colonization to Alfonsín.* Berkeley: University of California Press, 1987.

──────. *Politics in Argentina, 1880–1930: The Rise and Fall of Radicalism.* London: Cambridge University Press, 1975.

──────. "The Survival and Restoration of Peronism." In David Rock, ed., *Argentina in the Twentieth Century* (London: Duckworth, 1975), pp. 179–221.

Rossi, Clóvis. "FMI Pede que o Governo Argentino Reative Economia." *Folha de São Paulo,* 2 Oct. 1982.

Rotondaro, Rubén. *Realidad y cambio en el sindicalismo.* Buenos Aires: Ediciones Bermejo, 1972.

Rouquié, Alain. "Continuidad y cambio de los partidos en el proceso de transición a la democracia. La democracia contra los partidos: El caso de Argentina." In Carlos Huneeus, ed., *Para vivir la democracia: dilemas de su consolidación*(Santiago: Centro de Estudios de la Realidad Contemporánea, 1987), pp. 259–76.

──────. "El poder militar en la Argentina hoy: Cambio y continuidad." In Peter Waldman and Ernesto Garzón Valéz, eds., *El poder militar en la Argentina (1976–1981)* (Buenos Aires: Editorial Galerna, 1983), pp. 65–76.

──────. "Hegemonía militar, estado y dominación social." In Alain Roquié, ed., *Argentina, hoy* (Mexico City: Siglo Veintiuno Editores, 1982), pp. 11–50.

──────. *Poder militar y sociedad política en la Argentina.* 2 vols. Buenos Aires: Emece, 1981.

Roquié, Alain, and Ricardo Sidicaro. "Etats autoritaires et liberalisme économique en Amérique Latine: Une approche héterodoxe." *Revue Tiers-Monde,* 24, no. 93 (1983).

Rowe, James W. "Onganía's Argentina: The First Four Months." *American University Field Staff Reports,* 12, no. 8 (1966).

Roxborough, Ian. "Unity and Diversity in Latin American History." *Journal of Latin American Studies,* no. 16 (1984): 1–26.

Russell, Charles A., James F. Schenkel, and James A. Miller. "Urban Guerrillas in Argentina: A Select Bibliography." *Latin American Research Review,* 9, no. 3 (1974): 53–92.

Sábato, Hilda, and Marcelo Cavarozzi, eds. *Democracia, orden político y parlamento fuerte.* Buenos Aires: Centro Editor de América Latina, 1984.

Sábato, Jorge. "Notas sobre la formación de la clase dominante en la Argentina moderna (1880–1914)." Buenos Aires: CIAP, 1979.

Sábato, Jorge, and Jorge Schvarzer. "Funcionamento da Economia e Poder Político na Argentina: Empecilhos para a Democracia." In Alain Roquié, Bolivar Lamounier, and Jorge Schvarzer, eds., *Como*

Renascem as Democracias (São Paulo: Editora Brasiliense, 1985), pp. 155–96.

Santu, Ruth. "Poder Económico y burguesía industrial en la Argentina, 1930–1954." *Revista Latinoamericana de Sociología*, no. 4 (1968): 310–40.

Sasson, Anne Showstack, ed. *Approaches to Gramsci*. London: Writers and Readers, 1982.

Schvarzer, Jorge. "Cambios en el liderazgo industrial argentino en el período de Martínez de Hoz." *Desarrollo Económico*, no. 91 (1983): 395–422.

———. "Empresas públicas y desarrollo industrial en la Argentina." *Economía de América Latina*, no. 3 (1979): 45–68.

———. "Estrategia industrial y grandes empresas: El caso argentino." *Desarrollo Económico*, no. 71 (1978): 307–51.

———. *La política económica de Martínez de Hoz*. Buenos Aires: Hysamérica, 1987.

———. "Las empresas industriales más grandes de la Argentina: Una evaluación." *Desarrollo Económico*, no. 66 (1977): 319–38.

Schvarzer, Jorge, and Ricardo Sidicaro. "Empresarios y el Estado en la reconstrucción de la democracia en la Argentina." *El Bimestre Político y Económico*, no. 35 (1987): pp 5–14.

Selser, Gregorio. *El onganiato: La espada y el hisopo*. 2 vols. Buenos Aires: Carlos Sarmonta Editor, 1973.

Senén González, Santiago. *El sindicalismo después de Perón*. Buenos Aires: Editorial Galerna, 1971.

Serra, José. "Three Mistaken Theses Regarding the Connection between Industrialization and Authoritarian Regimes." In David Collier, ed., *The New Authoritarianism in Latin America* (Princeton, N.J.: Princeton University Press, 1979), pp. 99–164.

Share, Donald, and Scott Mainwaring. "Transitions through Transaction: Democratization in Brazil and Spain." In Wayne Selcher, ed., *Political Liberalization in Brazil: Dynamics, Dilemmas, and Future Prospects* (Boulder, Colo.: Westview Press, 1986), pp. 175–216.

Sidicaro, Ricardo. "Ideologías y violencia política." *El Bimestre Político y Económico*, no. 39 (1988): 4–8.

———. "Poder y crisis de la gran burguesía agraria argentina." In Alain Roquié, ed., *Argentina, hoy* (Mexico City: Siglo Veintiuno Editores, 1982), pp. 51–104.

Sigal, Silvia. "Acción obrera en una situación de crisis: Tucumán, 1966–1968." *Revista Mexicana de Sociología*, 40, no. 2 (1978): 375–420.

Sigal, Silvia, and Elisio Verón. *Perón o muerte: Los fundamentos discursivos del fenómeno peronista*. Buenos Aires: Legasa, 1986.

Silva, Juan, and Frans J. Schuurman. "Neighborhood Associations in

Buenos Aires: Contradictions Within Contradictions." In Frans J. Schuurman et al., eds., *Urban Social Movements in the Third World* (London: Routledge, 1988), pp. 45–61.

Silvert, Kalman. "Economics, Democracy, and Honesty: An Assessment of the Frondizi Regime." *American University Field Staff Reports*, 7, no. 1 (1960).

SPIRI. Stockholm International Peace Research Institute. *World Armaments and Disarmament Yearbook*. Philadelphia: Taylor and Francis, 1984.

Skocpol, Theda. "Bringing the State Back in: Strategies of Analysis in Current Research." In Peter Evans, Dietrich Rueschemeyer, and Theda Skocpol, eds., *Bringing the State Back In* (Cambridge: Cambridge University Press, 1985), pp. 3–43.

————. *States and Social Revolutions: A Comparative Analysis of France, Russia, and China*. Cambridge: Cambridge University Press, 1979.

Skocpol, Theda, and Margaret Somers. "The Uses of Comparative History in Macro-Social Inquiry." *Comparative Studies in Society and History*, 22, no. 2 (1980): 174–97.

Skupch, Pedro. "Concentración industrial en la Argentina: 1955–1966." *Desarrollo Económico*, no. 41 (1971): 3–14.

————. "El deterioro y fin de la hegemonía británica sobre la economía argentina." In Marta Panaia, Pedro Skupch, and Ricardo Lesser, eds., *Estudios sobre los orígenes del peronismo/2* (Buenos Aires: Siglo Veintiuno Editores, 1972), pp. 3–82.

————. "Nacionalización, libras bloqueadas y sustitución de importaciones." *Desarrollo Económico*, no. 47 (1972): 478–93.

Smith, Peter. *Argentina and the Failure of Democracy: Conflict Among Political Elites, 1904–1955*. Madison: University of Wisconsin Press, 1974.

————. *Carne y política en la Argentina*. Buenos Aires: Paidós, 1968.

————. "Los radicales y la defensa de los intereses ganaderos." *Desarrollo Económico*, no. 25 (1967): 795–829.

————. "The Breakdown of Democracy in Argentina, 1916–1930." In Juan Linz and Alfred Stepan, eds., *Breakdown of Democratic Regimes: Latin America* (Baltimore, Md.: The Johns Hopkins University Press, 1978), pp. 3–27.

Smith, William C. "Crisis of the State and Military-Authoritarian Rule in Argentina, 1966–1973." Ph.D. diss., Stanford University, 1980.

————. "Reflections on the Political Economy of Authoritarian Rule and Capitalist Reorganization in Contemporary Argentina." In Philip O'Brien and Paul Cammack, eds., *Generals in Retreat: The Crisis of Military Rule in Latin America* (Manchester: University of Manchester Press, 1985), pp. 37–88.

————. "The Armed Forces and the Bureaucratic-Authoritarian State in Argentina." Paper presented at the Inter-University Seminars on Armed Forces and Society. Tempe, Arizona, 1976.

————. "Heterodox Shocks and the Political Economy of Democratic Transition in Argentina and Brazil." In William Canak, ed., *Lost Promises: Debt, Democracy, and Development in Latin America* (Boulder, Colo.: Westview Press, 1988), pp. 138–66.

————. "The Political Transition in Brazil: From Authoritarian Liberalization and Elite Conciliation to Democratization." In Enrique Baloyra, ed., *Comparing New Democracies: Transition and Consolidation in Mediterranean Europe and the Southern Cone* (Boulder, Colo.: Westview Press, 1987), pp. 179–240.

Snow, Peter. "Parties and Politics in Argentina: The Elections of 1962 and 1963." *Midwest Journal of Political Science*, 9, no. 1 (1965): 1–36.

————. *Political Forces in Argentina*. Boston: Allyn and Bacon, 1971.

Sourrouille, Juan V. "La presencia y el comportamiento de las empresas extranjeras en el sector industrial argentino." *Estudios CEDES*. Buenos Aires: Centro de Estudios de Estado y Sociedad, 1978.

Sourrouille, Juan V., Bernardo B. Kosacoff, and Jorge Lucangeli. *Transnacionalización y política económica en la Argentina*. Buenos Aires: Centro de Economía Transnacional/Centro Editor de América Latina, 1985.

Spagnolo, Alberto. "Costo económico del conflicto de las Malvinas." *Le Monde Diplomatique en Español*, June 1982.

Spalding, Hobart. *La clase trabajadora argentina (documentos para su historia, 1890/1912)*. Buenos Aires: Galerna, 1970.

————. *Organized Labor in Latin America: Historical Case Studies of Urban Workers in Dependent Societies*. New York: Harper and Row, 1977.

Springer, Philip. "Disunity and Disorder: Factional Politics in the Argentine Military." In Henry Bienen, ed., *The Military Intervenes: Case Studies in Development* (New York: Russell Sage Foundation, 1968).

Stepan, Alfred. *Rethinking Military Politics: Brazil and the Southern Cone*. Princeton, N.J.: Princeton University Press, 1988.

————. "State Power and the Strength of Civil Society in the Southern Cone of Latin America." In Peter Evans, Dietrich Rueschemeyer, and Theda Skocpol, eds., *Bringing the State Back In* (Cambridge: Cambridge University Press, 1985), pp. 317–46.

————. "The New Professionalism of Internal Warfare and Military Role Expansion." In Alfred Stepan, ed., *Authoritarian Brazil: Origins, Policies, and Future* (New Haven, Conn.: Yale University Press, 1973), pp. 47–65.

————. *The State and Society: Peru in Comparative Perspective*. Princeton, N.J.: Princeton University Press, 1978.

Stiles, Kendall W. "Argentina's Bargaining with the IMF." *Journal of Interamerican Studies and World Affairs*, 29, no. 3 (1987): 55–86.

Sunkel, Osvaldo, and Pedro Paz. *El subdesarrollo latinoamericano y la teoría del desarrollo*. Mexico City: Siglo Veintiuno Editores, 1970.

Terán, Oscar. "El discurso del orden." *Cuadernos de Marcha*, 1, no. 2 (1979): 49–54.

Terragno, Rodolfo. *Los 400 días de Perón*. Buenos Aires: Ediciones de la Flor, 1974.

Teubal, Miguel. "Estimaciones del 'excedente financiero' del sector agropecuario argentino." *Desarrollo Económico*, no. 56 (1975): 677–98.

———. "La crisis alimenticia y el Tercer Mundo: Una perspectiva latinoamericana." *Economía de América Latina*, no. 2 (1979): 61–80.

Therborn, Goran. "The Rule of Capital and the Rise of Democracy." *New Left Review*, 103 (1977).

———. *What Does the Ruling Class Do When It Rules?* London: New Left Books, 1978.

Torre, Juan Carlos. "El movimiento sindical en la Argentina." Buenos Aires: Centro de Investigaciones Sociológicas, Instituto Torcuato Di Tella, 1979.

———. "El proceso político interno de los sindicatos en Argentina." Buenos Aires: Instituto Torcuato Di Tella, 1974.

———. "El programa de STIRAC-STIRAM." *Los Libros* (Aug. 1971).

———. "La democracia sindical en la Argentina." *Desarrollo Económico*, no. 55 (1974): 531–43.

———. "La tasa de sindicalización en la Argentina." *Desarrollo Económico*, no. 48 (1973): 903–14.

———. *Los sindicatos en el gobierno, 1973–1976*. Buenos Aires: Centro Editor de América Latina, 1983.

———. "Una nueva oposición social." *Los Libros* (Aug. 1971).

Tozze, Roger. "Perspectives and Theory: A Consumer's Guide." In Susan Strange, ed. *Paths to International Political Economy* (London: George Allen and Unwin, 1984), chap. 1.

Túrolo, Carlos M., Jr. *Así lucharon*. Buenos Aires: Sudamericana, 1983.

Ubertalli, Jorge L., et al. *El complot militar: Un país en obediencia debida*. Buenos Aires: Ediciones Dialéctica, 1987.

Unidos. 4, no. 15 (1987). Issue on the 1987 Easter military rebellion.

Urry, John. *The Anatomy of Capitalist Societies: The Economy, Civil Society and the State*. London: Macmillan, 1981.

Van Rijckeghem, W., and George Maynard. "Stabilization Policy in an Inflationary Economy: The Case of Argentina." In George Papanek, ed., *Development Policy: Theory and Practice* (Cambridge, Mass.: Harvard University Press, 1968), pp. 207–35.

Vanossi, Jorge Reinaldo. "Reflexiones sobre el nuevo régimen institucional argentino." *Carta Política*, June 1976: 41–50.

Vergara, Pilar. "Transformaciones en las funciones del Estado bajo el régimen militar." *Colección Estudios CIEPLAN*, 5 (1980).

Verón, Eliseo. *Imperialismo, lucha de clases y conocimiento: 25 años de sociología en la Argentina*. Buenos Aires: Editorial Tiempo Contemporáneo, 1974.

Vigo, Juan. *Crónicas de la resistencia*. Buenos Aires: Peña Lillo Editor, 1973.

Vilas, Carlos. "Política y conflictos sociales de la industrialización periférica: El primer peronismo." Manuscript, 1978.

Villanueva, Javier. "Economic Development." In Mark Falcoff and Ronald Dolkart, eds., *Prologue to Perón: Argentina in Depression and War, 1930–1943* (Berkeley: University of California Press, 1975), pp. 57–82.

———. "El orígen de la industrialización argentina." *Desarrollo Económico*, no. 47 (1972): 451–76.

Villareal, Juan. "Changes in Argentine Society: The Heritage of the Dictatorship." In Mónica Peralta Ramos and Carlos H. Waisman, eds., *From Military Rule to Liberal Democracy in Argentina* (Boulder, Colo.: Westview Press, 1987), pp. 69–96.

———. *El capitalismo dependiente: Estudio sobre la estructura de clases en Argentina*. Mexico City: Siglo Veintiuno Editores, 1978.

Villegas, Osiris. *Políticas y estrategias para el desarrollo y la seguridad nacional*. Buenos Aires: Pleamar, 1969.

Viola, Eduardo, and Scott Mainwaring. "Transitions to Democracy: Brazil and Argentina in the 1980s." *Journal of International Affairs*, 38, no. 2 (1985): 193–219.

Waisman, Carlos H. *Reversal of Development in Argentina: Postwar Counterrevolutionary Policies and Their Structural Consequences*. Princeton, N.J.: Princeton University Press, 1987.

World Bank. *Economic Memorandum on Argentina*. Washington, D.C.: The World Bank, 1984.

———. *Economic Memorandum on Argentina, Volume I, The Main Report*. Washington, D.C.: The World Bank, 1985.

———. *Economic Memorandum on Argentina, Volume II, Statistical Appendix*. Washington, D.C.: The World Bank, 1985.

———. *World Debt Tables, 1986–87*. Washington, D.C.: The World Bank, 1987.

Wright, Erik Olin. *Class, Crisis and the State*. London: New Left Books, 1978.

———. *Classes*. London: Verso, 1985.

Wynia, Gary. *Argentina in the Postwar Era: Politics and Economic Policy-making in a Divided Society.* Albuquerque: University of New Mexico Press, 1978.

Zorrilla, Rubén. *Estructura y dinámica del sindicalismo argentino.* Buenos Aires: Editorial de la Pléyade, 1974.

Zuvekas, Clarence, Jr. "Economic Growth and Income Distribution in Postwar Argentina." *Interamerican Economic Affairs,* 20, no. 3 (1966): 19–38.

Index

In this index an "f" after a number indicates a separate reference on the next page, and an "ff" indicates separate references on the next two pages. A continuous discussion over two or more pages is indicated by a span of page numbers, e.g., "pp. 57–58." *Passim* is used for a cluster of references in close but not consecutive sequence.

Library of Congress Cataloging-in-Publication Data

Smith, William C.
    Authoritarianism and the crisis of the Argentine political economy
       p.   cm.
    Bibliography: p.
    Includes index.
    ISBN 0-8047-1672-2 (alk. paper)
    1. Argentina—Economic policy. 2. Argentina—Economic
conditions—1945- 3. Authoritarianism—Argentina. 4. Argentina—
Politics and government—1955- I. Title.
HC175.S54 1989
338.982—dc20   89-31681
                                             CIP